Digital Master

Debunk the Myths of Enterprise Digital Maturity

PEARL ZHU

ISBN: 978-1-4834-2100-1 (sc)
ISBN: 978-1-4834-2154-4 (e)

Lulu Publishing Services rev. date: 1/14/2015

CONTENTS

INTRODUCTION

"The best way to predict the future is to create it." –Peter Drucker

The Digital transformation, like the computer technology revolution itself, is a long journey. The outlines of the fully digitalized world have long been sketched, now the phenomenon of digital is reaching the inflection point, yet we are now entering an even more rapid and extensive period of change. As this notion of "digitization" is now affecting all aspects of business operations from innovation within and around business ecosystem, to customer engagement, to business models and processes – and no industry is exempt. Hence, most companies naturally aim to move into a more advanced stage of digital deployment by tailoring their own unique strength and business maturity. They hope to outstrip competitors and eventually become the digital masters.

However, digitalization raises questions about leadership, strategy, culture, structure, talent, financing and almost everything else. Obviously there's no one-size-fits-all magic formula to digital transformation success. "Digital Master" is the guidebook to perceive the multi-faceted impact digital is making to the business, with the following nine chapters to help businesses navigate through the journey and avoid the "rogue digital":

1. **Digital vision**: <u>Digitalization is a constant game changer for the organization</u>. It is the age of customer; empathy is the core foundation in customer-centricity. The organizations of the future are increasingly exhibiting digital characteristics in various shades and intensity.

2. **Digital mind-set:** <u>The mind-set is far more important than talent.</u> Talent can always be developed by those with an open and

right mind-set. Leaders and talent with digital transformational mind are in higher demand, as transformational leadership is all about change.

3. **Digital strategy:** <u>The whole is superior than the sum of pieces.</u> A strategic vision for how digital will transform the business, understand the whole before you build out the pieces, and create a roadmap for implementing such transformation.

4. **Digital culture** - <u>The right culture is a prerequisite for implementing digital strategy.</u> A great culture can support a weak strategy, but a weak culture cannot support a great strategy. A strong digital culture promotes inclusiveness, empathy, creativity and agility.

5. **Digital Capability** <u>– In-depth understanding of the "recombinant" nature of digital capabilities.</u> The maturity of a business capability would be based on the ability to deliver on customer needs; or to achieve the desired capability outcome, catalyze organizational maturity and business competitiveness.

6. **Digital Innovation** – <u>Make a relentless commitment to innovation with expanded scope.</u> Innovation is more often composed with the full spectrum of light, focus on not only the "hard" innovation such as products or services revolution, but also the "soft" innovation such as culture or communication evolution.

7. **Digital Intelligence** – <u>Intelligence is nothing but the ability to solve problems.</u> A hallmark of digital age is the proliferation of data being generated. As businesses are moving slowly into an era where Big Data is the starting point - not the end. Digital Transformation concentrates on defining a comprehensive scope of change and then figuring out how to execute it with intelligence and speed.

8. **Digital Workforce** – <u>The "work is what you do, not where you go" shift is unstoppable.</u> And businesses must be alert to the digital dynamic environment, adapt their workforce planning and development strategies to ensure alignment with future skill requirements.

9. **Digital Maturity** – <u>The purpose of such radical digitalization is to make significant difference in the overall levels of customer delight.</u> Digital makes profound impact from specific function to business as a whole, the truth is that both the digital world and the physical one are indispensable parts of the business. The real digital transformation taking place today isn't the replacement of the one by the other; but harmonizing the hybrid nature of digitalization and making the well combinations that create wholly new sources of value and achieve high level digital maturity.

The shift to digital cuts across sectors, geographies and leadership roles, the digital transformation is now spreading rapidly to enable organizations of all shapes and sizes to reinvent themselves. But dealing with the challenge of digital change requires an accelerated digital mindset, taking an end-to-end response, building a comprehensive digital strategy, and rethinking the business and operating models, etc. The book "Digital Master" is based on numerous professional digital debates and enriched crowd-sourcing brainstorming. From doing digital to being digital, may this book share a few insights, throw some light on digital transformation, and create the value for encompassing your digitalization journey. It is the book which was born in digital era, targets to reach the broad and diversified digital audience, from business leaders and managers to digital professionals and knowledge workers, to help them shape the game changing digital mindset and navigate through the adventurous digital journey.

CHAPTER 1

The Future of the Organization

Go Digital, Like a Pro

Introduction

Digitalization opens new doors and connects silos, across walls, across streets, across the seas, and across the planet. When things connect in this way, entities wishing to negotiate successful journeys have to understand what the implications of this degree of connectivity means to them. They have to understand what it means within their business or organization. But much more importantly, they have to understand the external changing connected environment, and how they can proactively cultivate the set of digital capabilities to adapt to the continuous disruptions. A digital enterprise with organizational democracy is a means to that end; it means people enjoy sharing knowledge, values, and wisdom so divergent thoughts can converge into more objective decision making by wise leaders, who then can execute the well-crafted digital strategy and create values for all shareholders in the long run.

1. "VUCA" as Digital New Normal

Digital means changes.

VUCA is an acronym used to describe or reflect on volatility, uncertainty, complexity, and ambiguity of general conditions and situations (Wikipedia). Perhaps it's the best description of today's digital characteristics – VUCA as digital normality. It brings the new level of complexity, uncertainty, opportunities, and risks for digital businesses today.

- **V = Volatility**: It well describes the nature and dynamics of change, the trait and speed of change forces and change catalysts. Volatility means change with increasing speed technologically, economically, politically, and environmentally. It used to take years or even decades for disruptive innovations to displace dominant products and services and destabilize incumbent industries. Now, in the age of digitalization, any business can be at risk in any minute due to the disruptive innovation and digitalization. In such a new normal, efficiency and productivity no longer guarantee business's survival. Agility, the ability to change with speed; flexibility, the alternative options to do the things; and resilience, the ability to survive and thrive at volatility, are the new abilities for business to success.

- **U = Uncertainty**: The very basic nature of uncertainty is defined by Wikipedia as a term used in a number of fields (physics, philosophy, statistics, economics, finance, insurance, psychology, sociology, engineering, and information science) with as many variants as the number of fields themselves. It indicates the lack of predictability, the prospects for surprise, and the sense of awareness and understanding of issues and events. It applies to predictions of future events, to physical measurements already made, or to the unknown. To use the common term, uncertainty is the lack of certainty, a state of having limited knowledge whereby it is impossible to exactly describe the existing circumstance.

- **C = Complexity**: It is about the multiplex of forces, the confounding of issues and the chaos or confusion that surrounds an organization. The hyper-connectivity nature of digital organizations can bring the new level of business complexity. Complexity is a systematic thinking concept, and it's not the opposite of "simplicity." In systematic thinking, systems such as organizations, biological systems, enterprise as system, etc., can be characterized as being complex if they have nonlinear feedback loops; such systems can exhibit emergent behavior. Simple systems can have complexity in that they have nonlinear feedback loops that can result in emergent properties and outcomes. Complexity is diverse, ambiguous, and dynamic, with unpredictable outcomes. It is often erroneously confused with the term complication. Nevertheless, complexity and complication do not mean the same thing. Something that is complex is not necessarily difficult, but something that is complicated does have a high degree of difficulty. The complexity can be good or bad for you, depending on your strategy. Complexity Management is the methodology to minimize value-destroying complexity and efficiently control value-adding complexity in a cross-functional approach.

- **A = Ambiguity**: The haziness of reality, the potential for misreads, and the mixed meanings of conditions; cause-and-effect confusion. Ambiguity can be understood as being similar to business 'risk,' a term used to describe a circumstance in which an investment is made but the outcome is uncertain. Consequently, in times of organizational change or digital transformation, dealing with ambiguity is a leadership skill. Ambiguity may be used strategically to encourage creativity, and guide through the multiple ways to perceive organizational reality and future. At the senior management level, planning and decisions for action are always based on rough estimations of what the future conditions of execution would be. They can therefore not predict any accurate consequences of execution on the circumstances of the action to come; they also can have a certain level of ambiguity toleration to inspire innovation and new adventure.

In a world where change is significantly speeding up so that business leaders couldn't predict the future with certain degree of accuracy, and the strategy can no longer stay static, the business goals can no longer be well framed in advance. Business leaders must realize that breakthrough success in digital business requires not only forward-thinking strategies but also a transformation of the company's underlying functions and structure through weaving digital into the very foundation of business, in order to build the new set of business capabilities and adapt to the VUCA digital normality.

2. Digital Dawn

We are at the dawn of new era for radical digital transformation.

We are at the age of digital dawn; deserts, mountains, and oceans will no longer be the walls to cognizance of the diversity that have been the gene banks and engines of human creativity and invention because the natural barriers that separated the world's societies have disappeared, thanks to digital technology. However, are we on the way to unify the best of the best; recognize originality from mass, shift the old way of thinking; or simply blend the best or worst into monoculture? From a business perspective, companies that can proactively and effectively build core digital capabilities based on digital foresight, will gain unique competitive advantage and execute with high speed.

- **Digital mind shift:** Digital transformation requires mind shift. In addition to the set point changing, transformation requires first shifting mind-sets, then building new skills, reinforcing and embedding new practices or reflexes. Skills and situations have become more subtle, more multilayered, and therefore more complex, what's needed every now and then in any individual, team, organization, society, and on up to the entire planet's population, is a little or a lot of energy to refocus, kick-start, or 'game-change.' And evolutionary digital technologies or scientific breakthroughs connected to human communication dynamics are all wonderful, useful, and interesting in driving digital transformation.

- **Digital literacy:** Wikipedia defines digital literacy as the ability to effectively and critically navigate, evaluate, and create information using a range of digital technologies. It requires business to recognize and use that power, to manipulate and transform digital media, to distribute pervasively, and to easily adapt them to new forms. Digital literacy does not replace traditional forms of literacy; it builds upon the foundation of traditional forms of literacy. It is much more than a combination of the two terms. Digital information is a symbolic representation of data, and literacy refers to the ability to read for knowledge, write coherently, and think critically about the written word. At enterprise level, digital literacy requires cross-functional collaboration and interdisciplinary knowledge sharing. It requires the synchronization of information management capabilities, innovation capabilities, and business learning and growth capabilities, etc. Just like digital consumers, Enterprise can also be classified into digital natives and digital immigrants. A digital native business is the one that is founded in the digital age, like many technology startups; while a digital immigrant organization refers to the businesses that adopt technology later in business life cycle. Though simply being a digital native company does not make business digital literate or digital mature, it takes strategy and practice to master digital fluency.

- **Digital inflection:** More and more organizations are at the strategic inflection point of digital transformation. A strategic inflection point is a time in the life cycle of a business when its fundamentals such as talent, skills, process, and technologies are about to change. Inflection is a bend, a fold, a curve, a turn, a twist; such change can mean an opportunity to rise to the new digital height or a risk to hit uncertainty. But it may just as likely signal the beginning of the end. Digitalization implies the full-scale changes in the way business is conducted, so simply adopting a new digital technology may be insufficient. You have to transform the company's underlying functions and organization as a whole with adjusted digital speed. Otherwise, companies may begin to decline from their previous good performance. Inflection point is the moment when the way business is being conducted changes more radically; it creates new opportunities for businesses that are adept at executing and operation. It is the moment to be "paranoid" – as it's the act of inflecting or the state of being inflected.

We are at the digital dawn. Digital is not just about any digital technology, the products or the website; it is the mind shift and business transformation. It requires reorganizing and orchestrating the entire organization because digital impacts every aspect of the business and it is the core of organizational strategy.

3. Digital Master

What the caterpillar calls the end of the world, the master calls a butterfly.
–Richard Bach

Digital transformation is a journey. The terms "transformation" and "change" truly overlap in literal definition; people tend to carry their own associations with each. Transformation is definitely the more ambitious sounding term, and organizations' digitalization is surely a transformation journey; it has to permeate into business vision and strategy, mind-set and action, culture and communication, process and capability, etc.

THREE-LEVEL DIGITAL MATURITY

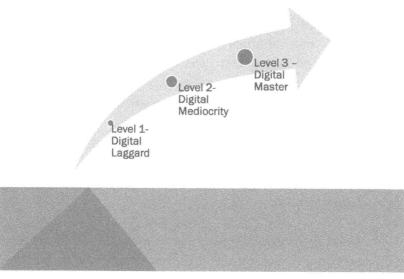

Figure 1: Three-Level Digital Maturity

(1) Three-level of Digital Maturity: Daily business change maybe mechanical, but transformation is more radical. "Change" can be a somewhat mechanical implementation of new or different ways to doing something, while digital transformation is more likely to be a sweeping approach to altering a culture, or parts of it, possibly even to parts of its value system, to embrace such change and help it become self-perpetuating. Although digital transformation is on every forward-looking organization's agenda, they may take different levels of altitude, attitude, and aptitude to achieve it. Here are three levels of digital maturity:

- **Level I – Digital Laggard:** These organizations probably use email, Internet, and various kinds of enterprise software, but they have been slow to adopt, or they are skeptical of more advanced digital technologies like social media and analytics. They don't have an overarching digital strategy to drive the transformation, and they have very limited advanced digital capability; they are pretty much still running with structured silos at industrial speed.

- **Level II – Digital Mediocrity**: This category of organizations understands the importance of digitalization and has built the digital strategy. However, these companies are still risk avoidant, deliberately hanging back when it comes to emerging trend or new technologies. They take a conservative mind-set or attitude to move with digital speed. Although their management may have a vision and effective structures in place to govern technology adoption, they lack leadership courage and business influence to pioneer the transformation. They prefer to wait and see, and follow the industry leaders.

- **Level III – Digital Master**: These companies, less than 15% of overall businesses, are digital forerunners and masters. They have both clear digital vision and well-crafted digital strategy; they are courageous to be in the vanguard of digital transformation with a quantum lead. But they also proactively develop more advanced and unique digital capabilities step-by-step, and build a digital premium into their very foundation of business, such as digital mind-set, culture, agility, intelligence, and structure, and they achieve high performance results through strong digital governance discipline.

(2) Decode Digital Master: Digital masters are organizations that have rich digital insight and high level digital capability, not only to initiate digital innovations but also to drive enterprise-wide digital transformation. They are the digital leaders in their vertical sector and business ecosystem. The digital transformation does not mean to only adopt the latest digital technologies; it refers to modification and internalization of new values, behaviors, and culture, when the need for significant digital shift is identified. It's generally naive to think it will succeed without transformation as well. The digital masters also have their very nature of digital influence or digital "persona"; they are strong digital business leaders or champions with their own unique strength and style. Here are nine types of digital master with decoded digital charm as **"CHASEHAIL."**

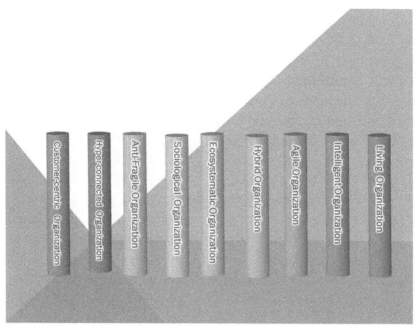

Figure 2:Decode Digital Master Style "CHASEHAIL"

- **C – Customer Centric Digital Business**: When companies adopt customer-centric strategies, customers become the primary drivers of "what" work should be done, "how" work should be done, and "who" should do it. These digital masters are customer champion.

- **H – Hyper-Connected Digital Business**: Hyper-connectivity is the key characteristic of digital organization for connecting the dots, both across and within organizational boundaries. These digital masters create deep "harmony" for strategy execution, and a business organization can only achieve high performance via seamless execution.

- **A – Anti-Fragile Digital Business:** Organizations with anti-fragility have better ability to tolerate volatility and thrive through it. Anti-fragility equals more to gain than to lose, more upside than downside. It equals asymmetry and likes volatility. An option is the weapon of anti-fragility. Option = Asymmetry + Rationality. Digital masters love options because digital is also the era of options.

- **S – Sociologic Business:** The digital paradigm that is emerging is the sociological organization, one that is alive, holistic, vibrant, energetic, responsive, fluid, creative, and innovative. These digital masters have transcendent business purpose and take hybrid and innovative business practices.

- **E – Ecosystematic Business**: It is critical that businesses diligently focus on the people construct and, through deliberate design, craft a more socially connected and dynamic people-centered ecosystem, taking full advantage of the massive shift from" push" to "pull" power. These digital masters are essentially a dynamic, people-centered ecosystem with agility and flexibility.

- **H – Hybrid Business**: A hybrid nature of organization well mixes the virtual social platform with physical structure to enforce cross-functional collaboration and innovation. These digital masters have a harmonized vision about overall business capabilities and maturities in an organization, and build customized structure to enforce open communication and collaboration.

- **A – Agile Business**: Agility must be built into an organization's very foundation, from mind-set to culture, from strategy to design, from processes to capability. These digital masters have strong business agility that provides them with solid agile pillars to respond in a timely, effective, and sustainable way when changing circumstances require it.

- **I – Intelligent Business:** Analytics becomes a decision discipline and innovation engine to pursue customer-centricity in high mature intelligent enterprises. These digital masters pervasively explore business intelligence and analytics applications cross enterprise to improve business agility and results. They are ultra-smart businesses.

- **L – Living Business**: These digital businesses have special attributes such as flexibility, responsiveness, passion, engagement, relationship, resilience, etc. These are more of what has been called the soft side of business for a long time, and they are the critical digital traits of living digital masters.

By becoming more cognizant of common digital traits and understanding of the digital uniqueness of these pivotal leaders as well as digital masters, businesses overall can build solid knowledge upon digital transformation and strike the right digital balance on the digital journey.

4. Digital Shift # 1: Customer-Centric Organization

Digital is the age of customer and digitalization is a constant game changer for the organization.

One of the key characteristics of digital organizations is customer-centricity. When companies adopt customer-centric strategies, customers become the primary drivers of "what" work should be done, "how" work should be done, and "who" should do it. Being customer-centric also needs to have more organic than mechanic structure to empower than control, engage than command, and dynamic than static.

- **Customer-centric organization takes outside-in customer view**: Customer-centric organization means very different things to different people. Customer experience comes from all touch points, yet organizations are structured by departments, which hinder their ability to create value. Customer-centricity is the description of the nature of the priorities in the organization. Unless the digital strategy, mind-set, culture, capability, and skills are continuously improved, then "customer-centric strategy" is a buzzword. Process, structure, behavior, and self-interest of individuals and groups are factors that interact in dynamic ways and powerfully impact the direction and outcome of the transitions and ultimate digital transformation. It's like a circle. Redesigned processes may require behaviors that may be out of one's comfort zone. Structural changes also may be necessitated based on extent and spread of redesign of processes. The consideration of digital design may include: How would you ensure that all structures, processes, and strategy alignment around an excellent customer experience to result in a profitable and evolving business? How would you model different value propositions to different customer segments, yet develop and offer the product and services using the same or similar business capabilities? In that manner, digital transformation doesn't become a one-time activity. Instead, it is a constant game changer for the organization.

- **Organizational design facilitates the customer-centric priority:** Customer-centric organizational design has to be much more "organic" in the sense that it's melded with process and even technology. For example, how customer-related data should be managed and on which systems often has significant organizational repercussions. Organizational design is the structure, and sometimes the strategies themselves, that facilitates the customer-centric priority. In customer-driven organizational design, the most important internal players are those understanding the "what," "how," and "who" – plus the "why." Technical organizational design knowledge may play a support role, but it's not at the forefront. Whichever group is shaping the strategy for an organization has a strong understanding of the organizational architecture and design. Organizational design is the ultimate expression of the organization's strategy because it reflects the resource allocation and configuration of the value-creating processes. From a structural perspective, whether it's "organic" depends on the culture of the organization, its life cycle and extent of rapid change outside the organization.

- **Customer-centricity takes both top-down strategy and bottom-up approach:** The strategic plan needs to be well articulated, communicated, made personally relevant to all employees, and sustained to reflect customer-desired outcomes. Customer integration, behavioral, emotional, social, and transactional design is well understood and practiced. Being customer-centric is not just a few best practices, or even high level customer interface; it has to go deeper to integrate all key business components to orchestrate a highly mature digital business that has key capabilities to delight customers. There's a pendulum swinging between people and process, engagement and efficiency, in order to adapt to the spiral changes facing in organizations. The problem usually is that when change is planned, the focus goes over to improving the process, and sometimes, one may forget that the real change has to come from the way people adopt new ways of thinking and, only then, new ways to work to achieve customer-centricity.

Being customer-centric is a transcendent digital trait and core of corporate strategy in today's digital organizations. An organic organizational structure that is melded with process and technology can sustain strategy and accelerate execution. It is a bridge to connect from serving customers to being customer-centric. Organizations have to exert considerable intelligence, do data analytics, look for insights, use imagination, validate, predict, try to inspire employees, and fight to make their business customer-centric, while keeping profitable for the long run.

5. Digital Shift # 2: A Hyper-Connected Organization

Hyper-connectivity is the nature characteristic of Digital.

Command-and-control comes through the industrial revolution and the perspective that everything, including organizations, can be viewed as mechanical in nature. The emerging digital era has also been referred as the "Birth of the Chaotic Age," due to its VUCA characteristics such as information explosion, volatility, uncertainty, connectivity, and ambiguity. It makes a very strong case that command-and-control organizations are inherently incapable of handling, processing, and managing the sheer volume of information they acquire. The crucial digital shift is to build a hyper-connected, widely-collaborative organization and business ecosystem.

- **Hyper-connectivity is the key characteristic of digital organization:** Connecting the dots, both across and within organizational boundaries, has always been a problem. Few organizations have found a way to reward the type of thinking that allows people to connect the dots. Dot connecting is knowledge alignment. Many people are capable of "connecting the dots" but, unfortunately, there's a lack of cultural support for independent thinking and contrarian positions often are prevalent. In short, it's often risky for people to stick their necks out, particularly when they may not have the concrete data to establish certainty. Therefore, the emerging digital organization must update the old fashion of stuff from management, culture, and process perspectives:

(1) Silos
(2) Autocratic management
(3) Individualistic cultures or a culture that must have winners and losers
(4) Bureaucracy
(5) Fear of litigation and making mistakes generally

- **Broad-collaboration across-business ecosystem**: An organization is about collaboration. Collaboration through the cloud and social media is already driving changes to enterprise systems to expose them to outside change. Use technology to enable integral design and holistic customer experience, rather than use it as a constraint. Complexity science and chaos theory, which demonstrate more of a biological model, are still fairly new and have not yet gained widespread acceptance or understanding.

Combine that with the fact that most decision makers grew up in the mechanical or command-and-control perspective, it's no wonder that we're not there yet. But many enterprises are learning to be much more considerate in order to build customer-centric, employee-satisfied, high-performing and sustainable organizations by getting the structure right.

- **Hyper-connectivity enhances transparency**: While people fight over the correctness and structure internally within organizations, the customers are turning to businesses that give them the control and power to maintain their personal data as source, though they understand that the digital normal is moving away from privacy and toward transparency. The cost benefits of maintaining data are in the design of the overall system, which includes people, process, and technology, not only the tools. That is why collaboration matters. Organizations need to move away from mantras like "truth is in the data and data must be in one place" as an excuse for creating barriers, gatekeepers, constraints, and overloads. And you do need to enable it in the design of the systems, with business goals to optimize business process and enhance customer experiences.

- **Create business harmony:** Collaboration is good, but it's not an end in itself. Creating a context where people can collaborate, where they are empowered, respected and make collective decisions, is the essence of information governance. It is the ultimate state of digital "harmony." A business organization can only achieve high performance through seamless execution by taking the collaboration road; the organization will not be blind to underlying the business challenges. Moreover, such a path should offer a more holistic view, hence allowing for the work design, pay and incentive systems, and decision-making structure. And the design of an organization will have significant impact on performance and how considerate the organization is. This is because dysfunctional sociopolitical contexts are representative of bad structure and not bad people. Thus, an organizational design structure that includes policy must be adaptable, take advantage of the latest digital technology platforms and tools, and provide the space for people to exercise their capabilities.

Hyper-connectivity is the very nature characteristic of Digital. At a hyper-connected digital organization, business execution, innovation, and transformation are fostered through high-degree collaboration, transparency, and business harmony, with laser focus on business values and people centricity.

6. Digital Shift # 3:
An Anti-Fragile Organization

"Antifragility is beyond resilience or robustness. The resilient resists shocks and stays the same; the antifragile gets better."
– Nassim Nicholas Taleb

Digital organizations are hyper-connected and interdependent so they can continue to adapt to the digital new normal such as volatility, uncertainty, complexity, and ambiguity. "Antifragile: Things That Gain from Disorder," written by Nassim Nicholas Taleb may provide another angle to perceive the future of business and its key characteristics.

- **Anti-fragility is beyond resilience or robustness**: Resilience resists shocks and stays the same; anti-fragility gets better. The anti-fragile loves randomness and uncertainty, which means a love of errors, allowing organizations to deal with the unknown, to do things without understanding them and do them well. By grasping the mechanisms of anti-fragility, people can build a systematic and broad guide to nonpredictive decision making under uncertainty in business and life in general.

- **Anti-fragile is organic and complex:** Digital organizations are organic, complex and living, whereas industrial organizations are mechanical and hierarchical. A complex system, contrary to what people believe, does not require complicated systems, regulations, and intricate policies; simple is more sophisticated in such circumstances. Complex systems are full of interdependencies, hard to detect and nonlinear responses; the simpler, the better. Complications lead to multiplicative chains of unanticipated effects.

- **Anti-fragility has a high degree of interdependence**: Digital organization as a whole is anti-fragile, but some parts maybe fragile. Anti-fragility gets a bit more intricate and more interesting in the presence of layers and hierarchies. A natural organism is not a single, final unit; it is composed of subunits and itself may be the subunit of some larger collective. Some parts on the inside of a system may be required to be fragile in order to make the system anti-fragile as a result, or the organization itself might be fragile, but the information encoded in the genes reproducing it will be anti-fragile.

Fragile	Anti-fragile
Mechanical, noncomplex	Organic, complex
Needs continuous repair and maintenance	Self-healing
Hates randomness	Loves randomness
No need for recovery	Needs recovery between stressors
No or little interdependence	High degree of interdependence
Time brings only senescence	Time brings aging and senescence

Table 1: Fragile vs. Anti-fragile

- **Anti-fragility has better ability to tolerate volatility**: Anti-fragility equals more to gain than to lose; equals more upside than downside; equals asymmetry, likes volatility; and if you make more when you are right than you hurt when you are wrong, then you will benefit in the long run from volatility. Thus, if a digital organization has anti-fragile characteristics, it can have much better ability to tolerate volatility, because anti-fragile means the harm from errors should be less than the benefits. Those that do not destroy a system help prevent larger calamities. The complication of traditional organizations is caused by layering, units, hierarchies, fractal structure, and the difference between the interests of a unit and those of its subunits.

- **Antifragility is self healing**: For the anti-fragile, shocks bring more benefits as their intensity increase. For the fragile, the cumulative effect of small shocks is smaller than the effect of an equivalent single large shock. At traditional organizations, treating a business organism like a simple machine is a kind of simplification, approximation, or reduction. Where simplification fails, causing the most damages is when something nonlinear is simplified with the linear as a substitute. Why is fragility nonlinear? The answer has to do with the structure of survival probabilities; conditional on something being unharmed, then it is more harmed by a single rock than a thousand pebbles. Nonlinear means that the response is not straightforward and not a straight line, so if you double the dose, you get a lot more or a lot less than double the effect – that is by a single large infrequent event than by the cumulative effect of smaller shocks. The difference between a thousand pebbles and a large stone of equivalent weight is a potent illustration of how fragility stems from nonlinear effects.

- **An option is the weapon of anti-fragility**: Many things people think are derived by skill come largely from options: Option = Asymmetry + Rationality. The difference between the anti-fragile and fragile lies there. The fragile has no option. But the anti-fragile needs to select what's the best option:

(1) Look for optionality.
(2) Preferably with open-ended, not closed-ended payoffs.

(3) Do not invest in business plans but in people; for example, look for someone capable of changing six or seven times or more over his/her career.

Time and fragility: Anti-fragility implies, contrary to initial instinct, that the old is superior to the new and much more than you think. No matter how something looks to your intellectual machinery, or how well or poorly it narrates, time will know more about its fragilities and breaks it when necessary. The foundational asymmetry is that the anti-fragile benefits from volatility and disorder, but the fragile is harmed.

Therefore, the digital organization with "anti-fragile" characteristics can better survive and thrive in volatility and uncertainty; it can well adapt to the business nature of complexity and interdependence, as well as lift business maturity significantly.

7. Digital Shift # 4: A Sociological Organization

The sociological organization is alive, holistic, vibrant, energetic, responsive, fluid, creative and innovative.

From a philosophical perspective, all things serve a purpose. We may not understand the purpose, but all things serve one. Humans demand to be served, so they create mechanistic and sociological systems to serve them. Enterprises demand to be served, so they create positions of employment and mechanistic systems to serve them. These systems have a purpose for which they act to fill. The digital paradigm that is emerging is the sociological organization, one that is alive, holistic, vibrant, energetic, responsive, fluid, creative, and innovative. Hence, a modern digital organization has a transcendent business purpose.

- **Mechanistic System vs. Social System:** Russell Lincoln Ackoff, an American organizational theorist and the pioneer of system thinking and management science, differentiates between "serving" a purpose and "demanding to be served." Mechanistic systems serve a purpose. They do not demand to be served. In this respect, the difference between the purposeless systems (mechanistic) and the purposeful structures (sociological) becomes clear, based on the definitions of mechanical and social as defined by Ackoff:

Mechanistic System	Social System
Where the whole has no purpose of its own and the parts have no purposes of their own.	Where the whole has a purpose of its own as well as the parts.
Example: Car engine, where neither the parts nor the whole can autonomously decide to have different ends or different means.	Example: Business enterprise, where the organization has purposes of its own and the people working there maintain purposes of their own.

Table 2: Mechanistic System vs. Social System

- **The hard vs. soft system**: The enterprise consists of an amalgam of socio-systems, techno-systems, bio-systems, and econo-systems. From an architectural perspective, the only factor that is introduced into design concepts is the question of what implications it has when the animistic aspects of your design behave differently because "their" purpose is not being served. The designer must not only consider the purpose of the enterprise; the considerations of the purposes of the employees must also be met, because the enterprise cannot fulfill its purpose without the employees. And unhappy employees will leave or not fill the purpose they are serving in the enterprise. You have to deal with the architecture of both hard and soft "systems."

- **Flexibility is a principle that guides system design:** It theoretically guides the original design and should continue to guide the evolution of the system. Flexibility would be important in many systems, but there are some systems for which flexibility is a much less important attribute than, for example, reliability. The challenge is that most enterprise architecture frameworks are very mechanistic in nature and do not know how to address business and people system dynamics. Flexibility would be embodied in the multiple system aspects differently. An often forgotten fact is that organizations consist of three types of intersecting and interacting systems: Social, technical, and cultural systems.

- **The architecture and design of a sociocultural-technical system is both art and science**: An enterprise is never going to be architected and designed like a building. The approach to architecting and designing social systems must be necessarily different than architecting and designing mechanical systems. First and foremost, because of the capacity of senior managers to override decisions made by enterprise architects, whether or not they grant authority to make decisions. And there is full knowledge of the distinction between design implementation and architecture decisions. Designing an organization, that is a sociocultural-technical system, is orders of magnitude more difficult than designing a "data-driven mechanistic system"; and a "data-driven mechanistic system" is but one of many technical systems. A good architecture is one that guides the total enterprise ecosystem to either generate wealth for shareholders or generate prosperity of constituencies.

Therefore, you have to look holistically at the problem domain to architect and design a sociological organization, and guide conversations based on the artifacts being produced. This is most challenging when, due to marketplace exigencies, radical culture and social structure changes are required.

8. Digital Shift # 5: A Digital "Ecosystem"

Digital organization is essentially a dynamic, people-centered ecosystem.

A digital ecosystem is a distributed, adaptive, open socio-technical system with properties of self-organization, scalability, and sustainability inspired from natural ecosystems. Digital ecosystem models are informed by knowledge of natural ecosystems, especially for aspects related to competition and collaboration among diverse entities (wikipedia). Increasingly, enterprises find themselves enmeshed in digital "ecosystems" whether they like it or not. For the most part, while they can influence and be influenced by these "ecosystems," they have limited "control" over them.

- **Enterprises have always been parts of simple or complex ecosystems**: That is the fundamental nature of the marketplace and the environment within which the enterprise functions. To function, an enterprise has to be linked to the many and varied "touch points" between itself and the marketplace environment of which it is a part. Why should it matter if the internal organization is hierarchical and the ecosystem is lattice? The enterprise is nothing more than a "switch" in the network lattice of the ecosystem. The aspect that matters is ensuring that the enterprise is connected to all the appropriate ecosystem, lattice or otherwise, touch points.

- **Digital organization is essentially a dynamic, people-centered ecosystem**: Hierarchical structures will be transcended to·the interconnected, network structure. Looking at all the elements (including the human element) as an integrated, systemic system that, at times, seems to be and functions as an organic living thing. "Individual" work and "group" work cannot be done as a segregated form, but within a "framework" of an entire system or business ecosystems that include systems, processes, policies, culture, work climates, customers, supply-side chain, society, laws, etc., an integration of across global business, social and political systems. The optimal internal structure, and the democratic nature of the enterprise is the one that provides the greatest effectiveness and efficiency, and depends, in large measure, on the nature and purpose of the enterprise.

- **Digital organization needs strong and viable DNA to sustain its agility:** Autocratic enterprises are limited by their DNA to take benefit of such ecosystems; after all, such systems are most likely to have a lattice-based architecture rather than a hierarchy. So, perhaps organizations now have an architectural mismatch wherein enterprises that are internally hierarchical have to operate in an environment where the external structure is a lattice. In a digital enterprise, it is not necessarily the case that a less structured and more dynamic enterprise means a diminished role for enterprise architecture. Such an organization essentially needs strong, viable DNA to sustain its operation and ongoing flexibility and agility. Enterprise Architecture (EA) is not only a mechanism; it's also a philosophy and methodology to enable such a best scenario. Enterprise architecture will assist it in determining what it needs to focus on and strengthen in order to attain this state. As long as the interfaces are provided and remain, why it should matter what happens:

  (1) Individual enterprises and the ecosystems they operate in are both complex adaptive systems. Such systems do not operate in a linear, predictable way as the whole notion of "master–slave" relationship does not work.
  (2) Such systems also have the added complexity of not just dynamic relationships, but also dynamic nodes. It probably comes to the conclusion that if one wishes to pursue enterprise democratization, then EA provides a philosophy, methodology, and mechanism to make it more visible about what is being decided, and therefore it will become a valuable tool.

A digital organization is a people-centric digital ecosystem. Business change is hyper-accelerating, especially as it relates to the people and value creation dimensions, and it is more important than ever to engage sharp thought leaders to help the enterprise chart the course and set a better sail. It is critical that businesses diligently focus on the people construct and, through deliberate design, craft a more socially connected and dynamically people-centered ecosystem to take full advantage of the massive shift from push to pull power.

9. Digital Shift # 6: A Hybrid Organization

A hybrid nature of organization strikes the right balance between "virtual world" and the human connections.

With the fast pace of change and emerging digital technologies such as social, mobile, and cloud, companies large or small are brainstorming the next generation of organizational structure design, how to take advantage of the new digital tools and how to improve productivity and enforce creativity as well as collaboration across the enterprise border.

- **Virtual vs. Physical**: A hybrid nature of organization well mixes the virtual or social platform with physical functional structure to enforce cross-functional collaboration and innovation, to strike the right balance between "virtual worlds" and "the human connection." While technology provides new frontiers for work systems, there also are challenges with issues of human "connectivity." What's intended to bring us closer together may leave us feeling further apart. But deep human connection may still be important, and the connection is not just about physical connection, but more importantly emotional connection. The impact of digital and social technology is that the future of the organization will become more virtual and that virtual organizational design expertise will become more important in the coming years.

- **Digital organization is hybrid, networked, and extended**. The emergent organizational models will integrate with social process models (both structured and unstructured social processes). Chaos theories and complex adaptive system will integrate with developmental processes. A digital organization is a hybrid, networked, extended modern working environment; the digital computing technology enables a more seamless virtual platform, enhances the physical organizational structure, empowers workforce sharing of thoughts and ideas, engages customers and partners to voice concerns and feedback, and encourages broader conversation and interaction with its business ecosystem and social value chain. But the supportive leadership has always been the basic premise of the organizational models. It's a matter of getting senior leadership to buy in to the practice, and that goes straight to ROI.

- **Centralized vs. decentralized design**: Organizational democracy will begin to become a fundamental management practice. Hence, organizational design needs to well reflect leadership competency: that democratic processes will overtake hierarchical control and that culture will become a more fundamental organizational asset through the impact of digital and social technology. The key is to improve business agility and enhance cohesive business capabilities. Functions that need the agility and customer intimacy can be decentralized and perhaps even embedded in business processes. Functions that are common to the enterprise or commodity services can be centralized to derive scale benefits. That said, the lower you go on the technology stack, the more it makes sense to centralize. The functions closest to the business are best federated; where the line crosses is driven by the complexity of the business model.

A hybrid organizational structure can bring greater awareness of the intricacies and the systemic value of organizational systems, processes, people dynamics, technological touch, resource allocation, supply side variables, market variables, economies of scale, etc. The challenge is to have a harmonized vision about overall business capabilities and maturities in an organization, and build a customized structure to enforce open communication and collaboration. This is a strong point of cost reduction and optimization of the technologies; in other words, it provides economies of all kind of resources (material and human). Still, people are the focal point of any organizational design; the purpose of a tailored hybrid organization is to produce deliverable quality, improve business productivity and agility, and encourage innovation and optimization as well.

10. Digital Shift # 7: An Agile Organization

An agile organization has seamless interactions between agile philosophy, principle, value, practices, methods, development, and management disciplines.

Agile is not just a software management methodology, but a business management philosophy, Agility is the dynamic capability that allows organizations to adapt to the digital new normal (volatility, uncertainty, complexity, and ambiguity). Doing agile is still not good enough because it is only a process; being agile means changing the way people think and behave, and embedding agility into the very fabric of an organization. Being agile means anticipating likely change and addressing it deftly, keeping business on course and customers satisfied. The point is, how to apply agile principle, agile practices, or agile methods to build a truly agile organization, from doing agile to being agile, from efficiency to effectiveness to agility, is an ultimate goal that organizations pursue to reach their digital maturity.

- **Strategic agility**: Since the digital context is changing all the time, organizations need to change the way they think of business strategy. The volatility of the digital dynamic complicates detailed planning and requires an even greater time commitment. Old methods work, but they are much too time consuming and too expensive to fit into the new economy. Therefore, strategic planning becomes a "living process," with regular evaluation, scanning, listening, revisiting, and potential course correction. It takes a combination of (a) recognizing and challenging the role of mental models in assumptions about the future and (b) having the means to reallocate priorities and resources nimbly when change occurs. Without that, strategic plans can actually be an impediment, and certainly become unsustainable.

- **System agility:** It is to establish and employ a comprehensive organizational learning system that looks broadly and deeply at the environment today and in the future. This reveals opportunities, risks, problems, and solutions. Business agility is the ability of an organization to sense opportunity or threat, prioritize its potential responses, and act efficiently and effectively. Forward-looking companies realize that the traditional management is marred by inherent strategic and organizational constraints, and they are looking for alternatives. It takes system agility to transform a traditional organization into an innovative enterprise.

  (1) To review and to reframe the core of the management system.
  (2) To apply methods including the collaborative mode of management.
  (3) To take Agile principal management practices.

- **Agile principles and practices:** The interactions between agile values, principles, and practices are tightly coupled. Understand the Agile principles first, but then to make Agile successful, you'll need a set of framework practices from other areas, such as organizational change, stakeholder management, financial management, IT management, risk management, etc. Without proper stakeholder management, the agile adventure will soon be over. However, the downfall of many framework practices is that people tend to view them as purely prescriptive. They happily adopt rituals with little understanding of why they are doing them, other than that a mystical methodology calls. The fundamental principles of being agile are about iterative communication and incremental improvement, to break down the silo thinking and enforce cross-functional collaboration in achieving the business optimization.

- **Agile problem solving**: Being agile means to solve business problems more effectively and collaboratively. Problem solving practice developed over many years shows that breaking big problems into smaller ones is the best way to solve problems. Break them down until you have small enough problems to solve and then solve those small problems. By solving many small problems, you solve big problems. The same applies to business goals: by breaking big business goals into smaller goals, each delivers a part of the big goal and you can more easily identify where the real value is and focus on the high value, cutting out the low value noise.

- **Organization agility**: Being agile also means to become a truly holistic organization. Organizational agility is only achieved when the organization changes, stops talking about IT and business as separate entities, recognizes that it is one organization with one set of goals and objectives, and starts to think about ways to achieve those goals, recognizing that there is always room for improvement. Agility is also the strategic balance of standardization and flexibility, targeted at those organizational pressure points where they're not only needed today but will most likely be needed tomorrow – to survive and thrive amid constant change and digital transformation.

The word "agile" is not a noun but an adjective. You need to build an agile organization with agile philosophy, agile principles, agile practices, agile methods, agile development, and agile management disciplines. An adjective applies a quality to the noun. If any of these nouns refers to something that is characterized by the habit of inquiring and adapting rather than predicting and controlling, it probably qualifies as agile. Also, every situation is different and you have to fit the solution to the problem. From doing agile to being agile, it is the transformation from methodology adoption to mind shift, from process toning to culture refining, from an industrial business model jumping into dynamic digital enterprise ecosystem.

11. Digital Shift # 8: An Intelligent Enterprise

An intelligent organization is not about the "cleverness" of one analytics team but the insightful nature of entire business.

Information is the lifeblood of digital business, and almost all forward-looking organizations are declaring that they are information and technology businesses. More and more organizations have "digital ambition" to become customer-centric, ecological, and smart businesses. Analytics become a decision discipline, a gold mine and innovation engine to pursue customer-centricity in highly mature intelligent enterprises. It pervasively explores analytics applications across enterprises to improve business agility and results. It is not about the "cleverness" of one analytics team or one IT division; the intelligence becomes the nature of the entire business and permeates into all key business process. Analytics becomes a core capability to impact business's survival and thriving.

- **The convergence of analytics technologies**: The convergence of machine learning, artificial intelligence, analytics and business intelligence, statistics, and decision science will make a direct impact on building an intelligent business. Talented people, particularly those in a position where they need a dramatic change to the status quo in enterprise computing, are seeking to exploit the value found in convergence of advanced analytics technologies with much more efficient returns, easier to use for the entire knowledge workforce on any device anytime anywhere, and to build a smart business based on:

  (1) The ability to make data-based, on-time decisions.
  (2) The ability to access the right data at the right time at the right location.
  (3) The ability to make context-based suggestions and recommendation.

- **Agile Business Intelligence (BI)**: BI agility is achievable through agile development and project management; the iterative process can significantly shorten development cycles and speed time to market for analytics requests. It is now possible to deliver analytics value to end users in weeks, not years. Agile BI also means the emerging analytics trends: the next generation of Agile BI such as social BI, cloud BI, or mobile BI., etc, are web-based, self-service, and deliver the insight or even foresight more dynamically. It helps organizations to make the right decisions through recognizing both opportunities and threats and responding to the customers' requests more promptly.

- **Cloud-Based Intelligence:** Cloud provides the alternative model to deliver Analytics-as a-Service, and improve business agility without hassle to upgrade hardware and software, though most of organizations may take a hybrid approach for in-house development and cloud-based analytics solution. Through leveraging the cloud capacity, organizations can have broader access to all relevant types of data, with updated approaches for mobile access to data and analytic results. BI in the cloud environment can provide users with SaaS-based, self-service analytics capability.

- **Mobile Intelligence**: Mobile is pervasive these days; it is a strategic imperative to leverage mobile technologies to share information and gather input to make on-time decisions. Mobile intelligence means taking advantage of the mobile platform to deliver and present information in a concise, user-friendly way by leveraging interactive and visual capability. It also means enhancing collaboration capabilities to open up strategy setting and performance management solutions, to seamlessly link the boardroom with operations across the organization. With the convenience to access information at any time, any location through mobile computing, both consumers and businesses can make better and faster decisions.

- **Social Intelligence**: Social media data can help enterprises understand their customers better, as well as their employees. Some hot social analytics trends, such as sentiment analysis, recognize subjective information that can be used to identify the polarity and determine the trends in public opinion, etc. Social intelligence also can provide companies a 360-degree view of business performance, paving the way toward true customer engagement, partner collaboration, and ecosystem connection, The momentum around social intelligence will continue to transform business models, strategy, structure, and management, so it will become a key cornerstone for all enterprise BI strategies.

- **Self-Service BI and Analytics:** Perhaps the only thing about self-service that is accurate is that analysts can engage with their tools or business users can click on their charts in a dashboard. Surely, it doesn't mean the analytics just serve up pretty charts and graphs. They must make it easy for business users to explore and correlate multiple dimensions of data. Visualization and intuitive user interfaces are making it possible for more people in the workforce to do the data exploration and self-service analytics and build a broader culture of inquiry to gain insight upon customer and business.

- **Big Data + Small Data**: Digitalization drives the massive cultural shift that is taking place at an increasing volume and velocity, producing a variety of data to pursue the value of information. An intelligent organization will develop an effective information management strategy to acquire, analyze and orchestrate both big data and small data, and continue to explore innovative ways to analyze, model, visualize, and extract value to formulate insight needed to solve complex business problems and weave the foresight to prepare for the future of the business. It's one of the most powerful tools to debunk the hyper-connected and overly complex digital world.

The beauty of a digital landscape is the fresh insight of business. An intelligent organization always looks for opportunities across the business to increase the usage of predictive analytics, social analytics, and collaborative decision making accordingly. Digital shift is a mind-set shift, which also comes with an information shift – a shift that will allow organizations to take advantage of information to gain knowledge and insight; a shift to drive culture and transformation toward a more intelligent enterprise; a shift from playing smart tools to being smart, intelligent, or even wiser within business and beyond. That is what a truly intelligent business stands for: to ultimately engage employees and delight customers.

12. Digital Shift # 9: A Living Organization

A Living Organization is flexible, responsive, and resilient.

With increasing speed of change and exponential growth of information, the hierarchical organization is no long effective enough to adapt to the changes, so how can one design an organization of the future to run at digital speed with an ultramodern leadership style, and how can one build up a dynamic, adaptable, and living digital business?

- **A Living Organization is organic, alive, and holistic**: The new paradigm that is emerging is one of a Living Organization, one that is organic, alive, holistic, vibrant, energetic, responsive, fluid, creative, and innovative, in relationship with its environment, customers, or suppliers, and above all enhances and supports the dignity of the creative human spirit. Because the current machine paradigm is not capable of addressing the needs of today's more dynamic, complex changing world, attempts to solve existing challenges through the lens of the old paradigm are also failing.

- **A Living Organization is flexible, responsive, and resilient**: Business attributes such as flexibility, responsiveness, passion, engagement, relationship, resilience, etc., are more of what has been called the soft side of business for a long time, and they are the critical digital traits. However, the current business paradigm is still essentially rooted in the mechanistic understanding or framing of the reductionistic view of the universe. Thus, it is no wonder we have a machine-like paradigm for organizing work. The organization of the future will be an "organically" and adaptively developed system, and empowered by an intelligent organizational design that puts values and people before rules and roles.

- **A Living Organization is fast, adaptive, and anti-fragile:** A Living Organization starts with a transcendent purpose that leads to a unique natural design, a design most fit to achieve the purpose under current conditions. The natural design allows the organization to morph as life conditions and organization capacities change to allow a better fit for the purpose. When that purpose is fulfilled, or a more compelling purpose appears, then the organization can morph again and move on to the next great purpose. Nevertheless, different rules for a game enable different expressions of the players. Providing a framework model based on a shared culture and on a valuable and well-defined purpose enables people to produce value with the least waste possible along the way, so the new breed of digital organizations are alive, adaptive, fast, and anti-fragile.

- **A Living Organization is an organic system:** A digital organization will be organized as an organic system with cells that have a function, and an infrastructure for input and output and for signaling. Does it need a brain? It might be its information management function. To achieve this, you will eventually break down the hierarchical structure of organization. But to do so, you must replace the "glue" of the hierarchy with something else. That something else will be the purpose of the organization, its mission, the deeply held core values, and the vision of the future it is creating. This compass or principle will guide all levels of the organization to operate more like the human body operates, with the cells (employees) and organs (department) of the organization being able to make decision in a very organic relationship with its environment.

- **A Living Organization is people-centric:** One key determinant of whether an organization can move to new digital structures is the development level of the people. So part of this journey is to prepare people for the new structures and to recognize this is a crucial step. People have to be ready to move to a more fluid structure, any ideas of what are the core qualities or competences determine if one is ready for fluid structure. This shift also will be supported by a new set of organizational processes such as hiring, sales, marketing, performance development, and the latest digital technologies such as social or mobile platform. A living organization embraces three "E"s:

  (1) **EMPOWERMENT** – to share power with all shareholders via true collaboration.
  (2) **ENABLEMENT** – to enable business innovation.
  (3) **ENCHANTING** – to enchant customer via digital touch points and tailored experience.

"Empowerment" and "engagement" cannot be new because they are tools of the existing world. Empowerment does not mean power giving. Power cannot be given; it can be shared. Power given is devolvement of responsibility from the power source.

The real digital shift means principles over rules, empowerment over control, engagement over command, and dynamic over static. The digital organization is a living thing with the ability to continually change as the world changes, perhaps much like the plants follow the sun.

13. Digital Management Shift: A Holistic Style

Holistic management style enforces business agility.

In the industrial era, a majority of organizations have been operated through such a classic management model, which is based on a tacit assumption that organizations can be compared to machines. Consequently, divide-and-conquer strategies are promoted both in organizational design as well as task responsibility and accountability distribution. As Peter Drucker stated: Classic management is about doing things right; it isn't about doing the right things: that's leadership.

- **Digital management is systematic**: Because of classic management, business units often do not work in collaboration; because they are driven by a culture of silos, they fight for limited resource to do what they believe is "locally" right instead of working together in order to do what is "globally right." This is also sustained by a tacit assumption that accountability cannot be given to a group but only to a single person. This is to be expected because most "classic" management principles date from the industrial revolution. The consequence of all of this is that "classic" management doesn't take a systemic approach to management.

- **Holistic management style enforces business agility**: While the characteristics of digitalization are hyper-connectivity, hyper-complexity, and interdependence, the classic management may not be the best fit to tone business agility that is the business capability to respond to the opportunities and risks, to ensure that the organization as whole is greater than the sum of its pieces. Holistic management (a Greek word meaning all, whole, entire, total) is a a digital management style and system thinking approach to managing resources, recognizing initiatives that take a comprehensive, anticipatory, design approach to radically advance human well-being and the health of business ecosystems.

- **Enterprise Architecture (EA) as a tool to tune digital management style**: "Classic management" is a significant part of the root cause of silo thinking, not because of its modernist metaphors but because it's all about power and control. Can Enterprise Architecture become the tool to transform the classic management style into holistic management style? One way to look at this is that EA is a difficult space to be in because it's countercultural to "classic management" and is "holistic" in its approach. However, such a perspective is not compatible with the simplistic reductionism implied by some popular EA frameworks and practices today. Only highly mature EA, which is truly the super glue between strategy and execution, can become an enabler to transform management style to run a digital business more holistically.

What is interesting is how resilient the classic management has been, from the industrial age to the information age, and now into the digital age; from business modernism to postmodernism, it is still there today. Which management style is the best fit may depend on the sector and nature of business. However, we are at a transformational time with more radical digitalization; thus, it is also the right time for a management shift from a classic industry management style to a digital holist management style.

CHAPTER 2

Decode 15 Digital Mind-sets

Changing the game is a mind-set.
– Robert Rodriguez

Introduction

We have moved into the new digital age when information is abundant and where creativity becomes a baseline competence. The race of human against machine is ongoing; the knowledge life cycle is significantly shortened, just as the "agricultural mind" lagged behind the industrial age earlier last century; and now, the industrial mind can also drag down the digital speed. The pace of information technology is so rapid that no one can rest on a static mind-set, past accomplishments, or the wishful thought that everything is perfect the way it is. Indeed, mind-set is far more important than talent. Talent can always be developed by those with an open and right mind-set.

Decode Digital Mind-set "ACCESSOFDIGITAL": Mind-set is important, so what is the major mind shift, and which mind-sets fit in best in the new digital era? How can one cultivate the digital-minded leaders and talent? This chapter will introduce the 15 decoded ultramodern "**ACCESSOFDIGITAL**" mind-sets (the abbreviation of first letter of each digital mind-set) to compete for the future.

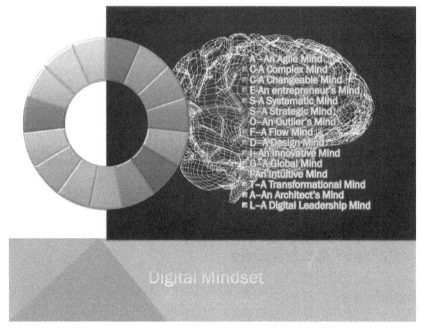

Figure 3: Decode Digital Mind-set "ACCESSOFDIGITAL"

(1) A –An Agile Mind: Agility is the ability to adapt to change. At its core, "agile" is a mind-set, a way of looking at the world and a way of thinking about work at hyper-connected digital world. This mind-set is influenced by twelve principles of the Agile Manifesto.

(2) C – A Complex Mind: Five major sources interact to drive profound changes in today's economic, regulatory, political, and social environments. They are diversity, interdependence, uncertainty, ambiguity, and flux. So the questions are: What is the mind-set to understand complexity in breadth and depth? What is the starting point to manage complexity? How can one change the strategy to dissolve the complexity? How can one be flexible enough to gain from moving into a deep forest?

(3) C – A Changeable Mind: Mind-set is a very broad term, and people are complicated, probably the most complicated "thing" on the planet. But this doesn't mean we can't change to improve who we are and what we're doing. An open, changeable mind-set is a prerequisite of any transformational effort.

(4) E – An Entrepreneur's Mind: An entrepreneur's view is usually positive, dynamic, creative, flexible, and resilient – keep hungry, keep foolish. As the world is stepping into the hyper-connected digital era, the entrepreneur's mind-set needs to be crafted to drive continuous mankind progress and spur the next level of innovation.

(5) S – A Systematic Mind: The characteristics of digitalization are hyper-connectivity, hyper-complexity, and interdependence. Traditional silo thinking is no longer fit for solving many complicated issues facing in business and humanity today. Systematic thinking is the process of understanding how things influence one another within a whole.

(6) S – A Strategic Mind: Strategic thinking is defined as a mental or thinking process applied by an individual in the context of achieving success in a game or other endeavor. It takes strategic mind to shape digital vision. The capability to "think strategically" is more a talent than a skill.

(7) O – An Outlier's Mind: An outlier's mind practices out-of-the-box thinking. Out-of-the-box thinking implies a certain level of creativity or unconventional problem solving. While the box is usually conceptualized as an intellectual boundary, an outlier's mind tries to make the thinking box much larger.

(8) F –A Flow Mind: Shift "mind-set" to mind-scope or mind-flow, so that it allows the mind to seek possibility. It requires that we move from one mind SET to mind flow, from closed mind to open mind, from fixed mind to growth mind.

(9) D –A Design Mind: It is type of agile problem solving mind-set: What is significant about the rise in design thinking is that it provides a counterpoint to the analytical, best-practice methodologies that define the 100-year-old industrial business model of management.

(10) I – An Innovative Mind: Creativity today asks for a new mind-set, a connected world image, the global consciousness, and cognitive intelligence; allowing "the creative flow" to open up for information abundance. The innovative mind or a creative state of mind may not be bound to any one "mind-set," but should be free to be expressed wherever it may pop up, if that makes sense.

(11) G – A Global Mind: Global mind-set is worldview that looks at problems or issues in such a way that a solution emerges through a collaborative multicultural approach involving global psychological capital, intellectual capital, and global social capital.

(12) I – An Intuitive Mind: At the age of Big Data, intuition is not less important, perhaps more critical. It's really interesting to know what intuition is and how we use intuition consciously or subconsciously; it's also interesting to know how to read between the lines and make the right decision, as well as how to listen to your inner voice and decide.

(13) T – A Transformational Mind: With many businesses are at crossroad, facing unprecedented change and uncertainty, they are also at a tipping point to significant transformations such as digitalization, globalization, radical management, and innovation. Leaders and talent with transformational minds are in higher demand because transformational leadership is all about change.

(14) A – An Architect's Mind: The modern architect's mind-set is both good at analytics and synthesis, abstraction and visualization, imagination and practicality, business and technology. All ultramodern leaders and today's digital workforce need to cultivate such mind-sets for better communication and to make multidimensional influences.

(15) L – A Digital Leadership Mind: In the digital age, leaders can make and amplify influence through multiple digital channels. Leaders not only consume the content; they also create content to convey the vision and leadership. The leader's influence is based on courage to inspire, confidence to assert, wisdom to negotiate, and uniqueness to bridge by taking advantage of expanded digital platforms.

1. Agile Mind-set

At its core, Agile is a Mind-set

Agility is the ability to adapt to the changes. At its core, "agile" is a mind-set, a way of looking at the world and a way of thinking about work at hyper-connected digital world. This mind-set is influenced by twelve principles of the Agile Manifesto. It is crucial for successful adoption of a better way of working that the people in the entire organization begin by embracing the values and principles, and then look at the set of practices that will work for them at the level they are at. The 12 Agile Principles and guidelines of Agile can shape 12 types of mind-set integrated into what is called Agile Mind-set:

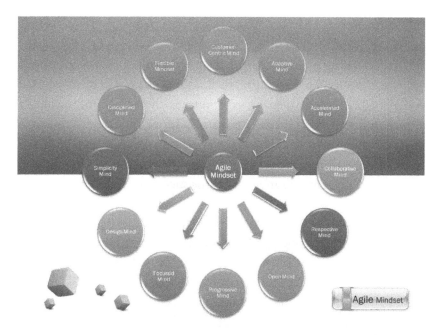

Figure 4: Agile Mind-set

(1) A Customer-Centric Mind: "Our highest priority is to satisfy the customer through early and continuous delivery of valuable software": One essential characteristic of digital organizations is customer-centricity. Being customer-driven is the key to running today's digital businesses. When companies adopt customer-centric strategies and mind-set, customers become the primary drivers of "what" work should be done, "how" work should be done, and "who" should do it.

(2) An Adaptive Mind: "<u>Welcome changing requirements, even late in development</u>." Agile processes harness change for the customer's competitive advantage. Identify the positive early adopters with adaptive mind-set and they'll help you convert the rest. Agile is, in its deepest and most profound sense, a philosophy of intelligent adaptation to constantly acquired knowledge and changing circumstances. It is a balance between what you know and not letting what you know hinder you in discovery of a new innovation as structures and preconceived "truths" are barriers to innovation.

(3) An Accelerated Mind: "<u>Working software frequently, from a couple of weeks to a couple of months, with a preference to the shorter timescale.</u>" With accelerating speed of change, the mind also needs to be sped up as well. From leadership perspective, the leaders with growth mind-set need to develop platforms that enable experimentation and learning, including opportunities to reflect on successes and failures. They should also align rewards with experimentation in a way that doesn't punish failure, but to encourage talent to grow and accelerate the talented individuals who can successfully navigate and harness the successive cycles of learning.

(4) A Collaborative Mind: "<u>Business people and developers must work together daily throughout the project..</u>" The most efficient and effective method to convey information to and within a development team is through open and in-depth conversation. Agile promotes the collaborative spirit to break through the silo thinking and encourage cross-functional interaction and iterative communication. Collaborative teams comprising a diverse range of individuals with cognitive difference will be able to draw on a wider set of experiences to do things both effectively and efficiently. It's meritocracy at its best – a highly diverse set of people collaborate seamlessly to represents nature of how successful digital organizations work today.

(5) A Respective Mind: "Build projects around motivated individuals." Give talent people the environment and support their need, and trust them to get the job done. People are willing to let go of their egos, and those with an open, positive attitude toward change tend to embrace it; those who dislike change, don't communicate well, or are overly defensive are at the other end of the spectrum. Leaders need to show staff that they respect them, understand their cares, and trust them in a safe environment. Help them not to fail, and if they do, show that you are trustworthy by supporting them. Respect others and you will earn respect from them.

(6) An Open Mind: "The most efficient and effective method of conveying information is face to face conversation.": An open mind-set enhances communication, or simply an openness to finding connections between people, ideas, experiences, etc., and making literally or figuratively something new from those insights. All snowflakes have different patterns – cool. Metaphorically speaking, all snowflakes received are valid and held sacred. To be innovative, see with a completely open and untainted mind. All problems can be improved through innovation until they are solved.

(7) A Progressive Mind: "Working software is the primary measure of progresses. We are uncovering better ways": Learning and discovery is constantly happening in agile organizations. The agile values and principles are a foundation on which being built – the practices are much more fluid and will evolve over time. Making progress is a core agile principle. A progressive mind-set is the most powerful force to drive business success and push the human world forward, and the correct assembly of knowledge, ability, and process is the golden goal to pursue.

(8) A Focused Mind: "Agile processes promote sustainable development. The sponsors, developers, and users should be able to maintain a constant pace indefinitely." Being focused is a key success factor to invite feedback and solve problems with synergy. Focus has to do with what one concentrates on. Values and focus make a couple like mind and heart or effectiveness and efficiency; you need both of them to achieve any sustainable success. Values are directing us to do the right things, things or projects we will not regret after a while. Focus gives the energy to complete a task or project we are engaged in. A mind with a progressive value and laser focus can move mountains and achieve goals.

(9) A Design Mind: "Continuous attention to technical excellence and good design enhances agility." The purpose of design thinking is customer-centric, agile, and collaborative problem solving driven by a "thinking out-of-the-box" approach, and looking at the organization from a 360-degree perspective with a key focus on customers. Design thinking is a type of agile problem solving mind-set: What is significant about the rise in design thinking is that it provides a counterpoint to the analytical, best-practice methodologies that define the 100-year-old business model of management that is taught today. It helps to think of problem solving as being on a continuum, with analytical, traditional business thinking on one end and design thinking on the other end.

(10) A Simplicity Mind: "The art of maximizing the amount of work not done is essential." When pioneering and solving problems, initial solutions often are more complex than required, and then adoption and progress come with simplification. Progress is in simplification, which often follows complexity. Simplicity means or is related to too many things such as manageability, availability, scalability, flexibility, reliability, robustness, sensitivity, comprehensiveness, speed, responsiveness, and agility.

(11) A Disciplined Mind: "The best architectures, requirements, and designs emerge from self-organizing teams." Being Agile takes more architecture, engineering or management disciplines, not less. Self-organizing agile teams do have a bounded authority to make their own accountability, organize and assign their own work. The digital paradigm is shaping work from being a place you go during set hours each workday to something you do in a dynamic, increasingly virtual workplace. So work is no longer the place you go but the accomplishment you achieve; thus, a disciplined mind-set is a more crucial successful factor than ever. Or we may say, digital takes more discipline, not less.

(12) A Flexible Mind: "<u>At regular intervals, the team reflects on how to become more effective, then tunes and adjusts its behavior accordingly.</u>" In short, being agile is not about methodology or process; it is about being flexible and adaptable. People who are looking for a fixed methodology or a heavily controlled process for agile will always realize less benefit, if not experience downright failure. The key words here are flexibility and adaptation. Flexibility is the alternative way to do things, and Digital is the era of choices. Talented people with flexible minds can discover the degree of "cultural coherence,"; they are more likely to find a diversity of perspectives and raise critical questions. For this reason, leaders and talent with flexible mind-sets can deemphasize hierarchy and accelerate strategic digital transformation.

Agile is a state of mind based on a set of values and principles. For Agile to work, it needs to be cultural, not an imposed afterthought. Ultimately, all aspects of the enterprise – from strategic planning to the most atomic level tasks – must embrace agile for optimal effect and achieve business agility.

2. Complexity Mind-set

Complexity is perhaps neither a problem nor the enemy; there are both opportunities and risks in it

Besides change, complexity is the most critical characteristics facing in digital business today, what will be the impacts complexity could have on businesses today and how to deal with it strategically? There are five major sources that interact together to drive profound changes in today's economic, regulatory, political, and social environments, they are diversity, interdependence, uncertainty, ambiguity and flux. So the questions are: What's the mind-set to understand complexity in depth? What's the starting point to manage complexity? How does one change the strategy to dissolve the complexity? How can one be flexible enough to gain from moving in a deep forest?

- **Complexity mind-set with four capabilities**: Complexity means increased uncertainty in things outside our control and uncertainty in the results of implementing strategies. Complexity thinking is best thought of as a form of perspectives, continually generating multiple perspectives on issues. There are four capabilities that form the pillars on a development bridge that can close the gap from your current mind-set to the complexity mind-set; they are: **Dynamic attention, integrated capacity, strategic clarity, and cohesive collaboration**. These capabilities expand thinking, improve performance, understand complexity systematically and support high-impact relationships.

- **Complexity thinking has affinity with strategic or scenario planning.** No one sets out on a sailing boat without checking out the wind; yet, most businesses have few procedures in place to routinely assess relative strength and direction:

    (1) Complexity is part of the day-to-day new normal of any digital business.
    (2) High complexity is associated with a high uncertainty.
    (3) The complexity is generated externally and has an impact inside of the business.
    (4) Before develop a business strategy, the organization needs to set the purpose of business and understand the business dynamic.
    (5) Evaluating the business environment via three dimensions: Predictability, Malleability, and Harshness.
    (6) Deciding on the best strategy for a particular business.

- **Complexity is new reality:** The biggest challenge for strategists with complexity mind-set is how to convert the outcome of the complexity analysis into an operational plan that will make the difference and aid achievement of their final goal. Complexity is tightly related with initiative. If you are a mover, complexity is your partner because it makes it difficult for your competitors to recognize your moves and address them adequately in time.

If you are a mere reactor, growing complexity makes growing troubles for you. Further, even with parity of information input and equal conclusion on the analysis between competitors in the same market, there won't necessarily be an advantage to one competitor over the other. But strategically speaking, coping better with complexity than the competition does provide a competitive advantage.

- **Mastering Complexity is a "must have" capability**: Complexity is perhaps neither a problem nor the enemy, there're both opportunities and risks in it. Complexity can be lessened as a problem or grasped as an opportunity with systems thinking and dynamic strategy, as well as adaptive talent with flexible processes. Organizations must learn to navigate uncertainty, innovate, and adapt to increasingly changing business realities. You cannot manage something that you cannot measure, but fortunately, complexity can be measured and there are techniques to understand how complexity can become a problem for your business and how it can be properly managed. The key is to align well the complexity thinking, governance processes, and a well-defined set of metrics.

Complexity is a nature characteristic, with color, with pattern, with theme, and it can create order as well as chaos; just depends on how you deal with it, and complexity mind is a an optimal digital mind-set to see both trees and forest, business and its ecosystem, to solving complex business problems more systematically.

3. A "Changeable" Mind-set

Mind-set is probably the most complicated "thing" on the planet

Open, changeable mind-set is a prerequisite of any transformational effort. But what is the closed mind? It is in human nature, people don't like the unknown because they fear; people don't like the ones who are not like them because they don't recognize them; people don't like new ideas because they fear to fail. This is what is called the state of the closed mind. So what's the opposite – changeable mind-set?

- **Mind-set is everything:** Change is accelerated in the digital era; embracing change requires a change of mind-set at every level and an understanding that things cannot stay the same. This is the groundwork that has to be done at all levels prior to initiating major transformation. Human beings are somewhat orthodox, get used to a comfort zone, and see changes as a threat. In the depth of individual and sociological funnel of behaviors, expectations, and group pressure, it might be difficult for a person to see with another pair of eyes, tone the tunnel vision, or cross the linear thinking, so how one shapes an open and collective mind-set effectively is critical for changes.

- **Mind-set is at the heart of one's belief system**: Mind-set is generated by years of experiences and sometimes takes new experiences to affect it. Everyone comes to work for different reasons; the alignment of those reasons with the objectives of the company is what keeps people active and involved in the business. Changing mind-sets is challenging; often if people have been in an organization for a long period of time, their mind-set may be one of "I don't want to change, and why should I?" Mind-set is at the heart of the belief system. These are beliefs that we all hold and have formed over time and through hard experience. If we agree with this, then we would have to say that we cannot change others' mind-set; only they can.

- **Change is about moving forward and improving:** It should be managed in a very grassroots way because not all change is an improvement. So, in some respects, those who resist change could argue that they do so because either the change will not result in an improvement or that the improvement is not evident to them. The perspective that "people resist change" has reasons. It is entirely possible that the resistance is symptomatic of a number of deeper causes, one of which is that the change has not been properly defined, aligned, or considered in respect to potential undesirable effects and appropriate mitigation strategies. Changing a mind-set is very important. It can be managed through active participation of the leadership demonstration that the mind-set is a part of the culture.

- **The management mind-set is the "mainstream" mind-set:** A critical mind-set that needs to change is the mind-set of management that says "I know best, and because I know best, you have to do what I say." It is the mind-set of trying to control the things that you cannot control; that is the foundation of these other mind-sets. Change that and you change everything. Another mind-set that needs to change is that of the "blame game," where blame always travels downward, like gravity. Try to adopt a behavioral approach that requires each person to take responsibility for his or her own actions, since ultimately this is what one can control. Business leaders or managers must first examine their own mind-set, craft the methodologies, and define the metrics to measure the progress:

  (1) Their mind-sets about how easy or difficult the change will be to achieve.
  (2) Their methodology about how change is done.
  (3) Their perceptions of the players who will be in the change initiative.
  (4) Their decision making about the direction of the change.
  (5) The degree, scope, and nature of the change required.

- **Sell the changes.** Mind-set is a very broad term, and people are complicated, probably the most complicated "thing" on the planet. But it doesn't mean we can't change to improve who we are and what we're doing. If you believe it's difficult, guess what? It will be. Resistance to any change is results of ingrained attitudes about oneself and about the company. People are egoists so they tend to cover the ignorance and weaknesses with exaggerated extroversive behaviors. These mind-sets can be described as defensive and resist or reject anything that affects cozy familiarity. Very often, they are founded on insecurity. To effect change, you need to think about how to sell the change to the team. This is done by:

(1) Talking about the need for change in relationship to the customer needs and the employee needs as well as the business needs.
(2) Including the people in the process so they don't feel that change has been imposed on them.
(3) Celebrating the successes along the way, not just overcoming objections to change.
(4) Encouraging the people who are on board, not just trying to convince the resisters to get on board.

A "changeable mind-set" is a success factor to any change management effort, a prerequisite to build a culture of innovation and trait in any high-performance businesses. Mind-set is everything and it is changeable.

4. An Entrepreneur's Mind

Keep hungry, stay foolish.
– Steve Jobs

An entrepreneur's view is usually positive, dynamic, creative, flexible, and resilient. As the world stepped into the hyper-connected, over-complex digital era, the ultramodern mind-sets need to be crafted continuously to spur the next level of innovation. Creativity today asks for a new global mind-set, a connected world image, global consciousness, and cognitive intelligence, allowing "the creative flow" to open up for information abundance. The creative state of mind may not be bound to any one "mind-set," but should be free to be expressed wherever it may pop up. If that makes sense, it has the following characteristics:

- **An entrepreneur's mind is like a digital river to keep running forward**: Minds are not closed if they are alive. Looking at the brain, the riverbed of our electrochemical synapse runs on branches into more complexity. Several things stop the mind's ability to expand branches and make changes. One of them is fear, when the larger common branch is deeper and more comfortable. People need to come out of ignorance and live with awareness. This will make them less fearful, which is very much required to challenge the status quo.

- **An entrepreneur has a curious beginner's mind-set**: An entrepreneur's mind is a beginner's mind that is a "learning" mind, just as a beginner's view is from a pair of fresh eyes: "Don't know" means keeping an open mind, fresh eyes, and responding or proactively interacting according to circumstances, not according to how we assume. People with beginners' minds naturally treat each situation with freshness and novelty; no matter how many times they'd seen it or done it before, they would enjoy exploring the new possibilities or pursuing different ways of doing things. An opened mouth might indicate a closed mind, unless it's opened to ask questions. An expert's mind hurries up for answers to show off knowledge, whereas a beginner's mind makes inquiries via curiosity. Though a beginner's mind doesn't mean negating experience, it means keeping an open mind about how to apply experience to each new circumstance, while not overburdened by previous experience. Lead by questioning, not answers.

- **An entrepreneur's mind is like an elastic spring**: It's hard to imagine that an entrepreneur never failed before; the up and down experiences make an entrepreneur's mind open, resilient, flexible, and strengthened. An open mind is one that holds onto its beliefs while being prepared to consider other perspectives or alternative solutions. An entrepreneur's mind is like a spring: bend in order to straighten up; retreat in order to move forward;

recharge in order to accelerate; driven, but not extreme; dynamic and elastic to more adapt to digital disruption.

- **An entrepreneur's mind is also like a growing tree**: Are you the one who always says "impossible" or are you the one who challenges the status quo? An entrepreneur's mind is positive and progressive; it is a growth mind that can tolerate the risks and focus on opportunities. Sometimes, opening our thoughts and behaviors requires a certain extreme experience, a wake up of something new; a growing mind is open and dynamic, stretching up and growing tall.

An entrepreneur who has a creative state of mind possesses even more things. It is about the differentiating eyesight between what we have and what we want, an attitude that "this is not good enough"; resilience – "nothing gets me down"; persistence – "I will not stop pursuing this"; and an inner need to feel that "we" can do better than the status quo or competition. It is the ultramodern digital mind flow to push the human world forward.

5. A Systematic Mind

System Thinking is a Discipline of Seeing Whole! – Peter Senge

From Wikipedia: Systems thinking is the process of understanding how things influence one another within a whole. In nature, systems thinking examples include ecosystems in which various elements such as air, water, movement, plants, and animals work together to survive or perish. In organizations, systems consist of people, structures, and processes that work together to make an organization healthy or unhealthy. The characteristics of digitalization are hyper-connectivity, over-complexity, and interdependence. The traditional silo thinking is no longer fit for solving many complicated issues facing in business and humanity today, so should system thinking turn to be mainstream thought process? How to apply system thinking to problem solving or strategy making?

- **System thinking is a set of habits or practices**: System thinking applies at the level of technology artifacts in the resource category as well as at the enterprise level across all the fundamental concepts. System thinking is not one thing but a set of habits or practices within a framework based on the belief that the component parts of a system can best be understood in the context of relationships with each other and with other systems, rather than in isolation. System thinking focuses on cyclical rather than linear cause and effect.

- **System thinking has been defined as an integral approach to problem solving**: It views "problems" as parts of an overall system, rather than reacting to specific part, look at business from an integral perspective rather attempting to understand it from a sum of the parts, understand how the parts fit as in subsystems. However, the overarching goal is to design an effective system rather than economical parts. A good strategy is always to set up choices and ensure that business as a whole is more optimal than sum of its parts.

- **System thinking is "a discipline of the seeing whole"**: At its core, system thinking is a belief that everything is interconnected and that it is the relationship between things rather than the things themselves that is the primary driver of change. In science systems, it is argued that the only way to fully understand why a problem or element occurs and persists is to understand the parts in relation to the whole.

- **System thinking is integral, which means comprehensive, balanced, and embracing**: When it comes to human beings, integral means maps, models, and practices that include the full spectrum of human potentials, often summarized as "exercising body, mind, and spirit in self, culture, and nature." – Ken Wilber

Most of today's methods make little or no mention of systems thinking. There are some voices for changes; indeed, it is time to change, to see both trees and forest, and to see wholeness rather than a sum of pieces, and system thinking needs to become the mainstream thought process at era of digitalization.

6. A Strategic Mind-set

Strategic mind is the right mind-set to shape digital vision.

Strategic thinking is defined as a mental or thinking process applied by an individual in the context of achieving success in a game or other endeavor. When applied in a strategic management process, strategic thinking involves the generation and application of unique business insights and opportunities intended to create customer bonding and competitive advantage for an organization. Statistically, only 5 percent of the population is natural strategic thinkers. Strategic thinking is the combination of three thinking processes and know-how:

(1) Predictive Thinking: Predictive thinking is a combination of imagination, numerical thinking and memory:

- **Start with the end in mind**: The biggest mind-shift in moving from operational to strategic thinking is switching from focusing on activities and solutions to thinking about outcomes. Outcomes are positive changes to a digital business. If you start all of your conversations with the outcome (Is our revenue growing? Are our customers happy? Is our market share increasing? etc.), you will start thinking more strategically.

- **See through customers' lenses**: The core of digital is all about customers from outside-in views. Getting in the habit of constantly looking at the business through the lens of a target customer might help clear predictive thinking. Managers get so focused on internal components that they forget about the reason a business exists in the first place – that is, to create value for customers. So it is very easy for an organization to become inwardly focused and fall into an operational mind-set. The day-to-day struggles of running an organization can become all consuming.

- **Strategic thinking means change:** It is not easy, but you need to explicitly carve out quality time from everyone's busy schedule to take a hard look at external forces, have meaningful dialog about how these forces are going to impact your business if they are not addressed, and build consensus about what you are going to do about it. Strategic thinking means change, and people don't like change. Only when the present circumstances are clearly seen as unsustainable will you be able to overcome people's resistance to change and sustain action over an extended period of time.

(2) Critical Thinking: Critical Thinking is reflective reasoning about beliefs and actions!

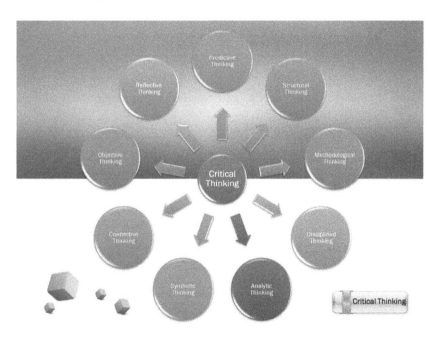

Figure 5: Critical Thinking

- **Critical thinking is an intellectually disciplined process:** It is the intellectually disciplined process of actively and skillfully conceptualizing, applying, analyzing, synthesizing, or evaluating information gathered from or generated by observation, experience, reflection, reasoning, or communication as a guide to belief and action. Establishing the strategic discipline based on critical reasoning will get people to move their thinking from operation to strategy and will get the whole organization to understand the importance of strategy over operation, or at least become aware of what is one, what is the other, and what is a stake when compromising.

- **Apply two schools of thinking – reflective thinking and predictive thinking**: On one side, reflective thinking is a part of the critical thinking process referring specifically to the processes of analyzing and making judgments about what has happened? How does this action help compete to win today? On the other side, it is predictive thinking: how will this action help us compete and win going forward? If both sides can be filled, this is a GO! if only one of the two sides can be filled, this action requires broader discussion because either the action is not aligned to the strategy of the company but worth doing because it is a tactical activity to drive short-term results, or just not to be done because it dilutes the equity of the brand the company wants to build and therefore potentially toxic:

  (a) **Identify** your most critical assumptions. For each one, do worst-case, best-guess, and best-case scenarios. See how that might influence your strategy.
  (b) **Define** the critical success factors.
  (c) **Understand** the barriers to execution.
  (d) **Identify** measures of success that are sensitive enough to quickly tell you if things are running as you desire.

- **Critical thinking is a foundational skill that wraps behind many other thinking skills**: It best applies to the multi-logical situations that are complex with many moving parts, or require multiple disciplines, or have multiple valid viewpoints. Critical thinking is a broad term that includes themes such as:

- Reflective thinking
- Predicative thinking
- Structured Thinking
- Methodological thinking
- Disciplined thinking
- Synthesizing, analyzing, and evaluating evidence and information
- Recognizing assumptions
- Identifying patterns
- Identifying and eliminating bias
- Drawing a conclusion that follows the evidence collected or evaluated.

(3) Creative Thinking: Creative thinking starts with big WHY.

- **Creative thinking is about connecting thinking dots:** Creative thinking is simply openness to finding connections between experiences, people, things, ideas, etc., and making literally or figuratively something new from those insights. Creative thinking is the way of looking at problems or situations from a fresh perspective that suggests unorthodox solutions. Thus, creativity is a key ingredient in strategic thinking in a hyper-connected, overly complex digital ecosystem.

- **Creative thinking starts with big WHY:** It starts focusing on why the tasks are necessary. When you begin looking at "why," benchmarks can be set for the improvement activities of the future. You will also drive greater innovation and change since you will find that you have more options available to solve your problems.

- **Creative thinking is both nature and nurtured:** From a behaviorism philosophy perspective, if the environment is stimulating and challenging, then the brain can thrive from new stimulus or ideas being generated, which is not suppressed but rewarded or reinforced by a positive response in a group work or team context, and motivation can function as a driver to encourage strategic thinking and create wholeness in harmony.

The capability to "think strategically" is more a talent than a skill. One can be taught tips and techniques to ensure that the right questions are being asked and the correct methodologies are being used, but in the end, the best "strategic thinkers" have a knack that others just don't seem to have. Strategic thinkers are the rare ones. They are the evangelists for change and opportunity. Strategic thinkers also have one more characteristic – "wisdom." They have reflected on the past, seen/identified patterns and effects, and underlying causes of those effects, understand linkages and are able to get to the bottom line – what's most important in terms of where to focus, as well as the top line–the long-term opportunities for growth. Therefore, a strategic mind is an ultramodern digital mind-set.

7. An Outlier's Mind

Where there is an open mind, there will always be a frontier.
– Dorothea Brande

An outlier's mind practices out-of–the-box thinking, which implies a certain level of creativity or unconventional problem solving. While the box is usually conceptualized as an intellectual boundary, it is most often an emotional one, with fear as the dominant emotion, because fear is the glue that holds the box together. With fear gone, people don't suddenly become creative – but they have a shot. An outlier's mind has the following characteristics:

- **An outlier's mind is open:** An outlier's view enables one to see through things from a nonlinear digital view and keep a certain distance from the environment you observe or experience. Just as the best photo of earth has been taken from space, the best analytics or solution of a problem is perhaps from an outside-in view; it has to keep your mind open, because an open mind is one that holds onto its beliefs while being prepared to consider other perspectives should they make sense. Our minds have been shaped through education, culture, historical events in our lifetime, the growth environment, the books and media we choose to follow, the "mainstream" mind-set of contemporary leaders; therefore, a human's thinking is somewhat boxed. We do categorize all phenomena in a number of boxes that are based on individual experience and cognizance. Some people may not have many boxes or they are not able to increase the number of boxes to adapt and accept other meanings.

- **An outlier's mind tries to change the thinking box for one much bigger:** More precisely, "out-of-the-box" thinking is the new box thinking. One question always asked is: what exactly is in the box? We often talk about getting out of it, but businesses regularly forget what's in it, especially digitalization by nature has extended boundaries. And then, look beyond the light: you see when you first jump out of the box for answers, not just what your eyes are still blinking at. But look around, look above, and look deeper. It is difficult to think outside the box from within. Invite others in, or get out of the box. For real creativity, take a look outside your industry, far outside your industry, if you want to pull the team out of the box. That's when the real ideas work. An outlier's mind is inclusive. An outlier's mind is magnetic to attract even a "polar opposite" viewpoint, because every wise thought always has an opposite thought not less wise. Inclusiveness doesn't over-control; let ideas flow.

- **Out-of-the-box thinking still needs to have logic:** While there may not be a box for digital business, there has to be a target. The most effective brainstorming is focused on a clear and targeted objective. The idea of brainstorming or the crucible of confrontation can be useful, but to "guide" the participants through its stages, you still need a structured process for unstructured thinking. Otherwise, things such as personal dynamics, seniority, grade, etc. will limit its potential. Maximum value can occur if one follows a logical process that incorporates brainstorming. An outlier may also be "skeptical" with a pair of scrutinized eyes, which tests everything and only accepts what is backed by reason and evidence. A skeptical mind is able to assess the value of new evidence and act accordingly. Although a skeptical mind may not be the same thing as open mind – just as being able to change your mind with good reason is not the same as having a completely open mind – there should be certain criteria for one to accept new ideas. But do not absorb everything; be positive and skeptical at the same time. It is still important to navigate solutions to problems through logic:

(1) What is the problem?
(2) What is the cause of the problem (in-depth thought often opens up the creative "outside the box" solution set)?
(3) What are the possible solutions?
(4) What is the best solution?
(5) Implement and repeat.

- **Laser focus on goals, not processes**: But don't get too restricted by logic processes. Don't constrain thinking by considerations that belong to one or more steps ahead. The real kicker during the "logical process" is restraining the group to not move ahead even subconsciously. Applying reasonable time constraints, but allowing freedom of "no-idea-is-a-bad-idea" thoughts in this process and have the team to solve a collective problem. Also, fundamentally, be sure to get all potential perspectives involved, so everyone has a say and no one can say they weren't asked. Management is really open-minded to implement fresh new ideas; it often comes down to two things: being explicit about purpose, and sincerity in problem solving.

- **The techniques in cross-functional brainstorming:** The other area for successful brainstorming is to make sure the people in the room are not intimidated and unable to participate. At organizations with hierarchical culture, it is useful to group people by "level" in the organization avoiding putting bosses and staff in the same group. This helps avoid the intimidation (despite how unintentional) that staff may feel when presenting ideas around superiors. The group can and should be cross-functional as appropriate; however, people are less guarded when they do not feel judged, and the reluctance to test ideas is reduced when people are concerned about appearing less prepared or that they will be judged. We are only human.

- **The emerging C – connecting digital workforce**: "Thinking outside the box" and "brainstorming"– these terms are still within the box and are not clearly understood by today's digital workforce, which is sometimes referred to as the "C – Connecting Generation." Thinking outside the box and brainstorming are approached very differently, as today's employees search for connections across many discussions at the same time, sometimes in short bursts at a time. There's also need to add another level to the discussion; that is continuous improvement. The native digital generation Y may solve problems differently than older generations – they view the "group" as very important and hierarchy is less identifiable. Indeed, we are all C – Generation now.

Digital innovation is the result of some kind of disruption; innovation can be defined as the collision between different perspectives, internal programming, mind-states of possibility and necessity, and thought patterns that result in creative ideas and solutions. Thinking "outside the box," is simply part of a well rounded paradigm. It is not only the ideas that are important; so are the challenge and willingness to try, the atmosphere in which the ideas are presented, the mind-set out of fear and mediocrity, and the culture to catalyze innovation.

8. A Flow Mind

The wise man does not grow old, but ripens.
– Victor Hugo

Many say an open mind is more important than talent. The critical step in change is to change one's mind-set. What does the open mind mean anyway: Is it like opening the window of mind to let the wind blow or brainstorm pour through? Is it like turning on the conscious or subconscious light to brighten the darkness of thought? Is it like a magnet to attract a wise or even opposite viewpoint? Or is it about connecting the neuron from left to right brain, from individual mind to collective mind-sets? Is it about mind-crafting, digging through, stretching out, or strengthening up? What are the states of an open mind? Perhaps our mind should never get "set" but keep flowing, to compete with the speed of the machine, the speed of wind, the speed of light. It is a shift from mind-set to mind flow.

- **Mind-set is at the heart of our belief system.** These are beliefs that we all hold and have formed over time through education, culture, or hard experience. It is in the individual's mind-set to either adapt or embrace the changes. It has been said that to embrace change requires a change of mind-set at every level and an understanding that things cannot stay the same. This is the groundwork that has to be done at all levels prior to initiating major change.

- **The flexibility of mind**: Shift "mind-set" to mind-scope or mind-flow, so that it allows the mind to seek possibility. It requires that we move from mind-SET to mind-FLOW, from FIXED mind to GROWTH mind. What is needed right now is continuous change and flexibility of our minds, completely away from being set in a fixed way. Put another way, our mind needs to be continually shaped and sharpened so we can adapt to changes.

- **Culture – the collective mind-sets**: The corporate culture is the collective mind-set of an organization: On one level is the organizational mind-set or culture; this is usually experienced as "the way we do things around here." It seems that this is the mind-set that can be altered by interventions such as system thinking or the "spirit from the top." The prevailing management paradigm can be moved from command and control to system thinking through intervention, and then results in the prevailing culture or organizational mind changing. By implication, those at the lower level of the hierarchy are liberated to think and behave differently by this change. You end up with people who view the design and management of work differently.

- **One's mind is not necessarily as old as one's age:** The world we see is dependent on the lens of proximity, the openness of mind, and the perception of eyes. The other level is the individual mind-set or "personal paradigm." This is much deeper. It is related to your functioning as a person – how you think about yourself and the world. Believe it or not, this is the biggest single contributor to how you act in a business situation. Changing this takes a substantial intervention on an individual level, working to expose and unravel the existing personal paradigm and then introduce a new paradigm.

- **The leader's mind-scope:** Leadership is a light to guide the change while people only changes when seeing the light or feel the heat. At a leadership level, mind shift from the top is prerequisite for any change management effort. Mind-set is very important, it can be managed through active participation of the leadership persons demonstrating that the mind-set is a part of the culture. However, at the staff level, there is a saying – "people only change when they see the light or feel the heat" – and it mainly seems to be the heat factor. Change in mind-set follows change in behavior; it does not precede it. Change in behavior usually follows change in the environment. Part of the challenge is the mind-scope of those initiating the change. Therefore, those who are leading the change must first shape the positive and creative mind-set.

Keep mind flow, changing mind-set is certainly the most important thing in effecting change and digital transformation – because the level of mind-set that is changed affects the scope and longevity of improvement in an organization. Be the change agent with a game-changing mind flow.

9. A Design Mind

Design thinking is the type of problem solving mind-set.

The discipline of design thinking in whatever iteration it is called has been around a long time; it is a problem solving methodology that businesses and professions can deploy. Design thinking is actually thriving globally and has now finally moved into the C – Suite: brainstorming for many forward-thinking organizations, as businesses strive to move up digital maturity.

- **Design thinking is a type of agile problem solving mind-set:** What is significant about the rise in design thinking is that it provides a counterpoint to the analytical, best-practice methodologies that define the 100-year-old industrial business model of management. This is because humanities and fine arts are teaching people how to solve problems in an increasingly volatile, uncertain, complex and ambiguous digital world. Design thinking addresses this in a nonlinear way that is more in keeping with the pace of technology. This is not to say that design thinking is a panacea. It's not. But it helps to think of problem solving as being on a continuum with analytical, traditional business thinking on one end and design thinking on the other end. Smart business leaders know this and balance their organizations with both.

- **Integration is the key:** Integrate design thinking into business strategy for organizational design, where it implements every business aspect into account (vision, mission, values, brand, marketing, sales, operation, business development, financial plan, and policy). More and more of work are less about design in its purity and more focused on holistic and strategic business initiatives. Business people begin to understand the design process. Designers begin to understand that they must design with all business realities in mind, not only those that affect the aesthetics of the end product.

- **Design thinking is not a process; it is a collection of methodologies:** It is an orientation toward life, powered by an ever-evolving collection of methodologies. Rather than focus on one method, as a team with broad expertise across a range of disciplines, there are choices of tools or methods appropriate for the challenge, and customizing tools and methods for the challenge will always yield a more desirable outcome. So focus on constantly building collective capability to think critically, solving problems creatively, seeing things systemically and engaging in conversations using a strategic mind-set.

- **Reliability vs. Validity**: The difference between reliability and validity also sum up the differences between traditional business thinking and design thinking quite nicely. Traditional business thinkers have a preference for reliability–getting the same result every time. Designers prefer validity; getting the right result this time. Design thinking is very reliable at producing valid solutions. The important thing is to identify shared principles and shared body of knowledge that will help raise design thinking from an inwardly focused semantic argument to the true, recognized professional discipline it has the potential to be.

- **Design thinking is a multidimensional professional discipline**: Design thinking turns to be a discipline with cultural, personal and strategic implications. It is having a major impact at organizations globally. There are many variations in tools, processes, and certainly descriptions, vocabulary and many are trying to "own" their own flavor and language. And given current predispositions, the forward thinking leaders understand how things like design thinking can fundamentally change organizations and their societal impact, first by demonstrating wins on simple products and services, and then on things like strategy, sustainability and social responsibility.

Everything is designed, so everyone is a designer, but very few are trained how to design well. Like many other expertise, it takes both aptitude and attitude. For design and design thinking to reach its full potential, organizations need to take disciplined approach to embrace design thinking and build such creative intelligence effectively.

10. An Innovative Mind

An innovative mind allows "the creative flow" to open up for information abundance.

As the world leaps into the hyper-connected digital era, the ultra modern mind-sets need to be crafted in continuous driving mankind progression and spur the next level of innovation. Creativity today asks for a new mind-set, a connected world image, a global consciousness, and the cognitive intelligence; allowing "the creative flow" to open up for information abundance. The innovative mind or a creative state of mind may not bound to any one "mind-set", but should be free to be expressed wherever it may pop up, if that makes sense, it has the following characteristics:

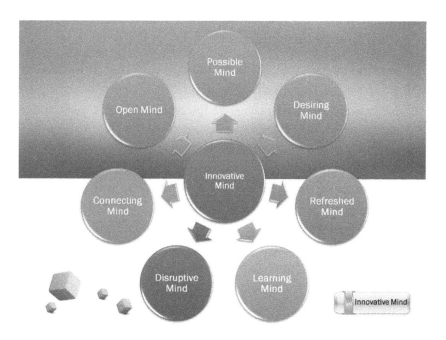

Figure 6: Innovative Mind

- **An Open Mind:** Or simply openness to finding connections between experiences, people, things, ideas, etc., and making literally or figuratively something new from those insights. All snowflakes have different patterns– cool; metaphorically speaking, all snowflakes received are valid and held sacred.

- **A Possible Mind:** A childlike state – anything is possible. By definition an idea is "possible," that is a step beyond "plausible," and it does take a mind geared toward innovation to take the concept from plausible to possible. Innovation requires a broad thought and action menu, the groups and companies that work to enable that type of environment do better.

- **A Desiring Mind:** Desire is the spearhead to motivation, which in turn creates the mind to wonder how to make your mission of change possible. It is the recognition that something is missing or something needs to be enhanced to get to the satisfaction level that you need or want. If you want to create a genuine innovation, which means that you can offer a solution that is not only an improvement of a former solution, but a complete new view of approaching the solution. You need to have strong desire and energy focus to both think hard and smart. Then use techniques of seeing things in different perspective, think upside down, inside out, think small, and think big, etc.

- **A Refreshed Mind**: It is a balance between what you know and not letting what you know hinder you in discovery of a new innovation. You have to empty your mind of how things "usually" are solved. Structures and preconceived "truths" are barriers to innovation. Avoid the "history of success" trap; unclog your memory from old knowledge. To be innovative, don't look to other products, ideas, and methods already in place as a starting point. See with a completely open and untainted mind. All problems can be improved through innovation until they are solved.

- **A Learning Mind**: Learning is necessary for innovation. The knowledge is the manifestation of brain energy because it is carried, transformed and stored by the interneuron superstructure of the brain. Creativity is part of imagination and part of knowledge; the pitfall is how you let it affect your innovative mind state when it can hinder not help. But, it doesn't have to "muddy" your innovation if you are aware that it can and you refuse to let it box you in.

- **A "Disruptive" Mind**: Innovation is the result of some kind of disruption; innovation can be defined as the collision between different perspectives, internal programming, mind-states of possibility, necessity and thought patterns that result in creative ideas and solutions. Only the disruptive mind can stimulate the radical innovation focuses to "replace" conventional value stream with new one, supported or filled with noble knowledge and idea.

- **A Connecting Mind**: The mind for innovation is also a mind that is free of psychological inertia. The mind needs to be freed so that it's connected to the rest of the universe and allows ideas to flow through. Every problem that we face has a similar or analogous problem in past; in some other industry; or in a leading area. One just needs to find that existing solution and adapt it to the current problem.

The creative state of mind means even many things. It is about the differentiating eye sight between what we have and what we want, attitude –" this is not good enough," resiliency– "nothing gets me down," persistency –"I will not stop pursuing this," and the inner need to feel "WE" can do better than the status quo or competition. It is the ultramodern mind flow to push the human world forward.

11. A Global Mind-set

Digital creates the new demand and dimension for global leadership mind-set.

The business world we live is in big digital shift and transformation: The global balance of economic power is shifting in a multipolar world; the change from a "multinational" organization that adapts the operations of each country or regional unit for local needs to a "global" firm with standardized, but agile, and horizontally integrated technologies and processes; there are leaders from the twentieth century whose profiles are very, very different than what is required for a leader now in a global, more uncertain, interdependent digital world with more distributed, multicultural, different business models and an incredible pace of information and innovation. However, when it comes to leadership substance or style, it turns out that many leaders of global corporations aren't so global leaders after all. Organizations must develop the capability to shape global mind-set and deal with global talent issues more thoroughly.

(1) From tactician to strategist with global mind-set: There are many multinationals, but few global companies; there is large quantity of international managers, but even fewer authentic and high quality global leaders. Digital businesses need global leaders at all senior leadership positions to deal with the level of complexity, to leverage its fundamental forces and have a positive impact in hyper-connected and interdependent global economy.

- **What is global mind-set:** Global mind-set is worldview that looks at problems or issues in such a way that a solution emerges through a collaboratively multicultural approach involving global psychological capital, intellectual capital, and global social capital. Being "Global" involves a personal intention to focus on being global. Companies don't exist in silos but within systems, especially global ones. Being global is about crossing not just borders but also cultural divides between business, government and social sectors.

- **How to cultivate a global mind-set:** Being multilingual, a culture master or having other global experience do contribute to shape the worldview with empathy, however, it is still not sufficient for the development of an accurate global mind-set. From leadership scholars and practitioners, there are many factors to shape a global mind-set:

  (a) **Three core competencies:** Self-awareness, engagement in personal transformation, and inquisitiveness.
  (b) **Seven mental characteristics:** Optimism, self-regulation, social-judgment skills, empathy, motivation to work in a global environment, multidisciplinary cognition, and acceptance of complexity and its contradictions.
  (c) **Three behavioral competencies:** Social skills, networking skills, and knowledge.

(2) From specialist to generalist with "globility": The global leaders are business generalist demand more comprehensive skills in leadership, strategic thinking, relationship building and management, crisis management and public relations in addition to finance, sales & marketing and HR, the common characteristics of successful global leaders fall into the soft skills bucket such as "emotional intelligence," "listening" and "authenticity." Thus, global leaders shall have "globility" (the hybrid word of "global +abilities").

- **Global capability**: It is about such set of capabilities to see the world through multidimensional lens; to understand and solve problems through multidisciplinary approaches; and to manage multifolded complexity through multifaceted practices. A global mind-set can strike the right balance, which means to raise your consciousness, bridge the difference, recognize the cognizance between left and right brain, between head and heart, and cooperate with others to adapt and manage. The qualities and competencies of global leaders include such as tolerance of ambiguity, cultural flexibility, learning agility, complexity handling, communicating virtually, and working across cultures.

- **Global influence**: The global leader's influence is not only about his or her expandable global horizon, but more about his or her very intention or effort to capture insight; the vision and wisdom to look forward. Besides being brilliant and master the functional skills, he or she must be a strong communicator and a strategic thinker, and know how to collaborate with stakeholders of all stripes. They are open from what's not optimal, and seeing all the limitations and blocks to a more inclusive and balanced view of people, life and the planet as a whole. And such transformational leadership transcends the issues of business strategies and professional development to create digital paradigm shifts.

(3) From analyst to integrator or synthesist with global culture empathy: For business leaders or professionals in global organizations, one single characteristic — "sensitivity and intelligence to culture" (so-called "cultural empathy") ranks at the very top of the requirement list. This rare quality can't be "taught" or injected simply by working in an overseas office. Surely, learning another culture deeply sharpens cognitive abilities, and speak a foreign language fluently notices how each language shifts one's consciousness and improve one's transcultural capabilities.

- **Global empathy**: Cultural empathy requires a degree of egolessness, because you have to surrender the notion that your country, or language, or point of view is best. Cultural empathy means that you have to not just see through the eyes of someone who is different, but you have to think through that person's brain. The empathy is the power of understanding and imaginatively entering into another person's feelings; or the intellectual identification with or vicarious experiencing of the feelings, thoughts, or attitudes of another. True cultural empathy springs from personality, early nurturing, curiosity, and appreciation of diversity.

- **Culture intelligence**: Culture is much deeper than custom, or a language. Culture is a collective programming of the mind that distinguishes the members of one human group from another. Cultural behavior is the end product of collected wisdom, filtered and passed down through hundreds of generations as shared core beliefs, values, assumptions, notions, and persistent action patterns; An authentic global leader can see the world with "fresh eyes", to create thresholds for possibilities that can result and expand into innovative thinking, The global leader with culture intelligence is transformational to create a vision of a new reality and inspire others to move toward the creation of this "reality" by both pushing and pulling.

(4) From bricklayer to architect with global-dimensional design and innovation: The world is moving from industrial age to digital era, now, the desert, the mountain and the sea will no long separate us, still, there're barriers in people's heart and there're silos in human's mind. A leader with global mind is an architect to bridge such gaps. The global organization blueprint is too important to be assigned only to specialist functions and regulated by specialist processes. However, those well designed functions and processes via holistic approach are needed, one in which every part of an organization and every individual within it is connected and animated by the need to foster global orchestration.

- **Global-dimensional design:** From a nontechnical enterprise architectural perspective, multinationals should consider diversity issues that range from factors related to their industry, operating geographies, culture, pace of growth and growth strategy, other elements of their business strategy (including all talent management aspects), sophistication of talent management practices, how people work and manage other people, workforce demographics and composition.

- **Global dots connection:** On the navigation dimension, have more antennae focused on the trends and what's going on in the world. And what group will have more diversity—conceptual diversity with diversity of opinion, independent thinking, decentralization, and aggregation. It takes world-class leaders who can connect global dots to both inspire and nurture the evolution of businesses that walk the talk when it comes to innovation. Businesses use inventiveness as a basis for achieving the kind of transformative change that propels global growth.

(5) From problem solver to global agenda setter with global leadership effectiveness: A global leader's "tolerance of ambiguity" and "cultural flexibility" has a strong correlation with global leadership effectiveness, they are good at identifying and articulating digital paradigm shifts, setting trend, not fad; and they are good at molding leaders that go out and promote changes in people's mind-sets and paradigms, to make influence through vision and insight.

- **Global leadership effectiveness:** The highly mature global leaders can lead effectively in an global business environment; articulate and embody the diverse values and culture of the organization; respect colleagues and reports with empathy; engage effectively with multiple internal and external stakeholders, customers and partners worldwide; make decision through leveraging variable factors; build new capability to expand global business growth; create working environment where global team and virtual team can thrive.

- **Self-initiated experience is valuable**: There's leadership study considers this topic in a more sophisticated way by examining whether the combined effect of personality characteristics and cross-cultural experiences predict a leader's effectiveness as a global leader. In this context, a global leader is defined as a leader who interacts with external clients from other countries, develops strategic business plans on a worldwide basis, and manages a global budget as well as foreign suppliers or vendors. Self- and organization-initiated cultural experiences contribute to global leadership effectiveness, but self-initiated experiences have a more meaningful benefit to leaders. To be effective, global leaders need high levels of both cultural flexibility and tolerance of ambiguity, and low levels of ethnocentrism required in jobs with complex international and multicultural responsibilities.

(6) From warrior to diplomat with global cognizance: There's an interesting research on a thinking skill called cultural meta-cognition, which simply means thinking about thinking; in this context, thinking about your cultural assumptions. If you can gain awareness of your assumptions, you can build trust and take your team beyond cooperating on a task to truly creative collaboration.

- **Global cognizance**: Developing global cognizance requires holistic thinking and forecasting capability, without such capabilities, companies can fail to increase value and competitive edge in a global economy. The well blended insight and foresight can make leaders more cognitive to drive competitive value and global growth. It is the capacity to empathize; it has to do with reaching people who differ from you and connecting to them not through the role hierarchy so much as through influence, so that you can act on a common purpose together. Hence, an authentic global leader is a diplomat with global cognizance.

- **Navigation capacities:** It is important to navigate through vision in a more volatile, uncertain, and globally distributed world because you need a directional guide; the global leaders need insight about the capabilities and expertise inherent in the talent they have now; more critically, they need foresight to seek out the potential and capabilities they'll need for the future development.

- **Self-awareness and self-correctness**: The global leaders can become more effective if you have a combination of self-awareness, awareness of the organizations, and then have the courage to be able to step into something that's unfamiliar and outside your comfort zone. Also you are able to self-correct if you are scanning the external environment and making sure that you're seeing signals, patterns, and trends that are going to have an impact on your company's ability to continue to thrive and grow.

- **A win-win proposition**. There's a transparency in the twenty-first century digital era; it's a global ecosystem of stakeholders that is going to determine whether or not your company or your organization can thrive. At global scope, the context of win-win is not about literally winning, it is about negotiating a reasoned and comfortable end point for all parties, to achieve ultimate satisfaction point. A win-win business deals are made through empathetic understanding, quantitative and qualitative analysis, "balanced" deal, or a masterful negotiation.

(7) From talent manager to global talent master to lead global mobility: High performance can be achieved and sustained by building the right set of competencies in the workforce and aligning and deploying these more effectively:

- **Global mobility**: The ability of global leaders to manage their global talent efficiently will mark the difference between success and failure. It is a strategic imperative to develop well-rounded leaders of the future, with a truly global perspective. It has also gained the sufficient recognition that an organization can benefit from a two-way transfer of knowledge, skills and experience. Every market is a fertile ground for new ideas, but also strikes the balance of global and local need. It is the extent to which business leaders allow organizations to pursue the optimal mix of local operating preferences and nuances along with established global standards.

- **Paradigm shift**: A 2012 survey by the Corporate Executive Board showed that 60% of organizations were experiencing a leadership shortage, an increase of 40 percentage points from the previous year, a "paradigm shift" — a fundamental change in thinking is required to tackle the global talent shortfall, and it's strategic to develop new digital capabilities for managing a global value chain for talent to deal with leadership development, workforce planning, strategy alignment, and workforce diversity capabilities.

In summary, global leaders are both nature and natured, cross-cultural competencies are also both created and shaped, and digital leaders' global influence are based on both the value that you bring and the values that you have. Such seven characteristics: global mind-set, globility, global cultural empathy, global leadership effectiveness, global design and innovation, global cognizance, and global mobility can become key leadership differentiators in the 21st century.

12. An Intuitive Mind-set

It is interesting to know how to read the lines and it is important to listen to your inner voice and decide.

With both business and the world becoming more complex than ever, how to make effective decision is perhaps one of the most challenging jobs for business leaders today, because making decision right is both art and science. We all know intuition plays important role in decision making. It's really interesting to know what intuition is and how we use intuition consciously or subconsciously; it's also interesting to know how to read between the lines and make the right decision, as well as how to listen to your inner voice and decide. The term intuition, according to Wikipedia, "is used to describe thoughts and preferences that come to mind quickly and without much reflection"; according to Oxford dictionaries, "intuition is the ability to understand something instinctively, without the need for conscious reasoning." Many may think intuition is opposite to logic, more precisely, intuitive mind could become complementary thinking process to logic thinking.

- **Intuition is an implicit cognition**: "Thinking, Fast and Slow" is a book written by Nobel Prize winner in Economics Daniel Kahneman (DK): What Kahneman calls "fast" and "slow" thinking, corresponds to what cognitive neuroscience and cognitive science today call "implicit" and "explicit" cognition. Implicit cognition is automatic, unconscious or intuitive (gut feeling) cognition. Gut feeling and other implicit cognition is very good at prediction as long as the environment is highly predictable and stable.

- **Business visionary is intuitive:** Business pioneers, who are ultimately accepted as leaders, are blessed with intuition. They introduce new business concepts, out of box systems and procedures for the efficient use of natural and human resources. Intuition, therefore, is the key to business innovation. It develops through advanced education, constant pursuit of knowledge and divine wisdom. When leaders learn how they have effectively used intuition in the past, they become more effective at harnessing this attribute for future decisions in their business and personal lives.

- **Intuition is like the inner compass:** It gives direction to the leader in making the decisions. For this inner compass to work correctly, the leaders should have the right balance of the depth and breadth of the technical and business knowledge. Such knowledge comes from combination of several things such as educational background, experience from the past successes or failures, observation, or cognizance etc. That means intuition is not lack of knowledge, or lack of training or education as a step-by-step process to acquire knowledge. Intuition, therefore, is a reflex expression of wisdom that is the first step in the right direction to provide acceptable answers to questions regarding social and natural sciences. Like many things, you have to train many times consciously, in order that it becomes automatic or unconscious.

- **Intuition is a result of self-training and observation**: The key is well balance of intuition and logic; think fast and slow with harmony. Einstein famously said: Logic will take you from A to B, but imagination will encircle the world. In business, if we only use the logical side, we're limiting our opportunities. We need to use both – our rational, logical minds and also our intuitive minds. Breakthrough ideas are always logical – in hindsight, but they are rarely or never logical in foresight. We need an intuitive approach for the logical breakthrough! The human brain can be a magnificent synthesizer of disparate pieces of nebulous information, and often formal techniques and procedures thwart and inhibit this mysterious mechanism from operating efficiently.

- **Quality of intuition takes more deep thought**: The big issue is that intuition needs some kind of catalyst; we need to be provoked to make our intuition work. Sometimes that can be as easy as asking a right brain-oriented question. An intuition should be taken as a new insight, a new idea, a new angle, but must be backed with sound reasoning in the end before putting it into action. And in the case of learning to access one's intuition, it's not just about hoping, relaxing, or going numb; it's about proactively opening yourself. And, there is some forcing: to step away from the normal noises and messages of life, which absolutely have their place but often drown out or override intuition. The entrepreneurs and innovators live and breathe in an intellectual world of their own. They read a lot; they discuss a lot; they analyze a lot; they debate a lot; they differ a lot. And they always end up with storing sets of agreeable and disagreeable options on every subject of their interest in the back of their minds, on their computers or in their note books. So quality of intuition takes more deep thought, not less.

- **Intuition is underpinning of judgment:** Business decision making is also such a "on balance" scenario, which needs to be supported by, but going beyond the data we can master. You need intuition (the wisdom of past experience and pattern recognition – in both conscious and subconscious ways) to take the final step. In other words, most business and other decisions involve some degree of "innovation." If this were not the case, we could program computers to sift all the evidence and decide things for us. Perhaps intuition is the food and underpinning of judgment. We do whatever analysis we can, then intuition helps us take the final, ambiguous step required for making a choice. More than 80% of leaders used their intuition; the business world can increase productivity and overall performance by systematically harnessing people's intuitive brain power.

So intuition is the quality or ability of having such direct perception or quick insight. It's about subconscious mode of evaluation that can help better understand the so-called "reality," in which we operate, maximizing our engagement with the broader and deeper aspects of our mind and our experience. That being said, even at today's analytic digital world, intuition has its unique space in decision making, innovation and almost anything we do, it's a keen and quick insight.

13. A Transformational Mind

"I only ask to be free. The butterflies are free." –Charles Dickens

As many businesses are at a crossroad, facing unprecedented change and uncertainty, the significant transformations are needed to digitalization, globalization, radical management as well as innovation. The digital-minded leaders are in high demand. Fundamentally there are two basic categories of leadership: transactional and transformational. Transactional, some call ordinary managers keep their organizations on the historical track, and exchange tangible rewards for the work and loyalty of follower; but transformational leaders, or some call extraordinary leaders inspire with vision and wisdom, engage with teams, focus on higher order intrinsic needs and raised consciousness about the significance of specific outcomes and new ways in which those outcomes might be achieved. Here are three "T" substances in transformational mind-set.

(1) Thoughtfulness: "Trans" is derived from Latin and as a prefix means "across, on the far side, and beyond." "Trans" connotes a bridging characteristic, thus, transformational leaders practice forward-looking, future-connecting thought leadership. They facilitate a redefinition of people's mission and vision, a renewal of their commitment and the restructuring of their systems for goal accomplishment.

- **Develop the vision**: The leaders with transformational mind-set must transform the organizations and head them down to the new digital tracks. What is required of this kind of leader is an ability to help the organization develop a digital vision of what it can be, to mobilize the organization to accept and work toward achieving the new vision, and to institutionalize the changes that must last over time.

- **Grow more transformational minds:** Success is much easier when shifting people's mind-sets to a transformational mind-set. Transformational leaders develop a relationship of mutual stimulation and elevation that converts followers into leaders and may convert leaders into moral digital change agents. Hence, transformational leadership must be grounded in moral foundations. It takes a leader to grow leaders with transformational mind-set.

- **Promote changes**: Change the game is mind-set. Transformational leaders inspire others to follow a vision. They create opportunities for people to show flair and to take responsibility for new ideas. They can provide the direction as vision, mission, and strategy, as well as leadership skills like delegation, decision making and monitoring. This role affects most through congruent behavior, continuous endorsement of the change and regular communication to keep the momentum.

- **Build trust**: Transformational leaders are said to engender trust, admiration, loyalty and respect amongst their followers. The transformational leader has to be very careful in creating trust, and their personal integrity is a critical part of the package that they are selling. In effect, they are selling themselves as well as the vision.

- **Drive mind shift**: Transformational leadership requires that leaders engage with followers as "whole" people, rather than simply as an "employee." In effect, transformational leaders emphasize the actualization of followers. Transformational mind-set is also based on self-reflective changing of values and beliefs by the leader and their followers. From this emerges a key characteristic of transformational leadership.

(2) **Transcendence:** The digital leaders with transformational mind-set are transcendent, because they are finding an appeal that can transcend unique leadership difference:

- **To create something new out of old**: Transformational leaders create something new out of something old: out of an old vision, they must develop and communicate a new vision and get others not only to see the vision but also to commit themselves to it; to build unique sets of capability to adapt to continuous disruptions.

- **To take leapfrog.** The revamping of the political and cultural systems is what most distinguishes the transformational leader from the transactional one. Where transactional managers make only minor adjustments in the organization's mission, structure, and talent management, etc., transformational leaders not only make major changes in these areas, but they also evoke fundamental changes in the basic political and cultural systems of the organization.

- **Four "I"s**: Transformational leaders have four common **"I"**s: Idealized influence upon building vision & goals; Inspirational motivation to attract more people to commit to the vision; Intellectual stimulation to encourage innovation and creativity, and Individual consideration through coaching to the specific needs of followers, and develop the structure to foster participation in decision making.

- **To elevate people to the high level of Maslow's pyramid**: Transformational leaders elevate people from low levels of need, focused on survival, to higher levels of purpose and mastery. They may also motivate followers to transcend their own interests for some other collective purpose.

- **Timing is everything:** Transcendent leaders have timely characteristics to handle ambiguity, deal with complexity and uncertainty, and identify themselves as change agent. "Observe due measure, for right timing is in all things the most important factor." –Hesiod .

(3) **Transdisciplinarity:** This is the ability to understand concepts across multiple disciplines to connect and effectively move between divergent knowledge disciplines:

- **To solve high complexity problems**: In the next decade, we will be confronting a number of high complexity problems in the hyper-connected digital world; the solutions will require integration of different sets of knowledge and fluency across multiple disciplines. Thus, transdisciplinarity – the ability to understand and work across disciplines will emerge as a key skill for the future of leaders and workforce.

- **To perceive "wholeness" of business ecosystem**: Transdisciplinary leaders will breakdown business functional silos, synthesize cross-disciplinary information to bridge the gap and enforce creativity. Transdisciplinarity will also be valued as a key driver of innovations.

- **"T-shaped" quality:** Transdisciplinary leaders are T-shaped specialized generalists, with both depth and breadth in their skill set. The vertical bar of the "T" represents depth in one field; the horizontal bar represents the ability to collaborate across other disciplines and to apply knowledge in areas of expertise other than one's own. Leaders with T-shaped quality are effective communicators to understand multiple dialects of knowledge disciplines.

Transformational mind-set is like butterfly, graceful and enchanting, built to change, and make sunny impact on humanity. "The fluttering of a butterfly's wings can effect climate changes on the other side of the planet." – Paul Ehrlich

14. An Architect's Mind-set

A master architect's mind-set shall well blend all excellent elements of mind-sets above.

An architect's mind-set is not privileged for enterprise architects only, it's the modern mind-set that is both good at analytics and synthesis; abstraction and visualization; imagination and practicality. As Enterprise

Architecture discipline not only embraces models, methods and theories of management and control; it also uses the same from systems engineering, linguistics, cognitive science, environmental science, biology, social science and artificial intelligence. Therefore, all digital-minded leaders and workforce need to cultivate architect's mind-set for better communication and make multidimensional influences.

- **Abstract thinker**: An architect's mind-set is full of good imagination, with capability to imagine enterprise and turn certain stakeholder viewpoints into views and then take it forward to reality. An architect's mind-set has capability of abstract or contemplative thinking, strong pattern-finding capability in order to design an effective "Enterprise Architecture," which is a "Structure of its data and processes (both computerized and noncomputerized) across the enterprise and within various silos providing an enterprise wide view of various relationships. Enterprise view further enables a framework for refining and optimizing processes, data interactions and interpreting change in business capabilities at various levels of an enterprise influenced and informed by enterprise goals and objectives."

- **Visual communicator**: An architect's mind-set can also translate the abstract concept back into the real world example, thus, it also has the "visual" ability to "see" an idea and express it in visual terms via interactive way. In addition, you need to have the ability to analyze problems and mentally iterate through possible solutions to find the best fit. As an architect, you need to take viewpoints of stakeholders and convert that into views and then enable design of those views as per real-world requirements. An architect's mind can synthesize / formalize / systematize / harmonize solutions from different enterprise related disciplines to be able to solve the complex and complicated enterprise problems.

- **Empathic persuader**: An architect's mind-set has the ability to zoom in and out of the bigger picture. Architects build bridges between strategy and implementation by communicating to the groups responsible for these two widely different activities and giving clarity to both. Therefore, an Enterprise Architect has to be in touch with the business forces through listening, questioning, connecting, and coaching, with the capability to know when to bend and when to make a firm stand. An architect's mind-set is coherent and persuasive, with the ability to reading the "ripples on the surface of the water"; aware of corporate politics and cultural pressure points; and identifies tradeoffs and negotiates them with all stakeholder to collaborate skillfully with empathy.

Imagination, abstraction, creativity, and coherence, etc., are some inherent cognitive and mental elements of architect-wise thinking. It is a type of digital mind to focus on long-term perspectives with outside-of-the-box mentality.

15. A Digital Leadership Mind-set

"Every generation needs a new revolution"
–Thomas Jefferson

More and more organizations are heading to the digital journey, it takes digital leadership to encompass the right direction, empower talent and enable the transformation. Digital leadership also does not come from one individual executive; all effective leaders need to cultivate digital mind-set and become digital leaders today. There are three D's in digital mind-set:

(1) Data-friendly: Digital leaders become champion to cultivate data-driven culture, embed data into business process and manage innovation through disciplines.

- **Digital leaders improve business's digital IQ**: As data turns to be one of the most valuable assets in business today, high performance organizations have higher digital IQ, which is a measure of how well companies understand the value of data or technology and weave it into the fabric of their organization.

- **Big Data turns to be a phenomenal mind-set issue**: Although businesses start to appreciate information as a strategic asset, they are overwhelmed with Big Data – from growing volumes and increasing complexity to the proliferation of unstructured data sources and a surge in external data streams. Big data isn't primarily a technology issue; it's more of a mind-set issue, because it has given business the opportunity and the need to start thinking in new ways. Digital leaders can take advantage of Big Data to think differently.

- **Digital leaders cultivate the culture of innovation to delight customer:** Digital leaders take practical and ingenious solutions that help the customer succeed. The boundaries of the corporation become fluid and permeable integration gives way to orchestration. Digital leaders take charge of managing big data and small data, capture insight about product or service trend, customer satisfaction, operational effectiveness and talent management as well.

(2) Decision Right: One of major responsibilities for leaders is to make right decision, digital leaders will naturally embrace data and streamline data-driven decision making.

- **Leveraging both data and intuition to make decision right**: First, changing attitudes on the role of data in decision making may still be a work in progress for many executives; digital leaders can leverage both pieces accordingly: The value from a gut feeling is probably setting the context of the problem up and making sure to use the right data. Secondly, it's always important to use more than one source of information analysis to drive decisions.

- **The art and science of decision making**: Digital leaders take consideration of simple data and more complex data analysis, in the mix with intuition and experience, a mix that collectively makes up the art and science of decision making. Humans may catch what a computer can't see as human eyes, with their ability to detect symmetry and adjacency, can see patterns in data that even sophisticated automated recognizers can overlook. So digital leaders need to think both fast and slowly to make the right decisions.

(3) Dynamic nature: Organizations have more dynamic workplace and global workforces at digital era than ever, it takes digital leaders' dynamic nature to embrace such new normal:

- **Digital leaders shape digital enterprise with agility**—doing things better and faster; **elasticity**–scale up and down seamlessly and **resilience**–a digital organization is empowered by digital tools and relying on a winning combination of face-to-face and virtual initiatives. It involves the creation of an interactively multichannel communication and sharing process to generate awareness about new digital tools and processes to accelerate and secure workforce buy-in.

- **Digital leaders cultivate digital capabilities of business**: Digital capabilities are fundamental building blocks for transformation in customer experience, operational processes, and business models. The unique set of digital capabilities will make high digital IQ organizations more competitive than laggards.

- **Digital leaders accelerate digital globalization**: Firms are increasingly transforming from multinational to truly global operations. Digital technology coupled with integrated information is allowing firms to gain global synergies while remaining locally responsive. They are becoming more centralized and decentralized at the same time.

Changing mind-set is challenging, from the set of constant such as fixed mind, closed mind, control mind, negative mind to the set of digital variables such as open mind, positive mind, growth mind, empowerment mind, etc. Change mind-set is a choice of life, because only you can change yourself that includes your mind-set. And that's the only way to make digital progress. A digital leader with such three "D"s will also be an insightful leader, a transformational leader, an adaptable leader, an effective leader and a true global leader as well.

16. Summary: Digital Mind Shift to Accelerate Digital Transformation

"A mind that is stretched by a new experience can never go back to its old dimensions."
– Oliver Wendell Holmes, Jr.

Human minds are perhaps still one of the most powerful and mysterious things in universe, because they continue to imagine and invent for changing the world; as a matter of fact, the digital world now becomes more advanced, complex and dynamic ever, while some types of mind-set may lag behind, should people now accelerate the mind shift in adapt to the change shaped by themselves?

(1) **From negative to positive mind:** What is positive thinking? It's the idealistic realism, also the cautious optimism, it's about value thinking and strategic pondering; it helps you conquer the current barriers so you can embrace the brighter future; it creates the energy and synergy in pursuit of the long-term vision and growth.

- **Positive thinking is the thinking capability**: It's the capacity (inward strength) and the ability (outward action) to reframe the experience of adversity: People with positive thinking convey strong will to make changes, and have a future orientation that makes them more prone to sacrifice immediate needs for future goals. And, importantly, they show a positive mind set about their circumstances.

- **Positive leadership**: Only positive leaders can look forward than backward, overcome barriers and bias, breakthrough ceilings, cross gaps, and bring the difference mankind need to make progress and move toward the future.

- **Positive thinking is superior**: "Squeeze an orange, you get orange juice. Squeeze a lemon- you get lemon juice. When a human is squeezed, you get what is inside – positive or negative." – Jack Kinder

(2) From fixed to accelerated mind: Fixed mind-set refers to those who approach the work with the assumption that their abilities are innate and not subject to change; accelerated or growth mind-set refers to those who solve problems or target the goals with growth mind; the belief that their ability level is nothing more than a snapshot in time and eminently changeable as they continued to learn and develop.

- **The accelerated mind is a digital mind-set**: In industrial era, fixed mind-set is OK to survive as the business and world are slow to change; however, at age of digitalization, knowledge is only clicks away, growth mind is needed to adapt to the changes and accelerated mind is needed to continuous improvement and transformation.

- **The accelerated mind is a focused mind**: Fixed mind-set sticks to the old way to do things while accelerated mind enjoys new thinking, though accelerated mind-set doesn't mean one should compete for everything, rather, it means one should stay focused, set discipline, enforce the strength, and unleash the potential, because the accelerated mind intends to understand human's difference and pursue the true character and uniqueness.

- **The accelerated mind accelerates leadership maturity**: Authentic, audacious, adaptive, aggressive when necessary, these business leaders have what we call the accelerator mind-set. Open, changeable mind is prerequisite of any transformational effort.

(3) From silo to connected mind: "My philosophy comes from a worldview that looks at the world as one. It's a holistic view that sees the world as interconnected and interdependent and integrated in so many different ways." – Dennis Kucinich

- **The connected mind is free:** It is the mind for innovation; it is also a mind which is free of psychological inertia. The mind needs to be freed so that it's connected to the rest of the universe and allows ideas to flow through. Every problem that we face has a similar or analogous problem in past; in some other industry; or in a leading area. One just needs to find that existing solution and adapt it to the current problem. The connected mind is open, insightful, innovative, and strategic, etc.

- **The connected mind shapes the new, bigger thinking boxes**: Optimize the whole, not the separate silos. Silo vision or thinking tends to hinder any efforts to systematically reduce operational complexity. Without a cross-functional, end-to-end perspective across the entire enterprise, managers tend to focus on their own functions or departments. This silo thinking is a source of process complexity.

- **The connected mind hardwires diversity into business:** Collective mind-sets are connected and superior to any single mind. To streamline processes and minimize costs, companies should capture collective insight, analyze all critical, cross-functional processes, and connect divergent factors in business ecosystem in decision making and business expansion.

(4) **From linear to multidimensional mind:** For most of the twentieth century, leaders led through variations of command and control with linear vision. That hierarchical, inward-focused style began to unravel at the end of the century. Still appropriate in certain situations, it is increasingly being displaced, because linear thinking leads to closed mind, tunnel vision and blunt communication.

- **A multidimensional mind can convey circular vision:** It is a perception through multidimensional lenses. Leaders transmit energy to variety of people, giving them a new sense of hope and confidence in achieving the circular and colorful vision with positive frame.

- **Multidimensional leaders are multidimensional thinkers**. They appreciate multiple values and see the world from multidimensional lens. They encourage people to think differently, engage diverse viewpoints and empower talent to reach potential.

(5) From exclusive to inclusive mind: Inclusiveness is the quality of the organizational environment that maximizes and leverages the diverse talents, backgrounds and perspectives of all employees. Diversity in the global context can be defined as visible and invisible differences, thinking styles, leadership potential, experience, culture etc. "No culture can live, if it attempts to be exclusive." – Mohandas K. Gandhi

- **Inclusiveness is the lever:** The world becomes more inclusive as the business functional border, the company border, and even the profession border are blurred at digital era; indeed, the world becomes more inclusive, admit of the inclusion of wide variety of specializations under one umbrella.

- **Inclusiveness encourages empathy**: Inclusive leaders have interdisciplinary knowledge and empathic cognizance; they always capture insight and substance, rather than look at things on the surface; they always put other people's shoes on, understand perspectives different from their own, and build networks with people outside of their organization.

As matter of fact, mind-set is the most valuable thing to shape every human progress and push the human world forward; but also the root cause of mankind problems. It's time to shift mind – from fixed to accelerate; closed to open; linear to multidimensional; exclusive to inclusive; silo to holistic; and reawaken your limitless mind, because changing the game is mind-set.

CHAPTER 3

Digital Strategy

Strategy is about living a holistic, integrative and transdisciplinary perspective.

Introduction

Some say there's a "strategy hype"–the variety of theories or best practices, books or white papers brainstorming about strategy, still, we have to admit at today's VUCA (Volatile, Uncertain, Complex, and Ambiguous) digital dynamic, strategy is more critical, not less, for a business's long-term success. The strategies have to respond to the turbulence in the digital business environment. In terms of practice, there is increased involvement of the stakeholders when formulating strategic plan. A digital strategy is cross-functional effort and multidisciplinary, multidimensional planning; it brings up new functions, roles and responsibilities, collaboration, demand for intuition and emergence, complementarities, philosophy, neutron sciences, and trans-disciplinary businesses. But these are not new per se. The frameworks of thoughts, consciousness and maturity assessments apply to strategy, then, now and in the future.

In a fast moving world where everything is touched by information and technology, businesses all kinds cross sectors are in the journey to digitalization. Company is part of a dynamic business ecosystem that connects digital dots or resources inside and outside of the organization to create value for customers. So the piecemeal strategy of bolting digital channels or technologies onto the business is no longer sufficient, because the strategic lenses have been expanded from inside-out to outside-in –seeing things from customer's perspective and making that view the core of your strategy; from current-out to future-in; getting to know more about the future and making digital strategy more future proof.

Hence, Digital needs to be well embedded into every aspect of business, the company must weave it as the very fabric of organization, and craft the digital version of strategy. And digital strategy needs to be shifted from top-down to organizational inclusion; from linear, static strategy execution scenario to dynamic, cascading strategy execution continuum; from a single strategy to an ongoing strategy portfolio.

1. Five Perspectives of Digital Strategy

Digital Strategy is like a GPS to navigate through your digitalization journey.

In a world where everything is touched by digital technology, businesses all kinds, cross sectors are at the journey to digitalization, they should not only include the digital aspects of strategy to their strategic plans, but put effort on reshaping the digital version of corporate strategy.

- **The digital touch point**: First comes to the digital strategy plan. The digital strategy is the strategic analysis of external environment, business capabilities, internal resources, and strategic objectives such as vision, mission and goals, strategic definition for platform, market, business model, culture, and strategic implementation of the digital business. The radical digital strategy shall not only put emphasis on defining how to take advantage of digital technology, but also better refine the broader digital effects, which include culture factor, agility traits or digital maturity., etc. Digital strategy goes for the whole organization and includes all kinds of digital touch points that help organizations get to the business objectives in a more effective, adaptive and cooperative way.

- **The digital focal point**: Digital strategy is the process of specifying an organization's digital vision, goals, opportunities and initiatives in order to maximize the business benefits of digital initiatives and digital transformation. These can range from an enterprise focus, which considers the broader opportunities and risks that digital technologies or methodologies potentially creates changes and often includes customer intelligence, collaboration, new product or market exploration, sales and service optimization, digital enterprise architectures and processes, innovation and governance; to more marketing and customer-focused efforts such as web sites, mobile, ecommerce, social site and search engine optimization. Digital transformation also requires the new focal point of strategy:

  (a) Low costs will matter less as a source of differentiation.
  (b) The human touch will become more central to competitive advantage.
  (c) Collaborative relationships will multiply and intensify.
  (d) Technology spending will shift to enabling knowledge workers to do their job better.
  (e) Organizational structures will change to become flatter.

- **The digital inflection point**: Digital strategy should look holistically into the business and how digital will impact and reach inflection of transformation in all the business aspects such as internal communication, organizational culture, supply pipeline, customer communication and innovation. Digital strategy answers questions like:

  a) **WHY** does the organization need to have a digital strategy, can, and how, digital optimize the business model or engagement model?
  b) **WHAT** are current business problems need to be solved, and how does digital impact different business practices such as sales/marketing, IT, HR, production, finance, etc?

c) **HOW** to set guidelines to enable integral digital platforms with mechanisms to build community, gamification, or social interaction?

d) **HOW MANY:** In terms of KPIs, how to measure the increase in sales, decrease of marketing and HR costs, optimized production, etc.

- **The digital decision point:** A combination of internal and external factors needs to be considered in order to achieve a winning digital strategy. The executives require thinking deeply in the business purpose and make strategic decisions to prepare for digital switch and maximize long-term digital value. Strategists know that any company has many factors affecting its position and direction. These factors sometimes are internal like staff, products, culture and so on. Sometimes are external factors like competition, customers, and regulations, etc. You have to consider a combination of People, Products, Customers, and Competitors (PPCC), because (P)s are internal and (C)s are external. Integration between these components will guarantee a good digital strategy to plan for, because they are more interwoven at digital business. Reduce cost without affecting negatively on (C)s, and Increase your sales without affecting negatively on (P)s. The challenge to reach the new digital horizon is how to grow sustainable profits in a way that does not violate core values and principles because an enterprise, and pursue short-term gain won't hurt business's long-term growth.

- **Strategy-As-A-Practice:** A company has to have both long-term as well as short-term plans that need to be strategized to adapt to digital disruption or achieve digital premium. Strategy needs to update when the underlying data changes, otherwise it will become outdated and no longer serve the purpose. Equally, there are some continuing efforts to marry complexity theory, which is focusing in particular on complex adaptive systems with the strategic management field. Digital strategy needs to be proactive, not reactive. Key topics are about repositioning companies, their value propositions, business models, game theory, theory of constraints, optimization vs. maximization of results, knowledge, resources management and wise leadership, etc., in order to remain sustainable. Some of digital trends will impact on business strategy and strategic management as well, there are a few critical issues that will press on the strategic consciousness of companies such as risks, boundaries, purpose and adaptiveness.

Crafting a strategy is like to grow a tree, to know the main path, to develop branches when necessary according to the futures events. It is not like tablets of stone handed down by senior management; it is an evolving thing about getting the best information you can, continuously update. A good strategy embraces three "C"s: Context, Cascade and Creativity.

2. The "IMPACTS" Components and "SMACC" Style of Digital Strategy

The real strategic differentiation is to create unique value, look forward and shine through.

Organizations large or small are heading to the digitalization journey; digital strategy is like a compass, to navigate the right digital path. More specifically, defining and planning how to shape digital mind-sets, taking advantage of digital technologies and methodologies to meet business objectives as part and parcel of what is being called "digital strategy." Strategy requires knowledge of "who we are," "where we are" and "our resources"; then a clear vision of "where we want to get to." The digital strategy is overall about how the business conducts of getting from point A to point B; from where they are now to where they want to go and how to get there. The digital business strategy is typically segmented into two perspectives: how does the digital world provide the business opportunities or new markets and threats to mitigate; and then on the other hand, how to promote the business through digital channels – search, display, social etc., tactical execution, and customer delight as ultimate purpose. Compared to traditional strategy, digital strategy needs to add certain special ingredients, as strategic design differentiates one company's products or services from competition and increases competitive uniqueness. Here are seven "**IMPACTS**" ingredients of digital strategy:

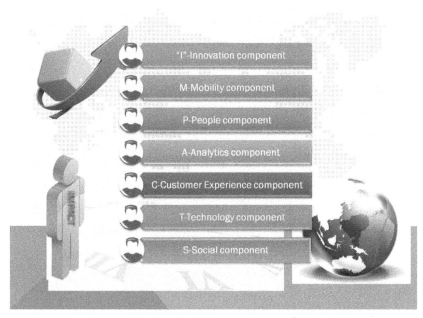

Figure 7: Seven "IMPACTS" Ingredients of Digital Strategy

- **# 1: "I" – Innovation:** Innovation refers to the creation process: How does the company create and transform the novel ideas and achieve its business value. Innovation must be a fluid process inside any digital organization; therefore, it will be addressed as part of the main overall strategic plan. Digital is an age of connecting the dots; an "innovation strategy" would encompass a repetitive or iterative process to create, discover, and experiment. Different innovation or creation strategies can exist, being top-down, bottom-up, user-oriented, internal, or outsource, etc.

- **# 2: M – Mobility:** Having digital mobility is not as simple as applying a mobile app, otherwise, every business is digital business already. It is about how to catalyze the digital ecosystems that are expanding due to the convergence and confluence of social, mobile, analytics, and cloud computing (SMAC); it is about how to enable digital flow for making effective decisions at rapid pace of digital dynamic; it is about how to enforce digital connection by integrating modular digital capabilities and streamlining digital processes; and it is about how to empower employees to be more creative and productive to engage in the digital transformation.

- **# 3: P – People:** In most of organizations, people are still the weakest link; therefore, talent strategy is a crucial component in digital strategy. The digital-minded leaders and managers are the corporate people architect to build up the business vision and implement strategy with their talent blocks; they are the human engineers to navigate the employees' potentials, energize their spirit, and identify their mojo, with the goal to amplify the collective capabilities for their digital businesses.

- **# 4 A – Analytics:** Strategists use "Big Data" + analytics to identify trends that will help an organization plan for the future and meet market needs in a differentiated way. Analytics capabilities need to be built in very foundation of organizations, because it lets organizations see the "real-time" cause and effect of business's actions and customers' responses, organizations that do so will be able to monitor people behaviors and market conditions with greater certainty, and react with digital speed and effectiveness to differentiate from their competition. It is strategic because it will lead innovation, which can improve processes cross-functionally or optimize customer experience life cycle based on personalization, targeted interactions and preferences, ultimately increasing customer and employee loyalty by following three "I"s: Insight, Interaction, and Improvement.

- **# 5: C – Customer Experience:** Customer Experience (CX) is all about putting design-led thinking into strategy. It is perhaps the hottest perspective in digital strategy today. Think about how important is contextual research and prototyping in helping think strategically. Delivering great experiences starts with research and strategic insights, with the findings and ideas flowing through conception, design, development, production and quality assurance. Without the strategic insight that CX offers, the best you can hope for is to design the wrong thing.

- **# 6: T – Technology**: Data and information is central to digital business today, although digital business does not simply mean the business that is using digital technologies, indeed, enterprise wide IT strategy is a key ingredient in business digital strategy. An effective IT management strategy will provide the framework to weave all digital components together to shape dynamic business capabilities. However, information technology strategy is a complex domain, and that the best approach requires to take the leaps of faith setting some of the right things in motion, delicately balancing and rebalancing the results toward urgent, but hard to predict outcomes.

- **#7: S – Social**: Social strategy is part of digital strategy, which is informed by the overall business strategy. A good social strategy will galvanize inspiration and gain traction on a powerful theme of digital conversation and renewal. Social strategy includes:

  (1) Social business strategy – answering the question of how does online social behavior change a business model, resources, product sourcing, service and the essence of the business.
  (2) Tactical promotion via social networks – how a business that is using available social tools must be coordinated with other components of the digital strategy, so as to avoid implementation conflict, confusion and risk.

Besides these special "IMPACTS" ingredients, digital strategy also has following unique "SMACC" styles:

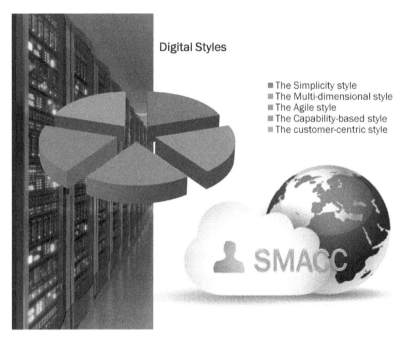

Figure 8: The "SMACC" Digital Styles of Strategy

- **A: Simplicity**: Build an executable digital strategy. Einstein said that every solution to problem should be as simple as possible, but no simpler. It means that a problem has an inherent, irreducible complexity; any attempt to simplify further than that will fail, and any complexity added to it is harmful.

- **B: Multidimension**: Digital strategy is a shareware with multidimensional perspectives. It fully meets and adheres to the assumptions that bound and guide the organization in achieving its vision and accomplishing its mission.

- **C: Agile**: An agile strategy embraces three Cs: Context, Cascade and Creativity. It is shareware, not shelf-ware; a dynamic planning, not a static document; and a good strategy always includes execution as part of strategy.

- **D: Capability-base:** Because capability is an acquired and organized "ability" within a company and takes hard work to put in place, so the capability-based strategy should be practical to implement, also unique to keep competitive, it's the good approach in strategic planning.

- **# E: Customer-centricity:** Customer centricity is about linking your strategy to the customer; linking your process to strategy and linking your technology to your process. Customer-centric strategy takes outside-in view, and put customer at the center of business strategy.

Digital strategy is about big picture–shared value collaboration. That is where the game is moving in the digital era with the new characteristics such as convergence, ambiguity, complexity and interdependency, etc. A good strategy follows a three-step scenario: Identify challenges – Set guidelines – Take coherent actions. And it takes cross-functional collaboration, cross-disciplinary pollination and ecosystem comprehensiveness. When it comes to digital strategy with such special "**IMPACTS**" ingredients and unique "**SMACC**" styles, the organizations can be more adaptable and dynamic upon such digital transformation.

3. Digital Strategy Component # 1: Innovation

"**Entrepreneurial innovation should be at the very core of culture and service at any business.**" – Peter Drucker

With the pace of change, frequent digital disruption and technological advances, businesses large or small have pressure to become more innovative in order to beat the competition or ride above the digital torrent. But what's the best scenario to practice innovation management and what are the challenges in innovation journey?

- **Challenge # 1:** <u>Does digital strategy include innovation or is there any additional need for a separate innovation strategy?</u>

It's situation-driven. A separate innovation strategy that is a subcomponent of overall business strategy can be effective if:

(a) if the company does not have innovation as part of its culture.
(b) if the current innovation program needs a significant boost, or the intention is to embed innovation in an organization as a new strategic initiative.
(c) if the company is under threat of becoming extinct due to fiery competition.

But for organizations that have already embraced innovation, then it's different because innovation is perhaps already a critical ingredient of strategy, it would be at the heart of everything they do and would run throughout the overall business strategy. But either way, innovation is a key element of business strategy, no matter it's a separate subcomponent or an integrated ingredient of strategy.

- **Challenge # 2**: <u>On the higher level, the question regarding strategy is often its width or narrowness ("too wide" = no strategy; "too narrow" kills innovation).</u> Look at innovation strategy as the stepwise process, by which a firm gains some sort of competitive advantage over other innovative products, processes as the case may be, but for strategy including innovation, it is about how the organization creates new novel ideas or reacts to incidents from competitors. On the operational level, one has to think who is going to contribute to the creation process, and how they are going to do so.

- **Take multiple ways to build innovation into strategy**: Innovation is what leads to differentiation. There are many ways to differentiate and therefore there are many ways to build innovation into a corporate strategy. Innovation must be included in a strategy; otherwise the company will fail in the long term. A good strategy will include what are the innovation gaps in the business, where the company plans to focus its innovation efforts (such as product performance, cost effectiveness, speed, business model, etc.), how this links to the rest of the corporate strategies, and the action plans that must be put in place to achieve the innovation goals.

- **Set innovation guidelines:** Innovation should be embedded in every aspect of the organization, including strategy. Even when the company performs well, that makes innovation more naturally become part of strategy. So, the innovation-driven organization should not only put more senior leaders to inspire and direct innovation through well-defined guidelines, but also have an innovation portfolio that holds all innovation initiatives. Even more operational or functional areas should move to a more strategic level. If a company pursues sustainable growth, through innovation lenses, a company really needs to exceed traditional boundaries. A strategy built around some clear value perspectives such as customer value automatically provides a basis for innovation and business development.

Not all changes are innovation, but innovation is a change. In this case, embracing innovation is a change and digital shift, and you need all the pillars of successful change management – a compelling vision and an effective strategy that addresses the following: committed leadership and team of champions, empowering employees, enabling collaboration across all the various functions, creating the right environment (culture), and providing the processes and tools to support innovation. Either an innovative strategy or an innovation strategy, a good strategy has to identify the gaps, take principles and practices, make the business choices and set the right metrics to measure execution performance.

4. Digital Strategy Component # 2: Mobility

Digital mobility is more about how to orchestrate underlining information and knowledge mobility that empowers mind flow and talent growth.

Having digital mobility is not as simple as applying a mobile app, otherwise, every business is digital business already. It is about how to enable digital knowledge flow for making effective decisions at rapid pace of digital waves; it is about how to catalyze the digital ecosystems that are expanding due to the convergence and confluence of social, mobile, analytics, and cloud computing (SMAC); it is about how to enforce digital connection by integrating modular digital capabilities, streamlining digital processes; and it is about how to empower employees with the sufficient knowledge to become more innovative in the digital transformation.

- **Diagnose the challenge**: Because the accepted industrial model of knowledge or process management is too hierarchical, too static, and the process is too silo for the fast-moving, increasingly social or collaborative digital enterprise of today, so it makes sense to create more fitting digital knowledge and process flow management.

- **Set the strategic guideline:** Digital mobility has been expounding many of the principles such as connect-collect-collaborate; ask-learn-share, interact-improve-innovate, and solving some of the pains underlying it, unlocking latent expertise, collaboration through communities, getting the right information to the right person at the right time to make the right decision and accomplish the right task.

- **Take coherent actions:**

(1) **Manage knowledge:** Digital knowledge management is not managing knowledge as an object; it is providing the management system that is dynamic to the changes.

(2) **Enable flow:** Create the environment that encourages the utilization and the flow of knowledge. Because knowledge does not stand still! It flows into the company, it flows out of it, it erodes; it gets created, and hopefully it flows to the customers of that company in terms of product and service delivery as well.

(3) **Bridge gaps:** Build the bridge from data to knowledge. Information is data with a purpose. Knowledge is information within context. Wisdom is ultimate insight from the knowledge you accumulate.

(4) **Assign responsibility**: Look at the organization chart to find out where in the organization the requested expertise might be sitting - part of taking knowledge seriously as a corporate asset involves assigning responsibility for knowledge within the organization. Data is collected continuously and is meaningless until it is processed into information. Knowledge is information put to use. It is about having the social skills to connect, share, find, on and off line with people who are very different to each other.

(5) **Converging processes**: It is important to achieve digital mobility via the convergence of unstructured processes and structured processes: The convergence of unstructured text messages with structured process entities will help create user-friendly process management applications handling structured and unstructured processes in a similar manner to enforce digital flow and mobility.

Therefore, digital mobility goes beyond applying fashionable mobile computing to the business, it is more about how to orchestrate underlining information and knowledge mobility that empowers mind flow and talent growth, transform modern business from static to dynamic, from efficiency to agility and from functioning to delight.

5. Digital Strategy Component # 3: People Strategy

Strategy is about putting a great team together to give you a multifaceted picture zooming into business's future.

Digitalization and globalization has huge impact in the business and world, and talent has become the defining theme of this new digital era, the talent demand for digital organization is never ending. However, the crux of the problems is that talent management is also at digital transformation at the moment, very few organizations have well crafted people or human capital strategy as integral element in their business strategy. But talent management is too critical to be assigned only to specific functions and regulated by silo processes or mechanical procedures. So what are the ramifications for digital Human Capital Management (**HCM**) strategy? Does the structure of the organization need to change to achieve the strategy? How will it impact on the overall digital capability (competency + performance) of the organization? What are the core digital competencies needed to achieve the strategy? Shall you need to unleash talent potential via training and development, or shall you recruit through alternative digital talent pipeline? How are you going to differentiate talent strategy, in line with the business strategy, that will ensure the business has the right skills, in the rights position, at the right time and for the right cost?

(1) **Diagnose the main issues in talent management:** Digital transformation takes both strategy and guidance on how to transform talent management with better education of the complete range of digital fits required in the business today and future. Start solving problems by diagnosing the symptoms, identifying the weakest link in your talent value chain, and digging through the main issues and root causes.

- **Hire for yesterday:** Somehow most companies experience a sudden, instead of planned shortage of people with specific knowledge or skill that can be workable in a very quick period of time and want them for "yesterday." On this scenario usually they hire the first person they are able to find that can join right away; Time, not quality, is the main driver. Also, project or short-term needs are considered more than profile fit for the organization's long-term needs. Or the organizations still follow the static industrial mind-set to hire certification, not ability. Certification is mainly as an indicator of good discipline to learn; but ability to pass exams is not always ability to put this knowledge to solve problems in context with team work efforts; and certifications are overrated by a whole industry of selling training and certifications. Now digitalization is shortening the knowledge life cycle significantly; what businesses really need are people who can learn new technologies and businesses, master creative problem solving, and communicate effectively with peers and users.

- **Employee disengagement**: The industry studies show that the majority of people are not engaged in their jobs because their talent is not being utilized; though every employee has individual reasons for not being engaged that is rarely revealed by engagement and exit studies. If you have people in roles where their natural strengths and talents are being recognized and utilized, they will be engaged. They will also have greater passion, because they are doing what they are good at doing. The studies consistently show the importance of using people's natural strengths and talents, although their process of doing this is not on target, the reality is that the organizational structures and relationships with and between employees were designed for a very different age, more often, workers are asked to be "engaged" inside and outside the company environment, at the same time, many companies don't have the mechanisms or interest in engaging employees outside the work environment. At the age of digital, businesses today need nothing less than a paradigm shift in their thinking about the fundamentals of how organizations work.

- **Lack of people development**: This is also a long-term view and one of the main causes of the broken staffing value chain.

Companies seem to be averse to continuous training of their employees. As a result, they either do not change or add technologies or they pigeon hole the employees with knowledge in older domain or technologies. It is important to create a culture on continuous learning for digital workforce, so their knowledge and experience continue to grow. But the real challenge is to build and retain a strong team when you don't have all the resources available at your disposal. Perhaps it is the time to adopt digital learning style combining traditional face-to-face sequences with digital platforms to train and develop talent.

(2) Five Aspects of Human Capital Management (HCM) strategy: A holistic HCM strategy needs to be well defined with all key strategic players, everyone knows exactly what is the recommended or agreed processes and the interdependencies of contributions becomes clear, a digital themed talent strategy can multiply talent effect, amplify talent influence and satisfy talent growth needs. Here are five aspects of HCM strategy:

- **A successful HCM begins with understanding your business:** The competitive environment, customers' expectations, strategic and operational goals and other factors affect your organization, build a people strategy based on gaps identified against whatever information available at hand and benchmarked against best industrial practices, legal compliance and progressive HR strategies. Defining digital talent strategy shall focus on strategic growth areas, future business needs and continuous measure and refine strategy. That means strategy must also be based upon the collective strength of the resources available. Connecting these potential strengths with the opportunities on the market place is a key driver for HCM.

- **Three "D" HCM strategy:** HCM strategy is about 3D – Discovering, Developing and Deploying the philosophy and signature processes for long-term talent focus. With continuous change and digital disruption, HR role these days is of talent enabling, facilitating, and collaborating to leverage opportunities and maximize investments. There are always a delicate balance to be achieved between corporate, business line and individual perspectives. In the end, business as a whole are all working toward achieving the same goal, managing change on a larger scale based on strong business imperatives and a sense of joint responsibility across the organization. People make a difference, as well as quality relationships.

- **Agile and resilient HCM strategy:** Because the digital world is VUCA, short-term guesses must be tested and revised more often and more quickly. The results of each test should be put into a management feedback loop to see if results are aligned to and supportive of longer-term talent strategy. It's less risky to fail fast and recover quickly. Managing strategy in the short term is analogous to agile software development methods or crowd-sourcing beta products and rapidly incorporating feedback in product revisions; it is very iterative. The talent strategy needs to be agile and resilient enough to accommodate fast cycles of strategy evolution. If the human capital management framework is perceived as too cumbersome to operate and to lag strategy cycles, then HR justifiably earns the "irrelevancy" anchor to wear around its neck.

- **Performance and capability framework**: The HCM strategy may also involve the development of performance and capability framework. The definition a performance management system is a system where the expectations are properly defined and the individual manager or employee can manage their own performance and utilize it as a regular reporting tool for empowerment. Under good governance principles, the development of performance management systems that are also reporting systems is essential. People management is complex; the effectiveness of people strategy depends on how it draws upon all the various HR or OD (Organizational Development) fields to come up with something integrated. And all the various levels or elements of strategy that flow from that – be it an overall HCM Strategy. Many HR functions don't think cross-functionally and holistically and as such, can't formulate an effective and comprehensive HCM Strategy to align with and support the business. Now, the available digital technology and tools enable the HR assets to be placed on the balance sheet. If the organization is using modern human capital management approaches, they will be able to plan, measure and manage the human capital more effectively.

- **From paperwork to living strategy**: From strategy on the paper to living on the strategy is a key step in business execution. The HCM strategy document needs to highlight broad strategy per talent management process, key components, deliverables agreed to the time term, main risks and control measures, supporting technologies noted and defined metrics. If HR understands this strategy, they can live and influence components within this strategy in their relevant sphere of influence, whether it is with local, regional or corporate business leaders. The follow-through from strategy to well-defined operational guidelines and buy-in of suitably equipped people in HR infrastructure is the key to move from a strategy on paper to living on the strategy. In many ways that is perhaps the most productive part – the strategy that comes out of it more like the icing on the cake. The more that dialogue to develop mutual understanding between HCM and business occurs, the better!

(3) Strategic guideline for digital people management: Strategically, the HR or talent management plays an integral role in acquiring new human capabilities through sourcing, recruiting, learning and development strategies; their ongoing involvement in C–suite "digital conversations" is more important than ever. Tactically, not only should today's digital organizations explore the best talent practice, but also it needs to continue to develop the next talent practices in order to strengthen the weakest link in organizations –People:

- **Define digital fit**: Business leaders and talent professionals need to take responsibility for ensuring the talent has the digital mind-set and presents digital fit. Because today's digital professionals have to be able to think, learn new technologies and relate what they have known in the past to create the new context and knowledge, due to the digital disruption and continuous changes. It means:

  - digital mind-sets
  - solve problems creatively
  - communicate with empathy via multiple digital channels
  - digital culture fit
  - digital competency
  - establish insight into approach and style in different situations
  - digital renewal (the ability to learn)
  - digital potential

- **Develop alternative digital talent pipeline**: Don't be afraid to look above, below, and outside of the talent pools that you are seeing. Be ready for the departure of top talent by trying to build a deep bench. Be open-minded to hire candidates that would be considered somewhat unconventional to others, but show a real desire to do the work that is required of them and have skillets that prove to be eminently transferable to their roles. Many great candidates can be recognized by wise eyes; otherwise they would have likely been given a pass by an automated HR system. Modern talent management not only makes "Apple to Apple" comparison but also manages "Apple to Apple Pie" style insightful scenario planning.

- **Empower digital talent to grow**: Don't get caught between the "hire the experience" vs. "grow your own" traps. Everyone in forward-looking businesses is to "grow your own," and regardless of past experience or success, providing the time and $$$ to educate, train, and retrain digital talent is a constant process that will never end. Look for people who are able to grow and give them the opportunity to do so, look at how to motivate and obtain the most out of the talent and look for breadth of experiences, internal rotational opportunities, individuals who are motivated to succeed along with leadership who encourages appropriate risk taking. Digital talent management will enhance the on-demand learning curriculum to develop the talent pool, and take initiative on growing employees' transformable skill set to fit in the future.

- **Enforce the positive organizational culture**: Take challenge to improve "Attract-Hire-Retain-Train-Organize" cycle; enforce cross-functional collaboration to reduce turnover; build creative and productive business culture; eliminate technology tunnel vision; introduce rotation programs, and increase employee productivity and efficacy. Talent mangers need to be visionaries who can articulate the strategic direction and personalize it to the staff. This is how to cultivate culture and organization, in order to overcome the weak link in staffing.

- **Improve talent supply chain maturity**: Increasing employee loyalty and training, taking care of employees, will eventually improve productivity and quality; sometimes the short term increased stress and oversight leads to long-term reward with a deep and talented bench. By analyzing the key problems, and manage next practices, talent managers can strengthen its weakest link and make its talent supply chain more mature, adding real value to both business's bottom line and top line growth. Modern talent management will evaluate the employee performance dynamically, as the digital technologies become the efficient tools to manage workforce with multidimensional focus, through better-tailored talent solutions.

A well-defined HCM strategy distinguishes actions to guarantee your workforce consists of the right people with the right skills in the right roles at that right time and are supported with the right information and tools to achieve your business priorities. One size does not fit all.

6. Digital Strategy Component # 4: Advanced Analytics

As an emergent digital strategy, there are both optimistic perspective and brutal truth about data analysis!

Strategy formulation becomes more complex as more factors must be considered simultaneously when the new digital phenomena emerges; Big Data is big by-product of digital business, the data and information created from multichannel conversations through customers, employees or smart devices need to be transformed into insight or foresight, then such data-based wisdoms need to be well integrated with decision making process, to develop the new products or service; to optimize customer experience or improve internal working process. Therefore, digital businesses all need learn how to swim at the sea of big data, to ride the wave, or avoid obstacles. The organization's Big Data strategy, which is key element of digital strategy, needs to make strategies more future proof in the increasingly dynamic digital ecosystem, because business has to draw on the insights about the future through their data, particularly the Big Data, and focus on exploring following business insight:

(1) Identify gaps: Every good strategy starts with identifying the key issues need to be solved, and the gaps needs to be bridged. Identify analytics gaps before putting much resource and making formal strategic plan:

- **Cross-organizational collaboration**: Data integration with multiple source systems is still one of the largest challenges. Analytics is the next step in achieving the holistic cross-organizational view. It has the potential to deliver enormous payback, but demands unprecedented collaboration. Where analytics is concerned, collaboration is not limited to departments within the organization; it requires integration of knowledge about customers, competition, market conditions, vendors, partners, products and employees at all level. Hence, an enterprise must nurture a cross-organizationally collaborative culture in which everyone grasps and works toward the strategic vision.

- **Well-identifying business problems**: Business is still unconvinced on the real bottom line value analytics can bring. Until the return on the investment made can be clearly articulated in revenue or margin terms, the problem will persist. Analytics has become far too much about the technical solution instead of focusing on the business benefit and the organizational problems that can be solved. From noble business purpose perspective, analytics helps optimize various business management, directly or indirectly related to long-term revenue, including traditional optimization, root cause analysis, statistical analysis, machine learning and data mining to boost efficiency of marketing campaigns, price optimization, inventory management, finance and tax engineering, sales forecasts, product reliability, fraud and risk management, user retention, product design, ad spend, employee retention and predicting success of new hires. And competitive intelligence leverages external data source, predicts new trends based on automated analysis of user feedback, and much more.

(2) Strategic guideline setting: Every organization has different strength and set different strategic focus to compete, the analytics strategy will also set the priority to focus on the best interest of company.

- **Customer insight:** Know what customers need before they know themselves. Big Data allows businesses to see customers' behavior pattern they have never seen before, it also uncovers the interdependence and connections that will lead to a new way of doing business, or engaging customers' feedback, do sentimental analysis or research on knowing what customers need before they even know themselves, and develop next generation of product, service or business model accordingly.

- **Decision making insight:** Businesses explore the power of big or small data to drive business decisions to create transparency in organizational activities, which can be used to increase efficiency, improve operational excellence and implement governance effectiveness. Big Data analytics also improves the quality of business decision making, requiring organizations to adopt new and more effective methods to obtain the most meaningful results from the data that generates value. Big Data also can help business to predict or detect fraud or bad behavior, break down functional silos to manage data more holistically, and converge IT governance with business governance to enforce GRC (governance, risk management, and compliance) discipline.

- **Talent insight:** It will always take sprint and long-term journey to identify, attract, develop, and retain the right people with the right capabilities at the right positions. Through Big Data analytics, talent manager can recognize thought leaders, social influencers or domain expert more easily; to transform from talent controller to talent multiplier, to make sure the right talent at the bus. Data analysis of employee and talent performances also allows experiments and feedbacks, make sure right talent at the bus at the right time. Talent managers start using data not just to monitor employees' behavior, but to ask and answer some hard questions that are at the heart of how employees contribute to business performance, predict employee preferences and behaviors, and tailor next practices to attract and retain talent. Develop predictive models and identify leading indicators to forecast business staffing requirements, track skills and performance, as well as maximize human capital investment.

(3) **Coherent action:** Take coherent actions to manage analytics portfolio, build analytics capabilities in very foundation of organizations. An analytics strategy can only be successful if it can be seen as key business capability or process. However, most people see analytics as tooling, software or any other IT application. This process has to be aligned with the organization's strategy, and therefore it has to be a component of the business capabilities. To be effective, it also has to be implemented in the management models and processes of planning and control.

- **Enforce data governance:** If you work to improve analytics effectiveness, you need to have high quality data; if you want high quality Big Data, you need data governance. Governance can be applied to content when it is collected. As you mine your content, you'll learn about other entities that need to be "promoted" to the governance model and standard for collection, creating a feedback loop, and improving your classification on ingest over time. However, governance doesn't always directly deal with classification or taxonomy or categorization issues in most deployments. It is most often a structure for what you are going to do or who is going to do it; how it is going to be done; and how it is going to be repeated. A corporate handshake if you would have involved between the parties.

- **Improve analytics maturity:** There are three steps toward "analytics maturity": Companies will start with simpler statistical analyses ("what happened?"); then move to predictive analytics ("what will happen?"); and finally prescriptive analytics ("what should we do next?"). There are also three parts to the analytics ecosystem: Technological-getting and storing the data; quantitative / interpretive; and decision support/decision making. Surely a simulation into what will or may happen is both predictive and prescriptive as it will almost certainly suggest appropriate actions.

Big Data is big part of digitalization, human and machine analysis of large data sets will also provide big insight beyond commercial value, it will have broad touch including social, political and economic intelligence, and it has huge positive impact for society at many perspectives in the future.

7. Digital Strategy Component # 5: Customer Experience (CX)

Digital age of business and world shall move up from apathy, to sympathy, to empathy.

Digital organizations are outside-in and customer-centric, how to build up a customer-centric organization takes both strategy and tactics. Should CX – "Customer Experience" – be part of strategy? The emerging experience strategy intends to really put customer at the center of business, from business transaction to customer experience management, to connect the dots between design thinking and service delivery; from customers' touch points to managers' decision point. Experience strategy is ultimately about the big picture. It ties closely to, and can often drive business strategy. It can also become the business strategy in an increasingly experience-driven economy.

(1) The goal of Customer Experience strategy: At customer-centric businesses, when setting Customer Experience (CX) management as your top objective, the goal of CX strategy, is to apply digital technology depending on at what time or lifecycle of touch point the customer is in internal employee collaboration. Enabling technologies for digital strategy are everything from online platform to social media, knowledge base tools, mobile, etc. Another subset of digital touch point would be the self-service channels (web, mobile, email, web chat) versus the other communication channels, etc.

- **Customer centricity is about how to sustain customer value:** Customer centricity is about linking your strategy to the customer, linking your process to strategy and linking your technology to your process. Customer centricity is about an attitude or a passion to do what's good for the customers. Customer-centric strategy shall serve the purpose of generating a positive customer-experience that contains commercial value. The customers experience is both an output and outcome as well as acting as input to future improvements and innovations. So innovation and customer centricity have to be built into the business strategy, the fundamentals of the business model and in the DNA of organization such as corporate culture. Because we have entered and exist in "the digital age of the empowered customer" with all the challenges that it brings, it is important to building a new model around sustainable customer value that aligns customer expectations with customer experience, staff expectations and corporate vision and values.

- **Customer Experience strategy attempts to design all touch points and subset experiences:** Service design is usually a tactic within a CX strategy. If the business model is based on service, the two become more synonymous and the services better be really well-designed and well-integrated into delivering the business and experience strategy. If there are many services offered, then they need to each be designed, and also integrated into delivering the big-picture experience strategy. Service design tends to look at the big picture, the businesses services should be designed and aligned to their overall strategy as a critical customer touch point. It defines and justifies the need for what service design is required as part of an overall experience design.

- **Customer Experience strategy output:** Outputs of customer experience strategy are about defining, communicating, socializing and fully understanding business goals at an enterprise level, from a human perspective, they are customers, employees, partners, affiliates, vendors, or users, etc. So "outputs" are really just communication tools needed to get the thinking behind the strategy expressed and understood by others. They can take the form of business models, prioritization matrices, roadmaps, experience principles, strategy diagrams, organization and change management models, content strategy and governance models, concept models, project plans, journey or experience maps, service blueprints, storyboards, videos, etc. It really depends on the audience and its vernacular currency of exchange.

(2) The strategic insight from Customer Experience perspective: Delivering great experiences starts with research and strategic insights, with the findings and ideas flowing through conception, design, development, production and quality assurance. Without the strategic insight that CX offers, the best you can hope for is to design the wrong thing. Therefore, CX needs to be well aligned with the business side of things. Though depending on the business model, CX belongs to different teams and has varying degrees of the strategic impact. It needs to have well alignment with business, because it provides more opportunity for moving up the pipeline and influencing strategy and direction. The strategic design effectiveness can be improved through a collaborative effort to improve processes and provide visibility across the teams.

- **Customer Experience is all about putting design-led thinking into strategy**: Think about how important is contextual research and prototyping in helping think strategically. If CX teams have been put inside the functional silos only, it will disassemble design approach, weakening CX effectiveness. CX strategy encompasses service design, product design, and more to cover all aspects of experience produced by a business. CX strategy might also use some service design tools to produce needed strategies, but that doesn't mean it is the same or on the same level as service design. Service design includes the relationship between a particular aspect of engagement and business goals, which scales service design up to a pretty comprehensive CX strategy.

- **Customer Experience is a disruptive force in business culture**: CX is at odds with traditional industry model of organizations that break projects into stages in a production pipeline. In digital organizations, more cross-disciplinary teams work with agile methodologies to develop a product or service over its lifespan. In that model, CX would play an equally important role throughout the life of the project. Despite how CX team is structured in real life, the best practice is to have it connected to a strategy or business unit. It can directly belong to that unit or at least have a dotted line there. For some, CX is closer to commerce and strategy in the process, in others it is closer to creative design. It's all about board level buy-in. Where can your CX activities gain the most support and ultimate revenues? It is important to remember that CX is practiced in many different guises and that fitness for function is ultimately important, and CX talent needs to be versatile and comfortable to work cross-functionally.

(3) Identify the gaps and build the customer centric capabilities: To build the customer-centric business, organizations need to identify the gaps, and think in terms of building business capabilities. A silo and disconnected organization could not deliver value effectively to its customers.

- **Resource gap**: A business capability is an ability of an organization to perform a particular type of work and may involve resources such as people with particular skills and knowledge, the effective process, defined practices, operating facilities, tools, software and equipment that work together for a defined purpose.

- **Business capability modeling techniques**: Basically, a business capability encapsulates all intangible or tangible resources, functional or cross-functional processes to perform a certain value added activity for customers. Apply business capability modeling techniques to align strategy with value proposition and to the business capabilities of the organization, as well as ultimately creating a capability driven roadmap for transforming enterprise from silo organizations to customer centric businesses.

Therefore, Customer-centric strategy takes outside-in view, and put customer at the center of business strategy. CX needs to be one of the unique ingredients in strategy of digital organization, and CX teams need to work collaboratively with the strategy team, to well embed design thinking into business culture, key business processes, and all business side of thinking and designs.

8. Digital Strategy Component # 6: IT– Information + Technology

IT is a holistic "digital brain" of organization.

Digital technologies are disruptors, and data is life blood in modern businesses today. However, from industry survey, a very real gap exists with just over one-third of respondents having an enterprise-wide information technology management strategy in place currently. What's holding these organizations back from building out an enterprise-wide information management strategy? What's needed to close the gap? Also keep in mind, information and technology strategy needs to be the key component of business strategy. The best strategies are living and ever evolving, and when deployed, it should provide the framework for business going forward. Information in itself isn't power; it's the ability to seamlessly access, analyze, and utilize data. Information strategy is a key ingredient of digital strategy that can enable executives to make data-based decision and build up an analytics-driven culture cross-organization.

- **IT strategy will leverage information and technology to empower businesses:** IT strategy is critical because it describes the future state and how to get there; how an enterprise will leverage information to power its business. But information and its lifecycle is complex, enterprises generally have governance and compliance rules on information. They want people to be able to find, reuse, publish, refactor, and republish. Information is the life blood of the enterprise, but if not properly managed, it becomes at worst case a liability and at best case an underutilized asset. An information management strategy can well define the principle, processes and best practices that optimize the value of information, while minimizing risk.

- **Do gap analysis before crafting IT strategy:** Do Gap analysis by framing the right set of questions and manage the flow: Vision-strategy-execution flow is from vision (where do you want to go, and what do you want to achieve) – Gap analysis (the current state assessment) –Strategy (how to get there, roadmap) – to Execution -Balanced Scoreboard (objectives, metrics):

  (1) What are the current functional capability, maturity and overall organizational capability and maturity? What are current IT capability and maturity.

(2) What things are in place that will enable the business strategy? What can be done to strengthen them?

(3) What things are in place that will inhibit or endanger the business strategy? What can be done to minimize them? Are the right skills in place? Are costs in line with the five year plan?

(4) What is the organization's capacity for change?

(5) What could cause you to fail?

(6) How to make assessments to allow IT to continue to monitor and modify the strategy?

(7) How to manage IT strategy flow seamlessly: Strategic objective – Strategic goal – Capability – Capability Increment – Project – (People, Process, and Technology).

- **Set guidelines to achieve business goals and priorities:** It outlines how an enterprise can achieve important business goals, such as innovation, process efficiency, increased employee productivity, or customer delight through information. It's those who proactively invest in strategic solutions today will be able to competitively leverage their own information going forward. There are real benefits to having a comprehensive enterprise-wide information management strategy in place to:

(1) Enablement –enables better data access and analysis by breakdown the silos.

(2) Efficiency – reduces costs and increases efficiencies.

(3) Integration – increases IT integration with the business.

(4) Innovation –enable cross-functional innovation.

(5) Enforcement –enforce standardization and governance.

Data and information is central to business today, a passive approach to enterprise information resources is akin to abdication of this duty. So the question is not why you shall have an IT strategy, but what the appropriate strategy is and how to build an effective one based on your organizational requirements.

9. Digital Strategy Component # 7: Enterprise Social Strategy

The high-mature social intelligence touches every aspect of digital business.

Digital enterprise is organic and living; social and mobile; always on and hyper-connected; being social doesn't just mean to use the consumer social network, a high mature digital enterprise needs to have a holistic social strategy, to diagnose the current issues such as silo functional thinking and process; or lack of culture of innovation, then set up the social guideline and take coherent action for building a truly digital business.

- **Social challenges**: New generations of social technologies, when coupled with clear vision, good planning, and effective execution, have the potential to change the way business is done. It is the optimal ways to encourage participation. However, one of the biggest challenges of social technology is how to manage or curate the volume and variety of artifacts that workers create using social tools.

- **Social guideline**: Enterprises that diagnose what's wrong with internal collaboration and prescribe a many-to-many cure are trying to weave social networking into the information fabric in a complementary way. They are also working on the organizational aspects of creating incentives, reengineering processes, and applying analytics to make the information flows relevant to specific groups and individuals. This approach promises three advantages:

    (1) A creative place to work, so people can be allowed to take risk and make mistakes.
    (2) A means of creating context, a significant component of knowledge sharing that's historically been lacking.
    (3) Bringing the social functionality to users in their familiar application environments.

- **Social rules**: Essential privacy and security rules, appropriate to the enterprise, need to be understood, and reinforced. There are tradeoffs, because the more that people share relevant information, the greater the benefit. However, some information is confidential and privileged, and the boundaries need to be set in advance. Social technology trials could be an opportunity to update the privacy rules and reconsider how the risk landscape is changing. Make social discovery, identify the social networks relevant to accomplishing the selected business objective.

- **Social Action # 1: Build social hub.** Social technology has the potential to address several perennial goals for enhanced, more efficient collaboration and effective communication in a flexible and low-cost way. One approach is to creating social hubs. These solutions pull activity and event information from enterprise applications into the social technology platform, to create a central hub for collaborative, task-based, and social activities. Enterprise builds the enhanced integration capabilities to support connections and interactions between individuals and communities; between individuals and information assets, and to facilitate enterprise activities in all of their possible combinations. The rise and advance of enterprise social technologies has the potential to dramatically alter the business information landscape and the organization's ability to more effectively leverage corporate data and information.

- **Social Action # 2: Meld communication and context for better collaboration**. Context creates relevance, aligns social technology's strengths with the way people learn today. The true value of enterprise social computing will come from bringing data, content, and people together in the context of business activities. Context is not just a general-purpose content management effort or a knowledge management effort. Social enterprise tools do meld communication and context for better collaboration, which is where the focus should be. The approach and style must synchronize to the realities of social technology and to the organization that the value in social technology will be in the effectiveness of information integration and pattern identification.

Enterprise social strategy is the integral component of business digital strategy, and it will navigate business's digital journey through collaboration, innovation and synchronization.

10. Digital Style # 1: Simplicity as Strategy

Strategy is for making progress; and progress is in simplicity.

Modern organizations spend significant time and resources to deal with complexity, the complex organizational structure, process or the hyper-complex business ecosystem. Which factors contribute the most to making organizations more complex? How to reduce unnecessary complexity or enforce effective complexity to increase business value? Is simplicity a digital style or part of digital strategy?

- **Complexity is neither good nor bad**. Einstein said that every solution to problem should be as simple as possible, but no simpler. It means that a problem has an inherent, irreducible complexity; any attempt to simplify further than that will fail, and any complexity added to it is harmful. So complexity per se is neither good nor bad. Some problems are simple in nature; others are complex. And it's a continuum, not either/or. The goal is to create elegant and practical problem solutions that accommodate a problem's inherent complexity. And depending on the system's nature as well as its audience, hide that complexity by abstracting up from it to a simpler level, without compromising the solution's quality, robustness, and enhanced ability.

- **Complexity is not the opposite of "simplicity":** Complexity is a systematic thinking concept, from such perspective, systems such as organizations, biological systems, enterprise as system, etc., can be characterized as being complex if they have nonlinear feedback loops; such systems can exhibit emergent behavior. Simple systems can have complexity in that they have nonlinear feedback loops that can result in emergent properties and outcomes. Complexity is diverse, ambiguous, and dynamic with unpredictable outcomes. It is often erroneously confused with the term complication. Nevertheless complexity and complication do not mean the same thing. Something that is complex is not necessarily difficult; but something that is complicated does have a high degree of difficulty. The challenge is able to see the simple elements that make up these systems, and understand the nature of the system, its elements, and the rules that govern them. This is not always easy. Once you have this understanding, the complexity still exists, but now you are in a better position to respond to threats and opportunities, and even modify the system, both its elements and the rules that govern them – to effect change.

- **Simplicity as strategy:** Complication is a better antonym for simplicity. Complicated systems will no doubt have layers of complexity as well, but can be simplified by reducing the number of components or changing the way they interact. Sometimes the way to do this is to make one of the elements of the system more complex, designed in such a way so that the complexity of other elements of the system is reduced. Some complexity factors cannot be simplified, you need to become more complex in order to serve, for example, customers. Other complexity factors do have less influence of external forces; these factors can be tackled and simplified in order to perform better. From the point of the business strategic changes, all tasks and requirements should be assessed and ranked in three dimensions:

(1) Criticality (value) for business of the task.

(2) Readiness (maturity) of business for this task solution.

(3) Feasibility (Effort/ Complexity).

Business is complex, human is complex, and nature is complex. There's beauty and harmony in it; also, it is dynamic, diverse, and distinct. So the purpose of managing complexity is not – actually impossible – to eliminate it, but on how to create synergy and build delight on it.

11. Digital Style # 2: Multidimensional Strategy

Strategic Thinking = Vision (insightful/directional/temporal) + **System thinking** (holistic/broad/synthetic) + **Creativity** (reframing /imaginable/ nonlinear).

An effective digital version of strategy is multidimensional. A successful strategy needs both breadth and depth of communication transmission that will create the sense of ownership. Everybody needs to be involved, at a certain point and at a certain stage of the strategy execution. Here are five dimensions of digital strategy.

(1) Height: A strategy is not always the oversight from 3000 feet + above; however, it does take a bird's eye view of the businesses in order to craft a good strategy.

- **Clear vision:** The "height" of strategy depends on how clear the business vision is; and a good strategy identifies its contribution to accomplishing to the organization's vision, helps achieve the organization's end-goal and overall mission. Therefore, work closely as a team to form a clear and concise vision for success, also have team members teach each other behaviors necessary to achieve the vision.

- **Ambitious objectives:** The height of strategy is also related to how ambitious the strategic objectives are. It is important that businesses get the best out of the people. And most people get the maximum motivation when the company they work at is very ambitious with their strategy. Often trying to be the best, the most innovative company pushes people out of the comfort zone. Of course, strategy has to be clear and achievable.

- **Potential roadblocks**: The higher the strategy is, the more roadblocks there are on the way to achieve it. Therefore, identify and clear obstacles, structures, or systems that may impede the vision, allow for risk taking, welcome failures, and share in the learning they provide and remove ambiguity of decision rights, immediately address inconsistencies.

(2) Length: There are always a right balance of long-term strategy and short-term business goals, the length of strategy is situational – five year, three year, one year., etc. Overall, a good strategy needs to well reflect business's long-term vision, with consistent and incremental business objectives to achieve it.

- **A good strategy is cascading and elastic**: The ideal length of strategy is long enough to well plan company's future with confidence, and short enough to sense the urgency to execute it. Strategy should be broken or breakable down into a series of tactical steps that further become nests of doable operational tasks. If people can see a direct link between the strategic goals and their everyday work, they can understand both.

- **Set the strategy milestones well:** The big picture of long-term strategy is translated into shorter-term details such as action or operating plans, and then given life in terms of resource allocations and short-term financial goals through the annual budget. As part of the strategic planning process itself, a detailed action plan needs to be prepared, it lays out the specific steps needed to accomplish the longer-term goals and objectives, establishes timelines, assigns responsibilities, looks at potential obstacles, etc.

- Break down goals into manageable and measurable chunks
- Track and celebrate the early wins, as well as larger milestones
- Use wins for credibility to buy-in the holdouts

- **Leverage incentives to fit the "length" of strategy journey**: More often, incentive and other compensation plans are all-too-often short-term-based and isolated from what the strategic plan is trying to accomplish. This problem will, fortunately, be somewhat mitigated if the strong linkage between strategy and operation exists. So internal communications strategies must incorporate the need to keep the long-term view within the short-term attention and focus of all key players and to facilitate change within the organization.

(3) Breadth: Strategic plans are often developed in isolation, in terms of who is and isn't involved in the process, what the context are (vision, mission, and values) as well as what the realities of the current business, market and competitive conditions are. With the new characteristics of businesses such as hyper-connectivity, hyper-digitalization and hyper-competition, the breadth of strategy needs to go beyond silo thinking, and touch the business ecosystem.

- **The hybrid strategic planning**: The well mixed top-down and bottom-up strategic planning can expand the breadth of strategy. The breadth of strategy is based on well accepted and acknowledged understanding of the organization's current reality, as well as how broad knowledge the people who make strategy have. Most strategic projects need experts from different departments, preferably the best resources, and fully dedicated.

- **Share widely**: Strategy breadth also means how to share the strategy widely cross organization. Statistically, majority (up to 90%) of employees do not know their company's strategy. The strategy has to be communicated and shared freely amongst all the organization, from the top executives to the lowest levels, everybody needs to know what is the goal and, by which means, which initiatives and how it is going to be achieved. They need to know what the top three strategic initiatives are as well.

(4) Depth: A good strategy is not "superficial", it needs to dig deeper and diagnose the root causes of business issues, make a set of choices and take actions accordingly.

- **Strategy translation**: In-depth business understanding and comprehensive technological solution is important to translate strategic goals into detailed business objectives. Once the strategic plan has been developed, it often remains in isolation from critical business processes and direct linkages are not made to important operating plans, budgets, HR decisions, and metrics, etc. Unless there is a direct linkage, resources will be misapplied, priorities will become confused and focus on the long-term goals of the strategic plan will be lost.

- **Strategy to tactics mapping**: From an overall portfolio perspective, there're nested relationships and close linkage between strategy and tactics:

  (a) The strategic plan drives an organizational project portfolio mix
  (b) The desired portfolio mix drives project selection criteria. This creates the linkage from strategic vision to implementation.
  (c) Project performance measures (success criteria) for each project are defined in relationship to the business strategy.
  (d) Performance measures for project team members are linked to the project performance/success criteria.
  (e) This linkage creates more resource engagement because it should be clearer to people how their work impacts the organization.

(5) Time: The fifth dimension of strategy is the realistic time-frames for actual delivery, not just published ones, but the right timing to harmonize strategic execution.

- **Create a sense of urgency:** Identify and discuss crises, potential crises, or major opportunities. Without strong motivation for achieving the goals, strategies will die on the whiteboard. It also has to create the stronger sense of urgency, the easier it will be to gain buy-in for the strategies.

- **Stay focus:** It is really important to focus on a few initiatives and priorities them. Senior executives should say "no" to many of the initiatives and just choose a few where they will put most of the resources of the company. Today companies very often say yes to all the initiatives, with the consequence lack of focus. This is then spread through the organization, and people no longer know where the priorities are.

- **Continuously revisit strategy timely**: Discussions of strategic plan issues must be ongoing and not merely a once-a-year exercise. The ability to revisit and reinforce what you have put into place at the start of the program consistently before moving on to new phases, just because you think its implemented does not mean it will remain implemented – you may end up working on the roof, whilst your foundation is rotting away. The project delivery needs to be on value, on time and on budget.

Therefore, a digital strategy is a shareware with multidimensional perspectives. It fully meets and adheres to the assumptions that bound and guide the organization in achieving its vision and accomplishing its mission.

12. Digital Style # 3: "Agile" Strategy

Strategic agility means that strategy planning becomes a "living process."

Agility is the ability of an organization to sense opportunity or threat, prioritize its potential responses, and act efficiently and effectively. While Agile as software project development methodology intends to enforce iterative communication, increase customer satisfaction and expedite project delivery, to scale agile effect, can such agile philosophy also retool business strategy planning, because the rate of change is accelerated, and strategy today needs to be more dynamic than you think.

(1) Strategy planning is a "living process": A clear purposeful "North Star" – a vision of what organizations wants to be, to achieve, and a good strategy compasses upon how to get there. Organizations must be proactive in keeping short-term and long-term strategy goals clear in sight, but strategic planning is a living process, not a static shelf-ware. It has such characteristics as:

- **Cascade:** Strategy Planning becomes a "living process" with regular evaluation, scanning, listening, revisiting and potential course correction. There is no "predictable future," but there are many possible ones. Long-term planning has its place, but linearity and over prescriptive-ness don't. If you laid all of the corporate strategists in the world end-to-end, you wouldn't reach a consensus.

- **Context:** Strategic corporate goals are sacrificed at the expense of reactively adjusting strategy. A proactive strategy has updated context, and accurately established strategy and goals should serve as general "borders" within which businesses utilize problems as opportunities for fine-tuning strategy.

- **Scenario planning:** Part of strategy is scenario planning. You never know for sure what is going to happen, but through continuously scanning the market, you should be able to identify different scenarios. After evaluating these factors, you need to use the different scenarios as an input for your strategy. The processes should not be rigid; you always need to be able to adjust. But by considering different scenarios into strategy, you are most likely to be prepared for these changes.

(2) A Good strategy embraces creativity: We are truly entering a digital evolution of the discipline, where strategy, innovations and change must converge dynamically; and where we should all be looking at any strategy, whether for product, service, or total business through the lens of "sustainable development," innovation and change.

- **Resilience**: Strategies that are overly prescriptive act as a cork on innovation and creativity. When a company can be quickly disrupted from a competitor from a different industry, businesses need strategy that is resilient enough to enable people to shift and adapt, and a good strategy embraces creativity. Companies experiencing paralysis from process and policy will find themselves unable to envision alternatives that fall outside the self-imposed boundaries they function within.

- **Feedback**: Any movement leads to feedback that allows strategy correction and refinement. A collaborative approach can help leverage the existing knowing upon how the organization enables teams grow beyond their limits and thus create solutions that can be implemented. While strategy should be a team effort, sometimes decisions simply have to be made, as being stagnant can be dangerous. No movement – Paralysis by Over-Analysis – will kill a product, project, and corporation faster than anything else. Staff and clients take inaction as fear and lacking a leader with whom the "Buck Stops."

- **Built-in mechanism**: Part of framing a strategy is to have built in a mechanism to correct the direction if the variables are changing or if there is an innovation that has disrupted the landscape all together –either in a big bang way or in a gradual manner.

(3) Execution is part of strategy: Strategy definition shouldn't be done without thinking about execution at the same time. Coming up with new strategies is easy. Executing them takes tireless effort and daily diligence

- **Communication**: Communicate strategy clearly. A good strategy needs to get feedback from bottom-up of the organization and helps in better communication and execution of the strategy. Strategy is not strategy if it does not take people, management and leadership into account and put it in perspective. In the networked society, strategy and execution are more and more intertwined.

- **Governance:** A necessary condition for the implementation of strategies is proper governance and, most critically, ownership by a resilient and empowered executive team that has the implementation of strategy as a "live" objective. This of course requires that the formulation of the strategy is a team effort, based on consensus reached by rational criticism. And a good strategy needs collaboration right from the beginning.

An Agile strategy embraces three Cs: Context, Cascade and Creativity, it is shareware, not shelf-ware, a dynamic planning, not a static document, and a good strategy always includes execution as part of strategy.

13. Digital Style # 4: Capability-Based Strategy

Capability-based strategy is to well bridge "as-is" and "to-be" state.

A business capability is a specific ordering of processes, people, resources, information and technology aimed at creating a defined business outcome, capabilities are often developed reactively to competitive threats, strategic opportunities, and environmental changes, so all businesses have certain capabilities, what matters is maturity, the high-mature set of business capabilities can make organizations more adaptable and agile, to fulfill their strategy.

- **Capability-strategy link:** Top executive team must have a clear understanding of the link between business capabilities and business strategies. Prepare a strategic plan that points the company in a direction where it can maximize its market position and reap as many benefits as possible. This direction must allow for economic, market or customer change and let business adapt swiftly.

- **Capability elaboration**: Enterprise Architecture is a mapping tool, in providing the visibility and defining the road map for strategic alignment. EA is also a discipline that helps organizations define and deliver business capabilities aligned with their strategic objectives. It is a process of progressively elaborating a set of capabilities through conceptual, logical and physical states, informing decision making at multiple levels, and helping to maximize the business value.

- **Bridge link**: Capability-based strategy is to well bridge "as-is" and "to-be" state, to breakdown the business capability blocks, there're skills (ability), knowledge (internal/external), policies/routines, business processes, any type of tangible/intangible resources, culture and forms of communications. The capability-based strategy is not only leading to destination, but also cultivating and optimizing the set of mature enterprise capabilities on the way.

- **Modular capability**: Modular business capabilities enable agile as well as flexible strategic planning and execution. Alternatives and adaptation are the key words to survival. You know where you come from, but you maybe never sure where you'll arrive precisely, so be well prepared for surprises! Most of enterprise capabilities need to be woven cross-functionally, it takes cohesive collaboration for business as a whole, and thus, making capability-based strategy should also take collective effort, to break through the silo thinking.

- **Maximizing value**: A good strategic planning helps organizations extract the maximum value from their portfolio of business capabilities, to inform decision making at multiple levels, and to drive strategic alignment and optimization. Use the capability-based plan to drive budgets and prioritization, which helps those stakeholders to articulate what they need in their natural language (and not be hung up about methodologies). This will get reluctant stakeholders to want to contribute in the next iteration; and gives IT enough time to develop good strategies to deliver them.

As capability is an acquired and organized "ability" within a company, and takes hard work to put in place, it can therefore not be transferred because of the degree of organizational learning and organization that goes with it, so the capability-based strategy should be practical to implement, also unique to keep competitive, it's the good approach in strategic planning.

14. Digital Style # 5: Customer-Centric Strategy

Being customer-centric is a transcendent digital trait and core of corporate strategy in today's digital organizations.

It is the age of customer; customer-centricity becomes the new digital fit. However, since there are many elements to customer-centricity, the key to success is focus on something that will "move the needle." For some companies, it's the customer experience; for others, it is product excellence, and some can build loyalty through low cost etc. So how do organizations craft their customer-centric strategy?

- **Customer centricity is about an attitude:** Customer centricity is about a passion to do what's good for the customers you target. Customer-centric strategy shall serve the purpose of generating a positive customer-experience that contains commercial value. As we have entered and exist in "the age of the empowered customer" with all the challenges that it brings!

- **Customer centricity is about how to sustain customer value:** The customer's experience is both an output, outcome as well as acting as input to future improvements and innovations. So innovation and customer centricity have to be built into the fundamentals of the model and in the DNA of organization – the corporate culture. It is important to building a new model around sustainable customer value that aligns customer expectations with customer experience, staff expectations and corporate vision and values.

- **Policy formulation is a crucial step in customer centricity.** An organization's policies are either customer centric or they are not. Process redesign should not take place until policy formulation has taken place. A move toward customer centricity can be delivered through policies that are taking the customer perspective, not the process perspective. Customer resolution is as much driven by the policy that informs or governs the process as much as by the physical act of the task at hand.

- **Customer centricity is built upon rigorous business's capabilities and processes.** In order to improve the process, questioning the reason of existence of the processes in the first instance, ask the questions: Should this process even exist in the first place? Or is it becoming an inability to imagine a different perspective that could be the big resistance to customer centricity taking a firmer hold? Process approaches fit for service, but don't restrict, they should support by getting the right information to the right people at the right time.

- **People are the wow factor in customer centricity.** There is a unique element in genuine "human connection" that cannot be standardized because of its very nature. Without that human connection, the outcome is far more dependant of task excellence. It is the element that can greatly influence the "memorable" part of experience for the customer, the part they deem worth talking about. Great people with poor processes can still occasionally give great outcomes; talented and engaged people can shelter customers from bad processes, although only with much greater effort, and therefore much greater cost to the organization. But disengaged employees will never wow a customer, no matter how great the processes behind them.

- **Action effect**: Action is always part of good strategy. It is incumbent on the organization to prove its capability to deliver a unique and differentiated experience consistently – to do that requires (1) a blend of strategic thinking –what do you intend to do in the future to create high contrast customer; (2) an ability to execute-demonstrable evidence that the business is actually doing something to build differentiation and (3) effect -as a result of executing against the plan, the organization is able to deliver a differentiated experience as well as generate improved business performance. The "effect" dimension often lags of course, but this is the determinant of a successful strategy.

- **Customer-centric score**: There's plenty of industry research to show that customer-centricity links to business performance. Customer-centricity has at least five dimensions: strategy, people, process and experience design, technology, and metrics. One thing to measure an organization's customer centricity score is the measurement of gap. On one side of the gap is how well you understand your customers, and on the other side is how well you deliver to your customers. The narrower the gap then the more Customer Centric (CC) you are. Once recognition of the gap exists, then the journey toward CC starts. Usually measuring how well you are delivering to your customers is relatively easy, but developing a true measure of how well one understands their customers is the hard part. It is akin to measuring the difference between somebody knowing something versus understanding something.

Customer-centric strategy takes outside-in view, and put customer at the center of business strategy. Customer centric strategy needs to be fully fledged and has objective and tactics assigned to various departments and measure business performance systematically.

15. Digital Transformation Executive Study Summary

Digital makes profound impact from specific functions to business as a whole.

Digital Transformation may already list at every forward-looking business's agenda, as the pace of pressure for change will continue to increase, leading to further pressure to transform their businesses; for some digital native companies, they are at smooth road, however, for many large traditional organizations, it's a bumpy journey with many roadblocks. There's a recent study published by MIT Center for Digital Business and Capgemini Consulting shared the findings from a global study of how 157 executives in 50 large traditional companies are managing and benefiting from digital transformation. The research also describes the elements of successful digital transformation strategy and show how to assess your firm's digital maturity.

(1) Building blocks of the digital transformation: The study indicated major digital transformation initiatives are centered on re-envisioning customer experience, operational processes and business models. Companies are changing how functions work, redefining how functions interact, and even evolving the boundaries of the firm.

- **Transforming customer experience:** Customers are becoming more demanding, the research provides executive insight from transportation and hospitality industry on describing urgency of changes and an "ever-rising tide of customer expectations" for service and convenience, they also share experience on how to create opportunities for digital transformation in three areas: Online presence, mobile customer engagement, and internal operational processes.

- **Transforming operational processes:** In a broader sense, digital transformation replaces limited one way vertical communication with broad communication channels that are both vertical and horizontal. CxOs can engage in two-way communication quickly at scale. Employees can collaborate in ways that were previously not possible. Performance transparency was a key highlight mentioned by several executives. Executives in most companies say they are more informed when making decisions. Transactional systems give executives deeper insights into products, regions, and customers, allowing decisions to be made on real data and not on assumptions. Beyond being better informed, digital transformation is actually changing the process of strategic decision making.

- **Transforming business models:** It is finding ways to augment physical with digital offerings and to use digital to share content across organizational silos. New digital businesses are introducing digital products or solutions that complement traditional product and services.

- **Digital globalization:** Firms are increasingly transforming from multinational to truly global operations. Digital technology coupled with integrated information is allowing firms to gain global synergies while remaining locally responsive. They are, in the words of many executives, "becoming more centralized and decentralized at the same time. Globalization also entails a different approach to policy: "fewer mandates from headquarters, but more guidelines."

- **Digital capabilities:** Digital capabilities cut across all above pillars. They are a fundamental building block for transformation in customer experience, operational processes, and business models. Although CIOs and existing IT departments are leading digital initiatives across companies, they hire extra skills or implement separate units to coordinate digital transformation.

- **Unified data and processes:** The most fundamental technology need for digital transformation is a digital platform of integrated data and processes. Large successful companies often operate in silos, each with their own systems, data definitions, and business processes. Generating a common view of customers or products can be very difficult. Without the common view, advanced approaches to customer engagement or process optimization cannot occur. Unified data and process is one reason that web-based companies are able to gain advantage through analytics and personalization much more readily than traditional firms. For many traditional companies, uniting data and processes is the first step in preparing for digital transformation.

- **Solution delivery:** Companies also need the capabilities to modify their processes or build new methods onto the data and process platform. A hospitality firm's executive said that knowledge of key emerging technologies is spread across silos of external vendors, making integration difficult. Several executives described knowledge gaps that existed after they ended a vendor relationship. And some other executives stated "It's time to harvest the data and turn it into insights." Combining integrated data with powerful analysis tools is seen as a way to gain strategic advantage over competitors.

- **Business and IT Integration:** With trust and shared understanding, IT executives can help business executives meet their goals, and business executives listen when IT people suggest innovations. Where strong relationships exist, executives on both sides of the relationship are willing to be flexible in creating new governance mechanisms or digital units without feeling threatened.

(2) Meet challenges in digital transformation journey: There are numerous challenges in digital transformation, how to overcome them is the key to success.

- **Initiation challenges include:**

  (a) Lack of impetus: Because impetus often starts at the very top of the firm, executives are justifiably skeptical of the benefits of emerging technologies.
  (b) Lack of awareness: Another concern can be lack of awareness of the opportunities or threats of digital transformation.
  (c) Regulation and reputation: concerns are being careful about mobile and social technologies because of security and privacy concerns.
  (d) Unclear business case: As with many innovations, digital transformation investments often have less clear business cases.
  e) Lack of culture of innovation: Friction accompanies any changes.

- **Execution challenges**: While a top-level impetus for transformation is important, it is often not enough. Interviewees cited three missing elements that threatened to prevent them from moving forward successfully: missing skill, culture issue, and ineffective IT.

- **Governance challenges:** Benefiting from transformation typically requires changes in processes or decision making that span traditional organizational or functional structures. Transformation, like any major organizational change, requires top-down effort to help employees envision a different reality, and coordination to ensure the firm moves in the right direction.

- **Coordination challenges**: Many firms fail to transform because of coordination difficulties across business units or processes. Units are able to make progress in their own areas, but are unable to influence practices in other units.

(3) How to make digital transformation success: Successful digital transformations in the study used a common set of elements, each is a lever executive can use to initiate and drive digital transformation in their organizations. Leaders diagnose the potential value of existing corporate assets and build a transformative vision for the future. Then, they invest in skills and initiatives to make the vision a reality. Fundamental to the transformation is effective communication and governance to ensure that the firm is moving in the right direction:

- **What and how:**

  (a) WHAT: The inner boxes, consisting of strategic assets, the digital elements, digital capabilities, and investments, are the shape of the transformation. They are the specific set of elements implemented by the organization, and the resources used to do so. Together, they represent, in essence, the digital intensity of the organization.

  (b) HOW: The outer boxes, consisting of digital vision, governance and engagement, are the ways in which leaders will drive the transformation to a successful outcome. They serve as a form of scaffolding through which leaders can ensure that the elements of the "what" are built effectively and that the organization understands customer's touch point.

Together, the "what" and the "how" represent the digital maturity of an organization. They can be thought about as digital "style" and "substance."

- **Digital transformation maturity:** Firms that are mature on both dimensions can drive powerful digital transformation that yields business value. Unfortunately, many firms in the study are mature at only one, or neither.

Conclusion

Leadership is essential. Whether using new or traditional technologies, the key to digital transformation is re-envisioning and driving change in how the company operates, how do you communicate the vision and engage the organization? How do you coordinate investments and activities across silos?

- **Envision the digital future:** How can you transform customer experience? Operation or business model? How can units work differently and work together differently in a more connected way?

- **Focus on the "how" more than the "what":** The most successful transformations from case studies in report focus as much or more on how to drive change as on the detailed content of the change. Build a compelling, transformative roadmap. Invest in digital transformation vision, with related engagement, governance and KPIs will allow people throughout the enterprise to identify new "what" to meet or extend the vision, and how to assess your digital maturity.

Digitalization brings a flood of opportunities and threats, raises the questions about strategy, leadership, structure, talent, finance, and almost every aspect of business. Digitalization won't happen overnight. And business capability optimization takes planning, experimenting and scaling up. Successful digital transformation comes not from creating a new organization, but from reshaping the organization to take advantage of valuable existing strategic assets in new ways.

CHAPTER 4

Digital DNA – Culture

Culture has been defined as "the collective programming of the mind which distinguishes the members of one group or category of people from another" (Geert Hofstede).

Introduction

There are many culture metaphors; culture is like soil, the glue, the fabric or the mixing colors of paint. The word "culture" stems from a Latin root that means the tilling of the soil, like in agriculture. People seem to have different ideas about what culture means for an organization. A company's culture helps define what a company is like – what it means to be part of the company, how to act in the company, what others in the company believe and strive for, even how others see the company.

Culture is the collective mind-set: attitude, behavior or approach to work adopted by or embedded among group of people in the conduct of business. Every organization has a culture, whether defined or not. Actual culture is a function of leadership, starting at the top. Culture is like the "glue" that holds and binds an organization together. It is the most invisible, but powerful fabric weaved in the organizations and surrounding the society as well. Culture is like water; it can keep the enterprise ship afloat and push it toward the right direction, or it can drag down the ship, even sink it. Culture could also be analogized to the "spirit" of the organization – much like the "soul or spirit" of a human being – and the spirit of organization comes from the top.

The Culture-Assessment Questionnaires:

(1) Why is culture so critical in business success?

(2) What are the symptoms of toxic culture?

(3) What kind of culture do you have and is it in alignment with what you are trying to achieve?

(4) If not, identify the culture gaps between what you have and what you want, and work toward that end.

(5) How do you effectively change and in what time frame do you make the transition? And can you?

Culture Eats Strategy for Lunch

A great culture can support a weak strategy, but a weak culture cannot support a great strategy.

Many of us like the witty quote from the management guru Peter Drucker: "Culture eats strategy for lunch"; culture is the most invisible, but powerful corporate fabric; it is both a "hard" competency and a "soft" asset of business. Effective execution of a digital strategy relies on a strong culture. A strong culture accelerates strategy execution and digital transformation. When does a weak culture "eat" strategy and undermine success? How shall you be mindful of culture?

- **Cultural coherence**: Strategy development requires understanding of the current environment, including the organizational culture. It requires an assessment of how the various factors including the culture help or hinder efforts to move to the desired digital transformation. A successful strategy must account for culture's impact on implementation efforts if the strategy is to succeed. Strategy implementation may have to deal with culture change as part of achieving the new end state.

- **Culture precedes strategy:** The right culture is a prerequisite foundation for implementing strategy. An organization's cultural orientation forms the basis for initiating and improving on strategies and sustaining it. A strong culture should have the characteristics of inclusiveness, innovation, learning agility, risk-awareness, etc. A too weak culture affects the ability to walk in one direction and fill in the digital gaps when formal artifacts – such as strategy, processes, and organizational charts are not good enough. Weak cultures rely on bureaucracy to enforce rules and regulations that undermine an organization's speed, simplicity, agility, and competitiveness. Great organizations live on their values.

- **Culture strength:** The strength of culture is reflected in the degree to which an organization performs as intended and desired without immediate, hands-on direction from its management. That doesn't happen unless people are bought into the strategic direction and have the internalized values of the organization. All changes, even those executed successfully, have been mostly messy experiences during transitions. Every major change at its core is a difficult emotional experience for those involved in making it happen. There are beliefs, assumptions, authority dilution, and rumors machines operating beneath the surface.

- **Culture catalyzes business execution**. Culture is collective human behaviors, whether they are aggressive or conservative, selfish or humanistic, collaborative or individualistic. If people are not in tune with an articulated and ingrained culture, their behavior will be less predictable. When people align with the company's values, there is less need for bureaucracy, which means an organization is able to move with speed, simplicity, and resilience, and possibly gain a competitive advantage. Simply put, executing a strategy in an enterprise with a weak culture is like trying to drive nails with a hammer that doesn't have a rigid handle. Culture undermines strategy by increasing the amount of time and effort it takes managers to initiate and execute a strategy, and possibly even the degree to which some of the tactical goals critical to the strategy's success can be achieved.

- **Be mindful of culture with differentiated workforce strategy**: To maximize execution against a strategy, you have to create that strategy while being mindful of the culture into which it will be introduced. How does an organization maximize strategy execution when players are misaligned with positions? To win and maximize strategy execution, an organization must have a differentiated workforce strategy, which requires aligning its strategic capabilities to strategy and aligning the right people in the right positions, to rejuvenate the culture of innovation.

Cultural behavior is clearly a critical capability to execute strategy under shared vision. However, execution effectiveness will be influenced not only by cultural readiness but also completeness of that strategy. For instance, strategy needs to be developed upon the understandings of organizational capabilities, and change management may be one of tools to promote strategy execution. When existing strategy is not working and new one is not defined, then "culture eats strategy at lunch."

2. Culture Pitfalls: Five Characteristics of a Toxic Workplace

Culture is what happens when the managers are not around.

One significant purpose for digital transformation is to create a more creative, healthful, and productive working environment. How to diagnose the problems existing in traditional workplace? It is crucial to measure the effects of a toxic workplace against the impact on people's lives in terms of stress, de-motivation, under-performance, diminished confidence, and also the effect of toxicity on company growth. Otherwise, our daily working experience and a large percentage of one's life is going to be challenging and potentially stressful. Though what's "right" can be subjective, is toxicity a natural part of any corporate or it can be avoided? Here are five characteristics of a toxic workplace:

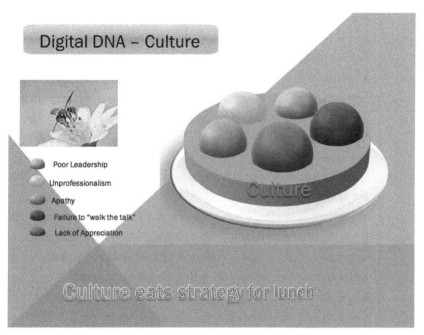

Figure 9: Culture eats strategy for lunch

(1) Poor Leadership: It doesn't take long for a workplace to become toxic. And because the spirit of an organization comes from top, the culture becomes "toxic" when leadership sets unrealistic goals, micromanages, and is non-inclusive with regard to the day-to-day running of a business. Like it or not, the leadership of a company drives culture and vision, and if it is doing so in a vacuum or without regard to its best asset (solid employees), things can turn toxic very fast.

- **"Skilled incompetence" is a symptom**: In upper management, too many unconsciously follow the mantra, "do as I say, not as I do." Breaking habits and learning new ones are just too difficult for too many people who run organizations, and with skilled incompetence running the show, it's almost impossible to have anything other than a toxic workplace.

- **Making decisions "blindly"**: One of the most toxic workplace characteristics is that of management making decisions without considering the people. Everyone can be guilty of it sometimes, but managers often take a "hands-off" approach to their staff, and so easily make changes and decisions that ride waves over the employees and alter their lives. And they often do so in a whim. What happens as we move toward larger and larger companies, with ever-more toxic management seeking to silence those who challenge the status quo? Turnover is today's cost. What will it cost in the future?

- **Lack of mentorship**: Leaders should coach teams on why they are doing what they do, and how it fits in with the company's objective. If management is taking the time to assign work, it does not take that much longer to say why the work is important. If this habit is followed on each and every major work assignment, then employees will gain some job satisfaction from understanding why they are important to the organization. Of course, this means that the organization as a whole has to know where it is going and why.

(2) Unprofessionalism: A toxic workplace is usually identified by the lack of morale evidences throughout the organization. A caustic environment will not attract the best and brightest hires.

- **Unprofessional characteristics:** Unethical conduct, unprofessionalism, unsatisfactory communication in general, back-biting and rumor-mongering, obsessive favoritism, discrimination (age, racial, sexual, etc.) harassment of any kind, abuse of any kind, and lack of teamwork are just some of the characteristics, and any of the numerous possible combinations thereof, that would make a workplace more toxic.

- **Interest conflict**: Organizations often are in conflict with the expectations of employees, regardless of what is said. It is necessary that they understand what the organization is doing, why it is doing it, and how each employee contributes to the whole. Companies need to understand the drivers behind attitudes and behaviors. Talent must decide where they want to invest the time, energy, and expertise. If it's with a company or organization, it's important that individual values are in alignment with that company or organization.

(3) Apathy: At traditional hierarchical organization, a lack of real support for employees can be an issue: Who do you go to if there's a problem with your boss or someone in a senior role? Often, there's an "elephant in the room" that no one wants to address until the problem begins to spiral. Unhelpful behavior that leads to general gossip can very quickly create a toxic environment.

- **Lack of support:** The "care-less" attitude perceived in corporations today may be simple responses to supply and demand, those two unforgettable axes controlling the consumption of all resources, human or otherwise. What level of toxicity existed in corporations during a thriving economy? Is the level of toxicity inversely proportional to economic health? Perhaps part of this toxicity comes from the financial crisis; everybody is pushed to the extremes and everybody is jittery. Pressure on top is released in the form of toxicity downstream. This does not excuse corporations spewing a toxic environment, but it may help them understand and deal with occurrences of toxicity.

- **Poor communication skills.** People can't communicate to their teams appropriately to keep them in the loop as well as motivating them to grow and develop. Leadership itself should be something that breaks down these boundaries and brings a more personable expectation to organizations and companies.

(4) Failure to "walk the talk": Toxicity is always spawned in the gap between what is said and what is done. Toxic culture is embedded into a toxic workplace.

- **Failure to "walk in its talk":** This happens when the behaviors that employees profess to value are not supported, but rather may even be punished, most often indirectly. The company literature says it values honesty and integrity, yet shoots the messenger more often than not. Or an organization says it welcomes diversity and entrepreneurial schools of thought, and then discourages such behaviors with an unaccepted culture that speaks far louder than the company literature.

- **Lack of trust that permeates everything**: This is usually indicative of a culture that lacks clear and realistic goals, does not provide "authentic" and balanced communication throughout the organization, and does not make employees feel as stakeholders and beneficiaries in the collaborative creation of equities created through their work.

(5) Lack of appreciation: Culture represents the "ethos" of the organization, as it has evolved since its inception. Toxicity is nothing new and it seems to have prehistoric roots.

- **Lack of "freedom"**: If individuals are to make change, the organization should have to give them some grade of freedom. No matter how hard one tries to diminish the effects of a toxic working place, one gets washed away. In this case, it is not possible to affect much. The organization is not in for change.

- **Lack of standard of excellence**: A "toxic workplace" has characteristics of not investing in its employees; accepting status quo as the new norm; not having a standard of excellence; thinking leaders have all of the right answers, all of the time; failing to acknowledge accomplishments, performance, and milestones; not leading by example; and not listening to its employees.

Toxicity needs to be eliminated. Respect, professionalism and perseverance are the values that are the foundation of the digital culture with positive and innovative traits, guiding talent in their daily work – how you relate to people and how you do business.

3. How to Assess Organizational Culture

Culture is intangible, but powerful; culture is invisible, but touchable.

Culture is the most intangible, but powerful element in business today and it is a key factor in running a high performing digital business. Besides identifying the toxic characteristics listed above, in order to improve and optimize organizational culture, the companies first need to know how to assess their organizational culture objectively and systematically.

(1) Identify culture attributes and gaps: You will have to identify the specific attributes of an organization's culture and which ones you wish to assess. With that in mind, you must decide how to do it. So the first question is, "what do you want to know?" Any cultural assessment starts on a premise that there is a particular angle on the organization's culture that is most important.

- **Identify the culture gaps between "as is" and "to be" states:** An organization wants to be more people-centric, which is driven by the data from a recent industry survey. A profile of the "as-is" culture shows what people perceive the present company culture to be across the following elements – overall brand, organizational characteristics, business leadership, management of employees, organizational glue, strategic emphasis, and criteria of success. Obviously, the perception is not absolute, but a relative perception of how people perceive the culture. An "as-is" profile is created; a future profile is also developed and discussed. The gap between the "as-is" state and the future helps leaders perceive what is needed to achieve that future state. A road map of change is then developed.

- **Take multiple dimensions of culture perspectives:** Some instruments assess culture from a value perspective; others assess culture by behaviors. Most culture experts believe that no instrument could possibly assess culture because it is too complex and overly focuses on the underlying assumptions, which is a deeper level of understanding. In fact, some instruments are measuring climate rather than culture. In the end, it comes down to which perspective you wish to take – values, behaviors, or underlying assumptions. Few instruments cover all three, which is why qualitative data are so important to pick up the richness and the "invisible" aspects of culture, underlying assumptions, and unwritten rules.

- **Make employee survey for feedback about ideal cultures**: The assessment measures are the underlying motivational drivers, whether an individual or collective organizational level that drives one's focus, mental map, decision making style, relationship to norms, time and change, etc., these patterns together ultimately drive behaviors, actions, and performance. One part of the assessment is to get employees to identify what the ideal culture would look like, and the instrument captures the current culture. It breaks down all cultures into constructive, passive aggressive, and passive defensive, and assigns behaviors to each of these categories. A problem statement usually drives the process to profiling and diagnosing the perceived "as-is" organizational culture and helps develop a future profile. Then, the prescriptive solutions can better fix the different matters more effectively.

(2) Assess current organizational culture via questionnaires: Most enterprises have a primary culture and many subcultures as well. Enterprise or business architects can play significant roles in assessing, analyzing, and redesigning culture; their task is not to completely design a complex structure like a culture but to redesign some aspects in an existing organizational culture. Start with the existing culture, analyze it, assess its effectiveness, and then redesign some aspects. The questions below help assess culture with in-depth understanding:

Q1: How is culture shaped and created?
A1: Culture is learned, knowable, measurable, modifiable, and manageable. Culture is shaped by the values and beliefs, etc., of the corporate founders in the first instance and subsequently by the values

and beliefs, etc., of the Board and senior executives. That said, the spirit of an organization comes from the top.

Q2: <u>What are measures on culture?</u>
A2: Culture can be measured and managed against some "model of the desired culture." Cultures can be considered to perform well or perform poorly according to the needs of the organization.

Q3: <u>Can you impose the culture of innovation?</u>
A3. Culture is an ongoing process and continuous journey. Culture is collective mind-set, attitude, habit and brand. You cannot impose your own thought or habit on someone else instantly; however, you could influence, inspire, and cultivate an innovative culture.

Q4: <u>Is heritage and the caste or class system prevalent in many countries part of the enterprise culture?</u>
A4: Societal culture and enterprise culture mutually influence each other; as people bring their values to work, working culture will also change individuals' behavior and beliefs and further influence the community and societal culture as well.

Q5: <u>Can culture be changed on purpose?</u>
A5: Culture can absolutely be changed on purpose with the right management strategy. To systematically change culture takes time, vision, and persistence by the senior leaders.

(3) Retool corporation culture through framework and methodology:
To analyze, assess, and redesign culture, the corporate culture designers such as enterprise architects need a conceptual framework and methodology to demonstrate that analysis, assessment, and redesign of enterprise business culture is possible and practical.

- **A framework within which to conceptualize, understand and structure the culture**: A conceptual framework can conceptualize culture as consisting of three parts. These three parts apply to all organizational cultures, irrespective of whether they are for-profit, not for profit, private, or public enterprises:

(1) The bottom part, which deals with the creation and maintenance of the culture.

(2) A middle part, which deals with how the culture is implemented.

(3) The top part, which deals with how the culture is expressed on a day-to-day basis.

- **A methodology to analyze, assess, and redesign culture in a consistent manner:** Conceptual methodology outlines a brief four-step approach:

  (A) **Analysis**: Identifies conflicts/problems and their causes.

  (B) **What:** Identify what needs to be changed, and why.

  (C) **How**: Determine the ways and means of effecting change: small step/success/reinforcement approach; identify dependencies and conflicts.

  (D) **When**: Step-by-step plan and road map to implement and realize change.

- **Social techniques**: Social network analysis is a technique that can be used as one of many techniques to analyze, assess, and change organizational culture.

  (a) **Culture is not one level, but many**: What sociology refers to as culture is a reaffirmation of values through totems, mores, and history. These values are driven by deeper primal motives, the mysterious need that humans have to connect with each other. The structure of these connections transcends culture and even values.

  (b) **Culture is what is internal to the group as these connections solidify over time**: You make reference to new members of a group being socialized. That is a second step that happens after assimilation. Before any values are passed, a person can be assimilated within the group structure. In many cases, an initiation period after assimilation starts the socialization process. This is composed of a set of totemic references that reinforces the group support for a common set of values.

(c) **Culture needs to be passed down**: The transition of an individual from one group or status to another group or status consists of three stages: orientation, transition, and incorporation. Every culture must be passed down to new generations and reinforced to existing ones.

Whether organizational or societal, culture is complex. Culture assessment is tough but it is worth the effort because strong, adaptive cultures with digital characteristics tend to nurture higher business performers compared to those with weak or nonadaptive cultures. The qualities that make up those cultures are unique and specific to each of those organizations so statistical validity, high correlations, rigorous design, etc., are all very important in selecting an culture assessment.

4. Debunk High Performance Culture Code

Culture is like water in the sea; it can either keep the business boat afloat or drag it down and sink it.

The culture of a company is basically "how and why we do things around here." Organizational culture is invisible, but powerful; organizational culture seems to be soft, but it's the hard asset of modern businesses. You have to understand what forms your organizational culture, before you can start dealing with it to improve the working relationships that optimizes the 'cultural' equation.

(1) The core components of business culture: Understanding how organizational cultures are formed and developed is a key part of organizational development. Two of the core determinants of organizational culture are leadership and demographics. The spirit of an organization comes from the top, so leadership plays a pivotal role in shaping an organization's culture. On the other side, culture is an organization's DNA; the "gene" is based on its demographic characteristics.

- **Leadership component**: The culture of an organization begins at the top, and filters down through the management team. Organizational culture is multilevel: the senior officers create the overall culture and rules of engagement while each unit of the organization tends to add onto these with "local" cultures that influence how work gets done, how individuals interact, etc. Goals must be clear; roles and responsibilities are unambiguous; an effective talent management process is in place, and the ability to delegate to your management team is unwavering.

- **Demographic component**: It includes age, gender, race, religion, cognitive difference, personality, etc. It needs to be matched by the leadership, strategic and operational approach to the business, as it looks at ways to ensure sustainable growth within its industry sector and for its specific target markets while optimizing the outputs from the organizational make-up, which includes "its culture."

(2) The art and science of culture development: The true organizational culture goes a lot deeper and is always multifaceted, especially in today's global economy and digital dynamic. Though the "spirit" comes from the top, culture is also like an organization's "habit," which cannot be dictated from above, but has to be developed and nurtured.

- **Culture defines many aspects such as:**

    - how failures or disappointments are perceived and handled;
    - how the customer (internal and external) is defined and handled;
    - the extent of cooperation and communication among different organizational entities;
    - having a "we can do it" or a defensive atmosphere; does the organization believe in long-term success and growth;

- how the individual feels rewarded or recognized for his or her contribution;
- how positions are filled and candidates selected; is cultural fit considered or only experience progression and educational background?

- **Culture is collective behaviors**: Active contribution of the leaders and "living by example" are important to the cultural evolution, but culture cannot be defined by the leadership team in a procedure. It starts at the top, but it has to be diffused downward to every employee. Messaging must be clear and done over time, with a consistent cultural or branding message communicated and practiced, not just preached. Only then can you hope that the culture will be pervasive throughout the organization; and it directly reflects business value.

- **Culture is brand**: It's a sign of a very strong leader and corporate culture when it stays intact throughout the world; when the "brand" and the "culture" are as one; when companies start to spread across the country or borders, then the culture gets diluted and starts to vary. At a global scope, the organizational culture is influenced by the local culture and, to some extent, the further away from the "head office" the employees are, the more they seem to adapt their own unique cultures being influenced by their own local environment. This doesn't mean that these "regional changes" in culture are always positive, but it seems the further away the office or branch is from the "core" (head office), the more it is influenced by local factors. Interestingly, the culture dilution has been mitigated in some large multinationals in a rather prosaic way by applying standard procedures or processes. Although procedures do not embody the culture, they may infuse it without "the spirit."

(3) Debunk high performance culture code – "AIRSHARE": High performance culture is a collective attitude and leadership quality that institutionalizes the true foundation for continuous improvement through operational excellence, sustainability, customer delight, and outstanding business growth. High performance ultimately becomes a way of life for the enterprise:

- **Overcome the obstacles**: Along the path are many obstacles such as high egos, envies, lack of vision, personal interests, dislikes for people, dislikes for customers, dislikes for following procedures, and outside factors such as certain negatives in local culture – all of which can stop high performance cultures or teams.

- **Walk the talk:** A company with high performance culture walks the way it talks. It takes time and leadership to develop competitive cultures. It begins with a mission and a vision, and follows with selecting and recruiting good people, plus retaining them. To develop and sustain a high performance culture, everybody in the organization must form a united front to achieve excellence and harmony. From upper management down to the most humble employee, a high performance company walks the talk; otherwise people lose focus and then lose excellence.

- **Debunk high performance culture code: AIRSHARE.** Culture is the "soil," to have a great harvest and grow the best crop (execute the right strategies flawlessly), you must prepare the soil to ensure that it is enriched. Culture is also like the air inside the organization; "AIRSHARE" is the digital, magic code to develop a high performance culture.

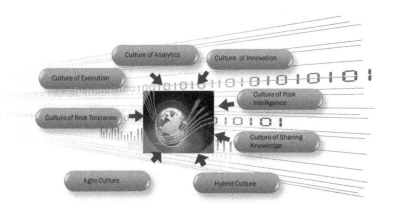

Digital Culture Code: "AIRSHARE"

Figure 10: Digital Culture Code: "AIRSHARE"

A – Culture of Analytics: An analytical organization not only measures the right things at the right time to facilitate quality decision making, but also measures for the sake of improving the business and customer services.

I – Culture of Innovation: Innovation comes from a combination of need and culture that is open to new things. Cultural change in an organization begins with the involvement of the top management and their commitment for change.

R – Culture of Risk Intelligence: Digitalization brings both significant opportunities and risks in organizations. In practice, risk intelligence culture is a risk awareness culture that thinks about managing risk as part of "how things get done around here," as well as risk management culture, which works to manage risk in intelligent way.

S – Culture of Sharing Knowledge: "Knowledge is Power." In the organization domain, knowledge is the context to make work well done. Thus, if the success of others is the value and cooperation is the expectation, then "knowledge-sharing" culture needs to be cultivated.

H – A Hybrid Culture Model: There are many culture masters and varying culture models around; however, in the age of digitalization, those models designed in the 20th century may have limitations to adapt to the rapidly disruptions, interdependence, and uncertainty facing in organizations today. Therefore, a hybrid culture model is the best fit.

A – Agile Culture: Agile is philosophy and principle, not just a software management methodology. It shapes business's collective mind-set to fit into today's hyper-connectivity, hyper-complexity and hyper-digitalization.

R – Culture of Risk Tolerance. It's easy to agree on the value of failure if the failures help expose the fundamentals needed to succeed. So, it is strategic imperative to create the culture of risk tolerance that enables learning from failure.

E – Culture of Execution. The right culture is a prerequisite for execution. Culture precedes strategy. An organization's cultural orientation forms the basis for initiating and improving on strategies for sustaining it.

A high performance organization dreams beyond boundaries to translate into realities through its own high performing cultures listed above. Every forward-thinking organization has to decode the myth of business culture and cultivate the right set of "digital habits" in catalyzing digital transformation.

5. Digital Culture Characteristic #1: The Analytic Culture

Success in analytics is more about the people than it is about the tools.

Information is the life blood of a modern organization; therefore, how to build up a digital business with a culture of analytics is a strategic shift to compete for the future. The point of analytics is not just to run the numbers or create new algorithms, etc., but to provide fresh and unique insights that drive decisions or strategies. Analytics is about the company's culture and whether or not your people are "curious." Do you have employees who are willing to get past the "what" part of numbers to wondering about the "why"? Is senior leadership in full support of adopting the changes in the culture necessary to get past the report or dashboard stage? Now comes the hard part – moving the organization to the next levels so that predictive analytics, forecasting, and optimization can be incorporated successfully. And the culture has to be right and open to accepting how analytics may change fundamental views about clients, processes, what is a profitable niche, etc. Here are the five principles in shaping culture of analytics:

- **"The why, what, and how" of analytics helps to inform strategy:** Analytics is about the "why." And you should care about the "why" because it will tell you tomorrow's "what." Analytics is not about getting to a point certain; rather, it needs to be used as a tool to reduce uncertainty in business. To make analytics pervasive within an organization, it needs to be promoted as a way to reduce, not eliminate, or explain uncertainty in both strategic decisions that executives make and the daily decisions that staff make.

- **Data-based decision:** Let the data do the talking. Analytics must drive employee decisions in the field without disclosing too much data – just enough to help staff improve by small steps. Analytics technology exists, and can be used to facilitate better communication with business leaders to reduce the aforementioned political problems. This leads to more fact-based decisions being embraced and implemented by the business.

- **Simplicity:** Because the people who are going to make the decisions based on the "why" do not have time to understand the process behind delivering the "why." They just need to know what happened and what caused it. Thus, keep the process simple and the tools easy to use with better visualization. Make sure the business decision is the first thing discussed. After that, create the analytic solution, methodology, and process, and work closely with customers to demonstrate how different types of analytics can be employed to provide insights into different types of business problems.

- **Creative problem-solving**: Analytics can redefine the box in such a way as to encourage and reward creative problem solving versus the same old methods that produce consistent results but fail to reach potential if only because the new definition of success has raised the bar. A report is used to answer questions that are known in advance. Analytics are about asking and answering the next questions, generally in the form of "why" or even better, "if/then."

- **Measures**: Measures are fundamental for anyone building a system and for a few more measures, more metrics via more angles are better to find and to fix problems. Leadership should demonstrate that it is leading, managing, and operating through measurements; that will influence greatly the rest of the levels in the organization. A truly analytical organization not only measures the right things at the right time to facilitate quality decision making; it also measures for the sake of improving the business and customer services.

Embedding analytics into organization culture is a vital step in building the digital organization, with competencies in data analysis, effective information management systems which communicate the results of analysis, support and understanding from the top about the value of data analysis, so that the effort is supported and promoted. People who work in the various data departments have excellent communication skills to link their work to the organization's objectives and outputs, and a governance structure has integrating mechanisms so that information is shared and valued by all departments. Thus, analytics culture becomes an organizational DNA in competing for the future.

6. Digital Culture Characteristic #2: Culture of Innovation

Innovation is like a plant, and culture is the fertilized soil.

Innovation is the key trait to differentiate digital leaders from digital laggards. Innovating is difficult. Innovating in a controlled environment is more difficult. So, can you impose a culture of innovation, or shall you build, cultivate, or foster it, and how?

- **Culture is an ongoing process and continuous journey**: Dissatisfaction is perhaps the first requisite to develop innovation as a culture. The second is to consider innovation not as a management buzzword but to define an ideation process with important organizational characteristics that help increase the number of choices for innovation management. Maintaining a culture of innovation in an ongoing and sustainable way requires leadership effectiveness and process agility. Every culture must be passed down to new generations, and reinforced to existing ones. Cultivating culture is a process that is ongoing and a continuous journey. You may also influence the culture through rapid learning that stands on its own as a separate point of influence. Especially where there's reluctance in an organization, trumpeting learning as an internal process is a powerful way to build proof and followers.

- **Tie the innovative culture to the organization's strategy**: This ensures that innovations will be supported by management and by all stakeholders. Lacking a positive strategic intent toward innovation in large mature organizations can become an issue; it is important to well define innovation as key ingredient in business strategy; and the three managerial tools for creating a culture of innovation are policies, programs, and processes. Get these steps right and you will be a world-class innovator with a strong culture of innovation. Get any one of them wrong, and your results will be suboptimal. Evidence exists that companies that have successfully tied innovation to their strategy actually have much better ROI than the ones that did not.

- **Innovation needs to be valued**: Values are a no-brainer; innovation is either valued or it's not. If not, any talented innovators probably had a short tenure with the company and went to the other pastures. This is pretty much a self-selection process. No amount of HR-speak or innovation vernacular will move the needle. When innovation is valued, the hiring and talent acquisition process reflects it; there is usually a history to point to when recruiting and the innovation culture will reveal itself to the candidates. Since innovation is typically won by the most persistent and passionately motivated talent, the typical descriptors for success need to be morphed to the descriptions that acknowledge what is learned and what doesn't work, and it is further enhanced by well-defined product or project performance and design parameters that create the target for what success looks like.

- **Culture change is pushing the really big boulder up hill**: Cultures have inertia. It is so much easier to sustain inertia than to alter the course of the already moving mass. The spirit comes from the top; the innovation leadership can set the right tone to foster and encourage an innovation culture. Even within progressive, "innovation-friendly" organizations, amazing ideas can wither on the vine when the passionate innovator reaches "the point of approval" – a manager or supervisor. If the innovation process leading up to this point is not well-developed, these managers will lack sufficient history and emotional bond to the innovation, to swiftly approve it or to avoid trenched conflict as the discussion escalates with the passionate innovator. Digital is about flow; then culture may be just like water, more easily permeating around when the innovation guidelines are well set from the top and innovative initiatives are warmly encouraged.

- **The metrics and reward system**: Digital is the age of discovery; employees should be encouraged to think out-of-the-box, go beyond their defined roles, and demonstrate their intellectual capabilities to bring positive changes. A recognition system and high visibility for all positive contributions will help create a culture of innovation. Innovation must be appreciated. Culture Index actually measures the ability of people to be innovative. Who can come up with the new ideas? Then, who can implement them? Who will embrace change; who will fight it? If you want an innovative culture, then fill your organization with people who are innovative and embrace change. The measurement of innovations must be in place to support funding of innovation work, to create positive environment and culture for innovation. After you get the management tools right and build a culture of innovation, you can benchmark your progress on the way to sustain the world class culture on these three parameters:

  (1) The company's definition of innovation is known and understood throughout.
  (2) The company dedicates sufficient human and financial resources to its innovation programs and structures.
  (3) The company's innovators apply the latest and best innovation tools and methods.

Culture is collective mind-set, attitude, habit, and brand, you cannot impose your own thought or habit to someone else instantly, however, you could make influence, inspire and cultivate. You cannot impose a culture of innovation, but definitely you can influence and putting the right innovation elements into your strategy and execution. Above are good foundational elements for fostering innovation. Further, these elements should be tailored for each organization. There is no one-size-fits-all set of policies, programs and structures as well, organizations have to keep exploring, experimenting and adjusting for fostering the culture of innovation.

7. Digital Culture Characteristic #3: A Risk- Intelligent Culture

Digitalization brings both significant opportunities and risks in organizations. Risk-awareness culture, which in practice means a culture where thinking about managing risk as part of "how things get done around here." The starting point in developing a culture of compliance and risk management is for the organization to have a common definition of risk management. That is, risk management should not be seen only as the "bad", but also as an opportunity to "gain." A common definition addresses risk management both as a value preservation and value creation tool. Without a strong risk- awareness culture, you will be unable to accomplish much in the way of a successful risk management implementation. In higher mature level, risk intelligent culture can manage both opportunities and risks scientifically.

(1) **Tone at the top:** For the culture to start talking the same language, the tone must flow from the top first. The executive team must champion the design, implementation and monitoring of an effective governance, compliance and risk management program.

- **Management attitude:** This is a make-or-break and 'goes to straight' culture, the starting point would always get an understanding of current attitudes to risk management at all levels, from senior executive team to front desk, and use the results to decide how to build a stronger risk-awareness culture.

- **Board leadership**: The top issue is having a strong, independent and inquisitive Board. It has control over management, not the other way around. The risk-awareness culture is indeed important, but it may not give you the full picture unless you also analyze the risk attitude of the top management.

(1) Oversight (organizational culture and governance, risk management).

(2) Clarity of the assessment structure and objectives.

(3) Ensure the sufficient resources to execute.

- **Collective attitude and behavior**: Everyone has to embrace positive attitude, as culture is a collective attitude. Everyone in the organization should have a common definition of risk management and a common understanding on what it does for the business as a whole. Everyone has to embrace positive attitude, foster the advocacy and execution of compliance and risk management. As the saying goes, you cannot force culture down people's throats; culture is collective behavior and everyone has a role to play.

- **Fitting in the culture gives different results than living it**. Risk is a too abstract concept for many to relate to. Try as one might, instituting a risk-awareness culture is just one more silo and administrative requirement that people often feel they need to deal with rather than embrace. There must be awareness from all people over organization. Besides top management commitment to building risk-awareness culture, all people must support it if they want to create risk management effectively in organization.

  (1) Senior management buy-in and sponsorship.

  (2) Ownership and accountability at all levels.

  (3) Non-retribution policy for risk identification and reporting.

(2) Enterprise Opportunity Management: A major part of the challenge in getting thinking about risk management embedded in the culture is being able to help people at all levels understand risk issues by applying language that makes risk management clear and relevant to each individual.

- **Effective communication strategy:** The key is for the risk management team to understand how different silos or departments are and manage the tailored solutions. It's important that risk managers compare their expert understanding of organizational risk with what is known, not known, or misunderstood in various silo or departments. Then effective communication strategies can be put in place to bring different perspectives into greater unison, which is an important part of improving communications and achieving risk-intelligent culture. The "experts" often learn quite a bit about their understanding of risk in this process as well.

- **From ERM (Enterprise Risk Management) to EOM (Enterprise Opportunity Management)**: As many organizations are at the journey for digital transformation, risk-awareness culture may not be strong enough to capture the opportunities in risk management, at higher maturity level, risk-intelligent culture needs to be cultivated, as every risk has opportunities in it, and every opportunity has risks within it. Therefore, Enterprise Risk Management has to be expanded and upgraded into Enterprise Opportunity Management.

- **WIFM principle**: If you can't answer the "What's in It for Me?" question when trying to engage people in thinking about risk, then it will continue to be regarded as "something done at headquarter" or seen only as a compliance issue at operational level. In fact, Risk Management needs to be well embedded in all key business processes, and it has to become opportunity management, as statistics shows that organizations with high mature risk management practices can achieve more than a 20% revenue increase over laggards.

(3) Risk-Awareness Culture Issues: Following are some of the important risk awareness and intelligence culture issues:

- Consistency of direction from management
- Employees' awareness of short and long-term objectives and strategies

- Alignment of objectives between business units and corporate
- Clarity of individual accountability for objectives
- Employees' understanding of policies
- Management's receptivity to messengers of bad news
- Employees' level of understanding of risk
- Management's emphasis on risk management and control
- Availability of processes to manage change
- Effectiveness of controls
- More information on risk culture assessment

The real advantage of risk management and compliance is that it gives the organization a competitive advantage. Culture is the collective mind-set, behavior, and business brand; therefore, it takes collective effort from top-down to bottom-up, effective strategy and efficient mechanism to cultivate a risk-intelligent culture, which is one of the key factors in running a high performance business.

8. Digital Culture Characteristic #4: Culture of Knowledge-Sharing

Culture of knowledge-sharing is to improve organization's learning capability.

It is the age of crowd-sourcing, which is the digital way to co-create, share and update knowledge to catalyze digital flow. "Sharing is caring" and "knowledge is power" – in the organizational domain, knowledge is the context to make work well done; thus, if the success of others is the value and cooperation is the expectation, then a "knowledge-sharing" culture needs to be cultivated because people need a common goal to be willing to share knowledge. What's a more systematic understanding than building a culture of knowledge sharing?

- **The success of Knowledge Management (KM) is mainly tied to culture:** Creating the right culture that fits both the organization and the employees is hence important. There are several elements that make the process faster, such as trust, mutual respect, sense of unity, and win-win. Employees should think of knowledge sharing as something they gain, rather than lose. Knowledge is more like a commodity, only a couple of clicks away in today's digital era with information abundance, only through sharing and updating, it can be refreshed and refined into insight and wisdom.

- **Three-step knowledge sharing behavior:** As a goal for leadership is to encourage and recognize talent, and make it practical for the members to help them do their work. It is often easier to have people sharing what they know, but more difficult to see people reusing what others has developed. To promote the "knowledge sharing culture" in any enterprise organization, a reward motivation program shall be applied along with KPI measurements exercise.

  (1) Learning before each event.
  (2) Sharing learning after each event.
  (3) And then co-creating the new knowledge and insight.

- **"Knowledge is power" as a part of "intrinsic motivation":** Knowledge workers with intrinsic motivation like to share their knowledge to learn more by themselves. Most of the times, knowledge workers are perfectly able to find a balance between sharing knowledge and ensuring sharing knowledge will not become a goal in itself. One's knowledge is the other one's information only, the ultimate business goal is to improve productivity and encourage innovation.

- **Three formats of knowledge – cognitive, psychomotor, and affective knowledge:** Knowledge is dynamic and multidimensional; it's not just spoken or transferred in hardcopy; it's also transferred visually and through emotions or feelings. There's a very wide range of knowledge to be considered.

Traditionally you have to look at knowledge transfer in three formats listed as following:

- Cognitive, intellectual outcomes
- Psychomotor-new physical skills
- Affective attitudes, values, beliefs

- **KM-Knowledge Management as the overarching umbrella:** It can include culture as soft, but key success factor; it is a management domain upon how information flows in the organization. People's beliefs and values are normally distilled through a long process of cultural cumulating socio-culturally and organizationally. KM methodologies or tools do play a major role. If knowledge is not flowing smoothly in the organization, figuring out the causes is a significant contribution to KM. Knowledge sharing becomes an effortless activity, if it is embedded in the work styles, and well-placed KM systems, it is not a separate exercise - one does it because every bit of information in the organization is tagged and flows through KM channels.

- **The holistic Knowledge Management approaches:** An effective KM platform or tools are efficient; however, many other aspects of knowledge management cannot be solved by technology only. KM needs to look at all the present collaborative processes already being used to evaluate them for improvements, and to enhance knowledge sharing, decision making, as well as follow on actions based on the decisions made. Innovation and knowledge creation, access and knowledge usage appear to be linked. And now at the age of information explosion, it is about managing information to create new knowledge with vast knowledge repositories available for talent to work with. The knowledge sharing culture is strongly influenced by both organizational and social structures.

Knowledge Management is not only about sharing knowledge. It is better to talk about the knowledge you need to do your job. Then you can determine what you need to do to get the right information or experience at the right time. Keep the end-the ultimate business goals in mind. If everyone already agrees that it is good to satisfy the customer, and they come to understand that by sharing knowledge, you help coworkers to succeed and so better satisfy the customer, and then the culture will begin to value sharing knowledge and the organizations move toward a knowledge-sharing culture.

9. Digital Culture Characteristic #5: A Hybrid Culture Model

Organizational culture is just like computer operation system, you need to reboot periodically to keep it running smoothly.

There are varying culture models around, however, those models designed in the industrial age of the 20th century may have limitations to adapt to the increasing speed of change, velocity, interdependence, and uncertainty facing any organization today. First of all, what are the good business culture models anyway?

(1) Different Culture Models

A: Lewis Model of Culture: The Lewis Model of Cross-Cultural Communication was developed by Richard D. Lewis. The core of the model classifies cultural norms into Linear-Active, Multi-Active and Reactive, or some combination. (Wikipedia).

Whilst Lewis' writings recognize these can only be stereotypes, he asserted that his model provides a practical framework for understanding and communicating with people of other cultures. Lewis Model emphasized this societal culture description:

- Cultural behavior is the end product of collected wisdom, filtered and passed down through hundreds of generations as shared core beliefs, values, assumptions, notions, and persistent action patterns.

- Culture is a collective programming of the mind that distinguishes the members of one human group from another.

- The iceberg of culture such as art, food, fashion, behavior, communication patterns, body language, mass media, custom is just about scratching the surface of in-depth culture discipline.

Digitalization is transforming the world, and the speed of culture change may also be expedited as the world becomes more hyper-connected and interdependent. Although each societal culture is unique, culture is also changeable, and it can be unified at certain level, to push the human progress.

B: Hofstede Organizational Onion Cultural model: Geert Hofstede (1991) sees culture as "the collective programming of the mind that distinguishes the members of one group or category of people from another." He proposes four layers, each of which includes the lower level. 'Culture' being like an onion can be peeled, layer-by layer. The figure below shows how Hofstede illustrates the differences between personality, culture, and human nature.

Layers	Description
Symbols	Such as words, gestures, pictures or objects, those carry a particular meaning that is only recognized by those who share the culture.
Heroes	Either real or imaginary persons, who possess characteristics that are highly prized in a culture and who thus, serve as role models for behaviors.
Rituals	These are collective activities, the ways of greeting and showing respect to others; social and religious ceremonies are examples.

Values	The core of culture is formed by values, which are slow to change and are significantly influenced by the history of the nation or culture. Values are broad tendencies to prefer certain states of affairs over others.
Practices	Symbols, heroes, rituals can be subsumed under the term practices.

Table 3: Hofstede's Culture Model

C: Hampden-Turner Trompenaars Two-Layered Culture Model:
Hampden –Turner Trompenaars model of national culture difference is a framework for cross-cultural communication applied to general business and management, developed by Trompenaars and Charles Hampden-Turner. (Wikipedia). In 1997, management consultants Trompenaars and Hampden-Turner adopted a similar onion-like model of culture. In their view, culture is made up of basic assumptions at the core level. These 'basic assumptions' are somewhat similar to 'values' in the Hofstede model. This model of national culture differences has seven dimensions:

- **Universalism vs. Particularism**: Universalism is about finding broad and general rules. When no rules fit, it finds the best rule. Particularism is about finding exceptions. When no rules fit, it judges the case on its own merits, rather than trying to force-fit an existing rule.

- **Analyzing vs. Integrating**: Analyzing, decomposes to find the detail. It assumes that God is in the details and that decomposition is the way to success. It sees people who look at the big picture as being out of touch with reality. Integration brings things together to build the big picture. It assumes that if you have your head in the weeds, you will miss the true understanding.

- **Individualism vs. Communitarianism**: Individualism is about the rights of the individual. It seeks to let each person grow or fail on their own, and sees group-focus as denuding the individual of their inalienable rights. Communitarianism is about the rights of the group or society. It seeks to put the family, group, company and country before the individual. It sees individualism as selfish and short-sighted.

- **Inner-directed vs. Outer-directed**: Inner-directed is about thinking and personal judgment 'in our heads'. It assumes that thinking is the most powerful tool and that considered ideas and intuitive approaches are the best way. Outer-directed is seeking data in the outer world. It assumes that we live in the 'real world' and that is where we should look for our information and decisions.

- **Time as sequence vs. Time as synchronization**: Time as sequence sees events as separate items in time, sequence one after another. It finds order in a serried array of actions that happen one after the other. Time as synchronization sees events in parallel, synchronized together. It finds order in coordination of multiple efforts.

- **Achieved status vs. Ascribed status:** Achieved status is about gaining status through performance. It assumes individuals and organizations earn and lose their status every day, and that other approaches are recipes for failure. Ascribed status is about gaining status through other means, such as seniority. It assumes status is acquired by right rather than daily performance, which may be as much luck as judgment. It finds order and security in knowing where status is and stays.

- **Equality vs. Hierarchy:** Equality is about all people having equal status. It assumes we all have equal rights, irrespective of birth or other gift. Hierarchy is about people being superior to others. It assumes that order happens when few are in charges and others obey through the scalar chain of command.

D: Deal and Kennedy's cultural model: Deal and Kennedy (1982) defined organizational culture as the way things get done around here. Deal and Kennedy created a model of culture that is based on four different types of organizations. They each focus on how quickly the organization receives feedback, the way members are rewarded, and the level of risks taken. In this model, culture has been classified into four categories:

- **Work-hard, play-hard culture**: This has rapid feedback/reward and low risk, stress coming from quantity of work rather than uncertainty; high-speed action leading to high-speed recreation.

- **Tough-guy macho culture**: This has rapid feedback/reward and high risk; stress coming from high risk and potential loss/gain of reward. Focus on the present rather than the longer-term future.

- **Process culture**: This has slow feedback/reward and low risk, leading to low stress, plodding work, comfort and security. Stress may come from internal politics and stupidity of the system. Development of bureaucracies and other ways of maintaining the status quo. Focus on security of the past and of the future.

- **Bet-the-company culture**: This has slow feedback/reward and high risk, stress coming from high risk and delay before knowing if actions have paid off. The long view is taken, but then much work is put into making sure things happen as planned.

E: Denison Organizational Culture Model: Daniel "Dan" R. Denison' model of organizational culture is widely known and used in academic research in organizational culture, effectiveness and performance. It identified four organizational culture traits that impact performance:

Involvement	empowerment, team orientation, capability development
Consistency	core value, agreement, coordination, integration
Adaptability	organizational learning, customer focus, creating change
Mission	strategic direction, vision, goal objectives

Table 4: Denison's Culture Model

F: Edgar Schein's Model of Organizational Culture: According to Edgar Schein, organizations do not adopt a culture in a single day, instead, it is formed in due course of time as the employees go through various changes, adapt to the external environment and solve problems. They gain from their past experiences and start practicing it every day, thus, forming the culture of the workplace. The new employee also strives hard to adjust to the new culture and enjoy a stress free life. Schein believed that there are three levels in an organization culture.

Artifacts	The first level is the characteristics of the organization that can be easily viewed, heard and felt by individuals collectively known as artifacts. The dress code of the employees, office furniture, facilities, behavior of the employees, mission, and vision of the organization all come under artifacts and go a long way in deciding the culture of the workplace.
Values	The next level according to Schein that constitute the organizational culture is the values of the employees. The values of the individuals working in the organization play an important role in deciding the organization culture. The thought process and attitude of employees have deep impact on the culture of any particular organization. What people actually think matters a lot for the organization? The mind-set of the individual associated with any particular organization influences the culture of the workplace.

Assumed values	The third level is the assumed values of the employees that can't be measured but do make a difference to the culture of the organization. There are certain beliefs and facts that stay hidden but do affect the culture of the organization. The inner aspects of human nature come under the third level of organizational culture. The organizations follow certain practices that are not discussed often but are well understood. Such rules form the third level of the organizational culture.

Table 5: Edgar Schein Culture Model

A majority of culture models listed above were developed based on the observation of the industrial business paradigm in the 20th century, so they may not completely fit in the digital dynamic in the 21st century. Still, these are valuable works that provide different angles to understand both national culture and organizational culture, and digital businesses today can well blend different culture models to tailor their own environment and overcome the culture challenges facing their organizations today and tomorrow.

10. Digital Culture Characteristic #6: The Agile Culture

Agile is philosophy and principle, not just a software management methodology, it shapes collective mind-set of organization to adapt to the digital new normal of hyper-connectivity, hyper-complexity and hyper-competition. How can Agile make influence on organizational culture, if it does, what are characteristics in it?

- **Agile promotes culture of open communication**. People are willing to let go of their ego and those with an open, positive attitude toward change tend to embrace it; while those who dislike change, don't communicate well, or are overly defensive are at the other end of the spectrum. Identify the positive early adopters and they'll help you convert the rest. It can also be hard to interface with other parts of the organization, as it is having differing expectations. But when open communication and cross-functional collaboration become habit for organization, part of the agile culture is shaped smoothly.

- **Agile promotes culture of continuous improvement**. Culture change is hard and it takes time. You can't expect immediate results. Learning and discovery is constantly happening in agile organizations. The agile values and principles are a foundation on which the organization is being built; the practices are much more fluid and will evolve over time. You start by improving where you can, enlist help, expand your influence, and repeat.

- **Agile promotes culture of self-discipline**: Agile is not taking less discipline, but more-either engineering discipline or management discipline. The digital transformation is shaping work from being a place you go during set hours each work day to something you do in a dynamic, increasingly virtual workplace. Self-organizing agile teams do have a bounded authority to make their own accountability, organize and assign their own work. They craft appropriate strategies to accomplish their goals, and make decisions with bounded economic and organizational impact.

- **Agile promotes culture of execution**: agile is an adjective meaning to be able to move quickly and easily. Applying agile principles to the process of agile adoption within an organization will definitely reap benefits. The more salient manifesto is being: "At regular intervals, the team reflects on how to become more effective, then tunes and adjusts its behavior accordingly." Provided adoption is also subject to the call to inspect and adapt, then barriers can be surmounted, minds changed, champions identified - and in time, successful delivery synonymous with project development.

- **Agile promotes culture of adaptability**: Agile inspires cross-disciplinary thinking, iterative communication and cross-functional collaboration, to allow decisions to be made at lower levels in the organization, and to reduce the time between stimulus and response. Agile culture can cultivate such collective mind-set that is able to correct itself through agile culture, such as entrepreneurial attitude, lens of diversity, and tolerance of ambiguity. See the work or project through the eyes of customers. As culture of agile needs to enable value creation, not just time or cost measures.

To sum it up, the adjective 'agile' is an orientation, an intention to be lightweight and low-structure without being ignorant or irresponsible. The culture of agile is the collective mind-set with customer-focus, adaptation to the changes, progression and flexibility.

11. Digital Culture Characteristic #7: A Risk-Tolerance Culture

Fitting in the culture gives different results than living it.

It's easy to agree on the value of failure if the failures help expose the fundamentals needed to succeed in digital transformation and business innovation. So why is it so difficult to create the culture that enables learning from failure? And what does it require by learning from failure?

- **Direct and indirect risks**: There are direct and indirect risks, where "indirect risks" are those associated with inaction and procrastination, in effect the risks of not taking risks, direct risks are proportional with business opportunities; the more risks you take, the better opportunities you get. Therefore, in order to fail, a company must take "direct risks" substantial enough that the potential for failure is real.

- **Scapegoating avoidance**: Excepting for blatant managerial incompetence, or malfeasance, failure must not lead to recriminations and scapegoating, which is a big cultural hurdle for many companies, as that is all too often the first and primary reaction to failure. The human tendencies of information silos, "protecting turf," undermining another's turf, positional power, etc., are enough reasons to kill innovation.

- **Credit and criticism:** Create a positive environment where true failures (unexpected or inadvertent one) are not punished. Do systematic failure analysis and learn out of the results. Most important thing for a company or organization can do to learn from their mistakes is to understand them within the context of how the organization works.

- **Effective communication**: Determine what went wrong and for which communication is the key. A great way to start this process is for the leader to tell the stories about how he or she made some failures early in their career and the lessons they learned. This is the power of storytelling – it can change a culture by sending a clear signal that it is OK to fail, if only you learn.

- **The positive tone:** When you reframe the word "failure" to be more positive tone, you open the door to learning. Failure is often viewed as falling backward instead of leaning forward. When someone fails, try asking them what they learned instead of focusing on what didn't work or chastising them for overlooking something or making a mistake. Curiosity is a great attribute to create the lure. When you are ready and willing to ask questions as to what was the source of failure, what worked, what didn't, why, etc., you are on the path to gaining value.

Too often, businesses want to blame someone or something for the failure instead of using it as a launch point for improvement. And a risk-tolerance culture is an attitude and leadership quality that institutionalize the true foundation for continuous improvement, ultimately becomes a way of life for the enterprise

12. Digital Culture Characteristic #8: Culture of Execution

The right culture is a prerequisite foundation for execution.

Digitalization accelerates the pace of speed in business environment. If strategy setting is more art than science; then strategy execution is more science than art, it takes systematic processes to set performance goals and achieve them step by step. But what is the better culture for execution? Setting reasonable objectives that can be achieved or setting stretch objectives that even if not fully accomplished? How about personal commitment or team performance, and how to shape a culture of execution to compete at digital speed?

- **Prerequisite**: Culture is a prerequisite for execution. Culture precedes strategy. An organization's cultural orientation forms the basis for initiating and improving on strategies for sustaining it. Both culture and strategy are important to an organization, it must have evolved its brand, as culture and strategy overtime maintain the brand as well as improve upon it. Culture is like glue through which the different components of the brand are binding together and aggregated to become the strategy for keeping that brand and culture unblemished.

- **Mobilization**: Strategy also "defines" the culture you need for execution. Culture is the one thing that other companies can't copy quickly, it gives you competitive advantage, it fosters safety, it generates innovation, it encourages leading across boundaries, etc. Strategy doesn't do any of those things, simply calls for them. Thus, focus should be on mobilization. Effective mobilization addresses strategy and culture, together as one. It combines the structure and direction of top-down strategy with the pragmatism and wisdom of bottom-up insight. This feedback loop reduces the resistance to change, and the proactive participation allows the strategy to be rapidly and efficiently implemented.

- **Goal-setting**: The greatest cultural impact on end-results comes from the goal-setting process rather than whether the goals are realistic or stretch. The more the person who has to achieve those goals is involved in the goal-setting process, the better the results. Too often companies take whatever budget numbers are presented and then arbitrarily add 10% "because of everyone's sandbags." That sets people up for failure and is a clear indicator of a bad culture that likely has extensive other problems including poor innovation, lack of growth, bad service, etc.

- **Balance:** Digital strategy-execution is continuum, not linear. Balance is the key. There needs to have a fair balance of "stretch objectives" and reasonable goals as well. Stretching goals need to be motivational, but not overly stressful. Stretching objectives should motivate people to think bigger, work hard and achieve more; as long as that baseline is communicated and understood, falling short of the stretch is better than sandbagging and setting mediocre goals. While "stretch" seems to be the obvious choice, if in each measurable period a company sets goals that are unreasonable and rarely achieved, the message to the team working to the goals is conflicted. Falling short could become acceptable or the norm. Thus, the balanced execution approach should be setting reasonable goals and stretch targets, and attach compensation to the achievement of both.

- **Commitment:** The other key element in culture of execution is personal commitment. Human achievements, often extraordinary ones, come from a deeply embedded desire to achieve. This in turn comes from identification with a worthy cause and a commitment to see that cause advancement. Collaboratively build individual goals that have a moderate stretch factor to them, and are highly attainable if the individual remains focused and leadership makes sure that the individuals stay on track while removing obstacles on the way to a successful outcome.

- **Correlation**: Strategy leads an organization to success according to a clear vision, a strong ambition, a right analysis of all issues and parameters with culture of course. So the two elements are correlated with each other. When conditions become grim, it's culture (ingenuity, innovation, perseverance, cooperation vs. competition) that will carry the day. A diverse, open, and questioning culture will produce a viable strategy; and culture of execution will accelerate strategy implementation. On the flip side, a great strategy in a corrosive culture is doomed. A great culture can support a weak strategy, but a weak culture cannot support a great strategy. A too strongly infused culture affects changeability negatively. A too weak culture infusion affects the ability to walk in one direction, and fill in the gaps when formal artifacts - such as strategy, processes and organization charts are not good enough, though that doesn't mean culture always shapes strategy.

Culture is one of the main factors that affect implementation of strategies. While successful strategy should also take account culture into enterprise even around the enterprise ecosystem. As shaping a culture of execution is one of the key success factors in building a high performing digital business.

13. Culture Debate #1: Is Culture Superior to Strategy?

Culture must match the strategy.

Culture is the mind-set, behavior, attitude, and approach to work adopted by or embedded among group of people in the conduct of business. Every organization has a default culture. Actual culture is a function of actual leadership, starting at the top. We all heard:

"Culture eats strategy for breakfast." Didn't Peter Drucker tell us that culture is "stronger" than strategy? Why is it stronger? Is it because people have accepted the culture internally, by definition, and it drives their actions? If they didn't identify with it, they would probably leave. And culture is more important because you can recover more quickly from mistakes in strategy if the culture supports these changes than you can from culture that is maladapted to the evolving needs of the business or industry. Of course strategy can guide changes in culture. In well-established organizations, this can take a long time; culture could be the place for strategy to start. A key to effective strategy implementation is to achieve the same level of internalization and sense so that the strategy is part of who we are. Then, the actions also will align with the strategy.

(1) Strategy and culture are inextricably linked: Being fully aware of the culture and its underlying values enables strategy to be input to, validated and executed across the organization. When strategy is developed with the insights of people stakeholders in the organization, then culture becomes the vessel that drives the ownership and alignment needed to guide the strategy. You can't guide a fluid book of business if culture and strategy are not inextricably linked. Culture is part of the strategy.

- **Culture assessment**: Strategy development requires understanding the current environment including the organizational culture. It requires an assessment of how the various factors, including the culture, help or hinder efforts to move to the desired end state. A successful strategy must account for culture's impact on implementation efforts if the strategy is to succeed. To put another way, culture may dictate the methods and resources needed to implement the strategy. Also, the desired end state will include a culture, either the current one or some new one necessary to succeed in the new environment. Strategy implementation methods may have to deal with culture change as part of achieving the new end state.

- **Culture-strategy linkage**: Strategies fail because they often do not address tough issues like culture. A strategy is very important, but will only be successful if it is embedded into a company's culture, and if the culture is designed to implement the strategy successfully. Conclusion: A company must have a strategy that is focused on serving its markets and segments with the defined services or products, and a strategy to mold the needed culture accordingly while culture is certainly part of the environment in which an organization operates, it represents the "box" in which actions and decisions occur. When an organization makes a logical decision to move "outside-the- box," then cultural change is certainly part of the equation. However, if cultural change is not part of the strategy-defining change process, then there are limits to the execution of desired change, and what normally happens is a sub-optimized result.

- **Culture strategy match**. Some organizational strategies set the tone for the culture they want to develop; other organizational strategies ensure the culture is continued. Every company has a strategy - implicit or not. Culture must match strategy. In the "age of discontinuity," strategies can shift, but culture must provide some continuity. So either you build a very strong culture that naturally evaluates and adopts presented strategic variables, or if such a culture is not established, you have to over and over again present and go through the key variables with all employees. But, of course, nothing beats the combination of a nurtured, functioning, and good working organizational culture with sound and well defined strategic variables.

(2) It can take a long time to change culture: There are interactions between the strategic fundamentals, the style of the leadership, the systems of the management, the structures of the organization, the culture understanding and the shared knowledge. Culture is tough and can take long time to change because it may require leadership and change management practices. Strategy on the other hand, can be regarded as the means to attaining and maintaining a position of advantage over adversaries through the successive exploitation of known or emergent possibilities, rather than committing to any specific fixed plan designed at the outset.

- **The challenges for culture changes:** Culture change is like any other change – sometimes it is welcomed, sometimes it is not by people in the organization. For example, a high avoidance culture, it is a cultural profile that is hard to change because the very behaviors that need to change, the avoidance behaviors, generate avoidance of changing them. The challenges are:

  (a) Analyzing and understanding the existing culture.
  (b) Assessing the effectiveness of the culture.
  (c) Understanding what changes need to be made in order to support the new strategy. It is imperative to understand what is/isn't working before attempting any changes.

- **Culture agreement**: Anyone deciding on changes to strategy in an organization need to ensure that they are either

  (a) Consistent with the current culture, or (b) making a knowledgeable decision to buck the culture and move into a new direction. If you decide to buck the culture, you really need a strong leadership team supporting your effort, or you will lose. Strategic success without cultural agreement is nearly impossible. Short-term change may occur, but the 'silent majority' in the background will immediately begin to find workarounds, and wait for their time to simply revert to their normal comfort zones.

- **Symbiosis between culture and strategy**. A strong bond between these two elements will lead to success by goal attainment. A strategy is the vision for how the goals or the "why" of an organization are achieved. Culture is the language in which it is expressed. A vision that cannot be effectively communicated will ultimately fail. However, culture without purpose is like an unbroken stallion. If those who are strategizing on change understand the culture clearly, and can estimate how that culture will evolve over some period of time, then they can use that timeline to their advantage in assuring successful change. In that instance, the effects of culture are not antagonistic or even competitive; rather, they become complementary, and should enhance success.

In summary, culture and strategy are inseparable. Without dynamic and positive organizational culture, no meaningful achievements can be attained with any strategy. A successful organization will create a symbiosis between these two elements to develop a cohesive realization of goals and communication of purpose. If there is no symbiosis between strategy and culture, the organization will not realize its goals. Worse, it may have difficulty in understanding why. Essentially; they are both equally important. And what is absolutely critical is that they are a matched pair.

14. Culture Debate #2:
Is Culture a Type of Competency?

Culture is corporate character!

Some believe that culture is a competency: it is something a company can be good, better, or worse at. According to this view, culture is something a company does; it's a set of behaviors that are closer or further from an ideal. On the other side, for those who believe that culture is not a type of competency: According to this view, culture is closely aligned to both what the company believes in, along with the practices and expectations associated with these beliefs.

- **Culture is organization's collective mind-set:** The word competency implies a learnable skill. Is corporate culture learnable? Change management gurus certainly think so. It also implies some set of metrics that provide ranking of an organization's mastery of the learned subject - culture - along with the relative benefit of various levels of mastery of the subject and ranking of various versions of culture one against another. Is one culture of greater benefit than another? Certainly there are various other cultural attributes that you can rank good, better, or best.

- **Culture is organization's fingerprint**: Culture of an organization is an intrinsic value system, a fingerprint of an organization, Culture can be a competency measured through performance. Culture of an organization is an indicator of the competency parameters at their best. Thus, culture is an indicator of the organizations capability to achieve results in competency parameters. Competency could be learned, but culture of an organization remains a fingerprint and an identity of the organization. If one were to write a case study of the organization's journey to success, the culture of the organization becomes a key element of interpreting the path to excellence, not as much the measured performance parameters. Management should reflect the values and positions established both through the mission statement and more specifically those competencies found in the governance statement.

- **Culture is organizational habit**: One of the respected culture theorists Edgar Schein's definition of organizational culture is: "A pattern of shared basic assumptions that the group learned as it solved its problems that has worked well enough to be considered valid and is passed on to new members as the correct way to perceive, think, and feel in relation to those problems." Culture by this definition is not highly malleable, and tends to be resistant to change, like habit. However, Organizations can learn, benchmark against, build competencies to improve business performance. Whereas the cultural aspect is an intrinsic factor that drives the organization's business longevity. An organization with an excellent culture is arguably capable to give great results in their competencies. Highest rated competencies could be very short lived if the organization lacks the culture to rate and retain the value system beyond the business results. More to the point, like "Seven Habits of Highly Effective People", certainly in a given strategic environment, a certain culture is a competitive advantage.

- **Culture is business brand:** Company culture is closely aligned to what the company believes in, along with the practices and expectations associated with these beliefs. Those beliefs are brought in by the people who make up the company: Both leadership and the members of the organization. There is not always perfect alignment between the two. However, the cultural competency arises in the manifestation of the company culture both internally and in the final analysis in the market environment. If the internal is not properly addressed, the external will also suffer. Corporate culture will therefore have an impact on the type of service or product finally created. Extrinsic reflection of culture is your business brand.

- **Culture is "corporate" character:** Either stagnant giant or small start-up, culture can be a critical component of a company's success. A company with a culture of openness, innovation, high standards in ethics and merit based compensation can motivate team member to work toward a common goal. Likewise, one that rewards yes-men or mediocrity, is patronizing or full of nepotism has the reverse effect. Creating and maintaining the right corporate culture is in itself a competency.

- **Culture is business attitude:** The concept of generic strategies also has implications for the role of culture in competitive success. Culture, the set of norms and attitudes that help shape an organization, has come to be viewed as an important element of a successful firm. However, different cultures are implied by different generic strategies. Build the capacity to intentionally shape the culture for business needs, rather than allow it to develop by default. Culture reflects your business attitude.

- **Culture is differentiator:** A mature culture can powerfully reinforce the competitive advantage a generic strategy seeks to achieve. Differentiation may be facilitated by a culture encouraging innovation, individuality, and risk taking. At high mature level of corporate culture, it is far easier to measure business effectiveness. Learning a corporate culture encompasses both what is found in the training manual and what is told around the water cooler. Some companies have taken a proactive approach to purposely creating a defined corporate culture and the competitive differences.

- **Culture is business asset:** Mastering upon the creation, development and leadership of a healthy, innovative and constructive culture is a strategic competency. Culture and the legacy are that the organization writes about itself through the times of decisions, dynamics and challenges. The fabric of "value system" and "credibility" differentiate an organization from others. A company's culture can be an asset. But assets are different from competencies. Certainly, some competencies are also assets, but not all assets are competencies.

- **Culture represents the "ethos" of the organization:** As it has evolved since its inception. Strategy represents the direction the leadership chooses to consider for future growth and orientation. Well-meaning strategy, which does not take into account the organizational culture, cannot succeed, unless the intended changes in direction are also expected to influence culture. Culture brings speed to market, competitive advantage and defines your brand. Once that culture is established as part of the DNA of the organization, then strategy can be implemented. A great culture can also help shape strategy, but you have to want to listen.

Business competency is both organization's capacity and capability; at the core of culture, it's about business leadership substance, enterprise strategy perception, talent management philosophy, and organizational brand and reputation. Culture is the "soil," – to have a great harvest, grow the best crop (execute the right strategies flawlessly), you must prepare the soil to ensure it is enriched. Setting up the "right" culture is also like a painter mixing the "right" color. How much competition should be mixed with collaboration, creativity with structure? The "right" culture is the one that achieves the objectives of the shareholders with a risk level appropriate for the shareholders; but at the same time compliments the culture of the community in which it operates and make positive impact for the whole society.

15. Culture Debate #3: Can Culture Be Measured?

Culture effectiveness is easy to tell, but hard to measure.

Company culture is unique and provides arguably the most sustainable competitive advantage an organization may have for distinguishing itself against the competition. Culture can make or break an organization. Talent is attracted because of culture, attrition also happens because of culture. It's easy to tell whether culture is empowering or toxic. However, is it possible to harden the soft factor like culture, to make it measurable, and how to nurture a high-performing, high-adaptable digital culture?

- **Culture is the process:** Anyone that is educated and has been involved in a corporate cultural initiative would know that corporate culture is created out of the systems, processes, human capital and associated continual development, organizational hierarchy, and strategy design of the organization. Through the design of the key company interdependencies and structure forms the way employees will work, interact, and use their collective knowledge to the benefit of the organization. Since this method of addressing culture is based on systems and processes, it could be measurable. The measurement of organizational culture can also present the purpose of showing mirror: How evolved the management is? Will it determine the initiation of corrective action to create sustainable competitive advantages? And how?

- **How to measure culture:** Culture is difficult to "measure", because the measurement of culture is not just one dimension such as financial or a technical point, it's a multi-dimensional assessment. Though it is hard to measure culture directly, there are logic steps in evaluating its impact indirectly:

  (1) **First, a sufficient understanding of the important culture elements.** It contributes to the way that the culture works to select appropriate measures. Culture is a unique characteristic of an organization that emerges from the combination of processes, best practices, synergies between departments and individuals, etc. – often unidentified characteristics. It is tempting to circulate the current hot tool or metric in an attempt to capitalize on the latest management fad or to use industry benchmarks as a means of assessing organizational success.

  (2) **Second, choose the right instrument.** Too often consultants, HR professionals, and other well-meaning individuals deploy their favorite instrument in an effort to understand something about the culture. These exploratory missions can be useful, but should be approached with caution since every measure implies some commitment to take action based on the results. Sometimes organizations create their own measures with little understanding of how measurement works. And there are tools and techniques that can help assess its impact:

Instrument	Description
Statement of values	This is to be articulated and communicated across the organization.
Employee feedback	The business line management is responsible to improve concern areas in the employee feedback

Degree of process transparency	What information is communicated and how frequently?
Degree of empowerment	How much delegation is permitted? What is the decision making freedom at various levels of hierarchy?
Participation in strategy and innovation by employees	Some organizations actively encourage everybody to comment, give inputs into these two areas in a secure fashion.

Table 6: Culture Instrument

(3) **Third: Three dimensions of culture perspectives**: They are multi-dimensional business values, behaviors and underlying assumptions. Some instruments assess culture from a value perspective. Others assess culture by behaviors. Most of culture experts believe there is no instrument that could possibly assess culture as it is too complex and overly focuses on the underlying assumptions that are a deeper level of understanding. Some culture instruments are in fact measuring climate rather than culture. In the end, it comes down to which perspective you wish to take - values, behaviors or underlying assumptions. There are few instruments that cover all three and hence why qualitative data is so important to pick up the richness and the 'invisible' aspects of culture, underlying assumptions and unwritten rules.

(4) **Fourth: Avoid the pitfalls to measure culture:** Culture is important, and it is supposed to be an inherent backbone of the organization. Cultural mismatch leads to separation. There are pitfalls when assessing culture only based on silo data, but not a holistic view. You are what you measure:

- The value of measures is very low compared to the cost of measuring culture.

- It will be grossly misleading. Culture like economies, societies and ecosystems, is a complex adaptive system that cannot be reduced to single metric perspectives. Singular reductionism approach vis-à-vis pluralism is a common flaw in approaching such constructs.

(5) **Fifth: There's a preplanned commitment to take action.** This is not to say that the exact nature of the action must be preplanned, but rather that the commitment to take appropriate action is needed before the measurement is undertaken. If this message is not followed up, it makes future measurement difficult and begins to erode positive aspects of the culture.

Leadership, organization structure, and employee engagement are the key drivers to corporate culture, so you can measure those drivers of culture in an organization and use those driver measurements to see if you are creating the digital culture that you want, and further review it to nurture cultural integrity and improve cultural maturity.

CHAPTER 5

Digital Capability

Increasingly, enterprises find themselves enmeshed in digital "eco-systems."

The definition of capability is "the ability and capacity to realize a measurable result in a specific operational context of conditions." A business capability is the abilities needed by an organization in order to deliver value. It's the ability of an organization to do things effectively to achieve desired outcomes and measurable benefits and fulfill business demand. In today's business dynamic, digital capabilities are a fundamental building block in digital transformations with which companies can transform customer experience, operational processes and business models, to reach high level business agility and maturity.

A business capability is a specific ordering of processes, people, resources, information and technology aimed at creating a defined business outcome. Organizational capabilities are delivered when various resources work together for a purpose to achieve an outcome. The business capability fulfills a need that is part of a value proposition. There is often a supported business scenario associated with the capability. Thus, capability is also defined as "the proven possession of characteristics required to perform a particular service and to produce a particular result with the required performance" – with attributes about historical, actual, and potential required performance in form of KPIs, metrics or measures.

Digital Capability Questionnaires:

(1) How to assess organization's business capabilities? Are there signs that traditional levers/capabilities that worked in the past are now falling short?

(2) How to do digital capability mapping?

(3) What alternative capabilities can drive high digital performance?

(4) How can leaders successfully implement these capabilities?

(5) What are the hot debates to brainstorm digital capabilities?

1. Digital Capabilities Assessment

Digital capability is synthetic in nature, embedding agility in processes and focusing on long-term competency.

The organization's digital capabilities are business competency to execute its digital strategy and deliver value to its customers. Every surviving business has certain capabilities; however, only very few high performing businesses have high mature level of capabilities, for not only running business today, but also competing for the future. Hence, from management perspective, it's important to assess business capability maturity accordingly.

- **Weigh business capability:** The maturity of a business capability would be based on the ability to deliver on customer needs or to achieve the desired capability outcome. Other criteria may be the importance of each capability to the enterprise; different weighting may be applied to the capabilities. Highlight the value of having good understanding of current and future capabilities. There is a case for only allowing changes that have a direct impact of these capabilities. One of the beauties of working with capabilities is that it keeps you from being dragged into all the detail of the processes involved too early. Clearly, the processes and then procedures also need to be understood to grasp the full impact of changes on roles, staff, and applications.

- **Assess effectiveness of capability**: "Adding value" and "delivering on customer needs" will be higher in a capability that is more mature. One way to measure "value" is by assessing the capability's effectiveness in achieving the desired outcome. This can be accomplished by measuring (a) the technology impact on capability effectiveness (service availability), and (b) the process impact on capability effectiveness (# of orders delivered, order cycle time), and so on. In other words, capability maturity can be measured against achievement of desired business or customer outcomes.

- **Identify gaps and conflicts in digital transformation**. Using business capability model, you can identify potential gaps and conflicts in accountability of execution and digital transformation. The capability map will provide you better coverage for accountability, and also in some cases, you will see overlapping resources to support the same capability. In some cases, you will discover no resource to support a business capability. The approach can be used for the entire enterprise, or for business units or for a team or even for stakeholders, and the time depends upon the complexity in the transformation project.

- **Digital capability maturity**: Business capability contains people, process, technology and infrastructure; capabilities have outcomes; they collaborate with each other and are enabled by processes. They include resources (manpower or raw materials), technology (systems) required and human capital. The maturity of a business capability would be based on the capability to deliver on customer needs or to achieve the desired capability outcome.

- **Seven-dimensional business capability**: Business capability is an acquired and organized "ability" within a company and takes hard work to put in place; it can therefore not be transferred because of the degree of organizational learning and organization that goes with it, and the set of business capabilities directly decide the overall organization's competency, and how well they can execute strategy and deliver the value to the customers. Establish sustainable and transformational capabilities based on the following key dimensions:

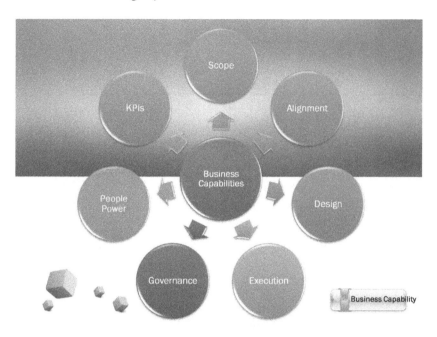

Figure 11: Seven-dimensional business capability

(1) Scope	Clear defined scope of the transformation engagement
(2) Alignment	Alignment to business and its strategy that is agreed by sponsors.
(3) Design	Design of the transformation comprising of people, process and technology through visioning and value map process.
(4) Execution	Execution of the transformation through collaborative approach using in internal and external organizations.
(5) Governance	Governance of the execution to manage and mitigate risks and intervention to ensure that strategic objectives do not drift.

| (6) People power | The commitment and belief in people who are part of the execution and governance will multiply the results of the transformation program. |
| (7) KPIs and Measurement | The procedure to set KPIs must be defined for the achievement of the objective and its measurement. |

Table 7: Seven-dimensional business capability

Business capability is an acquired and organized "ability" within a company and takes hard work to put in place; it can therefore not be transferred because of the degree of organizational learning and organization that goes with it, and the set of business capabilities directly decide the overall organization's competency, and how well they can execute strategy, deliver the value to the customers, and build long-term winning position.

2. Business Capability Mapping Process

The only problem about the future is that it is usually here before we are ready for it.

Business capability is the ability to achieve a desired effect under specified performance, standards and conditions through combinations of ways and to perform a set of activities. Capabilities describe the desired functionality of architecture. So what is exactly business capability mapping process? Is it about what business does to reach capabilities; or is it how it reaches its capabilities?

- **Business capability mapping:** It is the activity of making "reference links" between each capability in a "relevant subset" to specific processes, people (roles or teams), tools, and information. After completing mapping, then, you take information about those mapped elements and bring them together in one or more formulas in order to make a generalization about the capability.

Where that information doesn't exist, you may have to create evaluation criteria in order to generate that information.

- **Process underpins capability**. Business capability mapping is more as how the business reaches its capabilities; because what the business does is actually business process. Processes underpin capabilities; and capabilities are at a much higher level, and typically are easier to get consensus on. Mapping those capabilities to any other architectural entity (components, services, systems, resources, etc.) is what mapping is really concerned with. Mapping them and then defining formulas for determining maturity, importance and performance of capabilities in order to make a generalization. Each would invoke a formula that requires input of data attached to those underlying "mapped" things such as people, process, tools, and information.

- **Navigating through**: Business capability mapping answers questions such as "who," "what," "how," etc. A particular capability in an Enterprise Architecture model might not have been automated as such and still have manual processes associated with it. Although not automated, it is still a capability. The mapping would have to include the activity, the resource and the performer whether technology or a living entity to a certain degree:

  (1) **Activity ("how")**: Work, consisting of atomic or composite steps that transform resources to achieve an objective or provide a capability. Activities describe the processes and procedures carried out to actively change an effect object, a target resource.
  (2) **Resource ("what")**: Data, Information, Performers, Material, or Personnel types that are produced or consumed.
  (3) **Performer ("who")**: Any entity – human, automated, or any aggregation of human and/or automated - that performs an activity and provides a capability.

3. Decode Digital Capabilities: "DIAAMONDS"

Digital capabilities cut across all functional pillars. They are fundamental building blocks for business transformation.

Compared to industrial capabilities, digital business capabilities are more complex in design, with synthetic nature requiring cross-functional collaboration, embedding agility into processes for adapting to the changes, and the right set of unique digital capabilities directly decide the overall organization's competency, and how well they can make digital transformation, deliver the value to the customers and build long-term winning position.

- **Transformational leadership:** The key role of the digital leader is to be constantly challenging the business paradigm. It has much to do with the combination of pace and mind-set. The reality of senior leadership in many organizations is one of high paces and rapid decision-making. What is really relevant is a change mind-set and visioning pattern that allows these leaders to 'spot' the problem or symptom and constructively challenge the organization to support the digital transformation. In that manner, transformation doesn't become a one-time activity; instead, it is a constant game changer for the organization. In systems terms, transformational change comes from outside and the good businesses will always be seeking and embracing the influences beyond their own business. This requires a constant awareness of and challenging of mind-set and the inevitable rejuvenation of the leadership.

- **Dynamic capability:** It is the firm's ability to integrate, build, and reconfigure internal and external competences to address rapidly changing digital dynamic. Digital capabilities collaborate with each other and are enabled by processes; processes underpin enterprise capability, and capabilities have outcome. Identify those companies that consistently delivered best shareholder returns did so by focusing hard on the customer and re-designing their operations from the customer back into the operation. The maturity of a business capability would be based on the dynamic capability to deliver on customer needs or to achieve the desired capability outcome.

- **Decode Digital Capabilities: DIAAMONDS**: Digital capability of business is multi-dimensional, synthetic, dynamic, unique and hybrid. In approaching it, organizations need to determine what is value-added, what is unique that was missing, and how does it fit into the path of concept to customer-centricity. The often described business capabilities include such as robustness, speed, comprehensiveness, responsiveness, agility, improvement, sensitivity, optimization, resilience, etc. Following are what we collect the **DIAAMONDS** characteristics of digital capabilities that enable companies to compete for the future.

D - Dynamic Execution

I - Innovation Portfolio

A – Agile Learning Ability

A – Analytics Ability

M – Multi-faceted Change

O –Orchestration of Dynamic Processes

N –Nexus of Digital IT Forces

D –Delight Customer

S –'Simplexity' Management

Figure 12: Decode Digital Capability – "DIAAMONDS"

(a) **D – Dynamic Execution**: Execution is always critical, at industrial age, execution is operational capability for most of businesses; however, in the digital era, it is the strategic and dynamic capability in leapfrogging digital maturity.

(b) **I – Innovation Portfolio:** From portfolio management point of view, companies need both incremental product/service changes and small innovations to thrive, but also desire large, disruptive innovations for quantum leap.

(c) **A – Agile Learning**: The knowledge life cycle in the digital era is significantly shortened, the digital workforce today has to "de-learn" and "relearn" all the time, and a collective learning capability is strategic for company's long-term success.

(d) **A- Analytics Ability**: Information empowers businesses with the ultimate competitive advantage, data analytics is at the top priority of forward-looking businesses these days; it is the ability to anticipate and detect trends, offering business insight and prospect.

(e) **M – Multifaceted Change:** Change is the most significant trait in digital age, and it's multi-faceted. Digitalization is a transformational change; and thus, businesses attempt to characterize the differences, as managing changing is a strategic capability in digital transformation.

(f) **O – Orchestration of Dynamic Processes**. In digital working environment, the mix of traditional, highly-structured work shifts to a mix of unstructured and structured work in the industries where knowledge workers perform process steps, the unique digital capabilities are built through such hybrid process orchestration.

(g) **N – Nexus of Digital IT Forces:** There is an explosion of digital technologies related to business today, between cloud, big data, social, mobile and APIs, which are referred as the nexus of digital IT forces by Gartner. They are key forces to shape unique digital capabilities.

(h) **D – Delight Customer**: Digital is the age of customer; every company is a data company, how to delight customer becomes strategic digital capability to survive and thrive.

(i) **S – "Simplexity" Management:** Keep it simple to adapt to the complex digital dynamic. The hybrid word "simplexity" (simplicity + Complexity) well reflects the emerging digital paradox. Modern digital organizations spend significant time and resources to deal with complexity, the complex organizational structure/process or the hyper-complex business ecosystem.

4. Digital Capability #1: Dynamic Execution

Strategy execution takes both capabilities and disciplines.

A business capability is an acquired and organized "ability" within a company and takes hard work to put in place; it can therefore not be transferred because of the degree of organizational learning and organization that goes with it. Besides functional capabilities, an effective enterprise today needs to cultivate a set of strategic capabilities or business transformation capabilities to adapt to digital business dynamics in the 21st century. The problem is that things are changing so fast in the digital era, so what is the point of executing a poor strategy, and similarly, why waste valuable resources and time forming a strategy that is never implemented. It is the classic chicken and egg debate in strategic planning. Execution is always critical, at industrial age, execution is operational capability for most of businesses; however, now in the digital era, it is the strategic and dynamic capability in lifting digital maturity.

(1) Strategy-Execution Continuum: Strategy and execution represent the two sides of one and the same coin. There is no good strategy without an execution and there is no good execution to a bad strategy. The real strategists are also able to lead the change by themselves and adopt based on situations. And a "good strategy" is based on theories applied by great leaders in the industries. Its execution lies on the wisdom of the leader in applying it with considerations on the specific needs, conditions and goals of the organization. Hence, good strategies are good because they can be executed efficiently and effectively.

- **A living strategy**: At digital age, strategy steers execution and execution directs strategy – the evaluative approach. Strategy is becoming more a living entity, moving from the conventional approach of strategy plus execution to an evaluative management, the organization requires changing the underlying management practices and values that drive performance and organizational agility.

- **Strategy-execution continuum:** Execution is time critical, but you can't have smooth execution without the solid strategy. Execution has seemingly increased in priority as result of the rising frequency of digital disruption and turbulence today blurring the distinction between strategy formulation and execution. Many business leaders think they'd rather have great execution than superior strategies, but if you execute the wrong strategy, it is not going to get you where you want to be; on the other hand, if you have a great strategy, but fail to implement, it will also not lead you to the Promised Land either.

- **Two facets of the same coin**: While the strategy is oriented to the future and the decisions are taken by few, execution is oriented to the present and the decisions are taken by many. Strategy and execution are the two equally important facets of the same coin, and in order to reap the success in the fast-paced digital business, a clear and concrete strategy is needed with proper execution:

  (a) Strategy is associated with analysis; and execution with getting things done;
  (b) Execution is producing results in the context of those strategic choices;

(c) You cannot have good execution without having good strategy;

(d) The quality of execution depends a lot on the quality of strategy.

Strategy and execution are important and vital to the business. A digital organization must have strategic agility. Strategy and execution are composite; one is useless without the other. The challenge is that the environment changes so fast in the digital era that your strategy must be very flexible. Therefore, you need to have strategy before execution, but it must be an agile strategy, making this change requires a more fundamental and effective approach. It starts with creating a working environment that requires the change to take place.

(2) Execution Gaps: There are many pitfalls or hidden risks for strategy execution, besides "culture eating strategy for breakfast," there are more factors leading to poor execution of strategy.

- **Strategy creep:** Give lip service to the strategy. Similar to the damage scope creep can cause to projects. Strategy Creep can be indicative of larger planning issues such as poor due diligence in the planning phase, no alignment with vision or mission, lack of clear objectives, lack of clear goals, or lack of resources to support strategy.

- **Weak leadership:** There are list of reasons why strategy implementations fail, but every reason points back to weak or ineffective leadership. Implementing new strategies is difficult and is often met with great resistance. Leaders must be willing to display the courage and determination required to continually push the initiative forward to achieve the desired goal.

- **Lost in translation of strategy into goals:** Once a strategy is formulated, it has to be translated into goals. A strategy is a general outline of loose action items that create departmental goals; goals are concrete items with a measurable factor and deadlines; lost in translation of strategy into goals may cause failure to recognize and manage the devil in the details. When you designed the strategy, you may not have understood that the execution was going to impact other areas of the business in ways you didn't anticipate.

- **Poor prioritization:** Lack of prioritization of strategic objectives; lack of detail planning to support goal achievements. It is important to decide how to spend your time and staffing, what to communicate to the management team and troops, how your reward and what you recognize.

- **Poor communication and coordination**: Lack clear employee understanding of the strategy and what it looks like in action at each individual employee's level. And have absence of a clear strategy map. Let the wrong pressures into the system. "Get that product out there yesterday" to beat the competition, to discover that you managed to do their work and beat yourself in the process.

- **Lack of the governance structure**: The failure can often be linked with poor execution of strategy. You can have the greatest strategic plan in the world, but it will be worthless if the organizations are not accountable to anyone for execution of their tasks.

   - Organizational misalignment/poor strategy cascading (to business units, departments, and individual goal plans)
   - lack of active involvement in governance management at the executive and organizational leader level.

- **Failure to measure.** What gets measured gets done, especially when there is reward or recognition involved. Ensure you have something to measure. Execution of a strategy takes much longer to show up in meaningful metrics than originally conceived. Have measurements and track performance as part of governance practice; provide management and staff communication on progress, with recognition of milestones, misses and the people who are achieving the desired results. Measure! Reward. Recognize.

(3) Agility as key success factor in dynamic execution: With the accelerating speed of business change, more often than not, strategy is not static, but dynamic, the strategy execution phases will also be cascading, not linear steps. So alignment with the corporate strategy takes flexibility to rapidly change based on manifested conditions.

- **Agile philosophy:** Strategy-execution scenario should embrace agile philosophy. Discussions of strategic plan issues must be ongoing and not merely a once-a-year exercise, strategy execution will keep the speed at sync, and strategic planning and execution should keep the long-term view within the short-term attention, and all key players focus on facilitating change within the organization. That said, you are devising strategy, it needs to be relevant, but also general to deal with the changes the organization will naturally experience.

- **Agile ability**: Agility is the ability to think and act promptly to the changes. A successful strategy execution needs to have well-orchestrated plans, allocation of needed assets, time frame, market conditions, preparing 'what if' scenarios, analyzing impact on customers and competition, also setting the ultimate fishbone diagram planning for multiple forks in the road for quick agile ability to react.

- **Timely execution**: The success of strategy management undoubtedly lies in "timely execution," and this can be achieved only through continuous persistence and following up. There must be sense of urgency. Further, leadership at operational level must be competent, dynamic and smart to taste and digest the initiatives. Keeping fewer key initiatives increases efficiency and effectiveness. Apart from the buy in; one of the key factors that is often overlooked is the influence of performance metrics on other areas of operation that is not being monitored. A risk assessment has to be taken on the strategy implementation.

Strategy is both art and science; strategy execution takes both capabilities and disciplines. Organizations must have dynamic execution capability to achieve strategic agility and execution excellence.

5. Digital Capability #2: Innovation Portfolio Management

Innovation is about reducing the unnecessary complexity.

Innovation is important because it is the lifeblood of any business; without it, a company will cease to exist. An innovation capability is a strategic differentiator for business's long-term prosperity. But compare upcoming digital era to previous industrial era, does the content or context of innovation stay at the same or be different. From portfolio management point of view, companies need both incremental product or service changes and small innovations to thrive, but also desire large, disruptive innovations for quantum leap. So is digital innovation trying to reach the next level, what would it be? We will discuss "Digital Innovation" in chapter 6 comprehensively; here are a few highlight about the characteristics of digital innovation management.

- **Enriched context**: Innovation has more enriched context than ever today: Innovation is the process that transforms novel idea or knowledge into business value. The output from the process is the innovation. The exercise of deciding within each organization just what innovation is would be the single most critical activity of an innovation effort. Because the innovation capability- how an organization orchestrates to generate ideas; manages the activities, measures the results, etc. is determined by how that organization has decided to craft the innovation effort. There are many areas within a company where the innovation capability can be applied to create value, from communication innovation to culture innovation, from process innovation to business model innovation; the innovation context goes beyond the traditional new product invention.

- **Tipping point**: The business leaders reach the tipping point of new level of innovation flow and portfolio management. Companies have always had a flow of innovation, a flow sufficient for the needs of the company at that time. What has happened is that the flow from "before" is no longer sufficient to address the digital challenges of today. Hence, the importance of innovation has increased as business has the pressure to get more and better innovation. At tipping point, the processes for innovation will catch up to the business need and then, there will be something else that needs special attention. By then the flow of innovation will have reached a new level, a level that can address the business challenges.

- **Problem solving**: Innovation creates value by solving simple or complex problems. Opportunity for innovation tends to present itself when people are struggling with something. The luggage design improvement provides a great example of situation where people were struggling with their luggage while traveling; the new design of luggage with wheels is an innovation to solve such problems. Another example would be gears on a bicycle. In the past, there was one gear, and it's hard to get going uphill in the one gear. Someone thankfully took that opportunity to develop additional gears, which made it easier to go uphill in lower or higher gear. As we can see, innovation can address both simple and complex problems people face today. Hence, managing innovation is to improve business's problem-solving capabilities.

Innovation is the ability to transform any knowledge into society performance, performance for profit, for saving of resources, for satisfaction of users, etc. So innovation is the core activity of human progress. At corporate level, it's unique business capabilities to gain competitive advantage in face of fierce competition and digital dynamic today.

6. Digital Capability #3: Agile Learning

Learning becomes the life habit for digital talent, as well as culture style for the digital businesses.

Information explosion is one of the most important characteristics of the digital era, although DIKW continuum (Data – Information – Knowledge – Wisdom) is human artifacts since 17th century where modern scientific mind-set began to evolve. In fact, now the knowledge life cycle is significantly shortened, digital workforce today has to "delearn" and "relearn" all the time, and an agile learning capability is strategic for company's long-term success.

- **Brain power**: Human brains organize energy systematically and this has enormous implications for knowledge management. The knowledge is the manifestation of brain energy as it is carried, transformed and stored by the interneuron superstructure of the brain. The complexity of knowledge lies in what we know, not in how we know it. The complexity of knowledge has to do with the fact that we have the potential to interconnect and program up to 600 billion neurons. In addition, interneuron themselves connect in a number of ways. If we know the system, we can create a structure for knowledge that allows us to measure it qualitatively as well as quantitatively - the natural structure of knowledge.

- **Learning capacity**: Learning is a process and everyone has enormous capacity to learn. Limitations on learning are barriers invented by humans. Learning cycles assume that learning is a process, so the learning styles can be rationalized. Learning taxonomies try to explain the levels of learning and identify the domains or types of learning, as learning is multidimensional, dynamic, interactive, and integrated, and you can define learning through the knowledge it builds, there are knowledge styles reflective of the types of knowledge you build.

- **Learning agility:** It's the willingness and ability to learn; and then apply those lessons to succeed in new situations. People who are learning agile continuously seek new challenges, solicit direct feedback, self-reflect, and get jobs done resourcefully. They see unique patterns and make fresh connections that others overlook; a thoughtful and systematic knowledge management solution needs to explore the breadth and depth of knowledge, its prospects and practice to improve the collective learning capability in the organization to evolve working with knowledge.

- **Knowledge ecosystem:** Organizations can work toward a knowledge ecosystem view that incorporates the virtual aspects of the knowledge system, innovation, and intuitive behavior. It is important to cultivate the learning culture that has awareness and understanding plus setting a new behavior expectation for active knowledge participants. There are different levels of knowledge system models:

  - **Experiential:** Accessing information, exploring resource
  - **Transitional:** Refining knowledge; expressing ideas
  - **Transformational:** Shaping insight, foresight and wisdom
  - **Motivational:** Garnering attitude, gaining perspective and planning Strategy

Digital is the age of people. Talent people change each day; they grow, learn, and develop; so do businesses. This is organic change, it is unconscious. In effect, they want to change even though they don't realize it. But it is the organization that stops them. Therefore, knowledge management plays crucial role. Knowledge is information that has the potential to generate value. Knowledge management is management with knowledge as a focus, involves the use of technologies and processes with the aim of optimizing the value that is generated, and with the goal to improve organization's agile learning capabilities.

7. Digital Capability #4: Analytical Capability

We are moving slowly into an era where Big Data is the starting point - not the end.

Digitalization means big data, businesses are moving slowly into an era where Big Data is the starting point, not the end. Information empowers businesses with the ultimate competitive advantage, data analytics is at the top priority of forward-looking businesses these days; it is the ability to anticipate and detect trends. Analytics works best at the strategic level, and then the existing customer relationship part of the organization can benefit from these predictions. It is one of the strategic capabilities in digital organization.

(1) Five analytics insight: Back to fundamental, what is business analytics? Why analytics capability is strategic for digital businesses? What're the noble business purposes that can be achieved through deploying it?

Systemizing	Business Analytics is the systematic selection, transformation, and presentation of data, through technological and quantitative processes with algorithmic methods, to track the behavior of the past decisions and support the future business directions.
Examining	Business Analytics is the logical process of examining data, and applying management science to support decision making in an enterprise. Business analytics is a reliable process that transforms raw data into relevant, accurate and usable strategic knowledge with the purpose of increasing profitability.

Eco-system	There are three parts to the analytics eco-system: Technological component for getting and storing the data; quantitative / interpretive component; and decision support/decision making component. Business Analytics is the qualitative/quantitative scientific algorithm, or generalized algorithm from observable regularity to get the objective optimization at the given restricted feasible risk, assuming participation in the business tests or actions.
Insight	Big data analytics acts as revenue generating medium by offering business insight and prospect. If carefully nurtured, it can prove as a profit generating tool. One strategy to achieve this is to apply analytics to large data sets (big data) to identify hidden opportunities and threats. Once identified, you change something that could mitigate a threat, improve efficiency, effectiveness and optimize your differentiation in the market.
Maturity	There are three steps toward "analytics maturity." Companies will start with simpler statistical analyses ("what happened?"); then move to predictive analytics ("what will happen?"); and finally prescriptive analytics ("what should we do next?"). Surely a simulation into what will happen is both predictive and prescriptive, as it will almost certainly suggest appropriate actions.

Table 8: Five analytics insight

From business strategic perspective, analytics helps optimize various business metrics, directly or indirectly related to long-term revenue, it includes traditional optimization, root cause analysis, and statistical analysis / machine learning / data mining to boost efficiency of marketing campaigns, price optimization, inventory management, finance and tax engineering, sales forecasts, product reliability, fraud and risk management, user retention, product design, ad spend, employee retention and predicting success of new hires, competitive intelligence to leveraging external data source, forecasting new trends based on automated analysis of user feedback and much more.

(2) Analytics effect in decision making: Analytics is permeating into business's daily life, and it's one of key digital capabilities in shaping an intelligent organization. It's no surprise to see more organizations intend to adopt analytics in guiding decision making. Should analytics drive your decisions or should it be used to measure you decision's success?

- **Clear define business goals:** The first thing would be to identify clearly how and where you can apply analytics in business decision making in business. Firms would invest time and money in analytics when the goals and benefits of using analytics are clearly defined. Start with a problem that will allow you to do one of two things or both:

  (1) data-driven discovery.
  (2) theory-based exploration.

Apply that problem definition and then assemble a very skilled team to do a Proof of Concept. But, be very flexible to the "what if" analysis that is capable.

- **Properly done analytics should drive decisions:** Properly done analytics will give you information that you wouldn't have otherwise. Analytics are useful in guiding decision making, but always make sure that the recommendations suggested pass the "does this make sense" test. It is important to make sure that you are using the right inputs and a model that adequately fits the problem to carry out the analysis. Otherwise, the recommendations may not be optimal and it can turn out to be the classic case of "garbage in, garbage out."

- **Planning and validation**: Analytics is of paramount importance when planning and deriving results following implementation. If one uses the approach of defining a hypothesis for the problem space and the possible solution options, and then using statistical analysis to test and characterize the resultant set to the hypothesis, then analytics is required for both. Because once an approach is decided upon and implemented, a complete solution will include measures of the target results that validate success in achieving the desired business outcomes.

- **Analytics is to improve decisions as well as to drive measure**: focus on operationalizing analytics, meaning implementing predicting analytics results in operational systems in real or near real-time, analytics can

  (1) Drive (automate) decision making, and by monitoring those decision results analytically.
  (2) Measure-Analytics can be very useful to measure "success" or improvement between different scenarios, it is important to be sure that the right things are measured to come to correct conclusions about the performance.
  (3) Improve the decision and therefore the overall system and business performance over time.

Analytics capability is strategic because it is important to understand why things happened so those learning can be applied to the next iteration or project. Well designed experiments can yield great insights that never would have been uncovered if one goes with experience and "gut feeling." But at the end of the day, it is also critical to see if the outcome bears any resemblance to the predictions. Sometimes the differences are due to poor or great implementation. That all being said, analytics is important, but do not forget common sense.

8. Digital Capability # 5: Multifaceted Transformation

A systematic transformation takes step-wise scenario, and going from decision right to design intelligence.

Change is the most significant trait in digital age, and it is multi-faceted, the speed of change is accelerated, enterprise agility –the ability to adapt to the change, is becoming strategic capability in driving business success and gaining long-term competitive advantage. There is no shortcut for change. "Change management" is the overarching umbrella, that encompasses extensive planning, outreach, communications, creativity, discovery of concerns / objections / potential points of failure, addressing fears and resistance, developing a shared vision, communicating valid and compelling reasons for cooperation, recognizing sacrifice and incremental success, measuring outcomes in a shared, mutually understood and agreed upon fashion, being able to declare an end-point and successful conclusion. More specifically, how do you build an organizational change management capability?

(1) Transformation vs. Change: The terms "transformation" and "change" truly overlap in literal definition; people tend, though, to carry their own associations with each. Transformation is definitely the more ambitious sounding term; digitalization is a transformational change, and thus we attempt to characterize the differences, as managing changing is strategic capability in digital transformation.

- **Radical transformation**: Change maybe mechanical, but transformation is more radical. "Change" can be a somewhat mechanical implementation of new or different ways to doing something; while transformation is more likely to be a sweeping approach to altering a culture, or parts of it, possibly even to parts of its value system, to embrace such as change and help it become self-perpetuating. Organizational culture transformation is prerequisite for business transformation.

- **Mind shift**: Transformation requires mind shift. In addition to the set point changing, digital transformation requires first shifting mind-sets, then building new skills and reinforcing and embedding new practices and reflexes. People tend to need interpersonal transformation, then intrapersonal transformation to achieve organizational transformation. Skills and situations have become more subtle, more multi-layered and therefore more complex, what's needed every now and then in any individual, team, organization, society, and on up to the entire planet's population, is a little or a lot of energy to re-focus, kick start or game-change.

- **Nature and 'effortless':** Change can be dictated sometimes, transformation is a natural process and rather effortless to maintain. Change is "un" - natural activity, you need to focus and make an effort to maintain. Simple "Change" may involve dictated behavioral modification that is not natural and does not fit with the person's normal mode of behavior, values and beliefs. "Transformation" goes a step further, and involves internalization of the new values and conceptual model, so that the newly required behaviors don't require the same kind of effort and vigilance. Instead, the new established behaviors will be in harmony with the internalized values. Thus, transformation can more deeply touch people's heart and mind.

(2) How to build change capabilities: The change curve is a model of the states that people who are to change will go through. As going through the downs of the change curve has a negative impact on productivity, leadership is required to guide people through the different phases in order to flatten the curve and to minimize the impact on productivity.

- **Assessment:** It is important to first understand how much change capability is really required for the effort you are kicking off. Organizations can make major leaps forward in change capability by involving the entire organization in major change efforts that support key business strategies to drive performance improvement. The stage to start depends on how transformational the scope is. In some cases, it's best to start well before a project has even been conceived. On the other hand, if you want to build an enduring capability that will go on to support many projects, then it's never too late to start. An honest assessment of the lessons learned from a previous project could be a good place to begin.

- **Culture**: Real change and creativity is deprogramming old mind-sets, letting go of "the voices from the past," reprogramming collective minds with new values, norms and attitudes; establishing a new blueprint for how organizations want to create the future reality. Successful change is often linked to the DNA of the organization itself. The approach would require the following steps:

  (a) Seeding a culture of change- shared vision and values- leadership as a role model.
  (b) Clarity and transparency in communications of strategic initiatives, thereby nipping uncertainty, ambiguity, and doubt that reduce resistance when implementing change.
  (c) Continuous engagement through formal and informal methods.
  (d) Train employees across all levels as change agents / managers with leaders being enablers and facilitators.
  (e) Leaders actively and visibly sponsoring and participating in the change process.
  (f) Create CoE – Centers of Excellence – and high performance culture that can adopt and adapt to change during the change process.
  (g) "Harden" the soft – measure the culture via KPIs, and sustain the culture through change management and PMO practices.

- **Process:** Take a multistep process to get ahead of change curves. The goal of change and improvement should look beyond immediate problem resolution. However, energy usually gets focused on problem-solving, and realization becomes a rush where thoughtfulness about people and processes is a casualty of time. The focus should include actions designed to sustain performance improvement and anchor change as a new opportunity. It's getting into action in creative, positive, productive ways that educate, support and celebrate every emotional step of the change curve and collective transformation journey. The more complex the change, the more complex the solution.

- **Methodologies**: There are good methodologies that can provide a framework for building change capability within an organization. Without a quantitative tool to understand the individual behavioral tendency toward change, it would be very challenging to define who your target is within the organization. Different people will respond differently to change – understanding the behavioral predisposition and integrating that knowledge into your comprehensive change strategy can measurably increase the success potential for the change.

- **Creative mechanism**: Too often changes are made as a reaction to outer impulses, crisis and demands. This is the bureaucratic way of meeting the challenges. There cannot be any change without imagination that means creativity; being creative helps in finding new solutions in working differently and building a new world. When developing a change scenario, think of a creative mechanism that has the outcome to embed the change. Perhaps more so within the creative industries or organizations that has extensive innovative product development regimes. It would follow that the use of creativity would be more welcome in these areas. Indeed, in any business sector, creativity is incredibly useful, both in terms of making an impact with change management communications and tactics, because these days it is pretty tough to get attention, there is so much going on, but also in terms of strategies and solutions. It is creativity that is always questioning everything. To succeed, businesses need a united "one-sight" focus, a dynamic balance between the inner and outer, "yin" and "yang," dancing together, organizations need deeply to understand the relation and dynamics between consciousness (thinking), energy (emotions) and information, the manifested creativity is so important to change management; it can serve as a tool for cognitive dissonance to support adoption.

- **9-step Change Management life cycle:**

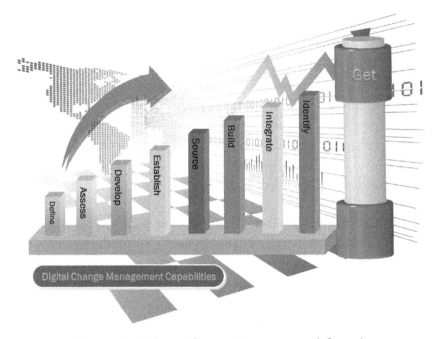

Figure 13: 9-Step Change Management life cycle

(a) **Define** the initial value proposition and determine demand and estimated pipeline;

(b) **Assess** current state capability in change management (people, process, technology);

(c) **Develop** the target state change management capability and identify the gaps;

(d) **Establish** change management capability leadership practice;

(e) **Source** appropriate skills to deliver desired capability;

(f) **Build** change management team and enable them with methodology, tools, products, services against value proposition identified in step 1.

(g) **Integrate** change management methodology into IT project management life cycles.

(h) **Identify** change agents within the business; educate champions and establish these as a key element for change management.

(i) **Get** early wins to demonstrate value and sustain the change for the long term.

The main perspective or change management focus is usually either the outside in; or the inside out. The outside-in is too often the approach for change management at digital age, the goal of change and improvement is more than discovering an elegant solution. It is upon how to build multi-faceted change capabilities, that includes both problem resolution and solution implementation. All stages must be handled with attention and proficiency to ensure success.

9. Digital Capability #6: Orchestration of Hybrid Processes

Future of BPM will have enriched digital themes; people are the focal point of digital processes.

With emerging mobile and social digital technology, and within hyper-connected and always-on digital working environment, the mix of traditional highly-structured work shifts to a mix of unstructured and structured work in the industries where knowledge workers perform process steps. Processes underpin business capabilities. So from business process management perspectives, how to well orchestrate such "hybrid" process environment, to not allow process mechanism kill innovation; but keep process flow with discipline.

- **People-centric:** People are the focal point of digital processes. To be more precise, it is people working together toward a common goal for digital transformation. These talent people cooperate to support the functioning of multiple business processes within a company. People move processes to streamline digital flow. People are creative, but with well-trained discipline; managing people well precedes managing process well. Business Process Management (BPM) will enable business agility. BPM is a powerful solution that enables interaction with humans, many other in-house or cloud-based systems. BPM is definitely an important asset for almost every business and size. The effective BPM shall become more people centric, going from functioning to delight; from standard to agility.

- **Rigor:** An agile and smart process should be rigorous to adapt to the changes. Process is key component to implement strategy. Changes in strategy are reflected in business policies. Changes in business policies are reflected in changes to business rules. The business rules should be externalized from the business processes. An agile or smart process is rigorous to adapt to the changes; it can handle ad-hoc and exceptional matter smoothly. A business process is "smart" when it accommodates controlled excursions away from what would otherwise be a rigid sequence of steps. A smart process follows process management principles, but encourages innovation as well.

- **Structure**: Business system always has certain structure: If you look at business in a systematic way and think in terms of digital eco-systems rather than silo processes, systems must have some sort of structured way of working processes in order to survive. If you don't have structure effectively, you have chaos. And chaos can only allow survival for a short time before things break down. Either within the system or between the systems, there are certain levels of structure exist, otherwise, the interactions between systems become chaotic and the system will start to break down.

- **Hybrid**: There is hybrid of structured and unstructured processes in digital businesses. Creative and digital knowledge workforces demand broader flexibility to be creative and to solve problems. Initially it may seem like they demand unstructured processes. But in fact, they want more latitude and greater power to make decisions. To accommodate that, the process segments may have to be defined less in terms of steps and more in terms of deliverable objectives, iterations and tollgates. The convergence of unstructured text messages with structured process entities will help create user-friendly process management applications handling structured and unstructured processes in a similar manner.

- **Social**: Social processes are unstructured by definition, though social interactions need structure. People move processes, all corporate digital processes are social, therefore to some extent, all corporate processes are unstructured and unpredictable. Definitely they have structured content. But they always have unstructured content as well - human tasks, discussions, assignments, etc. These unstructured process entities can be handled in the information system; or can be handled manually, but they are present in each enterprise process. Adding social interactions in the business processes will make them unstructured and unpredictable. The social BPM should handle such hybrid processes effectively.

- **Maturity:** As a matter of principle, in any organization, the hierarchical pyramid of strategic, tactical and operational business goals and business processes are related by "therefore-arguments," derived from paradigms varying per layer in the hierarchy. In order to harness business maturity, how can BPM be integrated into the overall governance and be aligned with strategy. BPM should not be viewed as an external alien that must be aligned to something, BPM itself is the way that governance will crystallize all over the organization. BPM is the easiest and best way to align efforts to digital strategies and final results as well, meaning that every single process effort must go in the same path to achieve what is expected. BPM ensures flexibility, efficiency, effective innovation, risk avoidance, continuous improvement, alignment and control to every effort within the organization.

Managing hybrid digital processes turn to be a strategic business capabilities; either managing structured or less structured processes, the focal point is on the deliverable quality along with the deliverable pipelines, to improve digital business productivity, agility, and encourage innovation and optimization as well.

10. Digital Capability #7: The Nexus of Digital Forces

The nexus of digital forces accelerates digital flow, improves digital fluency and bridges digital divides.

There is an explosion of digital technologies related to business today, between cloud, big data, social, mobile, consumerization of IT and APIs. At age of digitalization, the forward-looking organizations at all sectors claim they are at information business. However, most of IT organizations still run at industrial speed, with poor reputation as cost center. Hence, it is crucial to improve information management maturity as it is one of strategic digital business capabilities in today's business.

- **The Nexus of Forces**: Gartner refers to SMAC-Social, Mobile, Analytics and Cloud, as the Nexus of Forces and, of course, IT leaders need to pay attention. Cloud computing is changing how businesses think about infrastructure and application procurement. Big Data is changing not just traditional areas of analytics, but also how people manage the businesses in the future. Mobile is changing the customer relationship; the business is always on and need to be always available, always relevant, and always helpful. It's not enough to offer services on IT terms anymore – it has to be on the consumers' terms, when and where they want it.

- **Cloud**: Cloud computing is here to stay, and will only get bigger and more mainstream for IT organizations. For adopting cloud, the main focus is optimization of financial, technical resources and efficient IT service management. It is always important to focus on improving your business, especially during tough times.

Cloud provides ways to streamline OPEX and decrease CAPEX spending. It lifts up IT as a unicorn in today's world of IT, doing more with innovation is the key success factor for effective CIOs. So, they have to adopt cloud as a strategy, be it private or public, mostly hybrid, in how IT engages with people in business and on a personal basis.

- **Big Data**: Big Data is catching with mainstream. Digital is about Big Data. Though the foundation of businesses has remained the same, which is to provide quality services to their customer basis in an optimized and efficient manner. Big Data paired with social media can give consumer oriented company better insight into customer needs, desires, spending trends and lead to more profitable product introductions. Finding ways to get departmental and regular business managers access to the questioning is crucial to extracting full value from all these new technologies. There is a huge difference in how a data scientist views the world and wants to interact with data compared with a manager whose budget is adversely impacted by product returns and losing business to competing offers. As the tech matures and the technology becomes better understood by most of the enterprise, Big Data will get better understood and become more valuable.

- **Mobility**: Cloud handles the optimization part of digitalization, while mobility provides the efficiency, channel and segment, digital business is now always-on and hyper-connected, with multichannel, multi-touch points. APIs have been around and will always be around. They are the glue that sticks dissimilar tools together. One of the CIO's main responsibilities is to survey and keep themselves abreast of existing and future technologies available and see how they would be useful in their business environments. Adoption of these technologies has to be carefully considered in their particular business environments; sometimes what's good for the goose need not be good for the gander.

- **Portfolio Management**: With abundance of information and emergence of digital technologies, portfolio management is essential to successful corporate governance and as such, a comprehensive fusing of a firm's strategic capabilities, tightly coupled in one organization, would implement and oversee governance. Embodied in a portfolio management office, there are six programs - IT strategic planning, enterprise architecture, capital programming, assets management, risk management and projects management.

- **Social Influence**: Social makes the small world. While cloud is the provisioning medium, the mobile is the delivery channel; the brand engagement is where most of the strategy comes in. While big data and social helps identify the customer segment or preferences, the fundamentals of IT management will revolve around brand engagement that is social collaboration, customer relationship management. While cloud and mobility implementations are easier to justify, the impact of big data and social media are comparatively more difficult. These also need a great deal of effort, support and knowledge from the business community before the implementations bear fruit.

The current trends in Big Data, mobile, cloud and social indicate a set of technologies that are actively being pursued by organizations for implementation. A highly-capable IT is key business differentiator, but keeps in mind, IT digital forces are the means to the end, not the end, the end is to fulfill business's digital vision and execute business strategy smoothly and achieve the expected business result.

11. Digital Capability #8: Delightful Customer Experience

Quality in a service or product is not what you put into it; it is what the client or customer gets out of it. - Peter Drucker

To build the customer-centric businesses, organizations need to think in terms of building business capabilities. Too often, the customer centric effort is layered on top of the 'real' work so the customer mantra pales in comparison to the rigor of other areas of the operation, where there is measurable clarity of what needs to be done, by when and by whom. Therefore, having a strong sense of how to develop customer centric programs within the business means to build the integral and unique set of business capabilities to combine technology and business tactics, the smart or popular processes, and dedicated talent that drive customer value creation. It's about building competitive capabilities that create and sustain customer values. The challenge is demonstrating to a company how capable they are relative to where they know they need to be better than their competition.

(1) Knit key elements together into a great customer experience: A silo and disconnected organization could not deliver value effectively to its customers; and it has to learn how to collaborate across the business, network and ecosystem. A customer centric digital business is fluid, agile, flexible and resilient in knitting all necessary elements together into a great customer experience.

- **Leadership:** Success comes with leadership truly believes and commits to customer centricity. Many times, businesses generally don't have bold enough leadership and strategic movement to drive the change required to really develop customer centric business capabilities. Or the linkages between customer centric capability and sustained business performance aren't understood by enough executives. If senior management doesn't believe there is an acceptable return on investment, the race never starts in earnest. Most pay lip service to customer experience, but don't have the kind of commitment and guts necessary to show real results. Hence, everyone at the C-suite needs to be aligned on what customer-centricity really means for the organization. It's a fundamental shift in operations and philosophy. The reality is that without 'radical' change in organizational structure, culture and measures, nothing more than small incremental changes will transpire.

- **Talent**: One common element in all areas involved in creating the customer experience is the way people interact with customers and how proactively and promptly they solve their needs. The effective change management effort can convert many departments from rather inward-looking organizations to having an external focus and customer-centric approach. From top down, creating meaning and clarity of purpose for both management and people in frontline work, thereby addressing their thoughts, feelings, values, beliefs, and emotional needs, leaders lead through passion, teams have such curiosity to ask "Big Why", and gain customer empathy when following routine processes to serve customers, with ownership attitude to improve or optimize business process.

- **Process**: Businesses too often believe that customer experience management can all be done using existing resources and structures. The result is often that changes become silo driven – "that's a marketing /customer service/sales project," etc. Exceptional customer experience takes holistic approach with detected polarization around two themes. Firstly, the "horizontal," coordination approach and secondly the need for clearly designated "customer champions"; cross-functional collaboration and interaction are crucial in building true customer-centric organizations.

(2) Key components in customer experience capability: Besides leadership, passion, process, collective business capabilities are also crucial for optimal customer experience. There are quite a few paradigm shifts: Operation efficiency needs to be the solution to the customer problem, not create it; and profit is the byproduct of customer centricity, not the only goal business is pursuing; the key components in customer experience capability may include:

- **Amplified digital capabilities:** Web, mobile and social platforms offer multiple digital channels for customers to connect, engage, and have a significant effect on the customer's experience. How to integrate, enhance such digital capabilities more seamlessly will directly impact business's long-term growth; not just short term revenue increase.

- **Collective human capabilities:** Improving the capabilities of employees and influencing their mind-sets, so that they acquire the right emotional and technical skills to provide premium services; enlisting frontline leaders to serve as role models and to teach emotionally intelligent behavior, to enhance the intrinsic emotional intelligence of employees.

- **Holistic service capabilities:** The most essential aspect of CX (Customer Experience) is the need to establish the right customer-centric processes & capabilities throughout an organization. Build a service model that enables and motivates the average employee to achieve excellence, and to extend across the whole front-line network about the excellence of exemplary individuals, branches, and offices.

(3) Metrics and KPIs: Finally, the measurement systems must be put in place so that management is held accountable for customer service performance, and success is evident to the front line. The selection and usage of KPIs is a dynamic process that is relevant for measuring efficiency across operations, as well as effectiveness in achieving the financial and customer service goals of the enterprise through evaluating their current performance measurement tools:

- **Effectiveness metrics:** Enterprises should shift their focus from tracking KPIs that measure the efficiency of the customer centers to KPIs that measure the effectiveness of the overall customer experience via customer-level variables.

- **Strategic metrics:** These are highest-level metrics that matter to the senior executives. Typically they might be financial metrics, which include both top line revenue growth and bottom line business result; overall service image and customer retention, loyalty and satisfaction, as well as the customers' perception of the service and experience.

- **Operational metrics**: This is not a simple question to answer without a thorough understanding of the specific operational details of each business and a view into the broader customer service operation, management may ask what are those operating metrics that are going to drive financial performance, and drill down even further to front line metrics on a daily basis, and figure out how social or optimized process can enhance the performance in line with those metrics.

In essence, the digital era is the age of customer; building solid customer experience (CX) capability is a strategic focus and holistic company effort for any customer-centric business, which is agile to adapt to change, intelligent to make timely decision, resilient to business risks, and elastic to scale up and down seamlessly.

12. Digital Capability #9: "Simplexity" Management

Complexity is not just a phenomenon, it can be perceived as a property of a system.

Modern digital organizations spend significant time and resources to deal with complexity, the complex organizational structure, process or the hyper-complex business ecosystem. The hybrid word 'simplexity' (simplicity + Complexity) well reflects such emerging digital nature and paradox. However, simplicity should not be confused with simple-mindedness. The road to simplicity goes through complexity. And it takes complex mind-set with dynamic attention, synthetic understanding with integrated capacity, strategic clarity and cohesive collaboration to shape complexity management as a strategic business capability.

- **Every solution to problem should be as simple as possible, but no simpler. (Einstein).** It means that a problem has an inherent, irreducible complexity; many problems become more and more complex as we dig into them, a good system tries to accommodate as much of that range as possible, any attempt to simplify further than that will fail, and any complexity added to it is harmful. So complexity per se is neither good nor bad. Some problems are simple in nature; others are complex. And it's a continuum, not either/or situation. The goal is to create elegant and tactical problem solutions that accommodate a problem's inherent complexity, also depending on the system's nature and its audience, hide that complexity by abstracting up from it to a simpler level, without compromising the solution's quality, robustness, and enhanced ability.

- **Complexity is a systematic thinking and design capability concept:** Complexity is not the opposite of "simplicity." In systems thinking, systems such as organizations, biological systems, enterprise as system, etc., can be characterized as being complex if they have non-linear feedback loops; such systems can exhibit emergent behavior. Simple systems can have complexity in that they have nonlinear feedback loops that can result in emergent properties and outcomes. Complexity is diverse, ambiguous, and dynamic with unpredictable outcomes. It is often erroneously confused with the term complication. Nevertheless complexity and complication do not mean the same thing. Something that is complex is not necessarily difficult, but something that is complicated does have a high degree of difficulty. Some complexity factors cannot be simplified, you need to become more complex in order to serve for example, customers optimally.

- **Complexity is an emergent property and capability.** Sometimes "complex is as simple as it gets." System complexity arises from the interaction of dynamic components such as digitalization, and can be layered and intricate. At the core of these complex images or patterns are a few simple elements. The challenge is able to see the simple elements that make up these systems, and understand the nature of the system, its elements, and the rules that govern them. This is not always easy. Once you have such understanding, the complexity still exists, but now you are in a better position to respond to threats and opportunities, and even modify the system, both its elements and the rules that govern them, to effect change.

Business is complex, the human is complex, and nature is complex; there's beauty and harmony in it; it is dynamic, diverse and distinct as well. So the purpose of managing complexity is not to, actually impossible to eliminate it, but upon how to create synergy and build delight on it.

13. Capability Debate #1: Is Business Capability Equal to Business Process?

The Business capability is at a higher level than a business process, and it is in the conceptual layer.

There is no Wikipedia definition for business capability. However, they do define capability in general as the ability to "perform or achieve certain actions or outcomes through a set of controllable and measurable faculties, features, functions, processes, or services." Performing actions requires thinking about different "resource sets" an enterprise uses to perform the actions needed to achieve its strategy. The term resource is essential in power behind the notion of a capability vs. process thinking.

- **A capability is business capacity plus ability:** It is the ability of the business to consistently deliver an expected result to the marketplace. A business capability describes what a business entity is in the organization, what is their purpose and output to the enterprise. That output is generated by applying their internal business processes, and can also be combined at macro level to construct wider, cross-entity business processes. The process may show how capabilities are related. Whereas a "business process" evokes the notion of inputs, manage knowing from flowing, the sequence within which functional activities and decision points are conducted. The process brings clarity around the rhyme and reason for activities being performed in a predetermined order, illustrating dependencies, and the effect if certain activities are not done.

- **Business capability concept enables strategic level communication:** The problem is many business people are practical, pragmatic and processes or results focused, and they have difficulty in understanding abstract discussions. Business capability is Enterprise Architecture (EA) concept whereas EA is at abstract level; the idea of business capabilities to business is as a useful way to talk at a higher, conceptual or more abstract level about what the business can or wants to be able to do, and it enforces strategic level communication. Also organizations can look at both process and capability maps, and decides that capabilities are much more accessible, and thus aids the conversations between IT and its stakeholders.

- **The Business capability is at a higher level than a business process:** It is in the conceptual layer. It represents a conceptual service that a group of processes and people, supported by the relevant application, information and underlying technology, will perform. The capability represents the what, whereas the process and people represent the how. The Business process management provides a foundation that brings visibility, enablement and compliance, reduces errors and avoids cost, all important elements to the survival of an enterprise.

- **Digital capabilities have outcomes; they collaborate with each other and are enabled by processes:** It is the firm's ability to integrate, build, and reconfigure internal and external competences to address rapidly changing environments, an ability the corporation or company has to do a specific set of functional activities. Having demonstrated the ability to perform those activities, it now has that capability to do them again. Business processes are then a succession of activities that defines and supports business capabilities. For example, if you take "customer acquisition" as a business capability, it evolves many business processes, like "lead-to-customer," that support the "capability." At the same time, this 'customer acquisition' capability might also make part of wider business processes at the organization.

- **Defining your enterprise business capability is part art and part science**: Working with your business and leveraging industry reference models is the most effective way. A capability is comprised of people, process, technology and assets. This is a holistic and strategic definition and balances the various components of the capability. Business processes are enabled by technology and people within the framework of a capability. Capabilities can be an enormous help in understanding and prioritizing the change business and IT are attempting to create.

Business processes underpin business capabilities, and business capabilities underpin business strategy execution, therefore, they are both important to decide business competency and growth potential.

14. Capability Debate #2: How to Determine if a Capability Is a Core Capability

The core business capabilities are integrated set of capabilities contribute directly to competitive advantage of business.

Business Capabilities are essentially the learning processes that are embodied in the knowledge capital of a business organization. And core capabilities are integrated set of capabilities contribute directly to competitive advantage of business.

(1) A series of questions to determine the "CORE": "Capability" is a useful composite concept that is fairly specific in its bounds, and can be used as an analysis tool. The "core" capabilities can be determined via the questions and reasoning:

Q1: Is a capability core because it offers a competitive advantage in delivering and selling the product?
A: The core capabilities could be those that are identified as delivering the competitive product, services and customer experience than competitors.

Q2: Is it core because it supports your strategic direction?
A: Senior leadership defines a strategy. In order to meet that strategy, management in conjunction with Enterprise Architecture describes a set of capabilities needed to meet the strategy. The current environment is evaluated to understand which capabilities already exist and which must be developed or changed.

Q3: Is it core also because the company excels in delivering that capability? Must the core capability be delivered by the company itself?
A: In today's multi-sourcing and cloud era, the core capability does not have to be delivered by the company itself; the key point is the speed of delivery and overall business agility.

(2) The methodology to optimize the set of business capabilities: Overall, the problem is business capability optimization rather than picking core or non-core capabilities one by one. It requires a systematic methodology to look at options of internal, wholly owned subsidiaries, operational control, partners, vendors, even investment in related firms to create an effective or profitable ecosystem. The holistic approach provides the context for managing the complex organizations, and gives those organizations an open path to find a niche and become core. There is a methodology with logic steps to establish the core enterprise capabilities:

> **(a) Identify** what capabilities give your product or service a competitive advantage and align to the enterprise vision.

(b) **Choose** how to improve the capability based on your enterprise strengths either by investing in or renting a best of breed capability. Discover the business strength that can be transformed in a core capability if it aligns with the strategic direction.

(c) **Clarify** BCD: A more pertinent question would be the BCD (Base, Competitive, and Differentiating) classification. An organization would need to ask whether they need the capability at:

- Base level – to sustain the business.
- Competitive level – to stay competitive in the business.
- Differentiating level – to be the key differentiator for its business.

(d) Capabilities may evolve and move between categories based on the technology evolution, business driver, business model evolution, etc., move from base or competitive level to differentiated level. This happens when an organization decides to differentiate by taking an existing capability to the next level.

Business capabilities are different from the mere sum of individual abilities and skills of its members. It's about what you do as a company, how you do it, it's collective capabilities to ensure organization as a whole can achieve more even it is consist of group of normal people, and the well set of optimal or core capabilities can be cultivated via cultural coherence and continuous process improvement.

15. How to Map IT Capabilities to Business Capabilities in One Page

Business capability mapping is about measures of "importance," "maturity," and "performance" attached to each capability.

Business capabilities are a hierarchical decomposition of "what" the enterprise does. Business capabilities do nothing by themselves, all the work is actually done by business processes that are the "how" part of the question. All resources, business applications, etc. belong to business processes. While at age of digital, all key business processes are enabled by enterprise IT capabilities and digital technologies. Therefore, the crucial question needs to be asked: How to map IT capabilities to business capabilities in one page?

(1) Why is it important to map IT capabilities to business capabilities?

A: Go back to IT promises and see whether capabilities or processes provide answers to some of the questions you want answered, and if there is value then go ahead and provide these views. Some have questioned the validity of the capability matrix because they see IT as a support function, but the reality is that IT is a business enabler. This implies business is driven by technology. As it is an IT capability in most cases would be enabling one or more business capability. Such IT capabilities to business capabilities mapping is trying to assess and define how interconnected the IT organization is to the business, and trying to determine the return on investment (ROI) for their technical architecture (delivery - services costing) that is mapped to a business's capabilities.

- **Creating a one pager view of mapping relationship of business-IT capabilities:** It helps an organization to identify IT capabilities that are critical for running business. Organizations may also use this matrix to identify business capabilities that are neglected by IT; and these usually appear as business capabilities that do not have any IT enablers. Business could also go one step further to identify business capabilities that are over enabled by IT; and these usually appear as a business capability with so many IT capabilities mapped to it. It is the ability to use such a matrix to identify over extended IT or duplicate IT capabilities and solutions. Such a matrix is useful when planning or defining an IT Strategy that aligns to business needs and strategy.

- **Mapping business applications to capabilities**: It is important to first define what an IT capability is, as this determines whether all the above apply, identifying over extended IT capabilities would imply such an IT capability best represents an IT application. The relationship between business and IT capability is that of enabling. If you want to map business applications to business capabilities, you can do this by mapping all the applications associated with business processes to the business capabilities that use the processes.

- **Both capabilities and processes are decomposable**: Decomposing processes provides a deep understanding about how these granular functionalities connect to deliver the final business outcome (this is the language of business professions). Capabilities give additional views that are seldom available in processes, etc. These components are common and reusable across the enterprise (business units are silo organs and they do not give a lot of attention as to whether what they do is also replicated elsewhere). All this depends on business drivers though.

(2) How to map IT capabilities to business capabilities?

A: From a strategy perspective, the business capability analysis is based on current definition of functions instead of an organizational structure, as organizational structure is quite dynamic and frequent changes, which may create a chaotic process model, use the value chain or the supply/demand governance model to map the business capability. A pragmatic approach is to look at this from a 'value streams' perspective:

(1) **Identify** major business value streams (end-to-end processes that deliver customer value).
(2) **Map** information technology related services that support these or are missing (untapped capability).
(3) **Estimate** the 'capability leverage', preferably in dollars, provided, or potentially so, by of each of these IT services to each value stream (greater agility etc).

(4) **Assess** the business capability (preferably normalized to dollars) represented by each value stream.

Business-IT Alignment: Map IT capabilities to either at strategic work or tactical level in identifying business /IT alignment issues:

(1) What the business does – Capabilities.
(2) How the business does it – Processes/Functions.
(3) Processes are best if you are working at a tactical level.
(4) Capabilities are best for strategic work.

One page IT Capability Mapping: It is quite interesting if everything can be put in one page. It depends on the nature of the enterprise, such as sector, size, and the age of the business. So single page would include fundamental to any business enterprise with the questions of "what do we do?" and "how do we do it?"

(1) Vision.
(2) Requirements to deliver.
(3) IT capability.

The approach could be to draw an enterprise value chain and expose all the business capabilities beneath those functions, highlight the activities, identify the overlaps and gaps; and then, take to next level with lots of details in multiple pages. For all the capabilities, then calculate cost in three categories such as strategy, operation and governance. For all the foundational capabilities like HR, finance, customer service, sales and marketing, and then draw that at the bottom of the sheet across the whole enterprise value chain.

Conclusion:

Compared to industrial capabilities, digital business capabilities are more complex in design, with synthetic nature requiring cross-functional collaboration, embedding agility into processes for adapting to the changes, and the right set of unique digital capabilities directly decide the overall organization's competency, and how well they can make digital transformation, deliver the value to the customers and build long-term winning position. An organization's digital competency is enabled by its capabilities to perform effectively and efficiently with speed and agility. In short, business's strategic success to digital transformation is enabled by a set of DIAAMONDS type distinctive and dynamic digital capabilities. Therefore, in today's uncertainty and speed of changes, organizations face the ongoing need to identify and develop new capabilities to respond to emergent opportunities, changing customer demands, as well as competitive threats. Failing to do so can drag organizations down to the digital laggard; and doing it right is the key success factor in becoming a digital master.

CHAPTER 6

Digital Innovation

"Innovation is the specific instrument of entrepreneurship...the act that endows resources with a new capacity to create wealth."
– Peter F. Drucker

Generally speaking, innovation is how to transform the novel ideas into products and services to achieve its business value. Innovation has more enriched context than ever, and there are many forms of innovation - technology, application, product, design, process, business model, communication, management, culture and customer experience - just to name a few. Each has its own unique pathways.

It may be easy to split the term "innovation" into two categories, "incremental innovation" and "radical innovation." Incremental innovation has equal notion or concept with continuous improvement, focuses on improving a part of business process or capability. Radical innovation focuses to "replace" conventional value stream with new one, supported or filled with noble knowledge and idea. Innovation is progressive because it represents a new way of doing things, and it could be destructive because it makes previously valued skills or competitive advantage less demanded, with the potential of becoming obsolete.

Innovations at the digital age are coming at seemingly a much faster pace, more change, more potential disruption, but the patterns and rules of communication are pretty much the same. The broader the scope, scale and impact of the change, the more one leans toward calling such change an innovation. Some additional variables that might merit consideration are the scope, scale, and impact of the change. Significant innovations can catalyze organizational change. Innovation management does require not just interdisciplinary understanding to connect the dots and see what's possible, but also technical expertise to create the disruption.

1. Debunk Innovation Code

Innovation is more often composed with the full spectrum of light.

Why is innovation important or even more important at the digital era whereas technology becomes more advanced? Because innovation is the core activity of human evolution to changing of environment to reach performance for profit, for saving of resources, for satisfaction of users, for reducing the unnecessary complexity, and for pushing the human world forward. The speed of change is expedited, so does the speed of innovation.

(1) The science and art of innovation: Innovation is a systematic way of applying creativity in the real life. The first hint was coining of the word "retro-synthesis"; Wikipedia stated that "the noun synthesis refers to a combination of two or more entities that together form something new; alternately, it refers to the creating of something by artificial means." The science of innovation can be understood as retro-synthesis, which is planning a synthesis backwards, by starting at the product or service – the "target" – and taking it back a step at a time..." It implies to start with what you want to see or do or have; then think backwards from there to what the next simpler step is, then back to what are the next simpler components, back to what you have at hand. Simply put, creating is being able to think backwards (from product or outcome to components) and forwards (from materials or resources at hand) at the same time.

- **Innovation in general is surely a discipline**: It covers innovation management, knowledge and technology transfer, entrepreneurship and it is closely related to several other disciplines. It stands in between management, economy, psychology, sociology, and law, not speaking about disciplines that are related to technologies implemented by the particular innovation. Theoretical treatment of the discipline may give rise to a science. The bulk of data, methods and approaches involved as well as complexity of processes encountered speak in favor of scientific approach. On the other hand, the subject of the study is very subtle and difficult to distinguish from other sciences mentioned above - in a sense innovation would be a "cross-science."

- **Innovation is just the right mix of art and science**: The science is "the ability to produce solutions in a problem domain repeatedly." What defines science from chance is the ability to repeat a process with the same resultant solution every time, through the application of known facts. The core principles are the scientific method, using design of experimental approaches where a portfolio of options are pursued; knowing there will be pruning as new facts emerge. At the current situation, "innovation science", if there is such a thing, is rather more a complex set of rules, frameworks, processes, practices, and examples, etc.

- **Business innovation management is more science than art:** At individual level, innovation is a personal irrationality that is unique to every individual, it's one's inward creativity leading into outward innovation, we can describe the outer silhouette as a statistical percentile, but the crazy things that each of us do to arrive at a new idea will be different. However, at business scope, innovation expands its horizon and flexes its muscles, goes beyond creating the new things, it has enriched context, such as process innovation, communication innovation, culture innovation, management innovation, business model innovation, structure innovation. Innovation management is more science than art; it takes an effective framework, core principles, systematic disciplines, as well as the best and next practices.

(2) Decode Innovation serendipity – "SPECIALPR": Serendipity has been voted as one of the most popular words in the English language. It is also one of the hardest to translate. Conversationally, it is used as tantamount to luck, providence or chance. Serendipity will always play some part in the innovation effort, and there are plenty of stories over the years about great ideas evolving out of chance meetings, sudden flashes of insight, and sheer luck. However, businesses simply can't depend on happenstance, and the most successful ones understand that clearly, the better way is to crack innovation serendipity code, and manage their innovation portfolio more systematically.

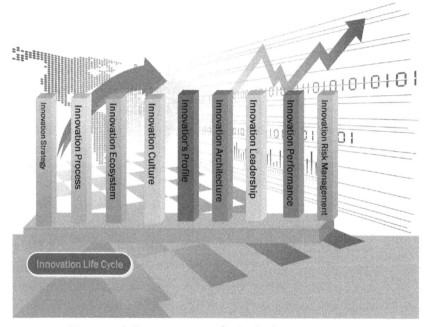

Figure 14: Innovation Life Cycle "SPECIALPR"

- **S – Innovation Strategy:** A good innovation strategy, either as a key ingredient of corporate strategy, or a subcomponent of strategy, is an inspiring mental model shared by the key stakeholders of a firm.

- **P – Innovation Process:** The term 'innovation process' implies openness to innovative ideas, with an accepted interface into the organization to actually develop and exploit the ideas as they come about.

- **E – Innovation Ecosystem:** There are many components in an effective innovation environment, each by themselves may not cause a good environment, but collectively they can and weave an innovation ecosystem.

- **C – Innovation Culture:** Companies whose strategic goals are clear, and whose cultures strongly support those goals, possess a huge advantage, especially for the areas such as innovation.

- **I – Innovator's Profiles:** For many, innovation is serendipity, and innovators are crazy ones. Indeed, innovators are among us and within us, it relates to leadership, empathy, idealism, process understanding, communication skills, cultural understanding, and definitely understanding in what is wrong with the status quo.

- **A – Innovation Architecture:** A systematic innovation approach is to depict innovation as a system (rather than a traditional process) whose performance depends on the alignment of its various components (people, actions, controls, resources, etc.).

- **L – Innovation Leadership**: A good innovation leader must be like a conductor leading the orchestra with a not yet written symphony. It takes creativity, openness for the new ideas, out of the box thinking, and very strong capacity of a rapid integration and digestion of abundant information coming from various sources.

- **P – Innovation Performance:** Innovation is about how to implement creative idea and achieve its business value. One can only manage what it's being measured. It is also true for innovation management as well.

- **R – Innovation Risk Management:** Innovation is a systematic way of applying creativity in the real life and it takes management disciplines to manage both opportunities and risks effectively.

(3) Decode innovation next practices – "SCORECHAMP": Due to the "creative" nature of innovation, there are no best practices or solutions to cultivate innovation; the structures and processes that many leaders reflexively use to encourage innovation are important, but not sufficient. Businesses just have to continue to experiment the next practices, here are a few:

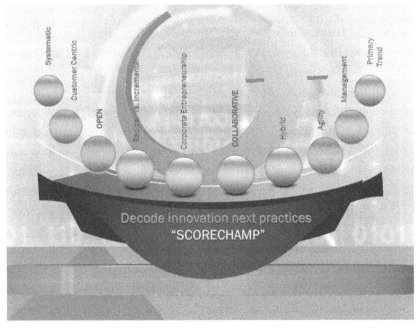

Figure 15: Decode Innovation Practices "SCORECHAMP"

- **Innovation Practice #1: S – Systematic Innovation:** It is a structured process and set of practical tools used to create or improve products/ services/process that deliver new value to customers or satisfy employees.

- **Innovation Practice #2: C – Customer-Centric Innovation**: When manage innovation life cycle, customer involvement at all stages often elicits highly valuable information.

- **Innovation Practice #3: O – Open Innovation**: The idea behind open innovation is that the problem/challenge/brief is put out for anyone to apply or contribute.

- **Innovation Practice #4: R – Radical Innovation vs. Evolutionary Innovation**: There are two types of innovations: (a) radical innovation that may be classified as breakthrough or disruptive; (b) evolutionary innovation that has two components - incremental and spiral.

- **Innovation Practice #5: E – Corporate Entrepreneurship**: Corporate Entrepreneurship is embodying risk-taking, pro-activeness and radical product innovations. Corporate Entrepreneurship has been recognized as a potentially viable means for promoting and sustaining organizational performance, renewal and corporate competitiveness over the past three decades.

- **Innovation Practice #6: C – Collaboration-based Innovation**: Digital hyper-connectivity can foster innovation through collaboration. In other words, try to digitally connect key resources and assets in their context to the resource rich innovation hubs across the business ecosystem.

- **Innovation Practice #7: H – Hybrid Innovation**: It is hard to think of any innovation as not a hybrid, a combination of something old with something new or a number of new things.

- **Innovation Practice #8: A – Innovation Agility**: Innovation agility is a critical business capability to manage innovation life cycle with speed; it's about to have a purpose stay ahead of competition in the delivery process. It's about to be able to get all the way around the task, to capture all relevant information, to see it from all interests; and to use collective wisdom.

- **Innovation Practice #9: M – Management Innovation**: It changes the way managers do what they do to improve organizational performance, where innovation is one of many management practices.

- **Innovation Practice #11: P – Primary digital innovation trends:** Compare the emerging digital era to previous industrial era, is innovation becoming more important or less, does the content or context of innovation stay at the same or be different, is innovation trying to reach the next level, but what is tipping point?

All humans are naturally creative. Either best practices or next practices, the goal is to create and nurture an environment in your organization where humility is appreciated, curiosity is encouraged, and creative thinking is rewarded.

2. Innovation Strategy

Innovation is what leads to differentiation. There are many ways to differentiate and therefore there are many ways to build innovation into a corporate strategy.

A good innovation strategy, either as a key ingredient of corporate strategy, or a subcomponent of strategy, is an inspiring mental model shared by the key stakeholders of a firm. It sets the direction and defines the broad boundaries of the creative space, within that these stakeholders can be inspired to generate new ideas and implement them to create new products, processes and business models.

- **In-depth knowledge upon business vision and strategy**: Before you can have an effective innovation strategy, you require a clearly communicated and understood overall business vision and strategy. A good innovation strategy supports a clear, and an ideally aggressive vision within the business. A vision is a mixture of the understanding of who you are as a company. What is your value, what is your external image, how others perceive you? Innovation strategy should then follow broader business objectives. Understand where your business wants to get its growth from and focus innovation strategy around it. Too often companies want hard and fast innovation that leaves them with new ideas that don't necessarily translate into business success because the objective of the project wasn't thought through.

- **The delicate balance of setting principles and having flexibility:** The key of innovation strategy is to give direction and set boundaries, but not at the cost of restricting creativity and inspiration. There must be different approaches, flexibility, and the possibility for Plan A to D: Is it a strategy that is focused at innovation sensitive opportunities; or is it an innovative way to weave defined strategic initiatives together or all of the above. You have to find out what makes sense to start with, but you don't have to absolutely stick to one line. You can think of it in term of the type of people you would like to involve in innovation. It's a delicate balance: Too loose and there can be much wasted activity; too tight and you can prematurely squash ideas. There are several important factors of a successful innovation strategy that should be pervasive in a company. The first is that every employee working on innovation efforts should understand how their assignment, the work they do each day, is essential to the success of the strategy. The strategy should be so compelling to them that they are fully committed to achieving their assigned objectives.

- **Digital business ecosystem understanding**: The ability to learn about the digital business environment and ecosystem is a more important characteristic of innovation management. As operating boundaries have become less clear attempts to 'protect' organizations from the uncertainties of their operating environments, the sustainability of an organization is dependent upon its ability to respond to the environment within which it operates. Mechanistic models and closed systems, approaches that attempt to 'protect' an organization from the uncertainties of its digital environment may have short term benefits (meeting targets, profitability); but in the long term they are likely to fail due to the lack of redundancy that underpins adaptive capability. A key feature of creating this redundancy, or slack, is the need to learn from the environment and to embed that learning into the knowledge stock of a digital organization.

- **Three core elements in innovation strategy**: Strategy in general is how a specific company will occupy a specific market space to differentiate from the competition. There are three core elements in innovation strategy.

  (1) **Source**: where do ideas come from?
  (2) **Scope**: what type of ideas would be considered relevant?
  (3) **Sponsorship**: How will you fund the selected ideas? Strategy in general is how a specific company will occupy a specific market space to differentiate from the competition.

  Building from this, the Innovation strategy is:

  (a) What the innovation effort is focused on - defending the core, penetrating the adjacencies, or entering the white space.
  (b) How the resources will be balanced across these domains; and how the company will do innovation - through internal development and organic growth, or though open Innovation such as partnerships and alliances, etc.

In summary, an innovation strategy should directly support the overall business strategy by creating a focused but balanced portfolio of projects that maximize the output from the innovation team, in terms of adding value to the organization by delivering solutions to the aforementioned attributes. So an innovation strategy should be all about focusing the creativity of the team to deliver the maximum positive impact for the overall business strategy.

3. Innovation Process beyond Oxymoron

The term "innovation process" implies openness to innovative ideas.

Innovation is both art and science. Innovation is a systematic way of applying creativity in the real life and business. In general, innovation is a discipline. However, should innovation processes be standardized? Or is innovation process an oxymoron? The term 'innovation process' implies openness to innovative ideas; with an accepted interface into the organization to actually develop and exploit the ideas as they come about. An organization that seeks to innovate must be able to make decisions on the innovative ideas and concepts, and then make both development as well as life cycle sustaining decisions. With maturity of digital technologies such as mobile, social, cloud and analytics, the organization takes significant portion of time and cost to experiment digital innovation, it sparks the new wave of creative idea sharing and implementation. But how to prioritize and manage the innovation process becomes the strategic imperative.

- **Innovation factors**: Idea creation, implementation processes, culture, governance, etc are all key factors to innovation. Any organization that innovates, but cannot move its innovative ideas forward, is an organization doomed to the status quo. An organization that excels at innovation development and life cycle sustaining is an innovation master. A digital master is more often an innovation master as well. In addition, culture is key success factor; it's easy for an organization to say "innovation is critical" or some other such trite phrase. Observation of the habits of the organization often reveals a culture that seems almost pathologically designed to stifle innovation. An organization that masters all these factors well becomes an innovation leader.

- **Innovation framework**: You do need some form of framework for innovation, to ensure that you can qualify ideas and direct the right amount of resources and investment to the most promising ideas. The key aspect is to ensure that innovation is not stifled by the underlying product management processes. A heavy innovation process is definitely an oxymoron, but you do need certain process and governance framework, as many good ideas have diminished in middle-management of many organizations because of lack of attention. The "process" could be any of the following; and the more, the better:

- unbounded, free of rules, and collection of good ideas;
- solicit ideas from anywhere within the organization, not just a specific group or individuals;
- allow for peer review and feedback;
- allow for management to contribute and encourage;
- have peer review "vote," as well as contribute or evolve the ideas.

- **Innovation process**: Innovation process needs to be rigorous, not too rigid. If the process in innovation management is akin to what would come out the PMP (Project Management Professional Certification) or CMM (Capability Maturity Model) school of thought, then the term might be oxymoronic. Try a very loose process that is not too time bound, but does prescribe a simple set of steps or gates that make things a little more systematic than they otherwise might be. In some occasions, the innovation process should be to solve a specific user case. Target the selection to address process, problem, new idea, etc. Have a time constraint; drive the results to be resolved within a specific period.

Organizations with rigorous innovation processes can manage innovation life cycle more systematically, and business with effective innovation framework, processes and governance tend to score high on both agility and performance.

4. Innovation Ecosystem

An innovation ecosystem is a systematic innovation methodological environment or a sort of innovation philosophy.

Innovation is changing to tackle the complexities of business dynamic at digital environment, but within itself, it needs to change as well. There is a paradigm shift that is taking place in generating innovation and building a scalable innovation environment, or innovation ecosystem. An innovation ecosystem should fully cover a wide enough direction. For example, cost optimization, waste reduction, quality improvement, problem solving, etc. When the designed objects scale up, it involves more aspects widely as well, so the businesses need innovation silver lining from specific tools rise to an overall problem solving system environment.

- **"Systemic" vs. "Systematic"**: "Systemic" relates to "from within" or the genes of the organization, hence, it ties to soft factors such as culture and leadership aspects; whereas "systematic" relates to capacities of hard methodologies, practices and tools, hence, there're demand for innovation methods or tools around, but they neither create nor replace the systemic factors such as culture, leadership, commitment, reward system, etc. in building systemic innovation.

- **The components in innovation ecosystem**: An innovation ecosystem is weaved by varying components. There are many components in an effective innovation environment, each by themselves may not cause a creative environment, but collectively, they can weave an innovation ecosystem; such as innovation leadership, culture, capability, practices, tools, recognition system, measurements, risk approach. Innovation ecosystem or the methodological environment should cover the whole innovation process, from processes in managing ideas or idea handling systems to idea implementation. That's why it is a set of means including methods that cover the process from problem's choice till commercialization.

- **Professional philosophy for innovation**: An innovation ecosystem is a systematic and methodological environment; or a sort of "professional philosophy" for innovation. An enriched innovation ecosystem enables systematic innovation management. It starts with innovation strategy that defines "what does the organization innovate" or "where should it innovate" to support the overall business strategy. The strategy is tightly connected to the business model and provides the context for the digital innovation. The organizational content is the innovation capability, which is how does the organization innovate.

- **'VCDC' traits:** Variety, complexity, diversification and collaboration are the new characteristics of digital innovation ecosystem. Organizations can no longer rely on a single individual or team to drive innovation. This is largely due to the fact that innovating in today's digital world has become increasingly complex in nature. Innovation needs to lay out different mind-sets, structures, processes, and solutions to develop its potential, where organizations are combining all that is available to them in imaginative, advantageous ways. That's why so many leaders have begun using collaborative methodologies as infrastructures to orchestrate their organization's talent and bring out the collective best thinking to accelerate innovation and optimize their innovation capabilities.

The business growth is accelerated by innovation, and their innovation is enabled by their ability to "systematize" process as opposed to rely on sporadic talent, therefore, the innovation ecosystem is for the long term and more of a catalyst for scaling up innovation.

5. Innovation Culture: Seven Cultural Habits to Harness Effective Business Innovation

Innovation has to become the philosophy, and part of DNA in an organization.

We spent the entire chapter 4 to discuss organizational culture. Indeed, culture is critical in business success. What is culture? Culture is how groups of people think and do things at organization. Culture is mindset, culture is attitude, culture is habit, and culture is brand. From an innovation report released by Booz earlier this year, culture is key to innovation, as they surveyed almost 600 innovation leaders in companies around the world, large and small, in every major industry sector, culture matters enormously. Studies have shown again and again that there may be no more critical source of business success or failure than a company's culture – it trumps strategy and leadership. Companies whose strategic goals are clear, and whose cultures strongly support those goals, possess a huge advantage, especially for the areas such as innovation. So what are the best culture habits to harness innovation?

"Seven Habits of Highly Effective People," written by Stephen R. Covey has sold more than 25 millions of copies in different languages. Though the book is more about individual self-improvement, the concept, philosophy and seven habits of essential can also help business improve organizational habit, to experience more successful innovation journey.

(1) Be Proactive: "Two people can see the same thing, disagree, and yet both be right. It's not logical; it's psychological." – Stephen R. Covey

Being proactive means people in the organization appreciate creativity, not just be compliant to order for survival; they are encouraged to be proactively questioning, connecting, collaborating and solving problems creatively. For business leaders, it means they may both push the new ideas proactively on how to leverage culture to drive innovation and increase business flexibility and agility; on the other side, they also cultivate the culture of "pull": proactively seek team feedback, deeply understand the potential business success factor and obstacles, to shape the culture that can harvest innovation.

(2) Begin with End in Mind: "We must look at the lens through which we see the world, as well as the world we see, and that the lens itself shapes how we interpret the world." – Stephen R. Covey

Innovation takes vision, vision may also help overcome culture inertia, as when everyone in the organization is collaborating to work toward the same goal; status quo, egos and silos no longer act as roadblocks, knowledge and creativity are unleashed to produce outcomes. Begin with the end in mind also means, innovation is means to the end, not the end, the end is how to delight customers or improve employee satisfaction, with such noble goals in mind, the culture can become more resilient to adapt to changes, employees are more easier to get buy in, and vision may also convey the good story telling to inspire culture of innovation.

(3) Put First Things First: "We see the world, not as it is, but as we are or, as we are conditioned to see it." – Stephen R. Covey

Culture is about how to focus – focus on a few things that matter for business, and business has the capability to do better than competitors. Isn't that what innovation is all about? Do it better, differentiate yourself from your competition, run, grow, and transform the business. The other thing to consider is it's not just about technology; it's about people, the partnerships, the process and capability. "Put First Things First" also means prioritizing, prioritizing the business goals that are most critical to your strategy; prioritizing the project investments that can help improve your key capabilities; prioritizing means to follow 80/20 rule: to put 80% of resources into 20% activities that can produce the best business results; from change management perspective: emphasizing just a few will allow you to move the needle on culture change much more easily, such as selecting a few key behaviors to change, rather than trying to create a completely different culture overnight.

(4) Think Win-Win: "When the trust account is high, communication is easy, instant, and effective." – Stephen R. Covey

Culture is also attitude, mutual trust is a good attitude to shape culture of innovation, to build up win-win relationship between employees and organization, business and customers; more specifically, it's about building up the culture of "reward success and failure" - the logic here is that you reward people for trying new actions, and doubly reward them for successes. If you punish failure, you shut down innovation immediately. Innovation is more about a process than a disruptive, enchanting new product these days, you need tolerate the failure, also make the effort on a "lessons learned" exercise to share. And, this entire innovation process area needs some oversight to make it not be a major business disruption. There are systematic ways to manage these actions effectively and to benefit business for the long term.

(5) Empathy – Seek First to Understand, Then to Be Understood: "Treat them all the same by treating them differently." – Stephen R. Covey

Business leaders may think ideally that employees are paid to make a difference, the reality is that in many hierarchical organizations, employees are trained to be compliant on the work being told to do, never to ask "why" or think independently, as employees' creativity is not evaluated fairly in business's talent agenda at industrial era. Empathy means business leaders and talent managers need to deeply understand the value, the motivation and the habits of employees, and take customized talent solution to encourage innovative behaviors. As most of creative ideas or solutions will usually come from the collective knowledge and experiences of the employees and the customers, not from the most powerful person or the smartest guy or gal in the room. And culture will be shaped by majority of people in the organization.

(6) Synergize: "Habit is the intersection of knowledge (what to do), skill (how to do), and desire (want to do)." – Stephen R. Covey

The creative team is usually composed of all sorts of talents, with heterogeneous cognizance, strength and skills, especially those roadrunner people who want to understand the whole game, the whole business, not just their job; people who think like business people and owners, people who shows curiosity to ask why, not like narrowly focused employees who follow rules and crave order only. The culture as habit here will harness the intersection of collective knowledge, wisdoms, and aspiration, synergize creative disruption, enhance interdependent, collaborative and even codependent culture of innovation, and channel such energy, enthusiasm and ideas.

(7) **Sharpen the Saw:** "Sow a thought, reap an action; sow an action, reap a habit; sow a habit, reap a character; sow a character, reap a destiny." – Stephen R. Covey

The culture is habit, the good habit is an attitude, and one may need to take most of his/her time to sharpen the saws, such as preparing the team, understanding the problem, and getting the right tool ready before approaching solutions or drawing conclusions. However, sharpening the saw is means to the end, not the end. Some businesses misunderstand the innovation purpose, may think innovation is implementing the latest and greatest technology, rather than using advances in technology or existing technology differently to provide innovative solutions for business now and in the future.

Like an individual's habit, cultural habit is hard to change, but it's changeable. Business leaders can take approaches of changing an organization's culture evolutionarily or systematically, as some conservative or negative culture encourage employees to be steadfast to the point that they'd become risk-averse, tolerant of mediocrity, and suspicious of outsider or new ideas.

6. Innovator's Profile

There's no innovation without disobedience. – French Proverb

For many, innovation is serendipity, and innovators are crazy ones; indeed, innovators are among us and within us, it relates to leadership, empathy, idealism, process understanding, communication skills, cultural understanding, and definitely - understanding in what is wrong with the status quo. Can you see yourself in the innovator's profile?

- **Dissatisfaction with status quo:** The profile that is most common and necessary is the rare being with innate curiosity to improve, at the risk of disobedience in positive sense -it's about the desire to make something better and the willingness to try. This intuition is doubled by courage and opportunities. Being impatient with the status quo and believing there is always a better way to do things. The next focus must be ideation that can be implemented and not just great wow ideas that one cannot implement.

- **Think differently (non-linear or different angle):** Innovators are at their very heart visionaries who also have the determination, dedication, motivation and passion. Innovation comes with a foresight to envision a need that others overlook or ignore, and a willingness to forge ahead to satisfy visions, in spite of a risk of failure. To the innovator, failure is just another opportunity for success. Innovators find more viewing spots than the rest. They find angles to wiggle through where most are unable to even envision a place where there is an angle. In short, innovators obviously think differently – problem solving is part of their DNA. They see the old problems and find different solutions.

- **Self-confidence:** If you're not sure of yourself, you won't be able to convince others to follow your leadership and vision. They have persisted because they were convinced to be in the right direction. And many times you also have to be willing to fail a lot and be very persistent and thick-skinned. Innovators usually have very active mind and a more fully operating brain. From curious to creative to critical, from analytical, assertive to adaptable, emphasis should be put new ways to improve surrounding and the world. For what can be called "implement-table innovation", the focus must be to ideate within existing resources. Ideas within that are usually innovative because innovative ideas are following with systematic processes and solutions.

- **Global view**: Be world-changing dreamer with critical and creative mind; be big picture thinker, but aware that micro-changes can also power big innovations. Be somewhere in the midst of borderless creativity and a revisited de/re-composition of existing ideas. Digital innovators have multidimensional mind-set; having a global view with both synthesis and analytics is most important, for it brings the ability to extract only the best and combine things. Able to listen and understand, and to depict whether and how innovation can be favored in a specific environment through empathy and global thinking.

- **Five "I"s and Five "C"s:** Influence, Imagination, Innovation, Implementation and Integration; Courage, Creativity, Curiosity, Concentration, and Customer-centricity are five 'I's and five 'C's of innovation team. Due to the complexity and dynamic of today's business, more often than not, innovation is team work than individual's effort through the collective creativity. Have the good sense and charisma to attract or to surround with the right people who can move the idea into action. And for teams to operate effectively in the innovation space, they need these core teaming skills, as a foundation for up-skilling their ability to generatively inquire, advocate and debate at high levels. They also need to know how to be collaborative, building upon trusted relationships, to develop mutuality or attunement with one another. In many large efforts, the people involved are often geographically disbursed, that requires folks to help create a new culture of innovation, so that complex innovation can become a true group effort with little need for the standard leadership models, leaving managers to identify opportunity, evangelize and fund raise.

Hence, an innovator's profile is colorful: Innovators are the one who can see things differently and positively, not negatively; dare to take risk, not risk-reverse; be courageous to 'disobedient' with good reasons; to push the world forward, not backward. Collaboratively, many minds can create many creative and different ideas, so working as a team can sometimes amplify creativity, with a balance in vision and implementation, responsibilities and privilege, opportunities and risks; as well as freedom and disciplines.

7. Innovation Architecture Framework

The framework of innovation is to highlight, not to restrict creativity.

A systematic innovation approach is to depict innovation as a system rather than a traditional process, whose performance depends on the alignment of its various components such as people, actions, controls, resources, etc. Enterprise Architecture (EA) is an important tool to describe enterprise; helps optimize all aspects of the business to increase profitability. All innovations mean change, although not all changes are innovation; and it is also obvious that such a change can only be achieved via corresponding change in EA. So which role can EA play to manage business innovations?

- **EA as a descriptive innovation management framework:** It catalogs the all of the tools and data available to the organization. EA is the body of knowledge. It is like an enormous box of Lego bricks. Innovation can then be driven by intelligent and motivated individuals from both IT and the business community seeing how these components can be assembled or utilized in new and hopefully better ways.

- **EA as influence power to enable innovation at people's minds:** Innovation requires a few elements under EA's custody or influencing power, which deals with how people must think in order to innovate:

  (1) a risk-free environment: So people can be allowed to take risk and make mistakes. EA should contemplate, consider, project, design and enable this element in every way.
  (2) A culture in which divergent forces are imposed on delivery/ production ability so to avoid 'compromises' solutions, which kill chances for business innovation
  (3) A drive to couple positive human emotions to the whole innovation lifecycle –for transforming the novel ideas and achieve its business value.

- **EA as culture catalyst and designer:** Innovation is more creative and spontaneous and should be encouraged more through corporate culture than only through EA influence. EA may be a catalyst toward enabling that cultural change if it does not exist; but it should be encouraged through the culture. Innovation does not come from technology or EA itself, but from a risk-free, divergent-thinking culture that is as spontaneous as it may seem, it needs breeding. There is a role for architecture in the designs, interactions and incentives that align with this culture, and this is a point in which it seems most methodologies are still narrow; they cover continuous improvement and incremental innovation, but shy away from disruptive innovation.

- **EA encourages holistic thinking:** The quality of EA depends on the quality of the information the enterprise understands about itself. Without any EA, Innovation is stunted by an incomplete understanding of what it is trying to do and what tools it has at its disposal. This then results in different initiatives often re-inventing the wheel, building new databases to store data that is already partially stored somewhere else or replicating functionality that is provided by another application. Advantages by applying EA as framework is that all concerns are visible, the substantiation for colliding concerns are discussed and a compromise will be part of the solution space. In short, all aspects of the business problem are addressed and will be handled, and the holistic thinking and solutions are encouraged to optimize complexity.

- **Simplification is the key.** EA is for clearing the sky, not for creating fog. It is easy to create the fog, to complicate things, to avoid direct answers to a question, to use terms arbitrarily, to invent absolutely meaningless terms. The real knowledge is not always simple, but it tries to simplify things, not to complicate them. It expresses its clear understanding by clarified ways. Innovation may transform the business and does not always need to involve technology or IT. IT is just another aspect of the business in terms of innovation. EA should be in a position to assess the ramifications behind the transformation, help maximize the potential and ensure the innovation transformation is in alignment with the enterprise strategic goals and objectives.

- **EA is a framework for enterprise opportunity management:** Innovation management is more culture and knowledge-management than EA as such, but EA can help in quite a few ways. One is that if it has a structure that describes the enterprise and its interrelationships, EA knows where an innovation might be tested out and put to use; if EA maps cross-links to people, such as in communities-of-practice, and social-network maps linked into EA, then also know who. But perhaps the most valuable thing is recognition that risk and opportunity are essentially the flip-sides of each other: if EA incorporates risk-management (which it should), it implicitly also incorporates opportunity-management. If you make that perspective explicit in EA, it automatically provides a stronger support for playing with innovation.

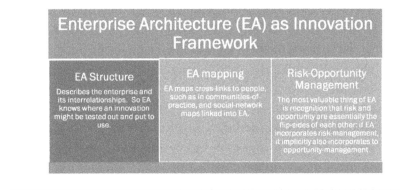

Figure 16: EA as Innovation Framework

Since there is far more philosophical scope in the "architectural" component of EA (architecture as blueprint, architecture as literature, architecture as language and architecture as framework. etc), the "schools of thought" in EA is an ongoing and emergent process. One recognizes that when you stand at a different viewpoint, you see a completely different problem, where viewpoints are based on one's role as a stakeholder. The innovative idea is in the head of an innovator, but having a good means for its realization is a great enabler, EA needs to play as such an innovation enabler.

8. Innovation Leadership

An innovation leader is a futurist, foresees the future and helps make it happen.

There are many common leadership qualities required between an innovation leader and those required from any good leader or any creative team member. However, being innovative leaders take more courage, creativity, adaptability, collaboration and concentration.

- **An innovation leader must walk the tight rope between diplomat and maverick:** On one hand, he or she will get faster results by respecting people, getting the best effort from the people. Listening and orchestrating as fast as possible. On the other hand, to deliver the innovation on time, he or she must be willing to take risks, and jump through some hoops. Knowing that success will reward and failure will punish. You cannot make omelets without breaking some eggs. Walking that tight rope makes the innovation leader a likable acrobat; a true artist; in short, an innovation leader.

- **An effective innovation leader must be like a conductor:** Lead the digital innovation orchestra with a not yet written symphony. It takes creativity, openness for the new ideas, out of the box thinking and very strong capacity of a rapid integration, and digestion of abundant information coming from various sources, including technology, service, business, financials, etc. Also an innovative leader has a skill to extract and impart learning from any situation, successes, failures, test, trial, networking and sense of humor. An innovation leader has to create, manage, and exploit innovation networks and business eco-system as well. Leaders, who can recognize innovative ideas, fight for resources and political cover, connect ideas and teams together to deliver an innovative result, are critical to achieving innovation excellence.

- **A strong innovation leader is like a bridge:** Innovation leaders emerge from many functional backgrounds, to network into non-conventional connections, out of the team's discipline and usual networks; with the ability to irradiate inclusion. It is important that innovation leaders and innovators understand both the digital technology they are using to serve customers and the strategy of the business. It's key to combine technology knowledge with business understanding in order to manage digital innovation portfolio seamlessly. Successful innovation team leaders offer the ability to provide:

Vision	Clarify the opportunity and articulate the vision
Process	Develop and manage the process of innovation
Culture	Promote a healthy climate for innovation
Portfolio	Inspire team members to create a portfolio of new ideas, concepts and scenarios
Practice	Coach team members on innovation management practices and how to overcome the barriers to innovation

Table 9: Innovation Leader's Ability

- **An innovation leader is a problem-solver:** In order to select the right people to drive innovation projects, you must recognize that in today's environment, you're no longer sourcing all the innovation inside your company. Innovation is a process that is cross functional and non-industrial specific. It is, at its heart, a problem solving process, and as such, you need to find someone who is able to network the firm to uncover the problems, to get problem owners on board with the innovation program, and then to devise the appropriate mix of processes, people, and tools to solve the problem and execute the solution. Innovative development team members need to exhibit qualities that make them better able to generate or discover good ideas, have the judgment to know what's important, and have the leadership ability to deliver.

- **An innovation leader's skills are varying**: The first question is what type of innovation your company's seeking. You need different types of people for various innovation objectives (incremental versus breakthrough, etc.) for different types of companies (solutions versus products, etc.). Aptitudes and skills will vary from front-end to back-end. Typically no one has them all and the first sign of a good innovation leader is that he or she will recognize his or her limitations and build a team to compensate. The desired skills may include but not limit to:

(1) **Listening**: A real capability to listen and integrate each function's inputs so that the projects get enriched and solid while progressing in its development.

(2) **Insight**: A deep understanding of key consumer or customer insights. An excellent memory and courage; not to forget those key findings when moving ahead in the execution when facing adversity.

(3) **Communication**: An effective leader needs a large and deep structure of soft skills like ability to communication, conflicts resolution, empowerment, motivational skills, control of criticism, etc.

(4) **Project and program management skills**: Innovation leaders may champion how new initiatives get framed, and then expertly guide engineers/ managers/marketers through cross functional development and commercialization stage gates to produce real results in a timely manner that lead to the creation of new business value.

(5) **Orchestration:** Facilitation skills to explore; promote and even translate new conversations to stakeholders at all levels that lead to new service or product programs.

(6) **Social intelligence:** Add in the elements of collaboration and social network experience. If you're doing this as a collaborative process, which any self-respecting innovation program should be nowadays, you need to be able to build, maintain, and engage internal and external social networks to provide new sources of insights, experiences, and ideas that drive value for the company.

Digital innovations are more disruptive and volatile; therefore, the effective innovation leaders must have both soft leadership qualities and hard business and technology expertise, with strong focus, perseverance and capabilities of doing the opposite of the crowd with confidence.

9. Innovation Performance Measurement

KPIs are critical to the test-and-learn process for innovation.

Innovation is about how to implement creative idea and achieve its business value. As say is going: One can only manage what it's being measured. It is also true for innovation management as well. However, due to the 'creative' nature of innovation and dynamic trait of digitalization, do KPIs kill innovation? It takes wisdom and practices to craft the right set of KPIs in order to stimulate digital advancement and manage innovation project more effectively. Innovation performance tools and metrics can help companies think systemically about business innovation.

- **Having in-depth understanding the innovation 'HOW' before measuring**: You need to know:

    (a) How company is performing in bringing new ideas (Inputs) and what are the sources of innovation, etc.

    (b) How company is processing the existing and new ideas that it is getting as inputs and how innovative are the process.

    (c) And then, how company is bringing the ideas into reality more related to commercialization, here it also deals with profits, learning etc (Outputs). So overall, company innovation performance can be measured around these three parts.

- **KPIs to focus on both innovation objectives and desired behaviors**. Further, before performance indicators are designed, the necessary and complete set of desired behaviors should be clearly established. If performance measures are to have the required impact, all of these behaviors should be assessed effectively. Otherwise, the behaviors that remain invisible will be sacrificed to raise scores on others that are being closely watched. A "good" KPI is judged both by its connection (even loosely or qualitatively) to the business objectives and by the behaviors it reinforces (or in some cases, discourages). But the even better KPIs are the ones that have been developed to positively reinforce desired behaviors.

- **KPIs metrics for the test-and-learn innovation process**. The starting point is to define what you want to measure to improve the innovation process; focus on thinking, effort and resource allocation. What's important is for the business to acknowledge that new KPIs, germane to the initiative, may need to be established and that these may fall outside current cultural norms and scorecard comfort zones. Likewise, for the process to be meaningful, it's vital that one is actually measuring and reporting KPIs, as opposed to just metrics. Pay more attention to dark side of KPIs, which discourages you to make mistakes. To quote Tagore "Where the mind is without fear and head is held high" for the river of reasoning to measure KPIs.

- **Quality of ideas as an innovation measurement**: Quality of ideas is measured by how well your ideas satisfy customer's desires and how much of the idea space your ideas cover. Innovative businesses have connected their funnel for collecting ideas (which consists of their own tools like portals, ideation platforms, social networking platforms and so on) with the product development process. All the ideas collected through this funnel pass through an automated filtering and then through a manual process of selection that qualifies ideas. The collected ideas then pass through business case preparation process. Some companies employ certain effective techniques like design factory method at this point and the results of this stage are then processed through regular design. In short, following are the steps:

  - Idea collection (funneling through multiple sources)
  - automated filtering of ideas (basically for elimination of the most obvious non-candidates)
  - manual assessment/filtering
  - business case preparation and validation
  - regular product development / design / product engineering

- **Personal innovation index**: Next step to drive the business growth and to increase creativity and innovation within a company is to introduce the Personal Innovation Index (PÏ). In relation to this index, the PÏ will indicate, top-down, the contributed economic value of each employee (executive/management, professional/expert) in relation to their innovative initiatives and personal activities, commitment, influences, impact and contributions. This indicator represents the innovation maturity level of an employee based on the personal impact and influences on innovation, the ability to innovate, the ability to network externally, the ability to integral innovation and the ability to accelerate operational processes.

- **Performance of delivering the ideas as another innovation measurement:** An organization's innovation performance could be measured in terms of its ability to convert the ideas that enter the 'Innovation Pipeline' into the desired output, propositions, process improvement, etc. Obviously, the performance of the pipeline depends on the quality of the ideas entering it and the organizational mechanics that evaluate and implement the ideas. Simple metrics can be applied to measure the performance of the pipeline at each stage. This would allow an organization to tune its processes to enhance the performance of the pipeline and measure the performance improvement or decrease. Innovation Quotient is the percentage of the total idea space covered by your products and designs. There are several types of Innovation Quotient to measure different aspects of the quality of ideas. For example, Vitality Index measures the contributing value of your new products or innovations as either revenue or preferably profit to your overall value, % of new product/service contribution to total value.

- **Pipeline metrics**: Once the innovation has progressed past a certain level of risk and uncertainty, it's gradually mainstreamed into the normal project pipeline. This may mean that it breaks into multiple projects owned and funded by different groups with the innovation team providing program management and oversight. But it ultimately becomes "just another project." Then track the ROI for reporting and keep the fingers on achieve the result:

New Users + New Product/Service =	Breakthrough/ Disruptive innovation
Existing Users + New Product/Service =	Evolutionary/Service Innovation
New Users + Existing Product/Service =	Product/Service Extension
Existing User + Existing Product/Service=	Product/Service Improvement

Table 10: Innovation Formulas

Given the dynamic nature of any organization and the complex mix of its resources, a well-defined standard set of innovation performance metric would need to be considered in better measures of innovation success, such as revenue sustainability, increase in knowledge, impact on brand reputation, customer satisfaction and loyalty, price elasticity, even attractiveness as an employer.

10. Innovation Risk Management

Innovation risk management needs to be innovative as well.

Innovation is a systematic way of applying creativity in the real life and business, it takes disciplines to manage both opportunities and risks; but what are the characteristics of an innovation risk management framework?

- **Flexible and applicable framework**: The innovation risk management framework would need to be flexible and applicable to a dynamic situation, where strategies are changing frequently and innovation in its basic nature is a high risk area; more often you are doing something that hasn't been done before. It follows that the primary focus of the risk management process would be to identify and control those risks that can be addressed, such as financing, market understanding, competitor analysis, identifying the space of opportunity, defining the scalability of the product, what timescale to allow before making a go or no-go decision.

- **Focus**: Innovation risk management framework needs to provide focus, level of details and tailored solutions for managing risks, the fact that innovation is defined across areas: There is claimed to be innovation in music, innovation in language, innovation in thought ... Therefore an innovation risk management strategy and framework must have focus, level of detail and meet the needs of the specific user of any such strategy toward the applicable innovation process he/she seeks to manage risk within, products, services, processes, and even in non-conventional areas outside of Product and Technology (P&T).

- **The next practice**: Innovation risk management is always looking for next practice, not 'best practice'. Companies compete on innovation, and depending on the company's position in the marketplace, regardless of how long they have been in business, they may be forced to take risks that others would not take to meet shareholders' expectations. It is inherently difficult to convince a company to adopt a defensive stance, or adhere to new codified precautions, in an offensive facet of their business. Innovation Risk Management means stepping away from the accepted "best practice" and asking whether a fundamentally different approach would provide more flexibility, more sensitivity, and more responsiveness.

The business competitiveness is catalyzed by innovation, and their innovation is catalyzed by their ability to "systematize" innovation. An effective innovation risk management will enable businesses to manage their innovation life cycle more confidently and systematically. Innovation risk management would be a trimmed down version of the status quo that focuses on the essentials. Innovation risk would also broadly need to consider both endogenous and exogenous drivers, and may not necessarily be best addressed by a lot of the formal ERM-Enterprise Risk Management standards, because innovation can be destructive, empowering, or even systemic, etc. in addition to its dynamic nature, etc. Therefore, innovation risk management needs to be innovative as well.

11. Digital Innovation Practice #1: Systematic Innovation

The Spark of innovation needs a framework to shine through and focus upon.

Innovation capability is strategic in digital organizations today. Accessing innovation capability of any organization requires a systematic approach. Innovation often has a lot to do with external circumstances, and people tend to focus on internal circumstances. But just because innovation is greatly influenced by external circumstances, it doesn't mean the innovation system of the organization is or should be unstructured. The robust processes and tools that enable any entity generate winning concepts on the consistent basis, is the prerequisite for sustaining advantage and growth.

- **"Systematic Innovation"**: It is a structured process and set of practical tools used to create or improve product/service/process that delivers new value to customers or satisfy employees. A systematic approach is to depict innovation as a system rather than a traditional process, whose performance depends on the alignment of its various components (people, actions, controls, resources, etc.). Organizations should ideally have a sustainable approach to innovation: The companies who get the most from innovation effort have the right ambition, good leadership and culture.

- **Innovation stages**: Innovation can be viewed as consisting of many different stages, some of which are more structured than others. For instance, creativity stage is generally accepted to be less structured than development stage. The latter is likely to be far more 'process driven' than the former. However, regardless of how structured stages of innovation are, stakeholders possess mental models (faulty as they may be) of 'how' innovation works in their ways. The key point is that the ideas being generated need a spark of creativity. But even here many innovations can arise from combining old ideas. Finally, while organizations can innovate without clear systems of innovation, the ability to achieve sustained innovation results probably does require at least some degree of a 'hard-wired' innovation system.

- **Visualization**: Visualization is crucial in innovation strategizing. Organizations find it difficult to depict or visualize innovation simply because it is difficult to visualize when innovation discussed in the abstract. Management can't just pick an optimum innovation strategy off a shelf and run with it. Neither can it just copy one from the firm next door. Instead, it must design a strategy that fits its own situation. But design requires an ability to articulate and reflect, which both are greatly assisted by visualizations. Visualization is crucial yet largely overlooked in innovation strategizing.

- **Multi-faceted nature**. Innovation in organizations is multi-faceted: Adhere to a broad definition of innovation (designing and implementing new and useful things, business model, process, etc.), then quite clearly, there are many avenues to get there. It is therefore unsurprising that people in organizations will consider only the parts of the process they understand and consider relevant to them. To depict innovation could be pretty difficult since it is mainly related to human being. In fact, as living people adapt themselves progressively to the various present and future situations when systemized processes enable to update themselves without the human touch.

- **In-depth understanding**: The systematic Innovation is based on the in-depth understanding business issues. Innovation process could be very loose on purpose, what is very rigorous and systematic is the analysis of the original business problem, product issue, opportunity, marketing dilemma, etc. The ability to innovate is ultimately dictated by the depth of understanding of the problem or issue to be resolved. It's the important step to identify, understand and evaluate the opportunities where important problems need to be solved or critical jobs need to be done (satisfying important customer needs), and then, the practice for systematic innovation can focus on translating from the innovation system to the business process.

- **Culture ready**: To develop a systematic innovation, you need to have the organizational culture correct underneath - many companies can put in place a good systematic approach in process terms, but if the underlying culture doesn't support risk-taking, collaboration, learning (often most via "failure") and self-empowerment, then it's very difficult to get the best out of the process. Get the two together, and it's the way you go. Innovation is a learning process that is vital for the organization as well as the individuals. Innovation generates value, both economic and social value. It opens up new possibilities of combining existing competencies in new ways that can form new capabilities as a stepping stone for doing more of the unexpected creative stuff.

- **Five key elements in systematic innovation**: "People" are the most important element in the mix. "Innovation" is a result of at least five main elements: Strategy, culture, people, process, and tools. These are important elements and missing only one of them will severely influence the sustainability of any intentional innovation effort. A structured approach with all key elements will improve the inventive thinking and the consistency of the innovation results by an order of magnitude.

Innovation is a journey and therefore it is not possible to pre-describe how it will work out, it involves luck, trial and error, groping, curiosity, experimentation, research, applying structured methods, tools, reviews, systematic analysis, debugging. It also requires a lot of listening and an enormous amount of convincing power. Still, a systematic approach can increase the chance to lead innovation success on the consistent basis.

12. Digital Innovation Practice #2: Customer-Centric Innovation

The more customer-facing the innovation, the higher the customer satisfaction would be.

One of the key characteristics of digital business is customer centricity. Thus, customer is absolutely a vital part of the overall innovation process. Customer-centric innovation accomplishes far more than incremental product improvement, it can also build evolutionary business models, as well as path-breaking products and services that establish new categories, and even internal process improvements arise from customer-centric innovation.

- **Proactive listening:** The customer (including prospects) should be studied and observed, innovators can use more inductive approach to gain deep understanding of what the customer wants to accomplish "next." This is where pro-active listening is very important and becomes vital link in innovation management efforts. It is not a question of whether the customer is right or not, it is more of whether you are truly and proactively "listening" to their needs. This involves gaining a deep understanding of the motivational construct of the customer through empathy and observation, in order that the innovator can become "anticipatory" of what the customer will likely "want next." Remember innovation must prove its value in the market. Customers must be willing to pay for this, be it product, process or service innovation. Thus, customers become important link in the innovation process.

- **Multi-dimensional view**: The customer should always be involved, but not be the main or the only driver behind the innovation process. The customer is only one of the stakeholders in the innovation process, certainly an important one, but not the final decision maker. As customers don't always know what they want and aren't always best informed. This is particularly the case with revolutionary innovations, and most especially when it comes to new technological innovations. That's why it is important to think when talking about innovation, not purely about technological advancements or breakthrough innovations, but also about different propositions, approaches to a problem or new interpretations. These can be achieved with empathy, looking beyond the direct customer problem, wish or request, taking the context into account and perhaps by using a wide network of experts to come up with these new propositions.

- **Customer involvement**: When manage innovation life cycle, customer involvement at all stages often elicits highly valuable information. In the innovation process, it is not really about whether the customer is "right." This kind of approach implies that the customer should be placed in a judgmental role, rendering a decision about an idea. Actually, this is not the best way to approach innovation. Instead, customers may not always know the "products" they want, but they clearly understand their needs and pains, so involve them as early as possible in the process. Customers cannot solve your problems for you, but insight into their goals, their process, their problems and their context is invaluable.

For a customer driven innovation, customers are major focus for innovation process and accomplishment. Listen to customers and involve them in the innovation process to gain insight and empathy, and then, innovators is to figure out how to solve the puzzle presented by differences between what is verbalized, what is acted out, and what is technically feasible.

13. Digital Innovation Practice #3: Open Innovation

Open innovation starts with an open mind-set and disciplined approaches.

Open Innovation in its simplest form is that a company recognizes the benefits of working with others to stimulate innovation. Is it too broad as a term or is it too vague as a concept? Is it a democratization of creativity, or just a cheap way for companies to underpay for good ideas? Here are more perspectives upon open innovation:

- **Crowd-sourcing for problem-solving**: The idea behind open innovation is that the problem, challenge, and brief are put out for anyone to apply or contribute. It can involve bringing in ideas from outside - from lead users (the ones that have passion and information to share), from wider user-community to drive features and understand the value-in-use of a product and service; or working with key suppliers or universities to innovate. You trust them and you both intend to learn and build knowledge. It can involve close-coupled relationships between organizations, with intent on exploring areas of learning that fit strategically for both companies.

- **Idea management**: At the heart of innovation is a life cycle of idea generation, interaction, selection and learning. The point of open innovation is to increase the odds of finding the next great new idea. Open Innovation is about ensuring that business have access to the maximum number of potential good ideas for new innovative products. This means having a very good internal program and it also means sourcing a lot of ideas from external partners. The goal isn't to be cheaper and it isn't to be just democratized, it is to ensure that as many of the good ideas as possible to flow in. The more different types of people and organizations that you can focus on solving problems for your customers, the better result you may get. Open innovation can improve idea generation, increase interaction and inspire learning.

- **System process:** Open innovation always intends to produce knowledge that leads to some value for those involved. Therefore, it can be a good thing. The goal of a good innovation program is not to minimize the expenses, but to maximize the chance to find the best idea and its market impact and profit. You will get different types of ideas internally and externally, and if you want to profit from both of them, you have to have a good open innovation platform, program and culture ready. Open innovation is more about the process - involving a wider stakeholder group, and everybody can vote and participate, but avoid these open innovation pitfalls as well:

- **Open Innovation pitfall #1: Lack of innovation cultures**. Most companies using or moving to open innovation often do not have the innovation culture ready for it, or they are not willing to spend money for change management needed. Mostly they spend a lot of money for their open innovation platforms. What's often missing is internal innovation culture to support these platforms and ideas coming from outside the company. "Open innovation mind-set" inside the companies is missing. It needs a complete new way of dealing with knowledge, willingness of sharing ideas and knowledge, etc.

- **Open Innovation pitfall #2: Lack of systematic processes**: Open innovation is sometimes overrated and often used as an excuse for not having an effective and efficient innovation process, and getting the "closed" innovation onto the market. Most of the companies are not prepared for open innovation, but believe it is a cheap way of getting fresh ideas and solutions from outside; they may see it as "outsourcing of ideation", but forget about the systematic innovation processes needed to be successful and profitable at the end.

Open innovation often is seen as the "holy grail" and solver of all the problems companies may have in new product development, etc. Open innovation is an important part of an innovation strategy, but it is just one methodology out of many for generating innovative ideas. If a company doesn't have a good internal innovation culture, it is going to struggle to get much value out of open innovation.

14. Digital Innovation Practice #4: Radical Innovation vs. Incremental Innovation

Incremental innovation is actually a critical part of breakthrough or disruptive innovation.

There are two types of innovations: (a) Radical innovation, which may be classified as Breakthrough or Disruptive, and (b) Evolutionary innovation, which has two components - Incremental and Spiral. Breakthrough Innovation and Incremental Innovation are not separated items, but it's rather a continuous line that it goes from innovations that break a market or create a new one to the simplest continuous improvement.

- **Radical Innovation is better with greater ROI, but with much greater risk.** Incremental innovation can be as rewarding as the initial breakthrough, especially if the incremental is based on a breakthrough technology you increase and create value. Research identifies the projects that ultimately break new ground frequently are fraught with uncertainty in many dimensions: technical, market, resource and organizational uncertainties abound. This requires them to be managed with a whole different approach: Processes that are fine tuned to deal with uncertainty, but not stomp it out immediately; metrics that take uncertainty into account; team members that thrive in conditions of ambiguity;

and a culture that is dramatically different from the operational excellence orientation that dominates incremental innovation.

- **Radical innovation differs from incremental innovation in number of ways**.

Incremental Innovation	Radical Innovation
Incremental innovation always starts with a small objective or aim to achieve.	Breakthrough innovation starts with a problem, having no solution in current situation .You know what you want, but do not know how.
Incremental innovation generally brings short term value additions or competitive advantage.	Radical innovation differs from incremental innovation to be a "game changer." Generally speaking, radical innovation is disruptive and will change your organization in many fields.
More often, incremental is top-down planning. It could either be functional or based on features, the final outcome or results of the "innovated" product or process is that it should be "better in terms of quality, faster in terms of its delivery capacity and cheaper in terms of cost."	Breakthrough innovation is most of the time bottom-up process. You need new technology, new processes, new consumers, new knowledge, and maybe a new business model. All that makes them very risky, but on the other hand, you will get very great chances and opportunities for new product lines, platforms, etc. They will need them in strategic long range view.

Table 11: Incremental Innovation vs. Radical Innovation

- **Out of box thinking vs. Inside of box thinking**: Radical Innovation is "anything new to businesses," really original; purist calls it "new to the world," something that no one else has done before. Incremental innovations fit into your core competencies and your core business. They are enablers to run your current business in a better way. Breakthrough Innovation is a radical new approach that leaves competition behind in some way. It's out-of-the-box thinking where incremental innovation is still inside the box thinking. Incremental innovation is what is used after the breakthrough to "touch" things up a bit. It is much more predictable, often the result of optimization efforts on the product or process. Radical innovation is the new s-curve, which mostly requires new technology. For incremental innovation, it is the improvement of existing technology. Breakthrough innovations, the radical changes, require cross-functional senior leadership commitment most of the time. Projects cross budget boundaries in the corporation can often interfere with pre-determined individual targets. These types of changes require a more thorough process to prototype, filter, test in a real world scenario, and ultimately add to the existing "new demand" project processes.

- **Revolutionary vs. Evolutionary**: Incremental innovation is evolution -improvement or change to something that already exists. Breakthrough innovation is revolution -something new that disrupts or replaces something else. Evolutionary innovations can be either incremental or spiral. Breakthrough innovation might be thought of as an initial innovation in an area, possibly the one that shows innovation is possible or gives a new route. Perhaps it is a major discovery regarding the area. It is generally not so predictable and may require a lot of luck, or advanced knowledge in one or more areas to accomplish. In incremental development, the end-state requirement is known, and the requirement will be met over time in several increments. Incremental innovation is also triggered and limited by the past, or something that already exists. On the other hand, breakthrough innovation is in the future with no necessary continuity with the past. Radical innovation can disrupt the industry. The differentiation between incremental and breakthrough innovation relates to the degree to which a particular innovation changes the competitive landscape, and potentially make entire industries obsolete, as digital photography did to the film industry. Innovation involves many steps: The generation of an idea, the demonstration of its feasibility, its implementation, its commercialization, and its diffusion. Those who study innovation find it helpful to differentiate between these stages. In some cases an incremental innovation in one area may be hailed as a breakthrough in another area.

- **Four key components of breakthrough innovation:** Innovation is the successful implementation and adoption of creativity or invention. There are cases where incremental innovation has resulted in breakthrough impacts. Perhaps the terms should be used in the context of the desired outcomes rather than as process descriptions or technological developments. Breakthrough implies a distinction in innovative solution at any type of innovation. Breakthrough innovations have four key components:

  (1) Takes advantage of emerging trends.
  (2) Provides for basic human needs.
  (3) Uses simple business models.
  (4) Build barriers to entry – by combining different choices about target markets, offerings, channels, and partnerships, breakthroughs are not easy.

- **Businesses need to build a balanced portfolio of innovation projects**, across the matrix of three types of innovation (process, product/service, business model) and three degrees of innovation (incremental, substantial, breakthrough). Managing this portfolio should be integrated with the annual strategic planning process and financial investment model. The size and mix of the innovation project portfolio depends upon the business situation, strategic objectives and severity of external challenges/changes. Generally, all businesses should have a handful of "bets" in the breakthrough category. What's important when developing the mix is to make sure:

(1) You're accepting risk for potential reward.
(2) You aren't ignoring specific types of innovation.
(3) Innovation is benefiting the widest possible audience within your organization.
(4) You aren't sacrificing the long-term viability of the portfolio for short-term rewards.

To put it another way, breakthrough changes how things are being created, and incremental improvements reinforce it. It's a continuous life cycle to manage innovation and achieve its business values.

15. Digital Innovation Practice #5: Corporate Entrepreneurship

Innovation is the only bridge to mind digital gaps.

Many established large organizations are struggling with innovations, due to the lack of culture of innovation or the internal business capability and capacity to support it. However, innovation is the only bridge to mind digital gaps. Especially for business model innovation, it runs up against a "not now, later" obstacle. As a digital business leader, you know you may be vulnerable and should do something, but you also know that, by definition, such innovation will be disruptive to the current business. So what are the strategies and methodologies to advocate business model innovation? Can corporate entrepreneurship be seen as a business model innovation?

- **Continuous adaptability**: Innovation culture cultivating and capacity building is a long journey, not a short fry in the pan. Leading organizations are not waiting until there is an immediate pressing task. Leaders realize that continuous adaptability is necessary in a continuously changing world. It will be disappointing for those who wait until the last moment of strategic or tactical tasks and then expect innovation to be forthcoming magically, but come up short. For strategic innovation, the leadership team has to become involved in that capacity construction.

- **"Visual thinking"**: Visualization enables people to bridge between the innovations of tomorrow with the business realities of today. The more tangible the innovation becomes in a visual form; the more it becomes evaluated on the execution alone. However, it's quite another level of challenge to develop visual thinking skills, the ability to see object-relationships and the ability to see object-relationships morphing through space-time are both marketable skills. Visual thinking is also the ability to see the "gaps" between object relationships and map these into the future.

- **Horizontal approach**: Road-mapping the future has much to explore through horizontal approach, such as portfolio mapping, scenario making and resource allocation. The 'art' of comparing and contrasting makes for great ways to inform, but so many organizations lack a focused view on competitors, changing situations, alternative solutions, and without such 'collective' place to gather around, you can't hold conversations around how their own set of propositions might evolve or is lagging behind.

- **Digital business model innovation**: Can corporate entrepreneurship be seen as a business model innovation, because if an established firm identifies a new value proposition that requires a change on the business model or the creation of a new one, then it's strategically safer to develop an independent venture. If this is so, you could say that every corporate venture comes with a business model innovation for the firm, but not all business model innovations need to become new ventures. The corporate entrepreneurship activities can improve organizational growth and profitability and, depending on the company's competitive environment, their impact may increase over time.

- **Culture of innovation**: Corporate entrepreneurship is embodying risk- taking, pro-activeness and radical product innovations. Corporate entrepreneurship has been recognized as a potentially viable means for promoting and sustaining organizational performance, renewal and corporate competitiveness over the past three decades. The empirical evidence is compelling that corporate entrepreneurship improves company performance by increasing the firm's pro-activeness and willingness to take risks, and by pioneering the development of new products, process and services through enriching its competitiveness. The entrepreneurial activities help companies to develop new businesses that create revenue streams. Corporate entrepreneurship activities also enhance a company's success by promoting product and process innovations.

- **Three challenges in corporate entrepreneurship:** The creation of corporate entrepreneurship activity is difficult, since it involves radically changing internal organizational behavior patterns. Many studies have attempted to understand the factors that accelerate or impede corporate entrepreneurship, which examined the effect of a firm's strategy, organization and external environment. It appears that the environment plays a profound role and influencing. There is consensus that the external environment is an important antecedent of corporate entrepreneurship. As a distinctive features of new businesses present three challenges:

  (1) First, emerging businesses usually lack hard data. That's particularly true when they offer cutting-edge products or when their technologies aren't widely diffused in the marketplace.

(2) Second, new businesses require innovation, innovation requires fresh ideas, and fresh ideas require mavericks. But many leaders are trapped by conventional thinking.

(3) The third challenge is the poor fit between new businesses and old systems. That's particularly true for budgeting and for human resource management.

There is no such universal way to do innovation; Innovation is the process of commercializing, not just coming up with ideas. The latter is actually in abundance - the entrepreneurial and intrapreneurial ability to deliver it. The creation of corporate entrepreneurship is to boost both soft success factors like culture and hard success ingredients like innovation, capability and capacity, in order to drive the business's long-term success.

16. Digital Innovation Practice #6: Collaboration-Based Innovation

Digital hyper-connectivity can foster innovation through collaboration.

Capitalism and innovation always has and always will be about collaborating and connecting; across the organization and outside of it. It's about having conversations that create something new, and being prepared to change what you are doing, not just "falling in love" with your idea. Digital technologies catalyze the age of engagement and collaboration. More often than not, innovation is a team work, not individual effort, and the effective approach to foster innovation is through talent engagement and social collaboration.

- **Sense of belonging.** Collaboration does create a sense of belonging. Collaboration is a fundamental part of what ultimately fuels the inspiration, imagination and innovation! Management must be supportive of any innovation or collaboration thrust, and teams must "own" their goals, also allows a team-member to "belong" and its team leader to learn, motivate, and persist.

Part of the innovation capability coherence comes through the sense of ownership, which is different from managers "owning" their people. Identifying shared goals is a crucial collaboration success factor, collaboration not only propels innovation, but it's the heart, soul, and DNA of innovation.

- **Hyper-connectivity**: Hyper-connectivity can foster innovation through collaboration. In other words, try to digitally connect key resources and assets in their vicinity or context to the resource rich innovation hubs and clusters across the business ecosystem. In doing so, you can create the collegiality and "shared context for learning." That, in turn, should lead to "inspirations" which will further fuel more collaboration in innovative projects and enterprises nascent to their communities or environments. In addition, innovation must be a multi-disciplinary effort. The innovation collaboration teams embrace multiple disciplines, and understand how systems work, and this yielded competitive advantage.

- **Cognitive diversity**: Diversity with cognitive difference can stimulate innovation. Since innovation is fundamentally about breaking assumptions, having more assumptions uncovered will lead to greater innovation. As we bring more people into the dialog, we increase the probability of those various assumptions surfacing as each person filters different things. Of course, that only works if those people are somewhat different from one another. Collaborating with entirely like-minded people probably won't yield results. The more diversified the team is, the more innovative the collaboration can turn to be.

- **Social innovation**: It is excellent to bring social media to this realm, to urge a sense of connection via virtual "conversations" beyond the confines of a blighted neighborhood. Organize around the vision and create new context for it. You are already having an impact. But consider starting new conversations that galvanize inspiration and gain traction on a powerful theme of renewal and growth. One other point: collaboration and innovation based learning needs patience and strategic support from management.

- **Intellectual harmony**: Collaboration-based innovation is built upon the intellectual harmony among humans (not clones), and it is a system that is not scalable or replicable. Every collaborative team will be different and hence produce different results. So, if you have a group that is doing exceptional work, it would behoove the company to maintain the balance of that group for as long as possible. If the collaboration is not bearing fruit, then by all means upset the apple cart and start anew. Find your own balance and you will find your innovation.

- **Innovation thinking**: Collaboration in the business and world requires a much higher degree on innovative thinking than competition and winning. It is easy to work alone and take the attitude of competition, but it is much more difficult to collaborate with different parties even competitors. Sharing is about innovative compromise. Win-win needs a lot of innovative effort. Recent neuroscience research has shown that our entire experience with our world is subjective, passing through numerous unconscious filters before we become aware of what we are seeing, hearing, or understanding. As a result, no individual has a complete view of what is really happening around him or her. Therefore, winning in the global economy means engaging innovative thinking, and strong collaboration.

Organizations build the enhanced integration capabilities to support connections and interactions between individuals and communities, between employees and information assets, and to facilitate enterprise innovation activities in all of their possible combinations. The rise and advance of enterprise social technologies has the potential to dramatically alter the business information landscape and the organizational ability to more effectively innovate either through incremental or radical way.

17. Digital Innovation Practice #7: Hybrid Innovation

The hybrid nature of innovation is a combination of something old with something new, with the mixed portfolio of incremental innovations and radical innovation.

Innovation is a management discipline, just like many other key elements in businesses today, such as leadership, culture, process, or technology, etc., hybrid is the digital fit style for managing innovation. Managing innovation requires leaders, either formal or informal, to shepherd an idea through several phases of development, knowing when to move forward and when to return to an earlier phase. More specifically, what is hybrid innovation and how to manage it effectively?

- **Hybrid nature**: It is hard to think of any innovation as not a hybrid, a combination of something old with something new or a number of new things. Probably, the more hybrid, the more old familiar things are combined, the less likely is any disruption, although all innovations are disruptive of someone or some behavior to some degree. You could consider all innovation as hybridized in that sense. That's precisely why it is an orthogonal concept to disruption.

- **Creative destruction:** Innovation is creative because it represents a new way of doing things and it could be destructive because it makes previously valued skills or competitive advantage less demanded, with the potential of becoming obsolete. Disruptive innovation is the most important concept in innovation because it can be demonstrated that virtually all real economic growth is driven by disruption. Disruptive Innovation brings something new to the party; something that couldn't have been possible without innovation.

- **Incremental-radical innovation continuum**: The incremental innovation always starts with a small objective or aims to achieve incremental innovation generally; brings short term value additions or competitive advantage. Radical innovation starts with a problem, having no solution in the current situation. You know what you want, but do not know how to get there. Incremental innovation is much more predictable, often the result of optimization efforts on the product or process.

- **Innovation portfolio management:** Innovations in the digital age are coming at us at seemingly a much faster pace, more changes, more potential disruptions, but the patterns and rules of communication are pretty much the same. The broader the scope, scale and impact of the change, the more one leans toward calling such change an innovation. Some additional variables that might merit consideration are the scope, scale, and impact of the change. Significant innovations can catalyze organizational change. Innovation management does require not just interdisciplinary understanding to connect the dots and see what's possible, but also technical expertise to create the disruption, unless it is so simple that anyone could do it.

- **Hybrid (cross-disciplinary) knowledge:** The radical innovators are adept at seeing ways to transfer knowledge from one field to solve a problem in another. They may or may not have as great a volume of knowledge as some authorities (an industry insider, vested in the status quo) in a field. But they perceive a key error or gap in the conventional wisdom and a way to resolve it. A corollary to this view of expertise is something like the old 80/20 rule: Only 20% of the knowledge in some subject usually suffices to solve 80% of the problems. So, a radical innovator does not need to master all or most of a subject. Rather, he/she is skilled at gleaning only the essential knowledge that is relevant to the problems, which the authorities have either bungled or overlooked. So the innovation ability lies with those who can see the gap between what is currently available and what is possible. This is of course facilitated by road of the interdisciplinary knowledge.

Hence, in order to manage innovation portfolio effectively, you do need some form of framework and processes to ensure that you can qualify ideas and direct the right amount of resources or investment to the most promising idea based on its 'hybrid' nature, incremental or radical, but innovation management process needs to be rigorous, not too rigid.

18. Digital Innovation Practice #8: Innovation Agility – How to Accelerate Idea Validation

Innovation agility is a critical business capability to manage the innovation life cycle with speed.

Agility is the key characteristic of high-mature digital business. From innovation perspective, the idea evaluation is a critical part of successful new product or business development. The basic goal of idea evaluation should be to quickly and thoughtfully weed out potential projects that are not a good fit for your particular business, so you can focus on the good ideas and commercialize its potential business values. It is also an important aspect to enforce innovation agility.

- **Three innovation disciplines**: So to accelerate a process, you need to create an environment that brings together the people from the inside and outside walls of the company in a collaborative way: the various "innovation activities" they perform and the information that they need. By using the collective intelligence of your audiences (employees, customers, partners, etc.) in the three front end disciplines – ideation, knowledge sharing, and prioritization – you will be able to work much more efficient in bringing ideas to implementation.

- **Front-end process**: A paradox is that you have to get the new products or services to the market as fast as possible; as a result, you may run the risk of compromising the comprehensiveness of the work you do and sacrifice the quality to get a product out of the door quickly to meet a market need; or in the other case, you can make the most visionary products that has no market yet; therefore, it is important to use a front-end innovation process between strategy and concept development, experiment, prioritizing and measuring what to invest to "value" the early ideas and unmet needs.

- **Information-based idea validation:** Information may be one of the most time intensive pieces to the innovation puzzle. Information is growing exponentially and it is humanly impossible to explore all of the "art" out there around a subject or technology. Big data analytics may provide certain customer insight or product foresight for drawing the beams of innovation light. Following are some critical pieces of information needed for accelerating idea validation:

  (1) Facts about business ideas: definition, benefits and shortcomings, applications, and competing technologies.
  (2) Root causes of business problems need to be solved.
  (3) Components or operations of ideas, what can interact with ideas, and what parameters the innovative ideas might have?
  (4) Who else is using such new ideas? Who are the industry players? You also learn what the trend of such new idea is. Identify important technology trends, including potential next-generation innovation waves, as well as the key players who are involved in their development.

Hence, innovation agility is a critical business capability to manage innovation life cycle with speed; It's about to have a 'purpose' stay ahead of competition in the delivery process. It's about to be able to get all the way around the task, to capture all relevant information, to see it from all interests, and to use collective wisdom. It's about creating a structure that delivers what your need.

19. Digital Innovation Practice #9: Management Innovation

Management innovation has both hard elements such as process and metrics; as well as soft elements such as communication and culture.

Compared to product innovation, management innovation is perhaps more intangible but radical in driving digital transformation. As management innovation changes the way managers do what they do to improve organizational performance, where innovation is one of many management practices. Most companies renovate instead of innovate: what are the underlining problems? Does that mean management innovation is perhaps the new angle to see through innovation management?

- **Cross-functional collaboration is imperative for management innovation**: The biggest problem is that the entire company is structured and organized to produce what they currently produce and it is staffed primarily to keep the current business humming. It is very difficult to have "Big Innovation" efforts vie for the same resources needed for implementation, especially when they lack the hard, historical metrics that companies are used to applying for their decision-making. More specifically, due to the fear of failure, most companies renovate rather than innovate because of a lack of alignment between IT, Marketing, and the C-Suite; therefore, management innovation must take place. The problem is that in a lot of organizations, many departments think in a silo and operate independently of each other. In order to better understand a potential innovation, you require brainpower from all the right areas of expertise to contribute their thoughts on that innovation's feasibility. Once this process takes place, the talent in charge has bought into this new strategy and, with the collective knowledge of your company behind you, it's likely you can accelerate the implementation of this idea and achieve innovation management as well.

- **Management style, tradition, and corporate culture play an essential role**: Or to put it straight, what is management renovation or even disruptive management innovation? Management innovation can be very powerful; it really comes with personal risks as you get close to the "core of power and control." To achieve that, the right atmosphere shall be created and maintained. The main issues of such atmosphere are:

    (1) **No fear**: Because when fear is present, brilliant ideas wait for better times, or just diminish.
    (2) **Reward innovators**: The person that brought the brilliant idea is not responsible to persuading the management of why is it a good idea, because, most brilliant minds in innovation are not strong in organizational politics. The organization shall do that task and credit the person with thought of the brilliant idea.
    (3) **The support process**: The innovation only begins with brilliant ideas. The organization shall develop the idea to the point it is a product or service.

- **Problem-solving mind-set**: Both management innovation and innovation management starts with mind shift. Rather than see Innovation as a goal, it would be best to see it as a set of tools to be used to address specific business issues in running a healthy and growing business. Many companies set out to innovate before defining the role that innovation will play in the business as a whole and where it fits in the overall strategy. It also needs to align innovation strategy with the development of an innovative culture or business eco-system, which requires grounding in values, behaviors, systems and artifacts as well as collaboration with key stakeholders. The other thing is that organizations can't afford risk of not engaging in disruptive innovation. So the point is not to denigrate incremental improvements in favor of "breakthroughs", but how to achieve both. In ambidextrous organizations, this is achieved by careful innovation portfolio management. So, without management innovation, companies tend to renovate rather than innovate, making innovations in other areas like culture, technology, service etc, move very slow.

- **Create space for dialogue:** Management innovation means to create the space for dialogue, and accelerate innovation at the multitude of levels; and debate about why it is important for their organization, developing a common understanding of it, creating the necessity and motivation for it. Enterprises that are able to successfully innovate at a breakthrough level can increase the likelihood that they will dominate and prosper in new markets that they create. Enterprises that restrict themselves to incremental innovation, on the other hand, risk unknowingly entering a vicious cycle in which they lag farther behind. There are a few dominant obstacles that stand in the way of driving higher returns from innovation. The first challenge is a conservative approach itself, focusing on individual line extension renovation rather than developing a broader portfolio. Renovation can limit innovation to small incremental improvements and fail to result in significant step changes and revenue opportunities.

Management innovation includes multiple elements such as communication innovation, culture innovation, process innovation, and leadership innovation, etc, management innovation and innovation management will mutually enforce each other and achieve full business values.

20. Summary: Primary Trends in Next Level Innovation

Innovation is the art at the eyes of artist; the science at the mind of scientist; and the bridge between the art and science.

If information is lifeblood of businesses; then innovation is important because it is the heartbeat of any business; without it a company will cease to exist. But compare the upcoming digital era to the previous industrial era, is innovation becoming more important or less? Does the content or context of innovation stay the same or be different? Is innovation trying to reach the next level and, if so, what would it be?

- **Expanded digital scope:** At corporate level, innovation is no longer equal to R&D department, it can happen anywhere, anytime; it expands both horizontally and vertically. It's the state of mind to think and do things from a new angle; it is business's unique capabilities to gain competitive advantage in face of fierce competition and business dynamic today. Innovation becomes simply "creating value by solving simple or complex problems across digital ecosystem."

- **Enriched digital context:** Innovation has more enriched digital context today as well, it is the process that transforms novel idea or knowledge into business value. The output from the process is the innovation. The exercises of deciding within each organization just what innovation is are the single most critical activity of an innovation effort. Because how an organization orchestrates to generate ideas, manages the activities, measures the results, etc. is determined by how that organization has decided to craft the innovation effort. There are many areas within a company where the innovation process can be applied to create value, from communication innovation to culture innovation; from innovation management to management innovation; from process innovation to business model innovation, etc; the innovation context goes beyond the traditional new product or service improvement.

- **Customer-centricity:** One of the key characteristics of digital business is customer centricity. Thus, customer is absolutely a vital part of the overall innovation process. Customer-centric innovation accomplishes far more than incremental product improvement, it can also build evolutionary business models, as well as path-breaking products and services that establish new categories, and even internal process improvements arise from customer-centric innovation.

- **Reduced complexity**: In the end innovation complexity has to be reduced to actionable, overriding variables, which must be managed. Innovation is about reducing the complexity to identify those critical variables, which are context, project dependent. This is why it is important to have an innovation methodology versus selected case studies to emulate. Often the case studies do not address the critical variables at hand for the current project.

- **Cocreation:** The hyper-connectivity nature of digitalization can foster innovation through collaboration; and innovation must be a multi-disciplinary effort as well. The innovation collaboration teams embrace multiple disciplines, and understand how systems work, and this yielded competitive advantage. In doing so, you can create the collegiality and "shared context for learning." That in turn, should lead to "inspirations" which will further fuel more collaboration in innovative projects and enterprises nascent to their business environments.

Innovation is the core activity of digital revolution and human evolution. That is why innovation is important or even more important whereas technology becomes more advanced. Are we reaching the tipping point of new level of innovation flow yet? Companies have always had a flow of innovation, a flow sufficient for the needs of the company at that time. What has happened is that the flow from "before" is no longer sufficient to address the business challenges of today. Hence, the importance of innovation has increased and the speed also needs to be accelerated, as digital business has the pressure to get more and better innovation. At tipping point, the processes for innovation will catch up to the business need. By then the flow of innovation will have reached a new level, a level that can address the business challenges at VUCA digital dynamic.

Conclusion: Innovation is a story book that has exciting chapters, with serendipitous cover, which can be flipped over to the next level-the systematic digital innovations now, but it is a book that never ends.

Innovation is future	Without it, you lose sight of tomorrow. When innovation outside your organization outpaces innovation inside your organization, it is time to address factors influencing business velocity, business performance, profitability and customer preference. Look to and listen to your data, use it to help you drive innovation.
Innovation is life	It is a continuous journey of transformation. It brings new energy, forces you to be at your best at all times. It is an alpha; it is the beginning of all things. It is also timeless - for our minds will never stop.
Innovation is oxygen	As with humans and oxygen, businesses cannot survive without innovation. You must differentiate yourself in the marketplace. It is air we breathe, it is like water we drink, and it's a nature element to keep you alive.
Innovation is growth	It captures the essential element of any business and quality within every leader. Innovation is an exceptional, exclusive and realistic idea that separates you from others without a second thought.
Innovation is converting a problem into an opportunity	The wheel was an innovation that converted the problem of weight lifting and transport into so many vistas of innumerable applications.

Innovation is the heart for improvement	Do something in a new way. Innovation is "incremental value creation," leveraging simplistic or intricate ideas into reality. It's the unexpected synthesis of an idea, followed by a lot of commitment.
Innovation is a double-edged sword	Keep aware of it and use both edges to your advantage. Innovation is the creative idea or a quick, alternative way of solving existing problem with affordable price to customer. Innovation is doing the conventional task in unconventional, simpler, much more efficient way.
Innovation is to reinvent business, but not to reinvent the wheels	Innovation is about reinventing the business direction and purpose at any time. It defines strategy, profitability and relevance at any given time. If you do not, you become commoditized and just like so many others who offer the same product or service. Innovation allows one to standout and above the rest.

Table 12: Innovation Story Book

Innovation is curiosity, creativity, urge, inspiration, intuition, need and necessity, instinct, survival of the fittest and larger good simple brilliance, boldness, logic, rationality, out of box thinking, etc. All contribute to Innovation – from a new idea, to a new method, to a new product to a new way, a new business proposition, a new and better deployment of resources – another way to achieve better results.

CHAPTER 7

Digital Intelligence

We are moving slowly into an era where Big Data is the starting point – not the end.

We are approaching the digital dawn: the age of the customer. Companies that can promptly and effectively build core business capabilities based on digital intelligence in their organization will gain unique competitive advantage. All forward-looking organizations claim that they are information and technology businesses. A digital shift is a mind-set shift, which also comes with information shift, a shift that organizations will take advantage of information to gain knowledge and insight, a shift to drive culture and transformation toward a more intelligent enterprise, a shift from playing smart tools to being an intelligent business, it's about building such cohesive, agile and intellectual capabilities to adapt to the continuous change and unpredictable disruptions.

1. Information as Lifeblood of Digital Business

Digital means flow: Data flow, information flow, knowledge flow, and mind flow.

Data are abundant; here are some statistics: Every day, more than 2.5 quintillion bytes of data are created through a range of activities including social media posts, purchase transaction records, cell phone GPS signals, supply chain and logistics data, as well as digital videos, pictures, and audio recordings, with 90% of the world's data created in the past two years alone. Data production will be 44 times greater in 2020 than in 2009. The volume of business data worldwide is expected to double every 1.2 years. Individuals generate more than 70% of all data; enterprises store and manage 80% of these data. The average business expects to spend $8 million on Big Data-related initiatives this year. Hiring growth is part of this spending. It is estimated that for every IT job created in the United States to support Big Data efforts, three Big Data-related jobs outside of IT are being generated. This equals literally hundreds of thousands, potentially millions, of new jobs. Global spending on Big Data is growing at an average annual rate of nearly 30% and is expected to reach $114 billion in 2018. So what are further perspectives upon such information abundance, and can we decode of digital intelligence:

(1) Information Value: Data is raw, unorganized facts that need to be processed. Data is simple, random and unorganized; on the other hand, information is processed data. Information is structured and present facts in context to targeted situations and conditions that facilitate business in making the right decisions at the right time. Given this assertion, there is no limit to the value of information in digital economy.

- **Information only has a value when it has been used**. Different information is required at different points in the decision and operational delivery chain. When information has been used to make an informed management decision to develop the right product or service, enter a new market, exploit a new channel or use the information to conduct day to day operations that have an output value etc, the enabling value of information can be captured in such a way that an information lifecycle will be developed from it; then information can be managed more systematically to build a data-rich, intelligent digital business.

- **The value of information is qualitative, measurable, and defined uniquely:** Digital organizations must bring to the table innovative solutions that meet customers' needs, while reducing cost to market, without the sacrifice of strategic goals. If done well, information achieves its value. On the flip side, information is also something that can hinder the achievement of strategic objectives if it is unavailable, lost, stolen, or compromised. Information risks have some direct impacts on strategic objectives, but most impacts are operational. Therefore, it is treated with all the other operational risks to the business and mitigated accordingly.

- **Information is not isolated**: Information does not live alone, but permeates to everywhere in the digital businesses. Thus, the value of information is not isolated. The effort of valuing information independent of its association to the value of related tangibles seems to be difficult, if it is not futile exercise. But it's a worthy effort to understand the logic behind information "scenes": First, work to identify how information is associated with the valued tangibles of businesses, products and resources; like information flows in processes by example, then, its own value will become readily apparent and quantifiable by association.

- **Information has potential**: Potential value of information depends on how the information will be used again in the future and this is often exceptionally uncertain. Information may never be used again or it may be used multiple times. Unless you can predict how it might be used again for tangible gain, it is difficult to evaluate its potential value. The art and science of information management is to optimize its usage and achieve its value as well as full potential.

(2) Information vs. Intelligence: The purpose of Information Management is to process raw data, abstract information from it, then gain knowledge and intelligence from abundance of information, in order to build a smart digital business:

Information	Intelligence
Information answers the questions	Intelligence questions the answers
Information is processed data	Intelligence is processed information
Information is a prerequisite for intelligence	But in order for you to recognize the information, you need intelligence
Information is what we know	Intelligence is what we do with what we know, it is actionable information
Information is a passive perceptual entity	Intelligence is an active cognitive entity
Information is just information without intelligence, or the right intelligence. The business success depends upon both	Intelligence is real-time wisdom, or wisdom is ultimate intelligence

Table 13: Information vs. Intelligence

(3) Intelligence is jewels on information crown of businesses: In the context of a business or organization, information is representation of organizational objects including human beings and processes. Intelligence is the understanding of the relationships between these objects, processes, patterns and derivation of associated value for the organization. The quality of intelligence depends greatly on the quality and quantity of information. If focused, the more we know, the more we can do. If not focused, we may know "everything" and still achieve nothing.

- **Information-intelligence-strategy**: Information is the grist for strategy; but it is intelligence that defines the strategy. With the introduction of information and application of intelligence, strategy may be developed, but execution is the stage even needs to have more real-time information and intelligence. In practical application, information is all that is used to create the intelligence that shapes strategy; as well as to test the results of strategy execution. Further, it is the aggregation and the assessment of the information that creates the intelligence required to define the rules that drive the business.

- **Intelligence as perceptional and cognitive ability**: Intelligence is to understand semantics associated with universal or worldly objects, and recognition of patterns in the universe and deriving value out of universal objects. Human cognition understands processes, but even processes need to be represented as objects for perception. So intelligence is your perceptual and cognitive ability to understand the objects and relationships or processes of entities of the world and recognize the patterns in them. Utilizing cognitive abilities to derive value for the betterment of human kind is intelligence, genius and wisdom.

- **Intelligence is nothing but the ability to solve problems:** Information is usually understood to be essentially "model-free" or just data. "Intelligence" implies the ability to make inferences or predictions from the information based on a model. Learning would go a step further, and implies actually adapting the model itself over time. Information is actionable; the issue of "actionable" is more a matter of whether intelligence generates value, rather than being a fundamental characteristic of intelligence. People or systems can be highly intelligent, but only when the intelligence translates into action is any value creation possible. Intelligence is your ability to solve problems. The larger or bigger the problem you solve in terms of its positive impact to the society, the more intelligent you are. And you can see how the breadth and depth of impact of such intelligence can have.

(4) Debunk digital intelligence code: WISEPRICARD: The abundance of data and information brings both significant opportunities and enormous risks in business today, as organizations can harness the power of data to provide the business with a more fact-based vision of where to aim and how to get there, through identifying the right data, validating it and communicating it to right people at the right time. Along the journey, many organizations intend to decode digital intelligence and move up the maturity curve from knowing "what happened" to "why did it happen" (with root cause) to what will happen (capture the trends).

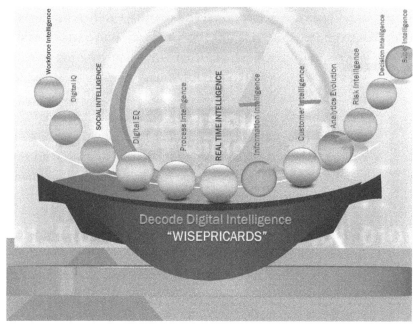

Figure 17: Decode the Digital Intelligence "WISEPRICARDS"

- **W –Workforce Intelligence**: Data-driven talent management will bring business leaders together across the organization to share their experience and insight wherever there is a GAP in the system, help streamline and identify root cause immediately. Integrating data-driven skills and tools into HR will challenge the organization to be more fact-based, objective and cost-effective.

- **I – IQ (Intellectual Quotient)**: Digital IQ is a measure of how well companies understand the value of digital technology and weaves it into the very fabric of their organization. The beauty of the increasingly digital landscape is that every single digital interaction that occurs brings fresh insights and outside-in perspective, analytics could be embedded directly into every key processes that drive the business and every touch point that optimize customer experience.

- **S – Social Intelligence:** The rapid increase in volume, variety and velocity of business information has changed how leading companies manage their compliance challenges and make social impact. Digital business is open and well-connected in the macro-social–ecological–technological environment, to create social value for community and society economically, culturally and environmentally.

- **E – EQ (Emotional Quotient):** Digital organization EQ means to have an ability to respond to emotions, the senses of people need to be engaged in organizational shifts, and cultivate a culture of innovation and learning, as culture is a socially transmitted process involving emotional values that drive core and sustainable business conversations, translate emotion into values driven goals and purposes, to achieve high performance result.

- **P –Process Intelligence:** With digital dynamic, it increasingly makes sense that business process intelligence and intelligent processes would be the choice for organizations that want to deliver the richest user experiences, as it can capture knowledge and provide a structure for collaboration and innovation.

- **R – Real-time Intelligence:** Real-time business intelligence compares current business events with historical patterns to detect problems or opportunities automatically. This automated analysis capability enables corrective actions to be initiated, or business rules to be adjusted to optimize business processes, and to improve availability or profits.

- **I –Information Intelligence:** Information Intelligence is business capability to manage data-information-knowledge-insight life cycle effectively, it also refers to a multidisciplinary approach to achieving organizational objectives by making the best use of knowledge in decision making across the organization.

- **C – Customer Intelligence:** Customer intelligence will gain insight upon analyzing customers' behaviors and shopping patterns, engage customers directly and on an ongoing basis to see how their goals are changing might be a good way to predict future behavior as well.

- **A – Analytics Evolution:** The evolutionary journey of data analytics reflects the trend moving from analyzing historical perspective into capturing business foresight, from operational perception to customer insight; from reactive intelligence to interactive intelligence.

- **R - Risk Intelligence:** Predictive Risk Analytics (PRA) intends to predict future event and gain foresight upon the potential business risks: What will happen? How to prevent the risks or what can be done to make business more resilient and well prepared for the possible disruptions.

- **D – Decision Intelligence:** Analytics is strategically important in guiding decision making, and decision intelligence becomes critical capability of an intelligent digital business. Either decision fast or decision slow; individual decision or group decision, it has to follow the decision principles, takes right information, organized process, efficient decision analytics tool, timely feedback, in order to make decision scenario more productive and effective.

- **S – Super intelligence through collective wisdom:** Collective intelligence is the emerging "super" business intelligence to overcome challenges and stretch business goals. The effectiveness of crowd-sourcing and brainstorming is that it enables you to bring a diverse population together and collectively pool of all the expertise at the discussion table, analyze as well as synthesize all sort of information from within and even outside of business boundary, and come out creative ideas or optimal business solutions with speed.

2. Workforce Intelligence

Data driven talent management will challenge the organization to be more fact-based, objective, and cost-effective.

An intelligent organization should have data orientation in anything they do, especially in talent management space, as people are the most invaluable asset in business, rather than following traditional subjective HR model, forward-looking organizations shall experiment, develop and mature data-driven talent management for leaping through digital transformation. Integrating data-driven skills and tools into HR will challenge the organization to be more fact-based, objective and cost-effective. Leverage analytics for global talent management planning, and well embed it into talent management strategy and key processes. Make sure you have an integrated infrastructure that makes these systems easy to use, secure, and available at all times.

- **Creating a vision and path for workforce analytics**: Data-driven talent management will definitely bring together leaders across the organizations to share their experience and insight wherever there is a gap in the system, and help streamlining immediately in identifying root cause, and give practical guidance for improving and ordering HR data as well as using it in creative ways to gain predictive insight and competitive advantage. Analytics-savvy organizations use a variety of internal and external data sources to make predictions about individual workers' actions and behaviors. Making decisions to identify, develop and retain talent relied on using data, analysis and intuition.

- Creating a vision and path for workforce analytics.
- Engaging workforce planning, deployment, development based on performance
- Doing social network analysis to improve effective communication and collaborative innovation.
- Embracing futuristic trend such as visualization and proactive presentation.

- **Balance of both data and intuition in decision making:** The organization should have the maturity to leverage and optimize the analytics or insights to make critical decisions, rather than looking as mere data and continue to launch and drive programs that operate as island. Data-based decision making may not completely replace the human decisions-making. You cannot actually deal with people-related decisions in the same way you do with engineering decisions. Human resources are related to people and people are not machines. Tools are innovative, important and useful, but they are intended for improving efficiency, adding value, making optimization or as a source of inspiration for new ideas. When it comes to managing people and to making human-related decisions, algorithms are not enough. There are a lot of additional parameters, correlations and context that should be taken into account. Talent-related decision is complex, using a blended, integrated approach with a selected set of data-driven tools and analytics capabilities will eventually provide competitive and operational advantages and support to the organization.

- **From talent controller to talent multiplier**: It will always take long term journey for identifying, attracting, developing and retaining the right people with the right capabilities at the right position, through Big Data, talent manager can recognize thought leaders, social influencers or domain experts more easily via their digital footprint and social influence; data analysis of employee and talent performances also allow experiments and feedbacks, make sure the right talent is on the bus at the right time. By creating an environment for people to come together, to interact, and to exchange different views on common topics of interest may create harmony, trust and eventually will benefit the organization.

- **Data-driven talent governance:** Talent managers start using data not just to monitor employees' behavior, but to ask or answer some hard questions that are at the heart of how employees contribute to business performance, predict employee preferences and behaviors, as well as tailor next practices to attract and retain talent. Develop predictive models and identify leading indicators to forecast business requirements and staffing requirements, track skills and performance, and maximize human capital investment. The data-driven approach in talent governance enables business to build effective indicators to get all the parties aligned to a common aspect for further discussions .When all parties agree with an open mind to look at something in common, it creates transparency, harmony and builds trust based culture over a period of time.

Workforce intelligence is crucial in long term business success, as people are still the most invaluable asset and capital investment in business today and tomorrow. Therefore, using a blended and integrated approach with a selected set of data-driven tools and analytics capabilities will eventually provide operational advantages and competitive uniqueness to the digital organization.

3. Digital IQ

Digital IQ is a measure of how well companies understand the value of technology and weave it into the fabric of their organization.

PWC's annual Digital IQ survey of nearly 500 business and technology executives in the United States confirmed that there is a fundamental transformation upon how information is used within the firm and in the marketplace.

(1) The definition of digital IQ: Digital IQ is a measure of how well companies understand the value of technology and weaves it into the fabric of their organization. An outside-in perspective is required to balance traditional thinking to better serving today's digitally empowered customers, employees, and business partners' will. It means turning your organization inside out to let in and accommodate the outside, market-driven trends being seeing in the global marketplace. Identified outside-in architecture, digital technology components, process components of the digital enterprise that affect how executives need to rethink their strategies:

New digital thinking:

(a) Everyone is mobile consumer
(b) Social media is a critical data source
(c) Moving business application to cloud can make firm more competitive
(d) Gain greater insight from business data by working from outside-in

Technology components:

(a) Mobility
(b) Social media
(c) Cloud
(d) BI

Process components:

(a) Strategic planning
(b) Mobilization
(c) Roadmap execution

(2) How can business raise digital IQ? Raising organizational digital IQ is critical; the way companies leverage digital technology and channels to meet customer needs as well as the needs of employees, and business partners will help you take full advantage of many of the recent changes in the global economy. In order to raise the digital IQ, executives should begin by framing the right questions. Growing digital IQ entails more than merely adopting the latest tools; it is about integrating technology into the way a company plans, innovates, measures results, interacts with customers and employees, as well as ultimately creates value in digital transformation:

- **Mobile**: <u>Are you prepared for the current and next generations of customer and employees, who are naturally adept with mobile devices?</u>

  A: To raise the firm's digital IQ, executives should take sharper focus on how to engage and support customers on their mobile devices. Put greater emphasis on creating mobile solutions for customers, engaging them wherever they are, and making it simple to do business with you. Remember that your employees are mobile customers as well.

- **Social**: <u>Do you have a social media strategy that extends past the marketing and sales functions?</u>

  A: The best companies integrate social media into their interactions with all their stakeholders. It helps adoption of change, it supports better, faster and more flexible work, anywhere you are at any moment of the day, it means you are connected not only to your department but also to the enterprise and to the outside world as well. From collaboration to social, it's more related to scale and scope, social means the abundance of collaboration in the broader environment with much faster speed. Customers can provide a wealth of information not only about their preferences, but how you can improve your products and services.

Social media should also play a role in corporate knowledge management and collaboration.

- **Cloud**: <u>Have you considered the role Cloud Computing will play in your next application replatforming?</u>

  A: Many firms are already starting to think about their next platform restructuring, and where their core systems will be managed. The cloud is an increasingly important part of the discussions. Those who think strategically will map out a cloud strategy that uniquely identifies the value proposition to the company and how cloud fits in.

- **Data Analysis**: <u>What sources of external information would most improve decision making and drive critical insight into operations?</u>

  A: Many firms still rely too heavily on only their internal data. Top performers understand that data is currency in today's marketplace. As a result, they are far more likely to be investing heavily in this area. Data provides opportunities to see relationships and correlations that offer access to new perspectives and new insights. But data analysis is not the end; it is a tool for end game, which is to make effective decisions.

- **Process digitalization**: <u>How much effort is applied to mapping out the process for and determining who will lead the execution of the firm's strategy?</u>

  A: Too many companies skip this critical stage in the process. Process underpins business capability. Digital business capabilities are more complex in design, with synthetic nature requiring cross-functional collaboration, embedding agility into processes for adapting to the changes, and the right set of unique digital capabilities directly decide the overall organization's competency, and how well they can make digital transformation, deliver the value to the customers and build long term winning position.

(3) The five behaviors that accelerate value from digital investments: If you want to boost your company's performance, redefine the way that digital capabilities are designed to ensure that the right decision makers and skill sets are engaged in idea development, designing, planning, estimating, and sourcing, raise your Digital IQ by developing these five behaviors:

- **CEO actively champions digital**. A digital CEO sets and steers the company's digital vision and addresses the inevitable challenges that come with new ways of doing business. CEOs must rethink the multiyear and annual planning processes to ensure that the proper questions are asked and answered at the right times to consider the potential of digital capabilities.

- **A strong CIO–CMO relationship**: Get explicit agreement between the CIO and CMO on who owns the initiatives, the role each leader will take on, and when and how they are expected to work together. Redefine the way that digital capabilities are designed to ensure that the right decision makers and skill-sets are engaged in idea development, designing, planning, estimating, and sourcing.

- **Outside-in approach to digital innovation**: Given the wealth of potential sources, outside-in innovation will generate a lot more potential ideas. It's crucial for companies to effectively filter and discern which emerging technologies will be the most disruptive to their unique company, market, and customers.

- **Significant new IT platform investments**: At what point in the strategic planning process does IT enter the discussion? Firms that put IT and its leaders at the heart of their strategies are more likely to be successful. Define the IT organization's role in planning, designing, sourcing, executing, and operating the new IT Platform. Determine and fill organizational skill gaps to realize and capitalize on the new platform.

- **View digital as an enterprise capability**: Do your parameters for successful execution include periodic measurement and a post rollout assessment of the overall value realized by the business? The company must begin broadening how they think about their digitally savvy resources, realizing that it is becoming essential to have a digital capability that is woven through business rather than only centralized in a single function and hidden in the shadows throughout the business.

With digital at the top of the agenda for nearly every company, raising Digital IQ becomes strategic imperative. It is about integrating "digital conversations" into every aspect of the business. The digital IQ surveys concluded that those with the strongest Digital IQ look to information technology for its power to alter business models and create new ones. Success in capturing value from digital investments starts with the senior executive teams and requires that company leadership agree on making digital an enterprise capability, then acting accordingly in everything they do. Those who do will reap the rewards; those who do not will fail to realize the expected returns from their digital investment.

4. Social Intelligence

Highly mature social intelligence touches every aspect of digital business nowadays.

Digital business is more open and well-connected with community and macro-social –ecological-technological environment, a business's reputation is no longer just the public relations department's job; customers and employees now have more voice and choice, the power to lift up your brand or thumb it down. Contemporary organizations need to build high mature social intelligence and create social value for business, community, and society economically, culturally, and environmentally.

More specifically, social analytics has been applied into almost every aspect of digital business:

- **Leadership**: Social activities and participation can help leaders sharpen strategic insight and extend strategic execution. As through social collaboration and collective wisdom, leadership can expand the tunnel vision, leverage collective insight, understand the future trend and what the customer need next, when executing it, social can amplify the positive leadership influence, enhance agile principles and improve communication and corporation.

- **Marketing:** Businesses are using social media, tool, and platform to improve customer relationship, monitor online customer behavior, create and support customer community and develop multichannel communications. Organizations start to use social analytics to make formerly invisible patterns of social interaction more visible; and apply such information to boost social engagement, find segmentations of populations with certain characteristics and understand their impact on others or what turns into certain actions such as purchasing, collaboration, and encourage behavior changes, with the ultimate goal for performance management.

- **Competitive intelligence**: Companies are using social analytics to monitor brand sentiment. But it goes beyond understanding what is being said to understanding who is saying it, what their influence networks are and where it is being said. The business also intends to understand where their competitors are getting negative sentiment. Social analytics enables business to track competitor on social media, and understand how competitors are leveraging social platforms for brand promotion or customer engagement.

- **Crowd-sourcing**: Innovative organizations are using social to source new ideas and refine current products or services, to manage different types of innovation, such as sustainable innovation, efficiency innovation and disruptive innovation in a more systematic way. Technically, crowd-sourcing through social platform is more critical to fuel ideas and contribution, provides inputs on customer preference, predict future trend, and capture collective insight.

- **Social influencers**: Social analytics helps pinpoint who knows what within or even beyond your organization, based on social influence and action rather than assertion, allow organizations to identify the strength of these relationships and how information flows within the groups, as well as enable companies to target group influencers who can best affect decisions.

- **Customer intimacy**: Social analytics takes track of customers' online activities, and interpreting customer sentiment; it has become a powerful tool for creating intimate and stronger relationship with a wider range of customers. Advanced social analytics can help organization collect feedback, analyze context and quickly draw inference from unstructured social media or enterprise data, and convert them into actionable customer insight. Doing so can be a catalyst for conveying the information and insights from social software and social analytics back to frontline employees themselves.

- **Operational excellence**: Social business allows knowledge or information to flow more seamlessly cross functional silos. The real impact of making the invisible visible, and then measurable, comes when companies find ways to use social to open communication channels from both top-down and bottom-up; from both inside-out and outside-in, and across the enterprise. Therefore, it can orchestrate enterprise wide collaboration and improve operational performance.

- **Social value chain:** Digital enterprise can unite the business with its value chain ecosystem more seamlessly, the borderless social platform unleashes great potential for business partners, even the competitors in certain circumstances to collaborate and solve challenges facing in the industry, make influence on the long term policy and investment or any other social, political and economic concerns. It optimizes social value chain through:

(1) Cross-functional collaboration
(2) Improving work effectiveness
(3) Voice opinions and share collective wisdom
(4) Build more interconnected communication platform
(5) Reputation and performance management

The world is leapfrogging from taxonomy to folksonomy. Though many businesses just start experimenting enterprise social tools, most of business leaders show enthusiasm and confidence about the potential it can bring up in the future. When amplify digital business effect into society, it is people brainstorming together to create the new chapter of innovation via collective wisdom and effort. Business with high level social intelligence can become more interconnected and interdependent with its macroenvironment by engaging conversation with partners, customers, community groups and industry experts. Only the businesses that can share the common social value and take leadership and responsibility to reboot economy are the true innovation engine for our society.

5. Digital "EQ"

Digital EQ has three dimensions: Emotional Intelligence, Execution Excellence and Employee Engagement.

Most organizations operate in a dynamic, unpredictable and ever changing digital environment, under such conditions; change must be part of normal day to day operations. And organizational level Emotional Quotient (EQ) means to have an ability to respond to emotions and cultivate a culture of innovation and learning, translate emotion into value- driven goals and purposes, to achieve high performance result.

Organizational EQ, which has three dimensions – Emotional Intelligence, Execution Excellence, and Employee Engagement – will become a key success factor in the digital transformation.

- **Emotional Intelligence:** Every one changes each day, they grow, learn, and develop. So do businesses. However, change is emotional, as it will disrupt the old mind-set and the old way to do the things; thus, high business EQ is the ability to respond to emotions and the skills to translate emotions into business goals. Indeed, organizational EQ is complemented with organizational IQ – the business policies, practices, processes, and digital technologies to provide necessary business capabilities for driving successful digital transformation.

- **Execution Excellence:** Execution is another dimension of corporate digital EQ. Execution is invisible; it has been taken for granted. It has been collectively decided that "execution just happens" so that all lights and eyes are taken off the process to focus on another strategy, idea, product, etc. Meanwhile, most of executions are in the dark, the haphazard execution happens and no one is there to see it. Hence organizations must have strong EQ – the business agility to achieve execution excellence. However, very few businesses have such agility, that's why execution excellence is so hard to achieve. The challenge is that the digital environment changes so fast nowadays that your strategy must be very flexible. Execution is difficult, also because all the key ingredients in it have mixed flavors. Most researches to date have pointed to key aspects of successful strategy execution, which include leadership, culture, and performance management systems or rewards; they all well mix the art and science of management disciplines.

- **Employee Engagement**: The third dimension of corporate digital "EQ" is Employee Engagement; statistically around 80% of employees in US are disengaged. High performance and satisfaction at work is most strongly related to the feeling that we can direct our own lives, learn and create new things, and do better by ourselves and our world; from talent management perspective, having an intense, passionate sense of ownership, fueled by empowerment, trust of management, HR systems of recognition and reward, which all reinforce the other two dimensions of EQ–Emotional Intelligence and Execution Excellence. As more often than not, the more engaged employees have higher collective EQ and better capability to execute collaboratively.

Hence, the high business EQ with such three dimensions will encourage system thinking, with in-depth analytics, enforce culture of learning and innovation, inspire the high EQ leadership, and energize the people of the organization – making them "want to be their best and give their best," to enable the execution excellence.

6. Process Intelligence

The processes that are programmed and adaptable are classified as "Intelligent Processes"; and such programmability and adaptability incorporated in the processes are what may be called as "Process Intelligence."

Digital is the age of the customer. The choice for digital user experience by process management is a choice for flexibility, adaptability and ultimately, much lower cost-to-maintain and the best possible user experience. The rate of change for deployed user experience systems is also increasing in the age of digitalization. For these reasons, it increasingly makes sense that business process methodology and technology would be the choice for organizations that want to deliver the richest user or customer experiences. Such leading-edge organizations will be constantly learning and adjusting the work that they support and improve overall business agility.

- **Process Intelligence vs. Intelligence Process**: Process Intelligence is information that is extracted from a process about the process, such as throughput times, bottlenecks etc. as the process could be a simple, badly designed or clever. Process intelligence can also mean process governance –the process to manage process, such as risk control, compliance, monitoring etc. Whereas Intelligence Process is the process by which information is converted into intelligence and made available to users. The process consists of six interrelated intelligence operations: planning and direction, collection, processing and exploitation, analysis and production, dissemination and integration, and evaluation and feedback.

- **The Process Intelligence as a tool to measure Intelligent Processes**: Intelligent processes are smart because they are well designed and self monitoring. Not only do they cleverly do the job they are designed for, but also they provide precise, predictive and important information from event logs to alerts. This allows them to be closely monitored by a process intelligence tool (using process mining or predictive analysis, etc). Ultimately they may be self-monitoring. The line between intelligent process and process intelligence is blurring: The processes that are programmed and adaptable are classified as "intelligent" processes, and this kind of programmability and adaptability incorporated in these processes is what may be called as "process" intelligence.

- **The intelligence of process based on management principles**: A smart process follows business management principles, but encourages innovation as well. An intelligent process is flexible, "knowing" enough to be able to handle failure effectively. An effective Business Process Management (BPM) can give you enough flexibility to execute the process. BPM should generate the process improvement alerts with historical data. Smart process needs to have dynamic aspects to it. Business rules in processes should not be rigid, but rigorous; it can handle ad hoc and exceptional matter so smoothly. A business process is "smart" when it accommodates controlled excursions away from what would otherwise be a rigid sequence of steps. It needs the ability to act more as a rules framework that can be used based on intelligence dynamically. To make process smart, the process solution specialist has to identify the failure points in the process and find ways the process should handle these failure points smoothly.

Process is one of the greatest tools for collaboration. The intelligence in a process comes from people. An intelligent process is therefore one that can capture knowledge and provide a structure for digital collaboration and innovation; intelligent process easily grows more intelligent. And intelligent workforce and intelligent processes are excellent combination to build an intelligent digital organization.

7. Risk Intelligence

Every risk has opportunities in it; and every opportunity has risks in it.

In today's digital VUCA environment, how to manage business risk is not only the bottom line management practice to keep the light on; more importantly, it's a critical business capability and intelligence to transform from risk management to risk intelligence; from reactively response to risk to proactively predict risks and discover growth opportunities from it, with the goals to improve business resilience and improve business robustness.

- **Predictive Risk Analytics (PRA) vs. Key Risk Indicators (KRI):** Predictive Risk Analytics (PRA) intends to predict future event and win foresight upon the potential business risks: What will happen? How to prevent the risks or what can be done to make business more resilient, and be well prepared for the possible disruptions. Key Risk Indicators (KRIs) involve metrics that move beyond upper- or lower thresholds or boundaries on plausible events within a business's value chain, that delve into deeper analysis of lead indicators of plausible events.

- **Business resilience and robustness:** PRAs focus on resilience whereas KRIs contributes to robustness. PRA has critical output – resilience. Resilience is a measure of how well a business (a system, a process) will resist shock, extreme events, or turbulence. Typically organizations have designed systems to prevent failure; however, business world is increasing in complexity, and it is more and more difficult to design fail-safe systems; to wit, zero-day exploits. It makes sense to focus on early detection and fast recovery or "resilience" as you accept the inevitability of failure. With the critical output from PRA, businesses are resilient to known risks that are predicted, but still there is an element of uncertainty with respect to unknown risks. To mitigate such element, it needs to take continuous monitoring without manual interventions.

- **From risk management to risk intelligence:** Manage the risks, but identify growth opportunities as well. Many of the opportunities are in the blind spots. When you are not looking at these blind spots, someone comes in and disrupt you over time. In business, every day is a risk, but when a company embarks on a growth strategy, the risk curve will always be greater than a business as usual approaches. And more than 80% of today's business value is based on their ability to embrace complexity, understand the future, identify opportunities, and develop risk intelligence, in order to identify opportunities and decide which one to go after and which one they will not go after, and clearly articulate forward the way value will be created.

- **Corporate culture and governance:** The "trust" factor will take new dimension to risk management. Many organizations lack of ability to understand complex risk models and also lack of "trust" in the fit of models on value chain level, due to "simplicity" of presentation and visualization in regular enterprise risk management and operationalization. Now the question is how to build the trust and acceptance for predictive modeling that proved to be effective at the higher end of the value chain, but not peculating down to realize the value addition expected out of these sophisticated operate models. Technology can enable such penetration to the deepest roots of the value chain, let it be Big Data analytics or risk intelligence developed from traditional models of KRI and audit findings. The trust factor and resilience need to be built into the business culture to ensure good corporate governance. They are the most sophisticated and swindling factors faced by the risk management. Building the models enabled with technology is a task that can be standardized and delivered. But, in the real world, only those who could build the models and integrate the same in their corporate culture found it effective in delivering value.

- **Continuous monitoring**: Stress-testing simulations assume that a differentiator between KRI and PRA is the extent toward which a risk impact model can be finalized and is well understood over through entire enterprise value chain. Some might see PRA data and KRI data as synonyms and one in the same. However, if you consider that the PRA data is merely a data feed and that the KRI consists of the historical audit trail of leading indicators with upper and lower tolerances. Use PRA and its current evolution (including continuous monitoring) to discover modeling fit to find potential weaknesses in a risk model and improve the model and its fit. Use KRIs to monitor events according to models that have been fit and are already understood and trusted on board level.

Thereafter, risk intelligence becomes key digital competency. The risk management needs to lift up from risk control to risk intelligence that can foresee the potential future risks, also identify the potential business growth opportunities as well. And a harmonic, forward-looking approach to manage opportunities and risks has to be put at the heart of the digitalization.

8. Information Management Intelligence

Information Management is to make sure that the right information is shared with the right persons at the right time in the right place.

From Wikipedia: Information Management (IM) is the collection and management of information from one or more sources and the distribution of that information to one or more audiences. This sometimes involves those who have a stake in, or a right to that information. Information intelligence is a business capability to manage data and the knowledge-insight life cycle effectively; it also refers to a multidisciplinary approach to achieving organizational objectives by making the best use of knowledge in decision making.

(1). Information Management: Digital means flow, data flow, information flow and knowledge flow. Information is structured and presents facts in context to targeted situations and conditions that facilitate business in making the right decisions at the right time, to ensure that accurate information is accessible and shared within relevant business units or across organization.

- **Connecting information dots**: The value of information is qualitative, measurable, and defined uniquely to an organization. Information only has a value when it has been used. Information Management is to connect people with the right information at the right time and location, to ensure that accurate information is accessible and shared within relevant business units. This information is open to interpretation accordance to the level of knowledge one has.

- **Process and access**: Information Management makes information available and useful. Information management is about process and access. It is about refining data into useful facts. There's no cultural or social context. Knowledge, however, is different – it is where the cultural and social context alignment (or misalignment) with the information that precedes it.

(2) Knowledge Management: Knowledge Management (KM) is the process of capturing, developing, sharing, and effectively using organizational knowledge. It refers to a multidisciplinary approach to achieving organizational objectives by making the best use of knowledge. Knowledge Management safeguards full understanding business processes, tools that are used to optimize business efficiency.

- **Knowledge is the application of information and experience.** Knowledge is information in use; that supports the decision making process. Knowledge is an expression of understanding – relating information and experience accumulated over time, about known facts and past events.

  Data = series of symbols written on a "support medium" (paper, electronic, audio, video);

  Information = data with semantics assigned by a language (interpreted data);

  Knowledge = a meaning used within an action whose value is justified (proven).

- **Knowledge Management is management with knowledge as a focus.** So the knowledge is about what is stored that can be applied by a user to overcome a problem. Knowledge is information that has the potential to generate value. Knowledge Management involves the use of technologies and processes with the aim of optimizing the value that is generated. Knowledge is an intangible resource that can be converted into tangible content and that can be utilized to produce measurable advances or progress in the business at hand.

(3) Insight: Insight is the vision through "mind eyes", the act or result of understanding the inner nature of things or of seeing intuitively in Greek called "noesis." When you learn to create inner space of clear calmness in the storming mind of thoughts, emotions, sensations, dreams and imagination, insights can be perceived. Insight is perception through multidimensional understanding. There are multilayer meanings upon insight.

- **Insight is the understanding of a specific cause and effect in a specific context**. Insight is being able to identify the root cause of a problem or the core issues of a situation that lead to understanding and resolution. Too often people may take easy path, think and work at a superficial level rather than spending time to understand what is going on underneath. Insight is an understanding of cause and effect based on identification of relationships and behaviors within a model, context, or scenario.

- **Insight is the ability to perceive clearly or deeply penetration**. It is about penetrating and often sudden understanding as of a complex situation or problem. Insight of situation requires in-depth understanding information available. It's about understanding of one's possibilities, adversaries, environments effects and other stakeholders' behaviors. The more complex the situation is, the more different approaches and role gaming is needed to reach for understanding. Insight is thinking into the box after thinking out of box. Thus, insight takes both creativity and analytics, the power of acute observation and deduction, questioning, connection, penetration, discernment, and perception.

Therefore, there is no limit to the value of information in digital economy. The purpose of Information Management is to process raw data, abstract information from it, then gain knowledge, insight and foresight from abundance of information, in order to build an intelligent business.

9. Customer Intelligence

Empathy is the core foundation in customer thinking and very purpose customer intelligence shall capture.

Essentially, digital era is the age of customer. The goal to architect a customer-centric organization is to bring value to customers in ways that are beneficial for them while also creating additional value for the company itself. How to achieve customer intelligence takes multistep effort.

(1) Customer experience life cycle: "Customer Intimacy" is a combined cultural, business, and technology issue. All three aspects need to be addressed in order to achieve "client intimacy." To be truly customer-centric, organizations need to refocus their thinking, culture, behavior, processes, and systems. Companies that have definition of customer experience and decisions could use this definition in everyday decision making. However, organizations need to determine the optimal balance point between adding value to customers and adding value to the company.

- **8-step customer experience life cycle**: From Wikipedia, customer experience is the sum of all experiences over the course of "a relationship" with a supplier, or more narrowly over "one transaction." It lists **awareness, discovery, attraction, interaction, purchase, use, cultivation and advocacy**" as individual aspects of a B2C (business to consumer business) customer experience. It means that an organization wants to optimize the experience of the customer through the entire relationship lifecycle.

- **Purposive expenditure of effort**: While the term "experience" includes financial value, quality value and other aspects of the customer–vendor relationship or transaction, businesses are interested in the strategic, technical, transactional, emotional aspects of the relationship. And the result of this definition is that the customer experience is a kind of "work," which is to say the "purposive expenditure of effort" related to changing states of objects in the real world.

(2) Customer Intelligence: Engaging customers directly and on an ongoing basis to see how their goals are changing might be a good way to predict future behavior. There is also lots of potential for customers to influence designs directly.

- **Analyze customers' behavior pattern**: Big Data and analytics allows businesses to see customers' behavior pattern they have never seen before. Approaches to building business intelligence on customers tend to look at the past behavior of individuals to try to determine the segments that they belong to and forecast future behavior (building intelligence on tastes and wants). It also uncovers the interdependence and connections that will lead to a new way of doing business, or engaging customers' feedback, do sentimental analysis or research on knowing what customers need before they even know themselves, and develop the next generation of product, service, or business model accordingly.

- **Optimize customer experience life cycle**. Big Data lets customer see the "real-time" cause and effect of business's actions and customers' responses, organizations that do so will be able to monitor customer behaviors and market conditions with greater certainty, and react with speed and effectiveness to differentiate from their competition. It will lead service innovation that can optimize customer experience life cycle based on personalization, targeted interactions, preferences and 360 degree view of customers, ultimately increasing customer loyalty by following three "I"s: Insight, Interaction, and improvement.

(3) Three levels of Customer Experience design maturity: User Experience (UX) is a philosophy, with perception upon design intelligence of business. Too often, it is limited to a methodology to be included as a technical process or marketing and visual effort as an afterthought. In order to truly live up to the UX way of thinking, an organization has to change the very foundation of what their goals are. Once you start to put the value UX design provided to users as the highest goal, then UX will finally evolve into what it is meant to accomplish, and improve customer intelligence and overall organizational intelligence to run business. Customer Experience (CX) maturity is dependent on how brand values, promises, and architectures need to be defined in order to deliver exceptional customer experiences. And companies that don't define them clearly can easily stumble due to lack of focus. Here are the three levels of customer experience design maturity:

Figure 18: Three-Level Customer Experience Design Maturity

Maturity Level	Description
Operational level	The designer is just an implementer, working on individual design tasks and creating design deliverables. It means businesses have made some investment and now have certain organizational capability, however, it may lack of architecture or systematic approach to design CX.

Defined level	The designer is an integral part of a product team and deeply integrates design into other product development tasks and processes. It means organizations accomplish most of what you can reasonably do with respect to building your organizational capability in the subject area and are in a state of continuous improvement and measurement
Optimized Level	The designer is a visionary or product owner who influences strategic decisions on how to evolve a product. The enterprise's vision, strategy and governance model should enforce alignment of the various silos toward customer-centric products and delivery mechanisms. This also provides the potential for enterprise effectiveness and efficiency. Organizations at this level are forward-looking, brainstorming and design the next generation of products or service even before customers knowing what they what, and CX becomes drive forces to sharpen its business brand.

Table 14: Three-Level Customer Experience Design Maturity

It's the age of customer. More companies put focus on customer experience, as it is the tangible interaction people have with a company and how closely it delivers against what the company brand promises. A strong brand can lend additional goodwill to a customer engagement, but more importantly, great customer engagements at every touch point support and grow the value of the overall brand.

10. Analytics-Based Talent Management

Information is the life blood of digital businesses, and makes impact upon all different aspects of the organization, especially in talent management space, as people are the most invaluable asset in business, rather than following traditional subjective HR model, forward-looking organizations shall experiment, develop and mature data-driven talent management for leaping through digital transformation.

- **The benefits of data-driven talent management**: Data-driven talent management will bring business leaders together across the organization to share their experience and insight wherever there is a gap in the system, help streamline and identify root cause immediately, and give practical guidance for improving and ordering HR data, as well as using it in creative ways to gain predictive insight and competitive advantage.

- **Balance of both data and intuition in talent management decision:** The organization should have the maturity to leverage and optimize the analytics or insights to make critical decisions, rather than looking as mere data and continue to launch and drive programs that operate as island. Data-based decision making may not completely replace the human decision making. You cannot actually deal with people-related decisions in the same way you do with engineering decisions. Human resources are related to people and people are not machines. Tools are innovative, important and useful, but they are intended for improving efficiency, adding value, making optimization or as a source of inspiration for new ideas. When it comes to managing people and to making human-related decisions, algorithms are not enough. There are a lot of additional parameters, correlations and context that should be taken into account. Talent-related decision is complex, using a blended, integrated approach with a selected set of data-driven tools and analytics capabilities will eventually provide competitive and operational advantages and support to the organization.

- **Integrated talent analytics approach:** People analytics is always important, but tools are not that strong. In many circumstances, Big Data or any analytics works well for the quantitative data sets and you may not find much usage on the qualitative side when especially it is related to people, as it will fail to capture emotions and circumstances. Now with unstructured analytical capabilities combined with social pulse, the organization has more visibility of people sentiments, and can work to make the motivated environment. The organization should have the maturity to leverage and optimize these analytics and insights to make critical decisions rather than looking at it as mere data and continue to launch and drive programs which operate as island. Using a blended and integrated approach with a selected set of data-driven tools and analytics capabilities will eventually provide competitive and operational advantages and support to the organization.

People are still the most valuable asset in any organization, and human capital has the best potential for a business's growth. It takes time to get matured for business implementing data-driven talent management, and it makes a big difference to the business's bottom line. However, integrating data-driven skills and tools into HR will challenge the organization to be more fact-based, more objective, more cost-effective, and ultimately producing higher performing business result.

11. Real-Time Intelligence

Real-time data denotes information that is delivered immediately after collection. There is no delay in the timeliness of the information provided. Real-time data are often used for navigation or tracking. Some uses of this term confuse it with the term dynamic data. In reality, the presence of real-time data is irrelevant to whether it is dynamic or static. But the data collection mechanism at the grass roots level is mechanical that there are delays in the time line of the information provided. This is because of absence of internet connection and other electronic data collection instruments. Here are three aspects of real-time intelligence:

- **Purpose:** Whether or not to run real-time data analytics depends on the need and purpose; you must consider whether you require real-time analytics or just real-time action. The reason for making the distinction is that a lot of value can be created from acting in real time out of calculations performed on a periodic basis. The reason you'd rather perform such calculations on a periodic basis rather than in real time is that doing so is a lot less complicated as well as less expensive.

- **Decision**: Real-time analytics could be useful in scenarios where you have to take immediate decisions. If you are in a consumer business setting prices, or running a call center trying to determine whether or not you have the right coverage on a calling campaign, then you probably do need real-time or real enough time analytics for "availability" or "profits." Real-time analytics is going to be useful where the volume that can vary dependent on things you can control. For example, product price availability or SLA (Service Level Agreement) in e-commerce, or brick and mortar environment. In each of these instances, real-time access may deliver a considerable portion of the value that could be delivered through real-time analytics. So you may wish to take a careful look at what you're trying to accomplish in order not to invest more time and resources than necessary.

- **Prioritization**: Real-time analytics can be a hard thing to implement; it should only be made a priority if it leads to actionable insights almost immediately. A nightly or weekly run of each customer's purchase history would allow the company to prepare for each customer's next visit by pre-populating a table with the right items. There's no need to do all these calculations in real time. Similarly, determining the correlations between the purchases of various items does not have to be calculated in real time, either. It's actually better in many cases for users not to have real-time data, simply because their ability to react to it in a useful way is constrained by the speed with which real-time data accumulate. There are at least two challenges in running real-time analytics:

- Having a system that can support quick changes and implement them throughout the entire business process.
- Having enough data to draw statistical significance.

So, whether or not to run real-time analytics depends on the situation and how rapidly things change, do it with clear business purpose and proven methodology.

12. Decision Intelligence: Analytics Effect in Decision Making

Analytics is permeating into businesses' daily life; it's no surprise to see that more organizations intend to adopt analytics in guiding decision making. Decision intelligence becomes a critical capability of an intelligent digital business. More specifically, what is analytic effect in decision making?

- **Analytics is important in guiding decision making:** Properly done, analytics will give you information that you wouldn't have otherwise. Analytics is strategically important in guiding decision making, but always make sure that the recommendations pass the "does this make sense" test. It is important to make sure that you are using the right inputs and a model that adequately fits the problem to carry out the analysis. Otherwise, the recommendations may not be optimal.

- **Analytics is scientific aspect of decision making**: Analytics is of paramount importance when planning and deriving results following implementation. If one uses the approach of defining a hypothesis for the problem space and the possible solution options, and then using statistical analysis to test and characterize the resultant set to the hypothesis, then analytics is required for both. Because once an approach is decided upon and implemented, a complete solution will include measures of the target results that validate success in achieving the desired business outcomes.

- **Analytics is to improve decisions and drive measurement as well**: At highly mature intelligent businesses, analytics is well embedded into key business processes; it means that implementing predictive analytics results in operational systems in real or near real-time. Analytics can:

  (1) drive or automate decision making, and by monitoring those decision results analytically;
  (2) measure – analytics can be very useful to measure success or improvement between different scenarios, it is important to be sure that the right things are measured to come to correct conclusions about the performance;
  (3) improve the decision effectiveness, and therefore the overall system and business performance over time.

- **Decision making is both science and art.** And both data analytics and intuition are important for effective decision making. Well-designed experiments can yield great insights that would never have been uncovered if one goes with experience and "gut feeling" only. But at the end of the day, it is also critical to see if the outcome bears any resemblance to the predictions. Sometimes the differences are due to poor or great implementation. It is important to understand why things happened so those learning can be applied to the next iteration or project.

- **Machine computation vs. human computation**: The difference between analytics and decision making is merely the boundary between machine computation for formalization and human "computation" for judgment and expertise, as well as the scope and complexity of the problem one is tackling. Hence, the degree to which a problem scope or boundary can be feasibly "encoded" into formalization versus left to expertise. Analytics is when the machine already suggests the best way, whereas in decision making, one considers options with different utilities assigned, at least inherently. It's like the distinction between two types of knowledge-based systems: Decision support systems output "what-if" evaluation and analysis devices with expert systems output "if-then" production rules. The difference is that even though both have knowledge bases embedded; only the second has reasoning and semantic apparatus embedded.

For any visionary company with complicated business territories and ambitions, analytics is strategic imperative and become more and more fundamental for companies to best utilize their data and make sound decisions. Analytics is important, but do not forget common sense.

13. Super Intelligence via Collective Wisdom

It's evident that large businesses are increasingly using crowd-sourcing to brainstorm new ideas and solve business problems in their management practices. Collective intelligence is the emerging business smartness to overcome challenges and stretch business goals.

- **Crowd-sourcing is an attitude**: New generation of social business empowered by digital technologies such as social platform, collaboration tools and analytics will extend the organization's physical boundary, enhance employees' participation and engage customers' feedback. Crowd-sourcing becomes the new attitude and reality, it also stimulates creative side of our brain and agility of our business to find better solutions for either old matters or the emerging problems, and apply collective intelligence to overcome business challenges.

- **Collective wisdom improves both quantity and quality of idea generation**: In an innovation study initiated by a group of researchers, who compared classic in-person, team brainstorming with a distributed idea generation model that had a team component with "hybrid structure" via a field experiment. The basis of their analysis is that companies want the best ideas, and to get those, they need to maximize the elements of extreme value theory, so they compare the following:

(1) The sheer volume of ideas generated.
(2) Average quality of all ideas generated.
(3) The level of variance in the quality of generated ideas.

And they found the distributed idea generation approach with "hybrid structure" generated both the highest quality ideas and a higher average quality overall, versus team brainstorming.

- **Crowd-sourcing brings cognitive minds and the pool of expertise**: Like anything else, the effectiveness of an activity like crowd-sourcing and brainstorming will depend on what it's being used for. The real value in these types of "group-based activities", when done properly, is that it enables you to bring a diverse population together and collectively pool of all the expertise at the discussion table. This is not something that can be done individually; hence, it's valued. However, the real problem with crowd-sourcing is that large group interactions often lack any underlining infrastructure or methodology. As a result, the loudest voice tends to dominate, hierarchical constraints limit freedom of speech, people lack alignment around issues, all insights aren't being harnessed to their full potential, and the list goes on.

- **Collective wisdom enables problem-solving**: It is true that some great ideas do come from brainstorming individually. Interaction with others, being able to build on each other's ideas can yield some amazing result as well. As an innovation manager, one should have a good idea when to deploy different methods and who should be involved. More often you would see, the amazing creativity "seeds" usually come from individuals and problem-solving more from groups. Not to say that creative endeavors can't happen in the groups, they most certainly can. However, different cognitive styles react differently within idea generating activities, and observing how people interact with one another in a way that protects privacy can provide managers with useful innovation process management insights.

- **Crowd-sourcing techniques**: The vast majority of ad hoc brainstorming sessions occur globally everyday now. Business should learn when, where and how each crowd-sourcing technique could be utilized to its full potential. Like so many techniques, brainstorming can deliver great results, if it is applied in the right context, and taking into considerations of its limitations. The techniques can be used to monitor and improve the social-psychological environment for creativity. It is also important to take advantage of methodology that allows large organizations to mobilize a large group of key players, tackle complex business challenges from all the right angles, and co-create the optimal solutions.

Collective intelligence is ultimate smartness of business. The digital businesses with collective intelligence are not just the sum of functional pieces any more, they do have the collective capability to analyze and synthesize all sort of information from within and even outside of business boundary, and come out creative ideas or optimal business solutions with speed.

14. Digital Intelligence Debate #1: Does Big Data Make Intuition Irrelevant?

"Intelligence is not only the ability to reason; it is also the ability to find relevant material in memory and to deploy attention when needed."–Daniel Kahneman "Thinking Fast and Slow"

"Thinking, Fast and Slow" is a book written by Nobel Prize winner in Economics Daniel Kahneman that summarizes research that he conducted over decades. The book's central thesis is a dichotomy between two modes of thought: System 1 is fast, instinctive and emotional. System 2 is slower, more deliberative, and more logical. What Kahneman calls "fast" and "slow" thinking, corresponds to what cognitive neuroscience and cognitive science today call "implicit" and "explicit" cognition. Implicit cognition is automatic, unconscious or intuitive (gut feeling) cognition. Gut feeling and other implicit cognition is very good at prediction as long as the environment is highly predictable and stable. From the case studies, it seems people are really good at guessing means, not so well at comparing them. Now, Big Data expands the new lens of machine intelligence, to complement humans' thinking, the interesting debate is: Does Big Data make "gut feeling" irrelevant?

(1). "Gut Feeling" is still special: "Gut feeling" depends on how we define it, and it can mean various things. Gut feeling is the key to really solving problems in some cases, as human factors can think outside the box. Big Data is what sets to make "gut feeling" increasingly relevant. Gut feeling means the form of human intelligence as expressed behaviorally as "subjectivity" – to make "operant" through "self-reference" as "sentiment" data-capture. The scientific study of subjectivity demonstrates the structure of gut feeling as a mathematical "fit" within specifically contextual human decision making processes. Gut feeling finds its expression in behavioral action, as expressed in hierarchical form through natural language processing- enables the modeling into Artificial Intelligence.

- **The vision thing**: An example of where humans' cognitive abilities seem to outperform any data driven methods is vision. Though "gut feelings" and vision might be pretty different animals, it is seemingly relevant to elevate the comparison to our cognitive systems' ability to process information into an actionable result quickly, without conscious cognition. Vision is one area where we seem to be much better than any "computer" thus far. Hence, gut feeling works very well for highly creative, visionary people, in particular, people are able to and not afraid to leverage contrarian views. It works badly for some others.

- **Intelligence of unconsciousness**: Following the psychologist Gerd Gigerenzer's assumption that "gut feelings" represents "intelligence of the unconscious," he makes the point that many moral judgments, and indeed the moral judgments of institutions, are made without full conscious awareness. In fact, it can be very difficult to express at times why we believe something to be "wrong" or not.

- **Senses of trust**: Many social interactions are based on "senses" of trust (or lack thereof) and "gut feelings," not logic. Big Data may not be replacing these sorts of judgments. That is not to say that Big Data might not eventually tell us something about when our moral or social intuitions are confirmed or not, that we simply observe the world as it is and make a conscious decision about it.

(2) **Big Data makes big difference:** Daniel Kahneman also suggested gut feelings are bad for driving decisions about highly complex interactive systems. In fact, our brains and sensory systems have built-in biases that may subtly (or not so subtly) influence both our perceptions and decision making. Statistical prediction and "intuition" will definitely not correspond in many cases due to various built-in biases (endowment effect, short-cut heuristics that are more sensitive to examples an imagery, risk-aversion., etc.) in human decision making. In other words, it is certainly true that analytic methods will be superior in many cases.

- **Signal vs. noise**: Are you looking at the "signal" or the "noise"? Did you find any of sample instances? How do you know? How do you know that you don't know? There are many instances when looking at the results of an analysis and it just didn't "smell" right - this isn't an "either–or" question. Data just are – we should definitely and clearly rely on analysis of that data (assuming rigor), and equally as importantly, remember that even our subjective experience has value as well.

- **New level of science-driven business management:** The result will possibly be a spectrum of relevance relative to the prevalent business culture and decision making process. Some companies and cultures are and have been data driven for as long as they have existed, they will be on the extreme side of the spectrum. Analytics and Big Data will just take them to new levels of science driven business management. On the other side of the spectrum, serious conflict may arise if Big Data leads to completely new insights or the need for serious business restructuring that conflict with what the gut says.

- **More brains and less gut:** Since we are talking about Big Data, the observations should quickly overwhelm the original gut reactions. So the predictions are like societal progress - over time, you see more brains and less gut. Some keys for communicating unintuitive results are:

    (a) Make really sure you are right. If other people start finding errors in the analysis you present, then you can lose credibility quickly.
    (b) Socialize your results before you get to the big meeting. And it also means that at least some folks in the big meeting will already be convinced.
    (c) Break down the analysis into parts that can be easily understood. It means you have to simplify your analysis and maybe weaken the results, but getting something done is better than not getting something done because you can't explain it.
    (d) Choose your battles. Convincing people of something that does not fit their intuition can be hard, painful and time consuming. Remember you have other stuff that needs to get done, as well as the goal is to successfully execute on as much as possible to deliver the most value possible.

(3) Hybrid solution: Combining technology with talent intelligence means how to use machines- advanced technology and algorithms analysis together with the human source- who can foresight trends and analyze them while understanding the market needs. There are many things machines can do, yet they do lack the human factors such as creativity and intuition, businesses can provide up-to-date ongoing information while using models and technological machinery, not undermining the human source that brings creativity among other important qualities.

- **Big Data and intuition do not exist exclusively to one another**: Data is always management tool, but not leadership tool. Intuition still plays crucial role in decision making. The data drives efficiency – doing things right; the intuition drives the vision – doing right things. If used exclusively, it will lead to decisions that are not best and could be a huge pitfall. Big Data gives us an opportunity to link intuition with the insights provided by data. There will be people who have previously used insight along, and it may take some time getting used to taking another form of sight in Big Data. But it is in the end just another tool that can aid business intuition by providing supporting evidence (or counter evidence) to the theories and assumptions adopted by the business. Big Data and business intuition are not the same thing, nor are they exchangeable; they are different ways to provide additional leverage in making decisions.

- **Big Data can broaden intuition**: In the end, Big Data provides a platform from that new and big thinking can spring ideas previously unthinkable. Like the printing press offered greater access to knowledge and ideas once limited to very few, the digital revolution manifest, in part, as the Big Data "movement" offers opportunity to broaden creativity, think unconventionally, and exercise human gift of intuition while being more aware that such a gift is not separate and distinct from data, but ultimately buttressed by greater insight.

- **Leverage both data and intuition accordingly**: Basing a decision on data, experience and previous failures is better than just data, no experience or no data and much experience. The value from a gut feeling is probably setting the context of the problem up and making sure we are using the right data. Secondly, it's always important to use more than one source of information analysis to drive decisions. Just using one method, gut feeling or data only to drive decisions is bad risk management; on the other side, Big Data provides opportunities to see relationships and correlations that offer access to new perspectives and new insights, which develop and certainly do not hinder intuition. The more ways in which the infinite points in the universe can be connected, the greater intuitive capacity we have. Any application of data sciences without a balance of "gut feeling" and business acumen would not do justice to the application of insights. The data can only tell you what has happened and what may happen, but it won't apply experiences and principles.

- **Measure it right**: Measurement as the traditional "hard" science concept is much more complicated in the social metrics arena. Human intuition is a decent thing to use to calibrate a model's real-world-ness. But making sure your data is measuring what you want, and measuring it in a relevant way should always be one of the first steps in building a model, and this step may be revisited throughout the design and build process. Furthermore, the measurement should be consideration for success of the team; such as a specific KPI has an impact on the company in revenue, customer satisfaction, employee retention, etc. and this is accomplished by defining specific measures derived from an analytics project conceived in the department, with a multidisciplinary team both technically and functionally.

- **Take balanced approach**: Data is factual and driving factors with which one can produce reports, charts and prepare concise material for analysis. The process to make decision is much more dependent on the skills, experience and belief system from data perspective of the decision maker. Those who have been brought up on "gut feeling" and corporate politics need overwhelming evidence to follow the data. Those of a more analytic/scientific bent need much less persuading and will follow where the data leads; but with the sapient touch, some of which turn out to be essential aspects of human nature, perception, cognition, choice, and satisfaction.

- **Big Data is not the end:** It is a tool for end game, which is to make effective decisions; Data is, after all, just data. It has no inherent meaning. It creates small world and makes us smarter not wise. Intuition will always play a part. It is a key part of being human. Context in and with the human experience provides data with meaning, which leads to information and ultimately supports enhanced insight. The key checking points include:

  - Do you believe what Big Data tells?
  - The "middle way" is to look closely at the results of the analysis
  - See if the data tells a cohesive story (no serious ambiguities)
  - See if the data conflicts with intuition for the environment.
  - If there are conflicts, go back and reexamine the data.
  - Accept the conflicts and search for explanations.
  - Make sure these results are reasonably transparent so they can be presented to decision makers
  - Socialize the results broadly.

In summary, analytics is increasingly important, but don't ignore gut feelings, and on the other hand, don't be a slave to them. Gut feeling is important, but this needs to be supported by good logic and data. Big Data has the ability to provide good reasoning and it can support when somebody having gut feeling is unable to convince with good data. In fact, people having gut feeling about any case can provide a good input for Big Data analytics. Hence, there is no reason for gut feeling becoming irrelevant. No matter how valuable the Data is, we still need the human factor in making final decisions.

15. Analytics Debate #2: Should Organization Build a Single Center of Excellence for Business Analytics?

More and more companies are realizing that analytics is a core skill and all the learning of analytics is applicable across the organization. In order to improve Big Data management agility, there needs to be a method for quantitatively understanding the uncertainties and risks; there needs to be a way to communicate and engage organizations in the effectively implementing a decision and managing the change as well. Big Data is leading companies to think further about the Analytics Center of Excellence (CoE). Should there be a central CoE Analytics that oversees and governs all business analytics, or multiple CoEs based on pillar, business unit, or domain?

- **The goal of analytics is to enable decision making**: There are high level corporate issues that need to be defined and passed to branches so there's some consistency in KPIs and decision processes. Analytics being performed to support decision making would be more effective if they are aligned closely to the senior managers making the decisions. The level of involvement from the decision makers would be quite high in business critical and time sensitive requests compared to an instance where the center is producing reports based on mature and established guidelines and processes.

- **A single source of truth makes sense**: Having a single Center of Excellence is ideal, but is not feasible for every company. A single source of truth makes sense as it brings more control, governance and flexibility. However, the success of a CoE will work best if the company is uniform in structure and the data that is required. It does not work so well when there is not any uniformity. Utilizing regional centers of excellence are more feasible when there is no uniformity, even in such a situation, it is important to have this regional or divisional centers work closely together ideally under one management.

- **It depends on BI maturity of organization**: Larger corporations require a more centralized structure to ensure basics; like data governance is complied to and ensure minimal disruption to operational deliverables. At the same time, every line of business should have its own analytical champion to lead the analytics for that specific line of business, and in very close cooperation with the Center of Excellence. But how feasible is it in any company of reasonable size where data is all over the place, and with different data owners and gatekeepers? The analytics team structure may also depend on the BI maturity of the organization, dynamics of the BI adoption in the enterprise. As organization matures toward "sage" stage in analytics, the goal is eventually creating a symbiotic federated system. You need to empower each organization with the ability to define what analytics are needed for their individual business situations for local, whether that's regional or departmental strategy and tactics.

- **Tailored analytics solution**: An Effective CoE Analytics may help unify the view, and target the customer with tailored, evolutionary analytics solution. Because you can discover a lot more "truth" about your business when you have a unified view across all silos of departments or business. Operational leaders need KPI-oriented analytics that are grounded in measurements, and they are owned by and used consistently in operations via business analytics. Strategic decision makers will need data scientists who build new models that identify trends and project them into the future via predictive analytics. Both need descriptive analytics that effectively standardize internal transactions across the enterprise and relate this to external sources for benchmarking with industry standards.

- **Setting objectives**: CoE Analytics or the data governance body such as "data analytics steering committee" shares the sets of objectives such as:

- **Ensure** information is consistently defined and well understood
- **Create** trusted data as an enterprise asset
- **Improve** the consistency of data use across an enterprise
- **Identify** external data to compliment internal data
- **Ensure** the availability of data at the right time and in the right format to enable data-driven decisions.
- **Create** vision for how analytics will be used in the organization and identify the specific capabilities necessary.
- **Formalize** the process of targeting as a collaborative process among business/IT/ analytic leaders. Focus on high value, high impact targets.
- **Set** the expectation that decisions will be based on data and analysis.
- **Promote and provide** delivery enablement through a consistent set of analytics skills, standards, and best practices.
- **Enable** repeatable successful analytics deployment through the development and focus of people, technology and process – in ways that makes sense to an entire organization or division, rather than just a "single project."

As an emerging digital deployment, there are both optimistic perspective and brutal truth about data analysis, whether setting up a central CoE or tailoring business solution, analytics maybe situation driven, with more mature data analysis tools and technologies available, high professional analysis talent get trained, and organizations can reap the fruits from their analysis experiment and efforts.

16. Analytics Debate #3: Why Analytics Fails to Deliver Its Promises

"Most people use statistics the way a drunkard uses a lamp post, more for support than illumination." – Mark Twain

Although analytics project is at the top priority agenda of any forward-looking organization, it has very low success rate to reach customer satisfaction. Why does analytics fail to deliver its promises, and what are principles to follow when doing analytics?

(1) **The Pitfalls to analytics success**: Far too often, the analytical work is started without a very clear goal of the actual problem, the business objective, and most importantly, the eventual deployment of the "answer"; lack of analytics talent, immature process and technology are all causes to fail analytics, more specifically:

- **No clear business purpose for the analytics model being built:** Fail to take a hypothesis-driven, rough-cut approach to the problem. What's the decision you're trying to make, or the problem you're trying to solve? The fatal failures always seem to result from the strategic or visionary side. A great analytical solution usually proceeds in reverse order from the implementation backwards to the data collection and aggregation stage. Quick and dirty analyses early on can simply keep the scope and focus considerably, before investing in more detailed modeling. Analytics is above all a practical discipline that should be oriented around solutions to problems; the techniques and technologies should be a function of what is needed to solve the problem, not the other way around.

- **Incomplete or ineffective leadership and sponsorship:** The analytics leader needs to have business insight. Analytics helps in driving better business decisions. So a leader should not only have a strong technical background, but also understand complex analytic equation in simple business term. Strong sponsorship is important, if a project appears to be stalling -slow data gathering, low project meeting attendance, etc., call for a sponsor review immediately to get clarity about the project's importance and help move things forward. If this does not work, consider communicating a clear "end date" at which the analytics team will stop working on the project, this can prompt client action.

- **One size fits all**: Ignoring ongoing structural change, insufficient understanding of data quality, or erroneous data conditioning, means existing data may have low predictive value. Predictive analysis assumes that history predicts future. This is a very strong assumption that might not be true all the times. Data sanity, data quality and data filtering can be issues. You need to focus on a few key points before starting an analytical project, which may help in finding exact results as per the client requirement:

– Predictive Analytics	vs.	Traditional Statistics
– Group level decision making	vs.	Individual evaluation
– Business Objectives	vs.	Analytics Metrics
– Low Incidence	vs.	High impact occurrences
– Effectiveness	vs.	Efficiency

- **Lack of Big Data talent or resources**: People tend to believe that by using past data, one can predict future, but that might not always be the case when the factors governing the results changes itself and many times modeler ignores many factors due to unavailability of data, resource, or many other reason. In addition, sometimes the best analysts tend not to be the best action translators or inspiring communicators and vice versa. An analytics professional is a translator of sorts. Their responsibility is to align the right data with the right analytical techniques to solve problems for the end user. In short, being insightful, that's the ability needed for data talent.

(2) The Golden Rules of Analytics: Data Analytics is a golden mine every organization is digging now, however, analytics is both art and science at the same time, perhaps not so many businesses understand these golden rules of analytics, shall you follow them?

- Question is more important than answers
- Accurately defining the problem is half the game won.
- Tell the story with analytics. Analysis is for effective decision making
- Don't expect automated tools to provide an optimal solution. There is no substitute for an experienced data analyst
- Correlation does not imply causation
- Never trust your data! Consider it always dirty and in need of extensive data preparation
- The analysis has to tell a story people understand and is relative to the problem.
- Right order of navigation: "Why" precedes "What" precedes "How."
- Garbage in, garbage out; fighting for clean and the right data never ends and understand your data quality and accuracy.
- Follow the "KISS" Principle: Keep it simple, stupid. The end-users must see, understand and follow it.
- Brilliant analytics does not trump bad decision makers.
- Your model should be as simple as possible, but no simpler. (Einstein)
- The only thing that is certain is there is no certainty, probably.
- Find regularity in a chaos, and recognize chaos in regularity.
- The actual model building (although critical of course) is the least important compared to business understanding, data understanding, communication and adoption.
- Data analysts can just find evidences. Who find answers are who asked question.
- Information is worthless, unless it has the power to change a decision.
- The three most important features of your data are metadata, metadata, and metadata.

- Observable variables are not the same as process variables.
- The continuous learning and improvement is available for all involved in the process from the data collectors to the analysts to the decision makers. Proper feedback mechanisms built into every analytical plan can be as informative as the results of the analysis.

"Not everything that can be counted counts and not everything that counts can be counted." – Albert Einstein

CHAPTER 8

Digital Workforce

Compared to a traditional workforce, the digital workforce is a new breed: more virtual and agile because the job is no longer the place you go, but the work you accomplished. The digital workforce has a multitude of varieties:

- **Multigenerations**: By 2020, there will be five generations of employees working together, the traditionalist; Baby Boomers, Generation X, Generation Y, Generation Z...

- **Multicultures**: Talent at every corner of the world can work as a virtual team to co-create context, co-solve the complex problems; and cooperate more closely than ever to overcome the unprecedented challenges facing humanity.

- **Multidevices:** Employees will choose the most appropriate device for the current task or situation based on device strengths and weakness, to improve efficiency and user experience across devices.

As the digital business is always on, interdependent and hyper-connected, for these reasons, more companies are adopting flexible working schedules and encouraging more employees to work creatively and productively via adopting "mobile" or "social" working lifestyle, and we all become the unified "C"- Connected Generation.

1. Future of Work: Connect the Forward Dots

The future of work is more fun, purposeful and intelligent.

Organization of the future is a digital organization designed openly for anyone with ideas on how human organizations ought to be contrived in the face of the strategic imperatives of the 21st century. The work is not only the place you paint only a small piece of large puzzle, but a live organization and an experiment lab you can connect the future dots. Here are five characteristics of future of work.

- **Autonomy**: The "work is what you do, not where you go" shift is unstoppable. The future of work will be shaped by changes that take place in the way people relate to themselves and to their experience of their environment and others around them, which will lead to greater autonomy and "self-generated" engagement. This will impact on the way people interact in organizations and how organizations interact with internal and external stakeholders. When the "parts" (individuals and sub-units of organizations) change their thinking, emotional processes and behavior, new patterns of activity will emerge. This will gradually replace notions of mechanisms of change achieved by hierarchical management and the emergence of more horizontal management structures. Such a shift will profoundly affect the way business will understand employee, team, organizational and leadership functions.

- **Collective wisdom**: New technologies and social media platforms are driving an unprecedented reorganization of how we produce and create value. Amplified by a new level of collective intelligence and tapping resources embedded in social connections with multitudes of others, we can now achieve the kind of scale and reach previously attainable only by very large organizations. In other words, we can do things outside of traditional organizational boundaries. We blur nations and cultures and we adopt global common practices. Probably the future passes by sharing different tasks and different jobs in different places at the same time and working remotely, eliminating transfer times with increase of productivity and work & life quality.

- **Forward-dots connection:** Fixed mind-set refers to those who approach the work through static mind-set, with the assumption that their abilities were innate and not subject to change; while accelerated or growth mind-set refers to those who solve problems or target the goals through mind flow, with the belief that their ability level was nothing more than a snapshot in time and eminently changeable as they continued to learn and develop. The future of talent management is not just to connect the backward dots when recruiting for the skill set, but blueprint to connect the digital forward-dots based on workforce analytics, discover the right talent with growth mind-set, and unleash talent potentials by encouraging staff to transform from "who you are" into "who you want to become." The work will be driven by the talent who shows more agility and innovation to propel themselves and their companies forward.

- **Social ladders**: The digital organization starts with a transcendent purpose, it leads to a unique natural design, which is most fit for achieving the purpose under the current conditions. The natural design allows the organization to morph as life conditions and capacity change to allow organization better fit for the purpose. Such nature design also inspires employees to explore their own purpose. Therefore, the traditional career ladder is perhaps too "steep", biased, or crowded to motivate employees "unhealthily" sometimes; in order to compete for the same position, whereas social ladders can have much open space and encourage talent to become who they are authentically, as it's open, transparent, and fluid, you are what you read and learn; you are what you are pursuing and creating; your unique value is in influence, your passion is in energy and your expertise is in the dots connecting!

- **Creative human spirit:** The new digital paradigm that is emerging is a living organization, one that is organic, alive, holistic, vibrant, energetic, responsive, fluid, creative and innovative, in relationship with its environment, customers, suppliers, and all above enhances and supports the dignity of the creative human spirit. What are the key attributes of a talent who is digital dream force:

- **Feel** comfortable with complexity, uncertainty and ambiguity; they can handle complex situations without reducing them to simple black or white cases.
- **Confident** in their own sense of self; recognize their long term needs are best achieved when the collective's needs are fulfilled.
- **Make** their teammates winners by "making the other look good"; they can be moved by and learn from the experiences of others.
- **Sense and respond** fluidly and flexibly to the environment; unite the heart, mind and hands when working.
- **Trusts** their own intuition; listens from the heart when situation calls for that level of connection; does not rely on authority, operates from a personal belief in the sense of things.

The future of work will remain "imperfect"; more stress, faster deadlines, reduced budget, etc. However, digital workplace is more flexible and productive, propelled by technology to affect where we work, how we work and at what time we choose to work. Our reach becomes global, distance disappears and connectivity increases, the future of work is indeed more fun, purposeful and intelligent.

2. The Future of Work Skills in 2020

The ideal digital workforce has T-shaped skills.

IFTF (the Institute for the Future) applies foresight as a starting point with a process called "Foresight to Insight to Action"; a process that enables people to take future visions and convert them into meaningful insights and actions they can take to be successful in the future. Their recent report analyzes key drivers that will reshape the landscape of work and identifies ten key work skills needed in the next 10 years.

(1) **Six Drivers of changes:** In the digital dawn, global connectivity, smart machines, and new media are just some of the drivers to shaping how we think about work, what constitutes work, and the skills we will need to be productive contributors in the future. Here are six disruptive shifts that are likely to reshape the future landscape:

Extreme longevity	Increasing global life spans change the nature of careers and learning. Multiple careers will be commonplace and lifelong learning to prepare for occupational change will see major growth. To take advantage of this well-experienced and still vital workforce, businesses will have to rethink the traditional career paths in organizations, creating more diversity and flexibility.
The rise of smart machines and systems	Workplace automation nudges human workers out of rote or repetitive tasks. Smart machines will also establish new expectations and standards of performance. We will be entering into a new kind of partnership with machines that will build on mutual strengths, resulting in a new level of human–machine collaboration and codependence.

Computational world   Massive increases in sensors and processing power make the world a programmable system. Every object, every interaction, everything we come into contact with will be converted into data. Thus, we will usher in an era of "everything is programmable" – an era of thinking about the world in computational, programmable, designable terms.

New media ecology   New communication tools require new media literacy beyond text. A new ecosystem will take shape around these areas. We are literally developing a new vernacular, a new language, for communication. At the same time, virtual networks are being integrated more seamlessly into our environment and lives, channeling new media into our daily experience.

Super-structured organizations   Social technologies drive new forms of production and value creation. Amplified by a new level of collective intelligence and tapping resources embedded in social connections with multitudes of others, we can now achieve the kind of scale and reach previously attainable only by very large organizations. In other words, we can do things outside of traditional organizational boundaries. It means to collaborate and play at extreme scales, from the micro to the massive. Learning to use new digital tools to work, to invent, and to govern at these scales is what the next few decades are all about.

Globally connected world	Increased global interconnectivity puts diversity and adaptability at the center of organizational operations. Globalization is the long-term trend toward greater exchanges and integration across geographic borders in our highly globally connected and interdependent world.

(2) Ten Skills for the Future Workforce: What do these six disruptive forces list above mean for the workers of the next decade? Rather than focusing on future jobs, this report looks at future work skills – proficiencies and abilities required across different jobs and work settings, and it has identified ten skills that they believe will be critical for success in the digital workforce.

(a) Sense-making	The ability to determine the deeper meaning or significance of what is being expressed. There will be an increasing demand for the kinds of skills machines are not good at. These are higher level thinking skills that cannot be codified. These are sense-making skills that help us create unique insights and synthesis process critical to decision making.
(b) Social intelligence	The ability to connect to others in a deep and direct way; to sense and stimulate reactions and desired interactions. Socially intelligent employees are able to quickly assess the emotions of those around them and adapt their words, tone and gestures accordingly. It's sort of "sense and sensitivity."

(c) Novel and adaptive thinking	Proficiency at thinking and coming up with solutions and responses beyond that is rote or rule-based. The employees with adaptive thinking have such "situational adaptability" – the ability to respond to unique unexpected circumstances of the moment, with adaptability to changing circumstances and an ability to sense and respond to new contexts.
(d) Cross-cultural competency	The ability to operate in different cultural settings. In a truly globally connected world, a worker's skill set demands specific content, such as linguistic skills or cognitive difference, cross-cultural competency will become an important skill for all workers, not just those who have to operate in diverse geographical environments. Organizations increasingly see diversity as a driver of innovation. Research now tells us that what makes a group truly intelligent and innovative is the combination of different ages, skills, disciplines, and working and thinking styles that members bring to the table.

(e) Computational thinking	The ability to translate vast amounts of data into abstract concepts and to understand data-based reasoning. As the amount of data that we have at our disposal increases exponentially, many more roles will require computational thinking skills in order to make sense of the information. In addition to developing computational thinking skills, workers will need to be aware of its limitations, as analytics and intuition are both critical in making effective decisions.
(f) New-media literacy	The ability to critically assess and develop content that uses new media forms, and to leverage these media for persuasive communication. The explosion in user-generated media including the blogs, videos, and podcasts that now dominate our social lives will be fully felt in workplaces in the next decade, so the expectations of worker ability to produce content using these new forms will rise dramatically.

(g) Trans-disciplinarity The literacy in and ability to understand concepts across multiple disciplines. Many of today's global problems are just too complex to be solved by one specialized discipline (think global warming or overpopulation). These multifaceted problems require trans-disciplinary solutions. While throughout the 20th century, ever-greater specialization was encouraged, the next century will see trans-disciplinary approaches take center stage. The ideal worker of the next decade is "T-shaped" – they bring deep understanding of at least one field, but have the capacity to converse in the language of a broader range of disciplines. This requires a sense of curiosity and a willingness to go on learning far beyond the years of formal education.

(h) Design mind-set The ability to represent and develop tasks and work processes for desired outcomes. Workers of the future will need to become adept at recognizing the kind of thinking that different tasks require, and making adjustments to their work environments that enhance their ability to accomplish these tasks.

(i) **Cognitive load management**	The ability to discriminate and filter information for importance, and to understand how to maximize cognitive functioning using a variety of tools and techniques. A world rich in information streams in multiple formats and from multiple devices brings the issue of cognitive overload to the fore. The next generation of workers will have to develop their own techniques for tackling the problem of cognitive overload, effectively capture the signal from noise.
(j) **Virtual collaboration**	The ability to work productively, drive engagement, and demonstrate presence as a member of a virtual team. Work is not the place you go, but the task you accomplish. Connective technologies make it easier than ever to work, share ideas and be productive despite physical separation. But the virtual work environment also demands a new set of competencies. Workers in the future will need to be adaptable lifelong learners. Place additional emphasis on developing skills such as critical thinking, insight, analysis and synthesis capabilities.

Future is not so far away, part of future is already here. To be successful in the digital age, individuals will need to demonstrate foresight in navigating a rapidly shifting landscape of organizational forms and skill requirements, cultivate the skills to adapt to the future. And businesses must also be alert to the digital dynamic environment, adapt their workforce planning and development strategies to ensure alignment with future skill requirements.

3. Digital Talent Philosophy and Strategy

The digital workforce pursues purpose, autonomy and mastery.

The digital talent philosophy is to accelerate employees to the top of Maslow's Pyramid 2.0: According to Maslow, once a person has fulfilled a need for one layer, they'll move up to a higher level. And numerous studies have shown that in the workplace, the revised Maslow pyramid 2.0 is a good practice; if you're going to motivate your people, besides compensation, fair and consistent talent management should be in place, acceptance, appreciation and affiliation can attract talent to have sense of belonging. In the digital era, and today's cross-generational, cross-cultural and cross-geographical working dynamic, the new generation of digital workforce pursues freedom, independence and autonomy, at the highest level, to find meaning, purpose, and mastering of work, so focus on what will matter most to your employees.

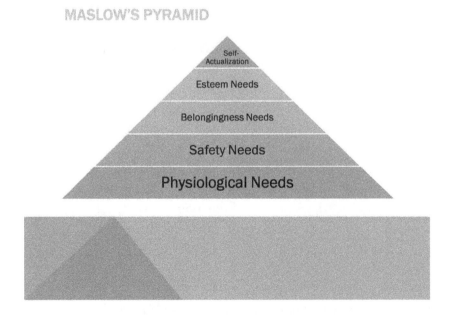

MASLOW'S PYRAMID

- Self-Actualization
- Esteem Needs
- Belongingness Needs
- Safety Needs
- Physiological Needs

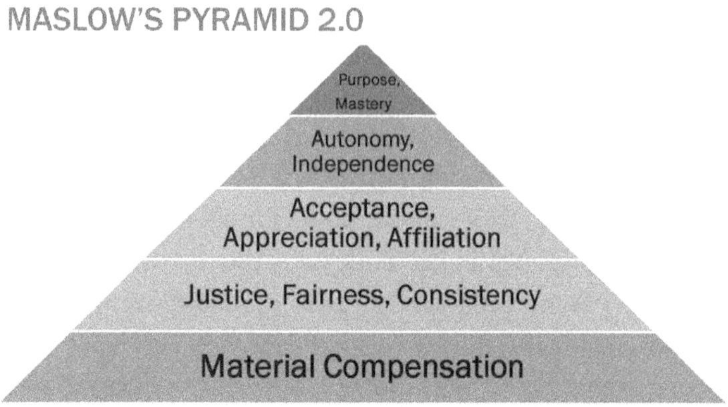

MASLOW'S PYRAMID 2.0

**Figure 19: Maslow's Pyramid vs. Figure 20:
Revised Maslow's Pyramid 2.0**

Digital Talent Strategy – People 2.0 Transformation: The varieties of industry surveys continuously show over 50% of senior executives across industries believe that their organizations have not fully leveraged the power of digitization in HR and recruitment. This has resulted in the HR function lagging other business functions in digital transformation, thereby emphasizing the critical need for change. Indeed, People 2.0 has been proposed as the behavioral, cultural, and educational transformation of employees and organizations driven by new technological paradigms. Digitization has triggered a transformation across the following areas resulting in benefits as well as transformational challenges.

(1) HR 2.0: Human resources have two definitions: One is the function within an organization responsible for administering to people and the other is the actual resource of people. The HR department plays a critical role with the dual responsibility of not only transforming itself, but also helping steer the transformation of work practices by leveraging technology. The challenge now for organizations is to most effectively communicate "what they stand for" and "what they offer" to prospective employees.

- **Digital recruiting:** A recent development in recruiting has been the use of social recruiting techniques to reach out a wider talent pool in real time. Employers need to realize the strategic imperative and benefits of the recruitment innovation initiated on social media and mobile channel.

- **Employee engagement 2.0:** Today, compensatory benefits, monthly town halls or annual retreats and other traditional activities are no longer sufficient to keep employees satisfied and motivated. They seek more visibility and involvement in the strategic objectives of the organization to drive constant engagement. Social listening within the organization is another trend that is gaining traction.

- **Performance management 2.0:** Performance management systems and processes are gradually moving away from a static, unidirectional, and time-bound avatar to a more dynamic, continuous, and interactive state of digital flow. Improved transparency, goal tracking, real-time feedback, enterprise-wide acknowledgment and recognition of achievements are some of the key drivers, which result in the adoption of digital and social performance management systems.

(2) Talent Management 2.0: Talent Management (TM) is the perspective of talent, TM is about building talent competency of business-finding, renewing and protecting the right of talent. TM is the practice of identifying, acquiring, developing, deploying, and retaining well-qualified people throughout an organization and managing business culture as well. The era of face-to-face, top-down management and communication; something that is reassuring for many traditional managers is beginning to change. Talent Management 2.0 is now all about transparency, active listening, and trust in the wisdom of the team, giving proper credit where it is due and constant experimentation. The adoption of a new generation of digital tools is providing organizations with potential better control over exchanged information by allowing it to be reviewed, moderated, and corrected by multiple stakeholders.

- **Collaboration 2.0:** Collaboration today is less about mere information and document sharing and more about leveraging collective intelligence. The increasingly virtual and dispersed nature of organizations, and the growing workforce of employees receptive to digital technologies, are two factors redefining collaboration practices both within the enterprise and with external stakeholders as well.

- **Learning 2.0**: Digital learning is about combining traditional face-to-face sequences with digital platforms to train and develop talent. Learning and development platforms with social features, for peer learning, coupled with web trainings /webcasts for diverse teams across geographies, are being increasingly adopted by companies across sectors.

- **Mobilization 2.0:** Mobilization is all about a new kind of Change Management, one empowered by digital tools and relying on a winning combination of face-to-face and virtual initiatives. It involves the creation of an interactive multichannel communication and sharing process to generate awareness about new digital tools and processes that help accelerate and secure workforce buy-in.

(3) Decode Digital Workforce: Digital workforce is dynamic, diversified, productive and creative; it is multigenerational, multigeographical, and multitasking, digitalization has erased the line between business brand and talent brand, as they are two sides of the same coin now. Thus, innovating digital talent brand is strategic imperative for any forward-looking business today; here are the digital codes of dream workforce:

Figure 21: Decode Digital Workforce – "EIGHTGAL"

- **E – "An Engaged Workforce"**: There are new digital ways to work together to accomplish a task and to provide an opportunity to engage employees. Think about driving enterprise social as a way to work out in the open style so employees can find a topic or area of the company or project to add value too.

- **I – "An Innovative Workforce"**: With increasing competition and emergent digital disruptions, there has to be the different talent assessment criteria that focus more on the **"digital fit"**– creativity, plasticity (fast learner); cooperation, and interdependence.

- **G – "A Growing Workforce"**: A game-changing digital workforce needs to cultivate a growth mind-set. One of the significant digital mind shifts is from fixed to accelerated growth mind. More organizations adopt "continuous learning model" – one in which people receive some amount of formal training, coupled with a significant amount of coaching, support by experts, developmental assignments, development planning, and management support.

- **H – "A Hyper-Connected Workforce"**: Today's workforce is hyperconnected; either you are digital native or digital immigrant, we all belong to generation "C"- the CONNECTED generation, as the internet and enriched digital tools make the business borderless and the world smaller than ever.

- **T – "A Transformational Workforce"**: The speed of change is accelerating in the digital era; however, most change management efforts fail to reach expectation. As the saying goes, "people don't resist change, they resist being changed." It is a strategic imperative upon how to build up a transformational workforce with collective capability to adapt to changes.

- **G – "A Global Fit Workforce"**: There are leaders and talent workers from the twentieth century whose profiles are very different than what is required for a global leader or digital talent now – in a hyper-connected, uncertain, dynamic and interdependent global world with more distributed, multicultural, different business models and an incredible pace of information and innovation. "Global fit" is a critical quality for digital workforce to thrive.

- **A – "An Agile Workforce"**: Today's workforce is more global, flexible, and virtual as the world becomes so volatile, uncertain, and ambiguous. Meanwhile, today's employees value different things compared to previous generations of workers. Therefore, talent management as a business-critical process needs to be agile in adapt to the accelerated change facing in organizations all over the world.

- **L – "A Learning Workforce"**: The knowledge life cycle is significantly shortened due to the velocity of digital disruptions, digital workforce today has to adapt to the new digital learning habit- "de-learn" and "relearn" all the time, and a collective learning capability is strategic for a company's long-term success.

With a well-accepted digital talent philosophy and well-set digital talent strategy, organizations are ready to hunt for the game-changing digital workforce.

4. Digital Dream Force #1: An Engaged Workforce

To engage employees takes both heart and mind, with empathy to know your employees deeper.

Statistically more than 75% of workforces in the U.S. do not feel engaged at work. There are many factors that can lead to employees being disengaged in addition to the company and role they work for. Disengagement can have as much to do with how one feels about their contribution in combination with the activities they are performing. So how to dig through the causes and what are the best management practices to engage talent and transform them into your dream force?

- **Root cause to disengagement**: There are external factors and internal factors that influence the engagement level of an employee. On the authority/responsibility matrix, low authority and low responsibility leads to apathetic employees. On the satisfaction/contribution matrix, low satisfaction and low contribution leads to disengaged employees. It indicates there are some things that are external to the employee (authority/ responsibility) and some things internal to the employee (satisfaction and sense of contribution). The organization can only control some of the factors involved with employee engagement, but these are often big factors. More specifically, a few disengagement reasons include:
  - The employee does not feel connected.

- The employee does not feel like they have an opportunity to contribute.
- The employee desires to have more visibility in the organization.

- **Keep employees informed with big picture of vision and strategy**: The best plan to get people engaged is for the business to have a well thought out strategy that is communicated throughout the organization. Then, managers should help employees find ways to link their activities to that strategy. By doing that, every individual should be able to see what they do in their job makes a difference to the company; and hopefully to the customer. Unless extremely self-motivated or driven, an employee will likely be disengaged if they find the work boring, are left out of the team and cannot see the difference they make to the company's bottom-line. So communication is the key. Some employees do make the necessary changes, but some do not. Then, it is appropriate to take actions on a case by case basis. Keep the employees informed of the state of the organization and the "real" picture.

- **In line with the organizational culture:** The employees should be able to take up challenging work just outside their comfort zone, included in the decision making process and kept in the knowing about how their actions impact the customers and translate to the business objectives. Employees are disengaged for various reasons. If quite a few employees are disengaged, then probably you have to reevaluate the organizational culture that is preventing these employees to actively participate, and hence they are disengaged. Keep in mind that you could have an issue with team chemistry where employees and peers do not have a good understanding of communication and work styles. Hence, it causes a lack of appreciation for different styles of work, and causes some of them to be disengaged.

- **Increase employees' authority, responsibility, and satisfaction**: More often, an immediate line manager plays a key role in engaging employees with the organization. When a manager knows about each individual in his or her team, knowing what challenges they face at work, their talent, career goals, etc., and employees' self-reflection is indeed important. So to have engaged employees, one of the most reliable methods is to increase their authority and responsibility, that the organization can control and work with them to increase their self determinations of satisfaction and contribution. And employees who are satisfied, who contribute, and who have the responsibility and authority to achieve both, are well engaged.

- **Take advantage of the latest social technology and collaboration tools**: There are new ways to work together to accomplish a task and to provide an opportunity to address these reasons for disengaged employees. Think about driving social enterprise as a way to work out in the open style so employees can find a topic or area of the company/project to add value as well. Working with social collaboration tools allows instant gratification and feedback on the best ideas. There are many tools to facilitate social collaboration; social enterprise is an open form of working together and thinking out loud to accomplish a goal or task. As employees would like to have their voices heard, their works appreciated, and their value recognized.

Therefore, to engage employees takes both heart and mind, with empathy to know your employees deeper, understand their career goals; but also with professional attitude as "it's nothing personal, it's about business." The goal is to build a high-performing business with your engaged digital workforce.

5. Digital Dream Force #2: An Innovative Workforce

Ultimately, if the company doesn't have "the expectation of innovativeness" in their DNA, innovation training is all for naught.

Traditional performance management in most of industrial organizations usually focuses on measuring employees' efficiency: Are they doing what being told to do well? However, going forward, with increasing competition and emergent digital disruptions, there must be different talent assessment criteria that focus more on the "digital fit"-creativity, plasticity (fast learner), cooperation, and interdependence. Should organizations today assess their talent's "creatibility" (the hybrid word of "creative + ability"), in order to cultivate culture of innovation and improve unique competency?

- **Innovativeness criteria**: First of all, you should give the employees knowledge on how to identify innovation opportunities. It also maybe that they haven't been asked to give ideas in a formal way. As marking someone "innovative" depends on many philosophical criteria, is it the number of ideas, usability of the idea, relevance of the idea in the present time or in the future, magnitude of the idea, implementation of the idea, etc.

  (1) Creating something new – new knowledge starting the long road to a new technology.
  (2) Improving capability or the process that makes it better.
  (3) Adapting the product or process to a new usage or situation.

- **Training and quantifying innovation into measurable if possible:** Innovation is very difficult if not impossible to achieve without an organization-wide culture of innovation. The other issue is that most people do not consider themselves as either creative or innovative, so mentoring and training should be put in place with quantified measurement before innovation is made as a key performance factor. Innovation training isn't as simple as yet another training program, as it involves process, networking, empathy to others, tenacity, alliance, and drives to see innovation commercialized. All the methods and techniques in the world won't eliminate human nature: You're asking people to feel comfortable with the unknown. That takes time. Ultimately, if the company doesn't have "the expectation of innovativeness" in their DNA, innovation training is all for naught. Better you create an atmosphere where staffs are encouraged to offer innovative, creative and insightful proposals for new products, and new initiatives in problem-solving or business growth.

- **Assessing innovation in performance review:** Set up certain level of standard for innovation performance. There most likely will be metrics assigned to a good portion of the workforce in the "goals and objectives" section of performance review. The innovation characteristic will go into the "traits and characteristics" section, such as the description for exceptional innovativeness is; brings in bright, original and creative ideas from outside the organization; has infectious enthusiasm for making things better; constructively challenges the status quo and has positive ideas for improvement; consistently acts to improve things in their own role or team; actively supports and adapts well to changes proposed by others.

How to encourage an innovative workforce may depend on the organization's willingness to motivate and accelerate the innovation and creativity, and there is a different approach in the mind of the people running the game. Innovation takes place in companies with the right culture and climate. Overall speaking, you need to make everybody innovative and set the proper rewarding system and provide the environment that hosts the stream of ideas.

6. Digital Dream Force #3: A Growth Workforce

A game-changing digital workforce needs to cultivate a growth mind-set.

One of the significant digital mind shifts is from fixed to accelerated growth mind. Fixed mind-set refers to those who approach the work with a fixed mind-set – the assumption that their abilities were innate and not subject to change; while accelerated or growth mind-set refers to those who solve problems or target the goals with growth mind-set – the belief that their ability level was nothing more than a snapshot in time and eminently changeable as they continued to learn and develop.

- **Strategic imperative**: A fixed mind-set sticks to the old way to do things while an accelerated mind-set enjoys new thinking, though it doesn't mean the talent with accelerated mind-sets should compete for everything. Rather, it means one needs to stay focus, set discipline, enforce the strength and unleash the potential; it means to understand humans' nature ability and pursue uniqueness. In industrial era, fixed mind-set is okay to survive as the business and world are slow to change; however, in the age of digitalization, knowledge is only clicks away, growth mind is strategic imperative to adapt to the changes and accelerated mind is needed to continuous improvement and transformation.

- **S-curve**: S-curve mental model indicates learning curves, exhibits a progression from small beginnings that accelerates and approaches a climax over time. It means the talent who can successfully navigate, harness the successive cycles of learning and maxing out that resemble; the s-curve will thrive in the digital era of personal disruption. As changes are expedited for both business and individuals, neither business nor life is linear these days, the capabilities to adapt to unpredictable are critical, and the best curve one can compete is the ability to leap from one learning curve to the next. There are five best practices to motivate talent grow in pursuit of autonomy, mastery and purpose:

  (a) Model the way.
  (b) Inspire a shared vision.
  (c) Challenge the process.
  (d) Enable talent to grow.
  (e) Empower employees to reach high level of passion pyramid.

- **Five-level empowerment**: People work best, and remain engaged and satisfied when work empowers and enables them to be fully who they are. Think in terms of the work acting as a strategic enabler and self-actualization where employees can improve and master with what they do with purpose, as part of something bigger than themselves. At the employee engagement and encouragement working environment, there are five- level employee empowerment.

  (a) Level 1: To be respected.
  (b) Level 2: To learn and grow.
  (c) Level 3: To be an "insider."
  (d) Level 4: To do meaningful work.
  (e) Level 5: To be on a winning team.

Digital business environment is dynamic and uncertain; growth and innovation are heavily dependent on having the right talent with growth mind-sets in the right places at the right time. The bottom line is that companies need to redefine themselves as platforms for talent development, creating positive environments where talent can develop and learn more rapidly than anywhere else; and talent with non-linear skill-set or learning agility can help build the culture of innovation many organizations intensively need now. That is the power of digital workforce.

7. Digital Dream Force Type #4: A Hyper-Connected Workforce

It is the time to tremendous awakening toward "inquisitiveness" with cross-cultural sharing through technology and inner insights.

We have entered a world with ever-increasingly instantaneous communication and hyper-inter-connectivity. It is true: Deserts, mountains and oceans will no longer be the walls to cognizance of the diversity that have been the gene banks and engines of human creativity and invention. Because the natural barriers that separated the world's societies have disappeared, thanks to technology. Today's workforce is always-connected and hyper-collaborated, either you are digital native or digital immigrant, we all belong to generation "C"- the connected generation, as the internet and enriched digital technologies make the business borderless and the world much smaller. However, from management perspective, how to manage such an emerging "C" generation effectively, what is the cultural inertia to improve productivity?

- **Connect-wise:** Driven by strategic necessity, digital technology, and cultural progresses, the connected workforce taking shape today, while divergent in many ways, shares a natural affinity for fresh perspectives, innovation and flexibility. The goal of such business connectivity is to unify the best of the best, recognize originality from mass, shift the old way of thinking, and take advantage of collective wisdom. However, don't embrace every trend or fad. Seek the business value before initiating support for the projects, products change, and forced migration may not be convenient to the business through timing or training perspective. Another facet could just be the control of when to implement change with cost effectiveness.

- **The root cause of "resistance to change":** People who are open-minded should adopt new digital process and tool despite their age. A good tool will be adopted by workers of all generations; just as bad ones will be avoided by all generations. It is rather the influence of the surroundings, the corporate cultures, past and present, in which they have worked, influences their possibility to adapt and use technology as a working tool. The nature of tool also decides how "hard" the adoption would be. Usually, it isn't the tool's online nature that makes adoption potentially difficult. It's whether the tool demands rethinking the patterns and menus that someone has learned. If a new on-line productivity tool demands rethinking the patterns and menus that someone has learned, the more resistant they are.

- **Digital unification**: Digital is the age of people, it is profoundly impacting how people interact, work and spend their time on. The new label of "C" generation can unify today's digital workforce and workplace, to appreciate the diversified point of view, and collective wisdom; to overcome the bias or out-of-dated perception upon today's multigenerational workforces; to allow management to look at the old problems through the new angles; to analyze the culture before criticizing the staff; to dig through the root cause before jumping to the conclusion; and to encourage innovation and improve productivity with both strategy and best practices.

It's the time to connect, to learn, to explore, and to experience mankind commonalities, and appreciate individual's uniqueness; it also is the time for tremendous awakening toward "inquisitiveness" with cross-cultural sharing through technology and inner insights if given to allow that to blossom, that is the beauty of emerging C-generation.

8. Digital Dream Force #5: A Transformational Workforce

People don't resist change, they resist being changed.

The speed of change is accelerating, large-scale transformation initiatives have become a fact of life at major corporations, and their success or failure often means the significant difference between long-term success and underperformance. Any successful transformation should start and end with a clear vision of what your transformed organization should be. But most of change management effort fails. Indeed, change is difficult, and usually people are the weakest link in change management, the primary reason for change failure is resistance to change, as the saying goes, "people don't resist change, they resist being changed." Therefore, the challenge is how to build up a transformative workforce with collective capability to adapt to changes:

- **Types of resistance**: There are two types of resistances that are expected: Personal and structural, and both need to be addressed effectively and efficiently. Change is inevitable, the differences between these two types of resistances are the reasons and goals behind the change and its scope, depth and breadth- why to change, what do you need to accomplish, and what does it consist of and what does it impact. Resistance to change isn't necessarily the problem either, since it's a natural human response to loss; fear of uncertainty or to hideous management of change. Overall, good anticipation in planning is important for a smoother execution, while regular updates and plan adjustments will enhance your chances of success.

- **Change capability**: Developing change capability in those who'll help drive and deliver the change, consider also the capability or ability of those impacted by the change to handle its impacts; their resilience will be massively increased if they are involved, included and educated as to what they should expect. Many people across the organization are at different stages of change involvement:

  (1) Involvement: Directly involved in contributing to the change effort.
  (2) Opportunity: Have the opportunity to participate and choose to hold back

(3) Update: At least listen regularly about the key change effort, the design, and progress made even if they have no direct involvement at all.

The key trait is credibility, no matter what level in the organization. Of course it is imperative to find a progressive executive sponsor, but you must also find other like-minded, well-respected individuals throughout the organization, take accountability on the change project or any transformation effort. They will serve the organization with more energy and determination.

- **Five personalities**: Change is complex and multifaceted these days, change the game is mind-set. Transformation requires first shifting mind-sets, then building new skills and reinforcing and embedding new practices or reflexes. However, people are complex and different; statistically there are five personalities: (1) pathfinder, (2) listener, (3) organizer, (4) follower, and (5) resistor (the lowest resistance = pathfinders and the highest resistance from the resistor). People look for WIFM – "What's in It for Me?" – given that change management needs to craft and deliver these messages at both the individual and group level, and more importantly reinforce these statements through consistent action.

- **Positive intent**: The person labeled a change resistor may even share the same purpose as the sponsors, it is wise to look for a "positive intent" behind a "resistor," collect feedback or opinion before making assumptions that it's just resistance to change. If someone is "resisting" change, what's that about? Are they perhaps interested in "certainty," "stability," "think things are on the right path" or is it something else? It's a good idea to get clarity around what the "resistance" is all about and look closer into reality of what's going on. Or they may just try to alert sponsors to poorly thought-out elements of their plan - or has better ideas. At a minimum, they need to be heard and understood, which removes some of the perceived resistance. People tend to need interpersonal transformation, then intrapersonal transformation to achieve organizational transformation. Better yet, engage people in the design of change solutions so that issues can be surfaced and addressed as early as possible.

- **Balanced approach:** Resistance to change is not a problem - it's a balancing mechanism. And it's also one of change's biggest opportunities. If you can tap into better understanding and work with the energy of resistance, you can also accelerate purposeful change. Resistance is a balancing mechanism that says something isn't aligned or set right. If approached or managed well, it will point to where important learning is needed to come up with strategies, goals, and actions that will actually work and, by virtue of engaging that part of the system productively, generate the buy-in needed to make something positive happen. The most important factor is multidimensional representation on your scenario team - management-bridges-finance etc. Most businesses need creative people, who can think outside the box and key stakeholders in parts of the process as well, in order to get an external viewpoint. There is understandably tension sometimes between the creative and the administrative staff.

Change capability is one of the strategic capabilities that underpin successful execution, and move organization from efficiency to agility. However, no change is for its own sake, there's always clear business purpose behind it, and people are the core to changes. It takes effective leadership - whether artistic or administrative- involves creativity, to build a transformational workforce by keeping people awake; keeping people engaged as well as keeping people informed.

9. Digital Dream Force Type #6: A Global Workforce

"In the end, we will conserve only what we love, we will love only what we understand and we will understand only what we are taught." – Baba Dioum

The business world we live is in significant shift of digital transformation. Talent can compete or collaborate from every corner of the earth. The global balance of economic power is shifting into a multipolar world; the change from a "multinational" organization that adapts the operations of each country or regional unit for local needs to a "global" firm with standardized, but agile, and horizontally integrated technologies and processes. There are leaders from the twentieth century whose profiles are very different than what is required for a leader now, in a hyper-connected, uncertain and interdependent global world with more distributed, multicultural, different business models as well as an incredible pace of information and innovation. "Global fit" is a critical quality for digital workforce to thrive:

- **Global mind-set:** It is a worldview that looks at problems or issues in such a way that a solution emerges through a collaboratively multicultural approach, involving global psychological capital, intellectual capital, and social capital. Being "global" involves a personal intention to focus on being global. Companies don't exist in silos, but within systems, especially global ones.

- **Globility (Global capability):** The qualities and competencies of global workforce include tolerance of ambiguity, cultural flexibility, learning agility, handling complexity, communicating virtually, and working across cultures. Besides being brilliant and mastering the functional skills, he or she must be a strategic thinker with circular vision and a strong communicator with empathy, also know how to collaborate with stakeholders of all stripes. The global capabilities can be shaped through seven mental characteristics: Optimism, self-regulation, social-judgment skills, empathy, motivation to work in an international environment, cognitive skills, and acceptance of complexity and its contradictions.

- **Global cognizance:** Developing global insight and foresight requires holistic thinking and forecasting capability, without such capabilities, companies can fail to increase value and competitive edge in a global economy. The global talent will have more cogitative difference – conceptual diversity with different opinions, independent thinking, decentralization, and aggregation.

The digital workforce with these global qualities can better connect global dots of innovation, and truly become ambassadors for their organization to be successful on the global stage.

10. Digital Dream Force Type #7: An Agile Workforce

Happiness seems like such an elusive thing to quantify. Maybe it's just one of those things that we know when we see it.

Today's workforce is more global, flexible and virtual as the world becomes so volatile, uncertain, and ambiguous. Meanwhile, today's employees value different things compared to previous generations of workers. Therefore, talent management as a business-critical process needs to be agile in adapt to the accelerated change facing in organizations all over the world.

(1) Agile workforce management: Employees are working anytime, anywhere through any digital device, if companies are to become nimble enough to respond to unexpected changes, they should see their workforce as essentially borderless. A borderless workforce is also multigenerational, multicultural, and multitasking with multi devices, but the question is how to manage them to achieve high performance.

- **Digital empowerment and engagement**: Agile workforces embrace culture of innovation; they need to be empowered to make right decision by accessing the right information at the right time. There needs to be broad management support for agile talent management, and an understanding that it means empowering staff to make data-based decisions. This is not always an easy transition for a legacy organization, but agile is the right way to go. A culture of passionate people that embrace change and seek understanding will be paramount. Share early and share often, cross-functional collaboration and iterative communication are encouraged to optimize business processes and improve business agility.

- **Human social system**: Focus on the fact that the fundamental nature of business consists of human social systems, which are partially designed or even architected, but are also evolved, grown, and matured. Not only that, the "components" of such systems include aspects of human beings:

  (1) **Purpose**: They have purpose, intent, motivations, etc., and they are perfectly capable of taking their skills and talents and hunting a new game to play in at any time.
  (2) **Attitude**: They have attitude to openness; need to be willing to present their results as well as failures; take full responsibility for their activities and goals.
  (3). **Motivation**: They are motivated and their motivation must be spurred by radical change and the aim for breakthrough innovation;
  (4) **Focus**: Finally, you need an audience and organization with a focus on people and results, which celebrates small successful steps, but keep the focus on long term objectives.

(2) Agile analytics in digital workforce management: Analytics savvy organizations use a variety of internal and external data sources to make predictions about individual workers' actions and behaviors. Making decisions to identify, develop and retain talent relied on using data, analysis and intuition.

- **Digital analytics tools**: The next generation of agile analytics tools is web-based, self-service, to deliver the insight or foresight upon talent and performance management. There are two ways to look at talent analytics:

(a) Bring analytics people into HR - benefiting HR

(b) Bring people analytics out of HR - benefiting the business that talent analytics has the potential to make a difference, as far as strategic decision making is concerned.

- **Six most important driver for applying workforce analytics:**

  (1) Identifying when, where and what type of workers will be needed in the future.

  (2) Recognizing candidates that will assimilate and perform well in the organization.

  (3) Increasing retention of critical workers.

  (4) Grooming future leaders.

  (5) Improving workforce safety.

  (6) Enforcing HR analytics, accurate/secure personnel data, data driven talent management.

(3) Agile project team and management: Agile project management is important digital methodology for today's businesses, it's essentially a trust exercise for many organizations that need to give agile teams enough rope to execute and build trust. For many organizations, this is a hard sell, especially those who are only comfortable with a waterfall model, or require a huge investment in project analysis upfront.

- **People dependent:** A process or methodology like agile is people dependent, agility is all about people and change, some failure statistics shall not become the excuse to be No-Agile again. A mature Agile team should take the following five actions:

  (1) Adhere to the process (by not skipping "inconvenient" steps).

  (2) Buy into the team concept (team wins, team losses - minimize personal ownership).

  (3) Show traceability (plan, execute, review).

  (4) Ensure everyone participates (full team participation, everyone contributes something useful).

  (5) Conduct early reviews, provide releases and gather early feedback (iterative, responsive, handle change).

- **Focus on providing the most value you can**: Get into the habit of delivering value as early as possible, even at the compromise of long-range planning. Agile project management inspires team democracy. Everyone has a voice and this voice should be used to suggest, collaborate, present outcomes (expected or unexpected), and contribute to planning.

Agile is the mind shift, the culture transformation, the management practice and the new way to manage talent and run business today. Is an agile workforce happier, more productive, or more creative? Happiness seems like such an elusive thing to quantify. Maybe it's just one of those things that we know when we see it. There seems to be so many variables to consider. Still, the very meaning of agile philosophy is to set the guidelines and build more productive and happy working environment for both individuals and teams, with result to bring happy customers as well.

11. Digital Dream Force Type #8: A Learning Workforce

Learning is multidimensional, dynamic, interactive and integrated.

Information explosion is one of the most important characteristics of digital era, although DIKW continuum (Data – Information – Knowledge – Wisdom) is human artifacts since 17th century where the modern scientific mind-set began to evolve. In fact, now the knowledge life cycle is significantly shortened due to the digital disruptions, digital workforce today has to adapt to the new digital learning cycle to "de-learn" and "relearn" all the time, and a collective learning capability is strategic for a company's long-term success.

- **Brain capacity**: Human brain has huge capacity to learn. Human brains organize energy systematically and this has enormous implications for knowledge management. The knowledge is the manifestation of brain energy as it is carried, transformed and stored by the interneuron superstructure of the brain. The complexity of knowledge lies in what we know, not in how we know it. The complexity of knowledge has to do with the fact that we have the potential to interconnect and program up to 600 billion neurons. In addition, interneuron themselves connect in a number of ways. If we know the system, we can create a structure for knowledge that allows us to measure it qualitatively as well as quantitatively - the natural structure of knowledge.

- **Learning cycles:** Limitations on learning are barriers set by humans themselves, as learning is a process and everyone has enormous capacity to learn. Learning cycles assume that learning is a process, so the learning styles can be rationalized. Learning taxonomies try to explain the levels of learning and identify the domains or types of learning, as learning is multidimensional, dynamic, interactive and integrated. Learning becomes knowledge building and we can define learning through the knowledge it builds, there are knowledge styles reflective of the types of knowledge we build.

- **Learning agility**: Digital learning agility is the ability to learn, de-learn and re-learn, and then apply those lessons to succeed in new situations. People who are learning agile continuously seek new challenges, solicit direct feedback, self-reflect, and get jobs done resourcefully. They see unique patterns and make fresh connections that others may overlook. A thoughtful and systematic knowledge management solution needs to explore the breadth and depth of knowledge, its prospects and practice to improve the collective learning capability in the organization to evolve working with knowledge.

- **Informal learning**: Informal learning is on the rise with the increase of social collaboration tools: The emergence of social platforms provides the new way to learn, share and collaborate through direct applications at the corporate level. The organizations with learning culture have implemented the set of social collaboration tools as part of the overall talent management platform. And, the social or informal learning will become mainstream learning channel and a preferred delivery method in the digital era.

- **Knowledge ecosystem**: Organizations can work toward a knowledge ecosystem view. It incorporates the virtual aspects of the knowledge system, innovation, and intuitive behavior. It is important to cultivate the learning culture that has awareness and understanding plus setting a new behavior expectation for active knowledge participants. There is different level of knowledge system models:

  (1) **Experiential** - Accessing Information, exploring resource
  (2) **Transitional**- Refining knowledge, expressing Ideas
  (3) **Transformational** –Shaping Insight, foresight and wisdom
  (4) **Motivational**- Garnering attitude, gaining perspective and planning strategy

Building a digital business with high degree "learning agility" is strategic imperative. People want to grow, develop and learn; in effect, they want to change even though they don't realize it sometimes. This is organic change, and it is unconscious. Therefore, knowledge management plays crucial role. Knowledge is information that has the potential to generate value and it is management with knowledge as a focus, involves the use of technologies and processes with the aim of optimizing the value that is generated, and with the goal to improve an organization's collective learning capabilities in order to develop an adaptive learning workforce.

12. Talent Debate #1: Why Aren't a Majority of Employees Engaged in the Work

Employee engagement takes mind, heart, and hands unification.

Statistically, more than two third of employees are not engaged in their work. Consequently, organizations have begun the survey analyzing the engagement level by function or by job: Is a researcher doing scientific statistics more engaged than a clerk checking thousands of invoices a month? Are people in strategy focused organizations more engaged than in process oriented organizations? What are the causes to employee disengagement, and how to engage talent for improving productivity and creativity, and overall employee satisfaction as well?

- **The talent not being utilized**: The studies show that the majority of people are not engaged in their jobs because their talent is not being utilized; though every employee has individual reasons for not being engaged that is rarely revealed by engagement and exit studies. If you have someone in a role where their natural strengths and talents are being recognized and utilized, they will be engaged. They will also have greater passion, because they are doing what they are good at doing. The studies consistently show the importance of using people's natural strengths and talents, although their process of doing this was not on target. Therefore, managers are important to making this happen, but you need a common language and a methodology so the individual and the organization know how to best utilize individuals, and their role on a team.

- **Lack of equal opportunity to success**: A lot of individuals' bias or perceptions on how the corporate world works will be based on that particular exposure. Some negative reasons upon employee departure are due to being mismanaged, not feeling appreciated, management's shortsighted vision or wrong judgment, etc. In order to be engaged or motivated, employees must believe the organization operates on a meritocracy bases and everyone has an opportunity to work hard and succeed, while at the same time the organization is contributing some sort of value and positive influence to society as a whole.

- **Dysfunctional structure**: The reality is that the organizational structures and relationships with and between employees were designed for a very different age. It's not just a leadership or management issue; most organizations are grossly dysfunctional, despite often noble attempts at change by the leadership team. More often, workers are asked to be "engaged" inside and outside the company environment. At the same time, many companies don't have the mechanisms or interest in engaging employees outside the work environment. In the digital age, businesses today need nothing less than a paradigm shift in their thinking about the fundamentals of how organizations work.

- **Out of balance**: If engagement is low, the team corner of the triangle (quality, process and culture) is perhaps off the balance, which can be reflected from the management. Organizations would benefit from creating a culture where employees feel safe in expressing themselves without reprisal, then listening to their internal partners before implementing change initiatives.

There are many factors that can lead to employees being disengaged in addition to the company and role they work for. Disengagement can have as much to do with how one feels about their contribution in combination with the activities they are performing. Hence, the influential leadership team can make difference. Implementing a methodology that teaches people how to use their strengths, and the strengths of others in the organization is necessary to get employees engaged. The few companies that catch this trend tend to have very visible, multiple ways where there's a much stronger benefit to the company's long-term growth.

13. Talent Debate #2: Employee Satisfaction or Customer Satisfaction: Which Is More Important?

Customer is the air; employee is the blood of the organization.

The purpose of business is to create a customer, but the brand of business is to satisfy customer, employee and shareholders. Here is another Chicken-Egg Debate: Employee Satisfaction (ES) or Customer Satisfaction (CS): What is more important?

(1)ES and CS as inter-linked elements of an organization: Employee Satisfaction (ES) is a company's ability to fulfill the physical, emotional, and psychological needs of its employees; whereas customer satisfaction (CS) is a company's ability to fulfill the business, emotional, and psychological needs of its customers. These two sources of information, ES and CS should be linked. Having high customer satisfaction should be reflected in a dynamic, innovative and agile workplace. Most employees would be satisfied if this was the case! In the scheme of things both employee satisfaction and customer satisfaction are:

(a) Indispensible elements of an organization's "strategic information architecture."
(b) Represent key "sensing" processes of an organization - a vehicle for "sensing" the external customer environment and "sensing" the internal employee environment.
(c) No single source of information is sufficient to make effective and efficient fact-based decisions.

(2) The Answer is based on "for whom" and "what for": The answer is perhaps situation driven, regarding who is your audience, and why shall you ask such question and what you are looking for:

(a) If you ask shareholders to get more value, the most probable response will be customer satisfaction.

(b) If you ask customers to get better products or services, the most probable response will be employee satisfaction.

(c) If you ask suppliers to sell their products or services, the most probable response will be employee satisfaction.

(d) If you ask competitors to get more customers for their business, the most probable response will be customer satisfaction.

(e) If you ask executives to achieve business goals and objectives, the most probable response will be employee satisfaction.

(f) If you ask complementors to get more business with your company, the most probable response will be customer satisfaction.

(g) What stakeholder is the most important in your business? If the customers is the most important stakeholder in your business, then they need the best value proposition (products/services and plus) from your business model. Employee Satisfaction is a key determinant for success.

(3). Explore cause and effect rather than trade-offs and priorities: If one accepts that sustainable business success requires satisfied customers, and that satisfied staff are more likely to satisfy customers, then you are exploring cause and effect rather than trade-offs and priorities. Perhaps the better sets of questions include:

(a) What investments can we make that lead to both staff and customer satisfaction?

(b) Should investments focus on staff satisfaction and capability as a means to deliver customer satisfaction?

(c) Or should investments be made directly in customer satisfaction?

(d) Does an investment directly focused on improving customer satisfaction, lead naturally to more satisfied staff?

Both Employee Satisfaction (ES) and Customer Satisfaction (CS) are about the culture of an organization. Both are important, however, sometimes they may not be connected as much as you think. The measures for each are very different, although typically they are subjective questions. So it is with "employee satisfaction measurement and management" as well as customer satisfaction measurement and management" - notice the emphasis in management, because in too many organizations, the discussion stops at measurement only because the organization merely plays a "numbers game." From outside-in perspective, customers are the focal point; from inside-out view, employees are the key to execute strategy, the successful organizations should look at both lenses, and leverage management practices in exploring cause and effect.

14. Talent Debate #3: How to Measure ROI on Talent Management

The business advantage lies in the hands of people with "KASH" - Knowledge, Attitudes, Skills and Habits!

People are the most critical asset in organizations today, business is moving from treating talent as human resource to thinking talent as human capital, not just the cost, but the investment for the future. There are clear linkages between strategic talent practices and improved corporate performance. However, what're the guidelines to measure ROI on talent management effectively?

- **Talent scoreboard**: The values ROI delivers in talent management must be a subset of the organization's own measure of created business value. Take a look at what is important to the senior team and figure out which metrics to use. Any talent management initiative can be measured with ROI to reflect the key set of business value; in order to make talent management a viable sought after area from the business leaders. And building a talent scorecard with metrics that they care about is the best way to measure ROI and the effective way to measure success and keep key stakeholders engaged.

- **Questioning**: A good starting point is to look at what you currently do and where do you want to be. Sometimes a guided questionnaire can help framework your intentions and therefore demonstrate clear logics, such as: Why are you implementing talent management processes? What's the reason you're tasked for making the investment in the first place? Once you've defined those clearly in the context of your organization, you should have the critical factors by which you can measure progress.

- **Micro approach vs. macro Approach**: Take macro approach to well align the talent strategy with the business vision and goals, then take micro approach to identify programs and initiatives within your talent management strategy, learning and development programs, organizational performance goals, succession planning objectives, and establish benchmarks. For example, you might be investing in leadership development programs because business unit is growing and don't have sufficient people to fill critical jobs there. If so, then the task is to look at the impact of that business unit being under-resourced. The more specific and linked to priority initiatives the better.

- **RoE – Return on Expectation**: The definable "Return on Expectations" needs to define what business results you are hoping to achieve, and this is essential for all business units to be consistent in their goal setting and measurement, it is a function of the vision and alignment aspects of leadership. Thereafter, once you've designed your activities to meet those goals, measurement becomes a matter of determining, "how well did you meet your collective goals." Just trying to measure ROI often confounds your contributions to the top or bottom line with everyone else's efforts. RoE is more definable, and therefore more measurable.

Measuring ROI on talent management is both art and science, talent management practitioners need to establish a set of strategic priorities and measurement guidelines, develop a roadmap of processes with well-defined benchmark, to build competitive capabilities they want to deliver, and make people a true asset and human capital of business.

15. Conclusion: Top Trends to Shape "World-Class" Talent Management

"Hire Mindset, build capability, harness creativity."

At today's highly dynamic digital business environment, now more than ever, talent practitioners need to design and implement a much more holistic strategic approach to manage talent with agility. It is also important to identify the top trends reshaping the future of talent management, and how talent practitioners can best adapt to create the most value for the business in light of the trends over the next five to seven years.

- **Digital talent trait #1: Agility**: HR plays strategic role in driving the adaptive and antifragile organization. As the world becomes increasingly unpredictable, organizations that can adapt to changing business conditions will outperform the competition. From Deloitte talent survey, there is a significant difference between the responses of high and low performers.

    (a) High performers are 60% more likely to identify talent as one of the critical factors for determining future competitiveness.
    (b) High performers are 50% more likely to see access to talent as a reason to enter rapid-growth markets.

- **Digital talent trait #2: Social workplace:** Social media drives the revitalization and democratization of work, instead of relying on solutions dictated from the top of the organization, businesses will be populated with knowledge workers who harness social media to create solutions in conjunction with each other, thereby, radically disrupting organizational structures, hierarchy, and job titles. Companies with wide adoption of social and mobile tools will find it easier to attract and retain the next generation of digital workforce, as they can collaborate and perform better, and their people can learn faster. From Deloitte HR survey:

(a) High performers are 43% more likely to be achieving flexibility through devolving decision making and 30% more likely to be seeking to improve their workforce skills as a result.
(b) Consequently, high performers are 16% more likely to have a concern about labor cost pressures.

- **Digital talent trait #3: Talent mobility**: It is not just enough to talk about it at leadership meetings, you have to take the plunge and invest. Developing a culture and set of programs around talent mobility is not easy. It takes work on behalf of the employee, manager, HR, and the top executives of the company. The top leadership team has to feel comfortable in letting people move around – creating a system of "continuous reeducation" of people.

- **Digital talent trait #4: Redefining engagement**. Focus on passion and the creative environment to consider Maslow's hierarchy of needs. Higher levels of engagement come from recognition, feedback, growth, and opportunity. While compensation and benefits are important, they are only the foundation. Top performers are looking for learning, growth, recognition, and career opportunities. Organizations should continuously monitor employee engagement through social communication channels with people at all levels. Build a sense of purpose and mission, and create a strong corporate brand to attract top talent.

- **Digital talent trait #5:Continuous learning**: More organizations adopt "continuous learning model"; one in which people receive some amount of formal training, coupled with a significant amount of coaching, supported by experts, work or project assignments, development planning, and management support. Learning includes development planning, rotational assignments, coaching, mentoring, and lots of expertise sharing. Companies that outperform their peers have an entire tapestry of learning occurring, driven by a learning culture that permeates all levels of management.

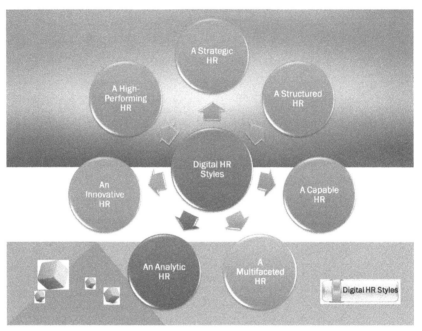

Figure 22: Seven-Style of Digital HR

- **Digital HR Style #1: A strategic HR**: HR plays role as a strategic partner to the top management for defining the proper organizational culture. There has never been a greater opportunity for a truly qualified HR who can be a strategic partner in scaling a business by finding and fitting talent into the organization. A strategic HR leads the change that results in high performing work systems with improvement in every performance measure (productivity, profitability, innovation, safety, quality, reduced labor issues, etc.). The traditional roles and the newer roles, when understood holistically and designed as such, together make HR into an amazing force for success with high commitment cultures.

- **Digital HR Style #2: A structured HR:** Talent practitioners need to think of all of the elements of talent management as one integrated "system," fitting into a total employee environment. Furthermore, there's a new opportunity emerging, the need to shift from "integration" to "optimization," driving new practices in almost every part of HR. These new programs no longer stand alone; they fit together into an integrated system, and HR organizations need to learn how to apply them to the business challenges in a highly customized way.

- **Digital HR Style #3: A capable HR:** HR has the most power and potential to impact an organization's future when it drives bifurcated strategy. The sets of ability to anticipate talent for current and future needs is a critical capability for any organization.

  (1) Sourcing, recruiting, and competing for talent
  (2) Building global leadership
  (3) Reengaging the workforce
  (4) Managerial excellence
  (5) Recognition and rewards
  (6) Career opportunities
  (7) A flexible work environment

- **Digital HR Style #4: A multifaceted HR:** Due to the globalization of the economy and digitalization of business, companies must be nimble in managing talent to have the right people in the right place at the right time. The multifaceted talent practitioners must handle talent paradox skillfully: Are employees truly satisfied? Or are they simply accepting their fate by "making do" with their current employers because of a difficult job market? Employees who believe their employers make effective use of their talent and abilities appear to be overwhelmingly committed to staying on the job, while respondents who said their job does not make good use of their skills are looking to leave. The talent practitioners must be capable of becoming:

(a) Animators – capable of breathing new life and energy into their organizations.

(b) Culture propagators – able to design people policies and processes to build a winning culture.

(c) Change agents – able to instill the beliefs and values in employees, and basic assumptions required for the organization to succeed.

- **Digital HR Style #5: An analytic HR:** Leverage analytics for global talent management planning, and well embed it into talent management strategy, key processes and information management life cycle (data-information-insight- intelligence). Data-driven talent management will bring business leaders together across the organization to share their experience and insight wherever there is a gap in the system, help streamline and identify root cause immediately, and give practical guidance for improving and ordering HR data and using it in creative ways to gain predictive insight and competitive advantage.

- **Digital HR Style #6: An innovative HR**: Talent practitioners must plan for the future of HR, through its particular lens into the business, as it has a unique perspective on the people challenges and opportunities. Therefore, talent practitioners must innovate, think outside the box and drive a view into the future, develop an understanding of future skill gaps, and take systematic approach to the art of people management.

- **Digital HR Style #7: A high-performing HR**: More organizations will make a bold step, reengineer or redesign the old fashioned performance appraisal process, and focus on enabling high performance. In many traditional organizations, their performance management, development planning, benefits, learning administration, and other HR applications and programs are simply too complex and reactive, not agile to adapt to changes or focus on the delivery of talent services, performance consulting, and deep expertise in management, coaching, and recruiting.

The dynamic economy will continue to present opportunities and risks in talent management, talent management needs to have a strategic impact. Take human, physical, economic, technological or financial assets as "pillars" of the organizational dynamics. The industrial leaders can outperform their competitors because they have coherent capabilities, a stronger learning culture, and a deep investment in leadership. These winning companies continuously invest in their team's technical, professional, and leadership skills. This "continuous capability development" approach makes them more innovative, responsive, and agile as their markets change.

CHAPTER 9

Digital Maturity

The effects of an increasingly digitized world are now reaching into every corner of businesses and every aspect of organizations. The business world is moving faster and becoming more global, more mobile, more social and more digitized. The shift to digital cuts across sectors, geographies and leadership roles, the digital transformation is now spreading rapidly to enable organizations of all shapes and sizes to reinvent themselves. But dealing with the challenge of digital change requires an accelerated digital mindset, taking an end-to-end response, building a comprehensive digital strategy, and rethinking the business and operating models, etc. Here are digital quotes from the prestigious consulting firms:

Gartner – Digital Dragon: "Digital business is the creation of new business designs by blurring the physical and digital worlds. What makes digital business different from e-business is the presence and integration of things, connected and intelligent, with people and business. In the IT industry, we have become inured and immune to new buzzwords and messages about how everything is changing. But this time it really is. All industries in all geographies are undergoing radical digital disruption – a 'digital dragon' that is potentially very powerful if tamed but a destructive force if not. This is both a CIO's dream come true and a career-changing leadership challenge."

Deloitte – Digital Strategy: "Today's digital and mobile devices provide unprecedented access to information, products and services across a variety of digital channels. Businesses need to create a seamless brand experience, projecting their brand clearly across the many touch points, channels and devices their customers use. They also need to leverage analytics and the wealth of data available in and around the business to sense and shape market opportunities ahead of their competition. Such a digital strategy is an important step toward becoming an intuitive enterprise."

Accenture – Digital Transformation: "High performers, more and more in lockstep with other executives in their organizations, certainly see digital as a strategic imperative – a tool of competitive intent. They aren't waiting for new technologies to be developed or to mature before they act. They demonstrate a higher order of thinking – a digital mind-set – that will, we believe, separate tomorrow's most able organizations from the rest."

MIT/Capgemini – Embracing Digital Technology: "The Digital Imperative, even in a connected world, it takes time, effort and willpower to get major transformative effects from new technology. Executives need to lead the process and make sure they're managing and coordinating across the company."

PWC – Digital IQ: "Digital IQ is about the CIO orchestrating rather than owning conversations. Social media, mobile channels and data analytics, along with the cloud, are making new business and operating models possible. Because enterprise responsibility lives across the C-suite for these issues, collaborative digital conversations are critical to bring it all together and evaluate and adopt these technologies."

EY – Digital Agility: "Digital leaders' advanced social listening programs, cutting-edge analytics and cloud-based infrastructure enable rapid deployment of new products and services, and offer the ability to quickly learn from and fix mistakes. This organizational agility is necessary to meet the demands of rapidly evolving digital consumer behavior. Digital leaders are well positioned for the future by using the power of mobile, social, cloud, and Big Data analytics in concert – working together – to make their organizations more agile."

McKinsey – Digital Enterprise: "Companies that want to hit their digital sweet spot need to do four things. Firstly, they need to understand, really, where is the value of digital? Is it in marketing? Is it in sales? Is it in automating operations or a combination of all of those? Secondly, they need to prioritize. There are always too many things to do in the digital portfolio, and focusing on the ones that count is important. Thirdly, they need to take an end-to-end view, ensuring that customers receive a joined-up experience from end to end and that all functions are working together. And then, finally, they need to look at their portfolio of businesses and understand what impact digital may have on valuations, and they should focus on what the needed or required capabilities are going forward and perhaps rebalance the portfolio accordingly."

Forrester - Digital disruption: "Digital disruption requires rethinking the entire business, not just one's technology portfolio. It requires first thinking and then behaving like a digital disruptor."

Altimeter's 2014 State of Digital Transformation: It defined digital transformation as "the realignment of, or new investment in, technology and business models to more effectively engage digital customers at every touch point in the customer experience lifecycle."

1. Decode Digital Maturity Factors

Digital capability has recombinant nature.

Digital makes significant impact on every aspect of business from people, process to technology and capability, both horizontally and vertically. Enterprises of the future are increasingly exhibiting digital characteristics in various shades and intensity. Digital makes profound impact from specific function to business as a whole, the purpose of such radical digitalization is to make significant difference in the overall levels of customer delight and achieve high performing business result. High mature digital organizations have high level digital capability not only to build digital innovations, but also to drive enterprise-wide transformation.

And they benefit from their actions. These high performing digital masters achieve significantly higher financial performance than their less digitally-mature competitors, and their key success factors can be decoded as "**SEABIRDS**":

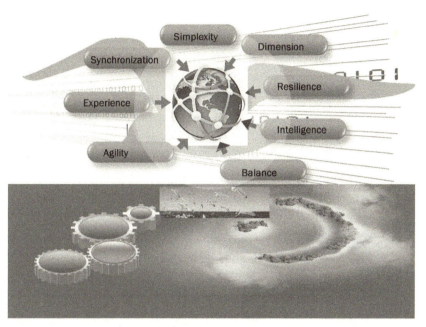

Figure 23: Decode Digital Master Success Factors "SEABIRDS"

- **Synchronization**: Digital synchronization is a digital trait of highly mature businesses that can function like a living thing that is organic, holistic, energetic, responsive, coordinate and consistent in relationship with its environment. Digital synchronization can be implemented through three Cs – Connectivity, Collaboration and Cocreation, as hyper-connectivity is the most critical digital characteristic. When things connect in this way, any entity wishing to negotiate a successful journey has to understand what the implications of this degree of connectivity means to them. They have to understand what it means within their business or organization. But much more importantly, they have to understand the external changing connected environment and respond it synchronously.

- **Experience**: Customer-centric enterprise's vision, strategy, and governance model should enforce alignment of the various silos toward customer-centric products and delivery mechanisms. At the heart of digitalization, it is people and how to build a customer-centric organization. Engaging customers directly on an ongoing basis to see how their goals are changing is a good way to architect customer-centric organization. By understanding customers' goals, digital organizations could also develop better interaction capabilities to enhance the customer experience. There are frequently fundamental differences between the organization's view of value and that of customers sometimes. Having a strong sense of how to develop customer-centric programs within the business means the infrastructure to combine technology and business tactics. Also having a clear understanding of how customer-centric approaches enhance the business model and by extension of profitability. It requires consistently digging deeper and having different level of metrics in place that keep a pulse on the inner workings of the business.

- **Agility**: It is a cultivated capability that enables an organization to respond in a timely, effective, and sustainable way when changing circumstances require it. The management literature increasingly refers to this ability as a "dynamic capability": The potential to sense opportunities and threats, solve problems, and change the firm's resource base, to achieve high level digital democratization. As digital enterprise democratization is to enforce culture of innovation and improve business agility. Enterprise democratization is in the first instance, a question of understanding and changing enterprise culture. The senses of people need to be engaged in digital shifts. Culture is a socially transmitted process involving emotional values that drive core and sustainable business conversations that leadership and middle management need to engage in and measure accountability.

- **Balance**: The majority of people will work in an organization that is somewhere between old and new; with the industrial pace and digital speed; in the physical building and remote environment; or will remain to be a mixture of old and new. Digital is also the sense of abundance. Abundance is the digital trend, the progress and the pursuit. In the information age, "abundance" means information flow; in the age of globalization, "abundance" means the beauty of diversity; in the age of crowd-sourcing, abundance means the multitude of point of views; in the age of digitalization, abundance means hyper-connectivity. When we approach others with a sense of abundance, working and living with that idea in mind, we're likely to be more creative, more innovative, more caring. But not to underestimate the challenge of balancing an awareness of current reality with the mind-set for what is possible, but the more abundance of the paradigm informs our behavior the better our future looks. It is the biggest management challenge to be a change agent with high mature attitude and aptitude, in order to take business from where you are to the next level of maturity. Hence, one of the biggest challenges in digital transformation is how to strike the right digital balance.

- **Intelligence:** The "why, what and how" of analytics helps inform digital strategy. Analytics is about the "why," and you should care about the "why" because it will tell you tomorrow's "what." Analytics is not about getting to a point certain, but rather it needs to be used as a tool for reducing uncertainty in digital business. To make analytics pervasive within an organization, it needs to be promoted as a way of reducing, not eliminating, or explaining uncertainty in both strategic decision executives make and the daily decisions the staff make. Organizations also start to use social analytics to make formerly invisible patterns of social interaction more visible; and apply such information to boost social engagement, find segmentation of populations with certain characteristics and understand their impact on others, or what turns into certain actions such as purchasing, collaboration, and encouraging behavior changes, with the ultimate goal for performance management. As computing resources have evolved, with advancing capabilities to better handle data size and complexity, companies start to reap many more benefits from analytics.

- **Resilience**: Businesses are faced with more opportunities and risks at digital era, being resilient is about failing faster, failing forward, failing cheaper and recovering more promptly. Digital resilience depends on how to manage the grey area effectively in today's VUCA – volatile, uncertain, complex, and ambiguous business environment. Business resilience is the business capability to make organization more resilient; not just controlling risk, but managing risk with intelligence. The key is balance, give enough autonomy to the business to make its own decisions on taking or avoiding risks, put in place a mandated risk tolerance structure through escalation requirements based on current risk ratings, and get the balance right should result in the future vision aspects, and also provide information to the assurance lines that evaluate the business risk profile for analytical breakthroughs.

- **Dimension**: Digitalization is not a single dimensional effort to using the cool digital technologies, but a multidimensional pursuit to embed digital into the very fabric of business. To stay competitive, companies must go beyond experimenting with digital and commit to transforming themselves into full digital businesses with multiple dimensional approaches. Digital technologies enable social behaviors to take place online, endowing these interactions with scale, speed and disruptive economics of the internet; provide platforms for content creation, distribution, consuming, cocreation, and transformation of personal and group communication into content. The real power of social technology also comes from the innate appeal of interacting socially and intellectual stimulation that people derive from sharing what they know, expressing opinions and learning what others know and think.

- **Simplexity:** It is a hybrid word to reflect digital normality (Simplicity + Complexity). Simplicity is the digital design of looking for what is common for maximum, reuse; simplicity is the building blocks of digital business. Certain aspects of the problem space may be inherently complex, complexity is the content put in the building blocks and the outcomes from interactions with the building blocks. Simplexity means or is related to many things such as manageability, availability, scalability, flexibility, reliability, robustness, sensitivity, comprehensiveness, speed, responsiveness, etc. With simplexity, the goal of digitalization is to adding clarity and purpose; removing unnecessary complexity such as assumptions or dependencies, but enforcing the good complexity and more clearly revealing the intentions of the architecture and its purpose.

Digitalization implies the full-scale changes in the way business is conducted, so that simply adopting a new digital technology may be insufficient. You have to transform the company's underlying functions and organization as a whole with adjusted digital speed. Otherwise, companies may begin a decline from its previous good performance. A digital organization with the key success factors listed above continues to climb up its maturity level from efficiency, effectiveness, and then to agility – the crucial ability to adapt to business dynamics.

2. Digital Business Synchronization

Digital synchronization occurs when all parts of the choir sing their respective parts in harmony.

Here is a nature phenomenon: When one starling changes, information moves across the flock very quickly and with nearly no degradation, in essence, that's the beauty of synchronization. Nature is full of beauty and mystery; murmuration is such a stunning nature phenomenon to take your breath away – sometimes from hundreds to tens of thousands of birds gather in flocks called murmurations. It exhibits strong spatial coherence and amazing synchronization, which seem to occur spontaneously, or in response to an approaching threat. So how could these masses of birds fly so synchronously, swiftly, peacefully and gracefully? Even more amazingly, the flocks of birds are never led by a single bird, but governed collaboratively by all of the flock members. It's such a nature example of collective leadership, fluidity of team motion, and harmony of collaboration. As the science researchers put it, the group responds as one, and cannot be divided into independent subparts. When one bird changes direction or speed, each of the other birds in the flock responds to the change, and they do so nearly simultaneously regardless of the size of the flock. What can businesses learn from murmurations? Shall you imitate nature to build such digital synchronization for their business transformation, talent management or organizational development? Digital synchronization is a digital trait of highly mature business that can function like a living thing that is organic, holistic, energetic, responsive, coordinated, and consistent in relationship with its environment. Through such digital synchronization, organizations can establish more sustainable and transformational capabilities based on the key dimensions such as scope, alignment, design, execution, governance, etc. Here are five types of business synchronizations in improving overall organizational agility.

- **Strategy–execution synchronization:** These days strategy steers execution and execution directs strategy in the synchronized way. Strategy is becoming more a living entity of strategy and execution, moving from the conventional approach of strategy plus execution to a synchronized management of iterative approach. Strategy and execution represent the two sides of one and the same thing. There is no good strategy without an execution and there is no good execution to a bad strategy. Strategy–execution synchronization can lead the smooth alignment process of ensuring all organizational action is directed to achieving common strategic goals and objectives. Basically, there is a main corporate goal from which you determine certain "action items." These action items become goals for business units. The business units determine action items from these goals, and these action items become the goals of the departments within each business unit. And so on, until each individual manager or supervisor has a goal, with action items and opposing metrics. Strategy–execution synchronization can also catalyze the flow of the right information to the right people at the right time to coordinate and execute strategy, tactics and risks. This means to translate strategy to operational terms aligning the organization to create synergies in making strategy everyone's everyday job, and a continual process mobilizing change through digital synchronization.

- **Business–IT synchronization**: Both business and IT get synchronized to stay on the same page about business strategy, and weave IT into business strategy and execution. It is about information management coherence. In order to build a bridge between IT and business, there must be a very clear understanding and agreement between IT and the business about the role of IT in the organization. If the business only regards IT as a support function, then the priority will be operational efficiency. If the business expects IT to be a driver of innovation and change, then the IT function needs to be flexible and responsive and even proactive to synchronize with core business activities. The business needs to know what IT can deliver and enter a dialogue about what best serves the goals of the business. IT needs to be telling business about the opportunities and possibilities and that means IT needs to really understand the goals of the business and synchronize with business goals, building the "right" bridge between IT and business to closing the gap is about doing the basics right to synchronize business and IT. Ultimately, you'd want to recognize that what most businesses need is an IT capability that is key component of building business capability, not "just" an IT department. Framing the right problem and therefore framing the problem right, it's often about digital business synchronization, alignment and implementation.

- **Data and information synchronization:** Data synchronization is the process of establishing consistency among data from a source to the target data storage and vice versa, and the continuous harmonization of the data over time. Inconsistent or broken business processes often result in significant data inconsistencies. Thus, streamlining and standardizing data management processes is an essential prerequisite to providing effective integration solutions and achieve data synchronization, and this is where the challenges lie to ensuring data quality earlier than later. Data quality is a multidimensional concept whereby a data expert provides a better definition of data quality as the extent to which the data actually represents what it purports to represent. Establish strong information and data governance is a critical step in synchronizing information. At a strategic level, the goal of strong information governance is to balance the long-term focus with some quick wins. Broad scope and long-term focus are great planning tools and overall targets. But you have to have smaller goals that are achievable in a reasonable time within the current business and IT environment. Nonetheless, to keep up with the competition, businesses cannot afford to complete an enterprise model first, before starting to harvest. They need to follow an incremental approach that ensures a return-on-investment within a reasonable period of time.

- **Change Management (CM) and Project Management (PM) synchronization**: A properly designed and implemented CM and PM systems are "must have" digital elements; Change management and project management are two sides of the same coin. Either one without the other, results in an incomplete transaction. Change management is one of many components of a project, and they should go hand-in-hand in a synchronized way. Projects follow change management processes and adhere to the policies in order to implement required design, new or changing implementations. CM and PM are also complimentary Ying and Yang. The interaction of these two objects causes everything to happen in any project environment. Furthermore, the size of the organization will influence the level of debate. In large enterprises, change management has a purpose in assuring that operation of the business is not disrupted by a single change, or a few changes. Project management is a plan to make changes; and to destabilize the current situation. In a large enterprise, PM should or must account for operational readiness, yet there are so many changes, that CM is required to funnel and manage a large number of changes to the operation. In a small business and many medium size businesses, there are fewer operational elements, systems, or players, so that PM and CM tend to blend together into project management.

- **Culture and talent management synchronization**: Culture is a collective mind-set, attitude and habit of an organization, in the digital era, HR plays role as a strategic partner to the top management for defining the proper organizational culture, and it is also a logical step in synchronizing culture and talent management to shape a high performing team. Culture is differentiator; differentiation may be facilitated by a culture encouraging innovation, individuality, and risk-taking. The culture of innovation or agility will attract more first rate talent to join the organization, empower employees to achieve more, and engage talent with synchronized process and platform in the place; on the other side, the strong talent management will further enforce the high-performing culture to synchronize talent's mind, heart, and hands to find meaning of work or mastery of work., etc. In the digital age, organizations need to redefine, reinvent, and digitalize their HR missions. They need to understand the extent to which digital technologies enable the people function to manage an integrated ecosystem of stakeholders and operate as an efficient and effective strategic business partner. They also need to work more closely with management and take a proactive and synchronous approach to purposely creating a defined corporate culture and the competitive difference.

Digital synchronization and strategic alignment occur when all parts of the choir sing their respective parts in harmony to achieve a higher business purpose, the music as a symphony of voice. Digital synchronization occurs on multiple levels, but it presupposes the ability of each "link" to articulate his/her "strategic intent." If strategic intent can be understood both within and beyond the organization, the alignment becomes an analytical "e-harmony" process where the actual configuration of the organizational strategy is a consequence of strategy design and implementation.

Back to the earlier story: When one starling changes, in essence, information moves across the flock very quickly and with nearly no degradation. The researchers describe it as a high signal-to-noise ratio. Starlings in large flocks consistently coordinate their movements with their seven nearest neighbors. They also found that the shape of the flock, rather than the size, has the largest effect on this number; seven seems optimal for the tightly connected flocks that starlings are known for. The nature is amazing; the nature is profound; and the nature is full of wonders, let's just learn from it.

3. Customer Experience Maturity

Digital is the age of customer empathy.

A high mature, customer-centric digital organization is agile to adapt to change, intelligent to make timely decision, resilient to risk, and elastic to scale up and down seamlessly. Therefore, the organization needs to define what the business does or must do to create value to customers. Once it is realized that the organization has to move to being customer-centric, how would you define the building blocks for business transformation? What tools and artifacts or road-mapping would you create to ensure that the business is evolving toward the customer-centric vision? The ultimate goal of a customer-centric organization is to architect an organization to bring value to customers in ways that are beneficial for them while also creating additional value for the company itself. The digital leaders with customer-centric mind-sets know that digital is not about being technology-led. The digital needs to be well embedded into the very fabric of organization, businesses have to think and rethink about how to be relevant to current and future customers, from building service model and differentiated capability to transforming entire businesses. And what are the key factors in customer experience management, how can companies do the better work when its scope is seemly so large, what's the better approach, and what's the methodology nailed?

(1) Six key factors in Customer Experience Management: There are many key factors in customer experience management. An enterprise would do well to qualify customer segments based on the incremental value that it is likely to generate from any of the customer experience strategies that it wants to adopt, to make the initiatives meaningful and profitable. But there are so many variables based on the nature and size of business, their vision and mission, the strategy and the culture, startup or well established company – just to name a few. The key factors in customer experience may include the products, the price, the distribution, the availability, the convenience and the branding, etc. The business decides where they're going to place themselves in each category to create an overall customer experience, and set brand tone as availability leader or the trend setter. The customer decides in most cases their own trade-offs.

- **Outside-in customer view:** A customer-centric enterprise's vision, strategy, and governance model should enforce alignment of the various silos toward customer-centric products and delivery mechanisms. It also provides the potential for enterprise effectiveness and efficiency. Customer experience comes from all touch points, yet organizations are structured by departments and it hinders company's ability to create value. Most organizations are organized in silos, how would you ensure that all structures, processes and strategy alignment around an excellent customer experience to result in a profitable and evolving business? Customers don't want to know how internally the business operates; they tend to think about what experience they would get when they buy a product from the business. How would you model diversified value propositions to different customer segments, yet developing and offering the product and services using the same or similar business capabilities? In certain case, different customer segments wants same experience, but they want it delivered through different ways and channels.

- **Customer value management:** Customer experience is an aggregate of all the different strategies around product or pricing differentiation, channel and any other activity that is intended to give the customer a unique experience. Values create value that a company stands for, the corporate social responsibility, sustainability; all add value to the shareholder, because they add value to the customer. One way is to measure Customer Value Added (CVA) and have it presented quarterly with the financial results. If CVA goes up, then the executives will reinforce it. If not, they will ask why it went down. They will see the correlation between financial and customer results as well.

- **Operational priority**: What does the brand believe its customers value at each point of the relationship by customer segment if this varies by segment? What does customer actually value at each leg of the journey? How well is the brand delivering on these values? What's going on in the competitive space? That is, how well or poorly are competitors delivering on their customers' operational priorities? Obviously, this can inform priorities or expose opportunities. How do you do this, concretely and efficiently? How do you prove you're getting these result effectively? Organizations are at the different stages of the business life cycle; some run down a diminishing returns pathway, others do the best they can with existing products and customers, and spend a lot of time on future products or customers. The strategic and operational priorities are key factors in Customer Experience management.

- **Design management**: The holistic customer experience design and management are what customer centricity is about; are they starting with the customer at the center or already have the infrastructure and want to define the customer experience around what already exists. The key elements in design management include:

   (a) **Design focus:** <u>Designing a customer experience for whom? Does the business have a clear point of view of design management?</u>

(b) **Customers' operational priorities**: <u>What are the most highly value you need and when you need it in the customer lifecycle?</u>

(c) **Funding mechanism**<u>: Do you know how you are going to afford to deliver the experience being designed? Do you know whether it will produce the returns they expect?</u>

(d) **Employee management system**: <u>Has employee management system been well aligned to your designed customer experience?</u> Compounding with the fact that most businesses are not staffed much further beyond managing the day-to-day operation, and that's why much of the customer experience is disconnected, siloed and left to chance.

(e) **Customer management system**: <u>Has service methodology been aligned to their designed customer experience?</u>

- **Decision management**: Approaches to building business intelligence upon customers tend to look at the past behavior of individuals to try to determine the segments that they belong to and forecast future behavior. Decision management manages customer treatment decisions as corporate assets and each customer decision is considered individually. These decision assets are identified, modeled, enhanced by analytics and business know-how, checked for compliance, evaluated for risk and delivered to the multichannel systems.

- **Customer experience matrix**: Competition and the lack of competition is a significant factor when evaluating where to invest along the customer experience lifecycle. In order for customer experience to be a differentiator as a strategic option, you must be able to map one company's experience versus competitors' customer experiences; this is part of why companies could examine the entire customer lifecycle from acquisition through disposal and isolate where in the experience they choose to invest, where they choose to compete and where they choose to innovate. Most companies think they are doing everything for a customer and do not know all they could be doing with knowledge blocks.

(2) Customer experience maturity: Customer experience is a customer perception about how they interact with a business. Customer experience is about the moment of truth. Firms engage in efforts that result in experiences. Whether or not the efforts are thought through or haphazard, the experiences are nevertheless delivered to customers. Individuals do not separate the research, purchase, receipt, usage, and post-purchase care of a product. Instead, they look holistically at the product, service, and the broader experience they have with the company that produced it.

- **The rising customer empathy**: Engaging customers directly on an ongoing basis to see how their goals are changing is a good way to architect a customer-centric organization. By understanding customer goals, organizations could also develop better interaction capabilities to enhance the customer experience. There are frequently "fundamental differences" between the organizational view of value and that of customers, and "customer-centric organization" means very different things to different people sometimes. Find out what the business means by this terminology and where and to which extent it is "real." It is unlikely that the business will commit to doing anything the customer asks for and it will be more evident in areas of customer communications, sales marketing and support, than in finance and manufacturing. In addition, you have to strike the right balance between customer retention and customer acquisition. An important distinction in putting a strong focus on customer experience is, are you doing this for your current customer base or are you diversified to the point where much of your future business is going to come from products or customers you do not presently have? This will vary widely depending on the business. Is it a one-sale-and-done product or a high transactional business with repeat transactions? These are some of the variables that limit any turnkey, "boxed" solution in designing the customer experience for every business.

- **Customer experience multiple touch points**: A customer experience is initiated by the customer and the experience is defined by the touch points, in which businesses leave an impression on those who come in contact with their efforts – the more contact over time, the deeper and quite possibly the more meaningful those impressions. As technology moves consumers from passive to active to proactive, it is where experience becomes what shapes perception. In addition, customer experience is the experience that only the individual customer can have, which will always be unique to that individual, whereas brand experience could be the planned experience for all customers. CX management can attempt to shape each and every potential customer experience (touch point/pain point/joy point) with its brand personality such that the firm provides customers with brand experiences that are unique to the brand as well.

- **Three levels of Customer Experience (CX) maturity**: CX maturity is dependent on how brand values, promises, and architectures need to be defined in order to deliver exceptional customer experiences. And companies that don't define them clearly can easily stumble due to lack of focus. As there are many tricky things related to the validity of the maturity models, one is that processes (many maturity models examine "process maturity") as such do not guarantee any level of usability. There are three levels of CX maturity:

  (a) **Operational level**. The designer is just an implementer, working on individual design tasks and creating design deliverables. It means businesses have made some investment and now have some organizational capability, however, it may lack of architecture or systematic approach to design CX.

  (b) **Optimized level**. The designer is an integral part of a product team and deeply integrates design into other product development tasks and processes. It means organization has accomplished most of what you can reasonably do with respect to building your organizational capability in the subject area and are in a state of continuous improvement and measurement.

(c) **Strategic Level**: The designer is a visionary or product owner who influences strategic decisions on how to evolve a product. Organizations at this level are forward-looking and brainstorming the next generation of products or service even before customers knowing what they what, and CX becomes drive forces to sharpen its business brand.

- **Employee development and empowerment**: Superior customer services are provided by dedicated employees; customer experience depends very much on employees' behavior and knowledge or skills they posses. Hence, the companies should develop training program to equip their employees to deliver the customer experience so that they could offer support and advice to their customers with the right information at the right time. Exceptional customer experience takes holistic approach with detected polarization around two themes: Firstly the "horizontal" coordination approaches, and secondly the need for clearly designated "customer champions," cross-functional collaboration and interaction are crucial in building true customer-centric organizations.

(3) How to measure an organization's customer centricity: More companies put focus on the customer experience, as it is the tangible experience people have with a company and how closely it delivers against what the company brand promises. A strong brand can lend additional goodwill to a customer engagement, but more importantly, great customer engagements at every touch point support and grow the value of the overall brand. The customer-centric company can be defined as one that adopts specific business practices that result in high levels of customer satisfaction and loyalty. That is, the concept of customer-centricity can be measured by what a company does to improve customer satisfaction and loyalty.

- **Make assessment on customer-centricity alignment**: The degree of customer centricity alignment includes: Customer strategy, process to strategy, technology to process, and organizational design to all tells the story. Consequently, building a customer-centric company starts with identifying those specific business practices that impact customer satisfaction and loyalty. These best practices essentially define and operationalize what is meant by a "customer-centric" company. It is equally important to see that the top management strategy is to be customer-centric, to have the acceptance of the lower level executable actions, and to have a measurable tracking and KPI system will highlight the importance of the customers to any organization.

- **Decide the scope to measure**: It is incumbent on the organization to prove its capability to deliver a unique and differentiated experience consistently. However, the other thing to do is to decide if you want an organizational level indicator or if you want to assess relative customer-centricity of different functions and business units. The latter might be desirable if your real goal is to begin the flywheel of awareness and change within the firm, rather than make an absolute statement about how customer-centric your company is.

- **Customer Centricity score**: An organization's Customer Centricity (CC) score is the measurement of gap. On one side of the gap is how well you understand your customers and on the other side is how well you deliver to your customers. The narrower the gap, then the more CC you are. Once recognition of the gap exists, then the journey starts toward CC starts. Measuring how well you are delivering to your customers is relatively easy but developing a true measure of how well one understands their customers is the hard part. It is akin to measuring the difference between somebody knowing something versus understanding something.

- **Net Promote Score (NPS)**: Customer Experience (CX) managers use tools like Net Promote Score (NPS) to build the case for CX as a discipline within an organization. Net Promoter is a management tool that can be used to gauge the loyalty of a firm's customer relationships. It serves as an alternative to traditional customer satisfaction research and claims to be correlated with revenue growth (Wikipedia). Customer experience as a set of practices and approaches to measurement extend and rejuvenate the longer-standing industry expertise developed around brand. The customer experiences they measure span the customer and product lifecycles of their companies. A truly successful customer experience is one that delivers excellence what the brand promises, but in a way that makes it unique or different for others. Collectively, customer experiences shape a customer's perception with regard to a firm, in turn defining the brand and its characteristics in their mind's eye.

- **Customer-centric culture assessment:** Culture is how groups of people think and do things in an organization, and the key challenge is related to measure the intangible power factor like culture. If you are going to create greater company-wide emphasis on customers, you need to know if you are making real progress. The larger challenge is upon how you create a common understanding across the business of what customer centricity is and more importantly how every individual can contribute. The employee's behavior must be linked to outcomes the customer cares about. Another important factor to refer is the social community data through which customers and employees share most of their important views and influential modeling makes a robust process to identify the key influencers of the brand and organization as a whole.

- **The "leading" measure:** Business needs to understand the maturity of customer-centric practices with quantified result across all measures at the overall business level and at specific section levels. Invariably, most businesses will demonstrate good performance in certain areas and "not so good" performance in others. The objective is to develop capability across all areas, as a customer-centric capability is a true representation of the value chain concept – you can only be as strong as your weakest link. This kind of measure is a "leading" customer-centric measure and is representative of how the organization is building capability for the medium to long term. The "leading measure" is enterprise-wide in nature, it doesn't just deal with satisfaction or loyalty, and it deals with capabilities and interdependencies in short, medium and long term. This is basically a framework that sits at the center of the business.

- **The "lagging" measure**: The "leading indicator" then needs to be balanced with a set of "lagging" measures such as Customer Satisfaction Indicator (CSI), Net Promote Score (NPS) and ES (Employee Satisfaction). These latter measures are a manifestation of the current capability of the organization and highlight immediate issues to be acted upon. Dealing with these issues is normally an example of a tactical initiative. There are various tools through which you can measure the performance of the organization for customer centricity. Customer centricity shows up to the customers as the amount of value they receive from the company, the benefits they gets in customer-centric products, services, treatment etc.

- **The "relevance" measure**: The other key factor on effecting customers' perception is that of relevance. First of all, you would look at how many of your KPI measure the end result from a customer perspective of outcome driven rather than output driven. Does the customer find what it is your offer relevant to their life, the life that they have or the life that it is they aspire to. If they do, then you build on it; if they don't, then the question that gets asked is: Why do customers not find the offering relevant? You need customers to help you answer this and that in itself is move toward customer centricity. The other important factor to look back and see while measuring the customer centricity of an organization is about the life cycle of the product as it plays a critical role in identifying the advocacy of customers to a specified store or brand.

- **The "REAP" metrics**: Those who meet higher profitability indicators over their lifetime – REAP (Retention, Efficiency, Accountability and Penetration) metrics are a powerful way to manage business and optimize value, particularly if the organization is able to operationalize segmentation – really and truly treat different customers differently. A REAP dashboard provides four core measures applicable to the entire customer base, however the emphasis and the principle focus may be different per segment. The dominant focus on high value clients, for example, may principally be around the retention and penetration lever, whilst efficiency may be the focus for lower value deciles. Segment managers are then best able to design appropriate programs and initiatives to meet the needs, characteristics and behaviors of their respective segments.

In order to improve the customer experience maturity, the key is to learn from the customers by gathering "actionable insights" from business interactions with them, then to have the processes, structure and skills to adapt businesses in response to these insights. This is not about the customer running the businesses, but about understanding customers' perspectives. In fact, the insight measurement of the level of "customer centricity" is crucial in achieving ongoing strategy and business focus for success. And organizations also need to cultivate the customer-centric culture that changes people's mind-set to appreciate that customer experience management can be a fundamental value driver in the business through well-defined KPIs to make such benefit tangible.

4. Digital Agility – Seven Pillars of Agile Organization

Agility is a dynamic capability to adapt to changes.

What Is Agility? It is a cultivated capability that enables an organization to respond in a timely, effective, and sustainable way when changing circumstances require it. The management literature increasingly refers to this ability as a "dynamic capability": The potential to sense opportunities and threats, solve problems, and change the firm's resource base. Your environment will change, one thing is certain: Change is no longer something that happens periodically, it's continuous – constant, unrelenting, and accelerating in the digital age. So anything that you do too far "up front" is likely to be wrong in the future, the agile practices address this using a short feedback loop (plan – try – test – learn); so that you never get too far away out on a tangent on the manifold of reality.

Agility is the dynamic capability that allows organizations to adapt to the digital new normal. Being agile means anticipating likely change and addressing it deftly, keeping business on course and customers satisfied. To achieve those goals, agility must be built into an organization's very foundation, from strategy to design, from capability to processes, from mind-set to culture, as well as supporting digital technologies. Here are seven pillars of high mature agile organization with debunked agility code: **BESTBIG**.

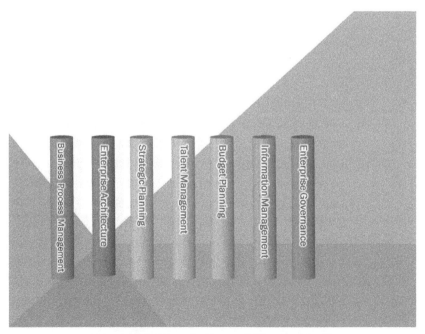

**Figure 24: Decode Seven Pillars of Agile
Organization – "BESTBIG"**

(1) Pillar #1: B – Agile Business Process and Project Management:
Agile is a natural transformation in software development processes to
adapt to rapid changes; Agile is an emerging methodology with many
advantages, such as faster release cycle, iterative communication, more
end-customer focus. It's the right way to do software and manage project
portfolio strategically, methodologically and tactically. In addition,
process underpins business capability, an agile process needs to have
dynamic aspects to act based on process intelligence. With the right mix
of process standardization and flexibility in place, business leaders can
efficiently anticipate and execute on change, turning scenario planning
from a theoretical exercise into a real decision shaper:

- **Digital discipline:** Agile requires well-trained engineering
  disciplines. It also requires strong business disciplines. Agile
  has to be continually tweaked for it to work. Because, as a new
  practice in many organizations, it also causes further concerns:
  Is Agile the cause for defect increase? Does Agile make most of
  customers more satisfied? Does Agile improve project success rate?
  What are pitfalls to adopting Agile? Agile disciplines allow you
  to really execute Agile well, as it has more effective control,
  communication, and metrics than waterfall.

- **Digital adaptation**: Create agile repeatable processes that
  can be changed quickly as needed. Create a common picture,
  understanding, and vocabulary of the way the enterprise operates.
  Identify additional capabilities, processes, and technology that
  may be needed to optimize operating costs, improve profitability,
  reduce process cycle times, and improve quality.

- **Digital balance**: Agility is the strategic balance of
  standardization and flexibility, targeted at those organizational
  pressure points where they're not only needed today, but will
  most likely be needed tomorrow. In order to survive and thrive
  amid constant change, companies must reclaim the right
  balance of standardization and flexibility and build strategic and
  operational agility into their business foundations. By developing

a business agility blueprint – a shared view of an organization that promotes deeper understanding of core processes, risks, and transformational opportunities – business leaders can approach change confidently.

- **Digital transparency**: By adopting agile practices, you can eliminate the "tunnel effect" and bring forth transparency into business processes. Digital develops more effective governance models, systems, and processes of improving agility and flexibility. Identify ways of realizing the end-to-end monitoring of key performance indicators and critical success factors.

(2) Pillar #2: E – Agile Enterprise Architecture: Incorporating agility into a business foundation or architecture requires new ways of thinking, new approaches to enterprise architecture and business process design. The failure to build flexibility into both organizational design and operations can threaten a company's survival, as your environment will change, hence, the Enterprise Architecture shall also be agile to adapt it.

- **Digital Design**: Enterprise Architecture needs to keep modular design and continuous planning. EA needs to be integrated with business dynamics so that they grow and evolve together. A good architecture should allow for dynamics in the business to be decoupled from design, continue planning and improving, and then fulfill EA purpose to bridge strategy and execution, to transcend business into next level of digital maturity.

- **Digital dimension**: Agility isn't inherited like some trait passed on through organization's DNA, you have to work hard to achieve it. It isn't permanent, either, once achieved; you have to work hard to maintain agility. One of the key things in the architecture space is the relationship between various dimensions of an enterprise. Agility isn't just synonymous with innovation and product or service development, agility can help improve performance across the entire range of organizational activities.

- **Agile principle**: If apply the agile mind-set to architecture development, whether it's EA or one of the architectural domains, the principles includes:

  (a) Balance: Bottom up approach needs to well balance out with top-down architecture foundation.
  (b) People first: People over process; high mature teams are key success factors.
  (c) Discipline: Agile is not lack of discipline, but need stronger architecture and management discipline.
  (d) Mind-set: Agile is both mind-set and methods; it means better communication, adaptability, and customer satisfaction.
  (e) Agile is not just about speed, also means high quality.

(3) Pillar #3: S – Agile Strategy: When the environment is so unpredictable, how can business apply the traditional forecasting and analysis that are at the heart of strategic planning? The volatility of the current market further complicates detailed planning and requires an even greater time commitment, preventing involved managers and employees from taking part in critical business activities:

- **Digital intent**: Strategy Planning becomes a "living process," with regular evaluation, scanning, listening, revisiting and potential course correction. There is no "predictable future," but there are many possible ones. Long term planning has its place, but linearity and over-prescriptiveness don't. If you laid all of the corporate strategists in the world end-to-end, you wouldn't reach a consensus. Effective leadership and a clearly articulated intent is essential in planning, otherwise you either end up getting nowhere over a long period of time, or you end up with something that does not actually meet the organizational needs. Continue to review agile strategic plan by asking: In what level, is "just enough" enough? Is planning adding another layer of complexity or bureaucracy, or is planning out of touch? The point where you have to stop is: When "planning" starts to interfere with "executing." So what is the "right level" of planning? It is whatever is needed to get us off the ground and running. In today's world, the business context keeps changing constantly, so plans will need to be revised constantly.

- **Digital mantra**: The mantra for planning success would be to follow agile principles and following steps:

  (a) Mind-set: Shape agile mind-set for planning and management via iterative communication, incremental business goals, and customer-centric views.
  (b) Navigation: Capture the bigger picture clear on what, when and how to achieve based on economical value and available resources.
  (c) Experimenting: Plan a little and try implementing to see immediate results to verify against the expectation; if time permits, plan completely first; then execute, monitor throughout for auditing and close it successfully to live up to the track record of successful relationship.
  (d) Mix and Match: In real life, there may be plenty of mix and match, and it is purely match and it is purely requirement based, amalgamated with constraints and KPIs of striving for perfection.

- **Digital choice**: Alternatively, companies can explore having a base strategy as well as a stretch plan; this dual approach requires clear top-down expectations for targets. It requires coherence of culture, strategy and leadership. Culture and leadership need to foster agile mind-set and behaviors, supported by well aligned policies and practice. Strategy needs to respond continuously to change with speed and through informed decisions.

(4) Pillar #4: T – Agile Talent Management: The digital workforce today is more global, flexible and virtual as the world becomes so hyper-connected and over-complex; meanwhile, today's digital generations value different things compared to previous generations of workers. Therefore, talent management as a business-critical process needs to be agile as well in adapt to the accelerated change facing in organization.

- **Digital ecosystem**: Focus on the fact that the fundamental nature of enterprise or business consists of human social systems, which are partially designed or even architected, but are also grown, matured, and evolved. A culture of passionate people that embrace change and seek understanding will be paramount. Share early and share often, cross-functional collaboration and iterative communication are encouraged to optimize business agility. Not only that, the "components" of such human social systems include aspects of human beings who have purpose, intent and attitude to openness, who take full responsibility for their activities and goals, and who are spurred to make radical change and aim for breakthrough innovation even facing failures.

- **Digital empowerment**: There needs to be broad management support for agile talent management and an understanding that it means empowering staff to make data-based decisions by accessing right information at the right time. And ultimately, you need an audience and organization with a focus on people and results, which celebrates small successful steps, but keep the focus on long term objectives. Organizations would also benefit from creating an innovative culture where employees feel safe in expressing themselves without reprisal, then listening to their internal partners before implementing change initiatives.

(5) Pillar #5: B – Agile Budget Planning: Are there really businesses out there that create financial budget forecasts and blindly stick to them regardless of the realities of the world happening around them? If there are, that seems to be a certain recipe for disaster. Does the dynamic digital economy calls for agile budgeting and real-time planning. Any efficient business leader or manager will routinely monitor his or her budget and create either formal or informal forecasts as the digital environment continually shifts. Changes to that forecast have to be communicated early and often so that you purposefully don't wind up with those big surprises at the end of the fiscal year.

- **Digital "rolling":** A shorter budgeting cycle puts the emphasis on speed, flexibility and results in less overall company coordination, fewer parallel and redundant activities, and less frustration. Effective planning and a more realistic outcome results from striking a balance between the setting of targets and light but frequent forecasting. The agile budgeting focus is on optimizing use of resources based on rolling forecasts and not adhering blindly to fixed annual plans and budgets.

- **Digital iteration:** Continually identify opportunities with the highest return, and allocate resources appropriately to profit from those opportunities. Some innovative organizations use iterative budgets based on continuous feedback from real-world events and actual operating results. The agile pioneers advocate doing quarterly or even monthly forecasts, instead of one big annual forecast and dynamic resource allocation based on emerging threats and opportunities.

- **Digital balance:** The wise finance people should find a way to balance the need to design good incentives with getting a flexible budgeting process that can keep up with a faster changing world. The incentives should simply encourage the behavior to increase company profits – in that way people don't get stuck with predefined targets for how to do their job, and they can keep changing what they do as long as it delivers the profitability levels that business is all about.

(6) Pillar #6: I – Agile Information Management: Information nowadays is a big resource and invaluable asset for organizations, and assets need to be managed in an agile way, to make sure that the right information is in the right place at the right time and shared to the right persons.

- **Digital effectiveness**: Information Management entails organizing, retrieving, acquiring, securing, maintaining, updating, distributing, sharing, publishing and finally archiving information. It is closely related and overlapping with the practice of data management. The key principles are to ensure that information management activities are effective and successful.

- **Digital alignment:** Information Management is the overall process of aligning the use of information through the MANAGEMENT (What data you have, in what format and the location or method it is held?), ASSURANCE (Data held is safe, secure and processes are legislatively compliant) and EXPLOITATION (Collaboratively enabled and fully support the business objectives) to achieve digital agility.

- **Digital synchronization**: Information or processes alone do not deliver product. It takes people, resources, information, processes and values to make a successful delivery. All of these must be reviewed in context together, if one is to find root cause and apply effective countermeasures, change management needs to go with agile hand-in-hand, with senior leadership support, cross-functional communication, and clear vision of Information Management.

(7) **Pillar #7: G – Agile Governance:** Corporate governance is the set of processes, customs, policies, laws, and institutions affecting the way a company is directed, administered or controlled. Governance will remain a difficult issue for today's digitalized organizations with extended business boundary in an increasingly flat world, and the desire for innovation will make governance issues even more complex. In order to survive and thrive in a "VUCA" digital environment, how do you manage unpredictability, rather than focusing on how to control the environment and how to make it more predictable or manageable, from managerial and governance perspective, how to become comfortable with turbulence or the unknown, and how to focus on the organizational "antifragile" ability to respond with the digital dynamic.

- **Digital "consilience"**: Good governance with the blended characteristics described in the hybrid word "consilience" (coherence + resilience), which can create good performance, especially for the long run. This is because that good corporate governance creates a highly mature decision making system and very effective controlling system, which can assure the corporation's operation under the right directions and behavior correctly. It used to be that we were seeing silos as marking the boundaries and territories of different lines of business within an organization. Agile governance is a holistic mind-set to bridge the silos, also leap the gap between the immediate outcome of the endeavor when you succeed in transforming the enterprise as intended and the outcome you ultimately desire.

- **Digital tradeoff**: In order to make changes to the planning systems, companies must acknowledge the necessary tradeoffs involved. One point of struggles is governance taking away liberties that are essential to people doing their jobs in a creative way, if there's a problem with trust, then governance will suffer, because motivations are not aligned across organizational boundaries. In addition, there might be very well differing opinions within divisions, among divisions, or between the divisions and corporate headquarters about the best direction to take. These differences have to be made transparent, and all relevant stakeholders must reach consensus on the best path forward.

- **Digital fit**: Corporate Governance is not about maximization, but about optimization, a term that could be applied to agile governance, which is the agile structure and processes of authority, responsibility, and accountability in a business or organization. Businesses need very different styles of governance depending on where the piece of work sits on a spectrum from classic "waterfall" hierarchy (control governance) to a self-management "agile" style (loose governance). Define the spectrum of governance from waterfall control to free-form agile, and the conditions that apply to change projects and experiments at each point along that spectrum. Here is a set of questions to ask in order for organizations to manage governance:

a. Can it be automated? Can it be dispensed entirely?
b. Is it possible for an organization to be highly decentralized and synchronized?
c. Can you get discipline without disciplinarians?
d. Are there ways of combining the freedom and flexibility of self-management with the control and coordination of traditional hierarchies?
e. Can you reduce the performance drag of top-heavy management structures without giving anything up in terms of focus and efficiency?
f. To what extent can "self-management" or "peer-management" substitute for manager-management or command-control?

Therefore, Agile is mind-set, management discipline, and governance practice. Agility is a cultivated dynamic capability that enables an organization with solid agile pillars to respond in a timely, effective, and sustainable way when changing circumstances require it.

5. Digital Balance: How to Strike it Just Right

Digital balance harmonizes the hybrid nature of digitalization.

Organizations are being experiencing the dynamics of the most significant business transformation since the industrial revolution. And they are also at a different stage of such digital transformation. It is the biggest management challenge to be a change agent with high mature attitude and aptitude, in order to take business from where you are to the next level of maturity. Hence, one of the biggest management challenges in digital transformation is how to strike the right digital balance.

(1) The balance between long term vision and short term perspective:
Nowadays, companies have huge pressures to survive and thrive in today's hypercompetitive economical dynamic. The digital normal-volatility, uncertainty, complexity and ambiguity may also bring certain digital "side effects" such as:

- Ambiguity effect – the tendency to avoid options for which missing information makes the probability seem "unknown."

- Bandwagon effect – the tendency to do or believe things because many other people do or believe the same.

- Near-sight effect – the tendency to focus on short-term goals, because the future seems to be so hard to predict.

Businesses have to achieve certain financial targets quickly, but they are in many instances, unsustainable. It's not until we can make lasting process improvements to meet or exceed long term goals. A good leader is someone who doesn't lose the sight of long term or "big picture" and expends majority of his or her time, efforts, and resources on achieving the short term goals. The digital harbinger gives a balanced focus on achieving both short term and long term objectives. The critical thing here is that short term goals should be aligned to the "big picture." A transformational leader should be able to immediately ascertain which term would benefit the situation most as he or she becomes aware of each unique objective.

(2). The balance between "local" and "global": Because of classic management, the business units often do not work in collaboration, as they are driven by a culture of silos, they fight for limited resource in order to do what they believe is "locally" right instead of working together in order to do what is "globally right." There are quite many silos in traditional industrial organizations:

- Geographical silos – arise with difficulty in collaborating when different parts of the organization are in different geographical locations.

- Project silos – occur when best practice isn't shared between groups working in similar ways toward similar goals.

- Functional silos – arise when there is uncertainty about peoples' roles within an organization and lead to redundancy and feelings of under appreciation among members.

- Information silos – exist due to barriers in sharing of information freely across organization.

Silos results in overlapping functions, increased costs, duplicated efforts and inconsistent decisions among entities. The digital leaders have to bridge both industrial silos and digital divide today; with emerging digital technologies, organizations can now have better opportunities to share best practices and next practices, the collective wisdom and cultural quintessential; it is true, deserts, mountain ranges and oceans will no longer be the walls to connectivity and collaboration, it is strategic imperative to strike the right balance between local and global; to bridge the silo and think globally.

(3). The Balance between digital speed and industrial speed: Majority of well-established companies today are running at both industrial speed and digital speed; the silo structures and legacy infrastructure limit the pace of their digital transformation; but every forward-looking organization also explores the new arena to speed up with digitalization:

- **Digital democracy**: It's from within the massive gray area between these two styles that the digital management comes from, and helps push this shift toward flatter hierarchies, and empowerment of employees, which in turn leads to the radical speed and efficiencies seen in agile companies today.

- **Digital shift**: Until business leaders come to terms with the reality that digital structures are really smarter and faster than "pure hierarchies", managers who understand the paradigm shift have to find ways to resolve the manager's paradox, strike the right balance between digital speed and industrial speed, build optimized processes and capabilities to accelerate execution, and create a better business result.

(4) The balance between "virtual world" and "the human connection": A hybrid nature of organization well mixes the virtual platform with physical functional structure to enforce cross-functional collaboration and dot-connecting innovation. The impact of digital or social technology is right on:

- **Go virtual**: The future organization will become more "virtual" and that virtual organizational design expertise will become more important in the coming years. But deep human connection may still be important, and the connection is not only just about physical touch, but more importantly as an emotional connection. While technology provides new frontiers for work systems, there are also challenges with issues of human "connectivity." What's intended to bring us closer together may leave us feeling further apart.

- **Resolve paradox**: Bridging the paradoxical gap between virtual workforce and the human touch; between digital strangers and a growing workforce of digital natives is the single most important management task for today's digital leaders. The successful managers are those who resolve this paradox by learning how to navigate the digital divide skillfully and keep balance upon digitalization and manageability.

(5) The balance between the standardization and flexibility: In order to survive and thrive amid constant change, companies must reclaim the right balance of standardization and flexibility, as well as build strategic and operational agility into their business foundations:

- **Agility**: Agility is competitive capability to keep businesses strive in the digital age; agility is the strategic mix of standardization and flexibility, targeted at those organizational pressure points where they're not only needed today, but will most likely be needed tomorrow. By developing a business agility blueprint, a shared view of an organization that promotes deeper understanding of core processes, risks, and transformational opportunities, business leaders can approach change confidently.

- **Balance**: In an era in which every tweet has the potential to plunge a company into a global reputational crisis, the demands for corporate transparencies are unprecedented. It's so easy to focus on the bad; it's so easy to see faults and mistakes, instead of seeing the positives, recognizing good and bringing those to light. Thus, today's digital leaders have to balance the optimistic spirit and cautious attitude; balance openness and standardization; balance discipline and flexibility; and balance effectiveness and efficiency.

How to strike the right digital balance is critical upon digital transformation, it takes both strategic planning and tactical mechanism; and it has to well align the right talent, the optimized process and the effective technology in order to reach the next level of digital height.

6. Five Digital Impacts in Highly Mature Businesses

Digital is about flow.

Digital makes significant impact on every aspect of business from people, process to technology and capability, both horizontally and vertically. Given the power of cloud, social, mobile and analytics technologies to fuel business innovation, capability orchestration and employee collaboration, digital becomes the very fabric of high performing businesses, being outside-in and customer-centric is the new mantra for forward-looking and high-mature organizations today.

- **Knowledge flow**: Digital means flow, data flow, information flow and insight flow; knowledge does not stand still. It flows into the company, it flows out of it, it erodes, it gets created, and hopefully it flows to the customers of the company in terms of product and service delivery as well. There is a shift from more traditional knowledge management approaches to techniques that involve enhancing the "flow" of knowledge within a high mature digital organization to improve access and use. As the accepted industrial model of knowledge management is too hierarchical, too centralized for the fast-moving, increasingly social or collaborative digital enterprise of today, so digital knowledge management has been expounding many of the principles such as connect-collect-collaborate; ask-learn-share, and solving some of the pains underlying it, unlocking the latent expertise, collaborating through communities, getting the right information to the right person at the right time; geographically-distributed teams are connected by technology, there arises an opportunity to analyze and reuse the data they create as they go about their activities, and from that to generate valuable knowledge that can be shared to help everyone in their work and keep talent grow. Hence, digital makes impact on knowledge management significantly.

- **Complexity optimization**: Complexity has increased exponentially and has become the part of digital new normal. Imagine the complexity that comes in due to these characteristics such as less structure, rules and regulations, diversity, volatility, ambiguity, unpredictability, lack of linearity and increased flux working and impacting together. The emergent digital complexity includes hyper-connectivity, hyper-diversity and the non-linear complexity such as less structure and multidimensional views, or design complexity such as highly-productive complexity, value/cost/risk ratio complexity; digital enterprise democracies are inherently and intensely complex. Moreover, these changes and more do not happen in isolation from each other in predictable ways. They act as a complex and unpredictable system, feeding, amplifying or ameliorating the effects of others and shaping enterprise architectures. There are unknown interactions and very high inner dynamics in complexity. It becomes complex if things do interact, particularly in case of "nonlinear" interaction, you can't separate things properly or you cannot predict the actual effect of interaction straightforwardly. The complexity can be good or bad for businesses depending on your strategy and capability. Thus, Complexity Management is the critical digital capability to minimize value-destroying complexity and efficiently optimize value-adding complexity in a cross-functional approach. And organizations must learn to navigate digital uncertainty and complexity via complexity mind-set, innovate and adapt to increasingly changing digital realities.

- **Structure design**: Majority of organizations are designed to improve functional efficiency in the industrial age; and many of traditional organizations today are running at two speeds, with the industrial speed, it can continue to keep the business light on; and with the digital speed, it will adapt to the more frequent digital disruptions, wired to change and designed for better innovation toward long term digital transformation. High mature digital organizations integrate organizational design (OD) into the process design and organizational reengineering. Hence, digital makes impact on the speed to run business, the empathy to their people and the orchestration of their capability in high mature digital organizations. In reality, fewer companies are truly using OD resources. But more often, the successful process improvement initiatives to digital transformation shall have representation and input from organizational design people management. It helps establish early buy-in and support through analysis of how the digital "initiative" impacts the people in the organization. Besides, realigning functions, structure and management should be there to support the people -the most important asset of any organization, and not the other way around. Therefore, both organizational design and process are important elements in digital transformation. The leadership team must understand that the road to achieving any effective and efficient business model is business process management with leverage of organizational design management, and reach the ultimate goal to build a high-mature, antifragile and outside-in customer-intimate digital business.

- **Digital "Horsepower":** Gartner refers digital technologies SMAC – Social, Mobile, Analytics, and Cloud as the Nexus of Forces, and, of course, IT leaders need to pay attention to their huge impact. Cloud computing is changing how businesses think about infrastructure and application procurement. Big Data is changing not just traditional areas of analytics, but also how people manage most things in the future. Mobile is changing the customer relationship; the business is always on and need to be always available, always relevant, and always helpful. It's not enough to offer the flat services. In the new age of consumerization of IT, digital customers and employees expect applications to be as intuitive and task-oriented. It's that consumers and employees are using the same technology devices for similar activities. It represents a merging of corporate and consumer capabilities within the organization. It blurs the line between professional life and personal life, it also transforms the monolithic enterprise IT infrastructure into mosaic digital backbone, and catalyze the new business culture. People can work anytime, anywhere, to access any necessary information to create any innovative idea now with partners outside organization, sustainable innovation means products and services need to be improved via continuous conversation and open loop feedback from customers and partners. This digital convergence of devices and services are creating new business models and revenue source as most companies across industries are being forced to become technology companies and run information business.

- **Change agent:** Changing the game is mind-set; people are always the weakest link in any change or transformation effort. Digital make huge impact on talent management. The emergence of social platforms provides the new way to learn, share and collaborate through direct applications at the corporate level. The organizations with learning culture have implemented the set of social collaboration tools as part of the overall talent management platform. The social or informal learning will become mainstream learning channel and a preferred delivery method in the digital era. On the other side, change agent is critical in radical digital transformation, as they have been an invaluable source of knowledge, business direction, insight and support etc. There are a few change agent roles:

(a) **Transformational leaders** can provide the direction as vision, mission, strategy, as well as leadership skills like delegation, decision making and monitoring. This role affects most through congruent behavior, continuous endorsement of the digital transformation and regular communication to keep the momentum.

(b) **Change specialists** are the people who stand outside the political hierarchy of the change area, a cross-functional specialist, an insightful outlier, or an outside consultant, their main skills are understanding the change mechanisms and human behavior, as well as providing appropriate measures for facilitating change.

(c) **Change champions** have a specific skill set in the field of the change additionally to the specialist knowledge. This role affects as a role model, an example that pulls the rest of the organization into the right direction. If necessary, organizations shall mobilize a change agent network- the network is a group of people integrated with the execution of the digital strategic plan and who own the required transformation so that the change and digital transformation can be orchestrated via cross-functional collaboration and iterative communication.

If necessary, organizations shall mobilize a change agent network- the network is a group of people integrated with the execution of the digital strategic plan and who own the required transformation so that the change and digital transformation can be orchestrated via cross-functional collaboration and iterative communication.

Digital business with organizational democracy is a way of designing organizations to amplify the possibilities of human potential and collective human capabilities for the organization as a whole. Enterprises of the future are increasingly exhibiting such characteristics in various shades and intensity. Digital makes profound impact from specific function to business as a whole, the purpose of such radical digitalization is to make significant difference in the overall levels of customer delight and achieve high performing business result.

7. Digital Resilience

Digital resilience can be achieved via risk intelligence.

Businesses are faced with more opportunities and risks in the digital era, digital resilience is the business capability to make organization more resilient, not just controlling risk, but managing risk with intelligence. Digital resilience also depends on how to manage the gray area effectively in today's volatile, uncertain, complex, and ambiguous digital environment, being resilient is about failing faster, failing forward, failing cheaper and recovering more promptly. Digital resilience can only be achieved through "resilient mind-set," enforced governance discipline, and proven risk management best practices and next practices.

- **Reframing resilient mind-set**: More often, business is still fundamentally looking at risk in a negative context, but adapting that context at the point of analysis to identify the upside from a specific uncertainty one is threatened with. Business has objectives that may have potential benefits, but whether that business strategy is successful or not in the future is uncertain and achieving that objective might have negative outcomes that need to be controlled. Even better, businesses can turn negative outcomes into potential future opportunities. Hence, there is nothing wrong with reframing, if you can reframe the thinking and try to recover positively from that uncertainty. And a resilient corporate mind-set is fundamental for digital transformation success.

- **Resilient attitude**: Resilient attitude starts with the right attitude to communicate. Resilient attitude is a critical element in collecting, analyzing, and synthesizing information to "influence" decisions. Regardless of what methods or indicators are used, the key is to express risk in business terms that can really make an impact. It's the management ability to communicate the extent to which it wants to take on risk relative to a specific objective. Businesses have to acknowledge a level of subjectivity to determine risk appetite and risk tolerance in real life, and it varies depending on the organizational strategy, culture and business orientation. Risk attitude shall meet "prioritization and escalation criteria." The purpose of assessing risk against consequence criteria is to determine what risk must be managed, and who needs to be involved in that management.

- **Multidimensional governance**: Corporate governance is not about maximization but about optimization. Optimization could be term applied to good governance. Governance is a neutral term that is useful in having the ability to discuss bad governance with terms such as waste, corruption, inefficiency, etc. Governance is the structure and processes of authority, responsibility and accountability in a business or organization, the ability of boards to oversee and advise management so as to ensure the best fit between short term profitability for shareholders and long-term sustainability for stakeholders such as employees, customers, and society. It is important to emphasize that governance is fundamentally about having a systematic approach to making decisions within the corporate entity. There needs to be a framework within which decisions are authorized to be made at each level, and supporting structures and conventions support governance bodies and officers of the company to make good decisions, ranging from strategic to operational decisions. Four key dimensions of corporate governance are accountability, strategy, policy, and monitoring to understand accountabilities of environment; developing business strategy; making business policies that offer further constraint or guidance to implementation of strategy; and monitoring performance and managing risks across all domains of interest. A governance system includes the following logic steps:

- **Plan**: Always be aware of what needs to change.
- **Do**: Execute well.
- **Check**: Evaluate if we're still on target.
- **Act**: Make necessary course corrections along the way.
- **Repeat**!

- **Innovation risk management**: Highly mature digital organizations inspire and enable innovations. Enterprise Risk Management (ERM) for innovation would be a trimmed down version of the status quo that focuses on the essentials. Innovation risk will be a critical, but not necessarily the only driver. Innovation risk would also broadly need to consider both endogenous and exogenous drivers, and may not necessarily be best addressed by a lot of the formal ERM standards, because innovation can be destructive, empowering, or even systemic, etc. in addition to its dynamic nature, so innovation risk management needs to be innovative as well. Innovation risk management means stepping away from the accepted "best practice" and asking whether a fundamentally different approach would provide more flexibility, more sensitivity, and more responsiveness. An innovation risk management strategy and framework must have focus, level of detail and meet the needs of the specific user of any such strategy toward the applicable innovation process he/she seeks to manage risk within products, services, processes, and even in nonconventional areas outside of product and technology.

- **Governance vs. Management:** Management and governance are interdependent discipline. Governance and management have different role in the business and IT project success and failure. The role of governance is to ensure that projects are properly monitored and tracked to make sure that cost, quality and time are maintained and a framework to ensure right kind of projects are being pursued and prioritized. Management, on the other hand, should ensure right resources, such as, people, technology, and skills are provided, operationalizing the product in the organization and measure various metrics for ROI. The management structures and project organization are supposed to separate to the governance of a program. Too often in some organizations, the project organization structure and the governance bodies (typically steering groups, etc.) are shown on the same diagrams and mentioned in the same breath. It is the lack of clarity for responsibility and decision making that can derail projects, and these can be both a symptom and cause of confusion between governance and management.

- **Crisis Management:** Organizations across the globe face more pressure and ambiguity in the digital age and the media continue to report many prestigious companies having reputational "surprises" resulting in material loss of valuation and future uncertainty. A company's brand is one of its most valuable assets; "reputation" is as the same as "brand" in this context: what's your brand reflecting to, the value and business purpose. Some say, reputation risk is not a risk, but a consequence of the public and media reacting to all the other risks. When someone talks about managing reputation risk, they are most likely talking about the post-risk processes of damage control and remedial steps involving corporate communication and public relations programs. And generic risk management includes how organizations manage economical, legal, political, social and human risks, and how to become more digital resilient, etc.

The more diverse, the more regulated, the more geographically dispersed an organization is or becomes, the more resilient it has to become for adapting to the digital speed, and the more important an integrated or federated risk and governance approach needs to become to be closely aligned with top-line strategic, financial and reputational goals, and seen as a "business enabler" rather than a cost center. An organization's success is, in large part, driven by how wisely it takes risks and how effectively it manages the risks, so find ways to create and leverage programs that facilitate revenue goals; easy to use digital tools for external communication, interaction, and collaboration with the ultimate goal to achieve digital resilience.

8. Digital Dimension

High mature digital organizations stretch out in every business dimension.

Digitalization is not a single dimensional effort to applying the cool digital technologies, but a multidimensional pursuit to embed digital into the core processes of business. To stay competitive, companies must go beyond experimenting with digital and commit to transforming themselves into full digital businesses. There are five dimensional maturity in differentiating digital master and laggard.

- **Differentiation from strategic dimension:** The strategic differentiation is the key step in such radical digital transformation. Coherence has a deliberately close alignment among the company's strategic direction, its most distinctive capabilities, and most or all of its products and services. However, a dichotomy often exists between vision and "doing." Strategies need to be first and foremost long-term, specifically because they are directional and need to allow for the organization to knock the rust off and move coherently in the described direction. Secondly, strategies need to be descriptive, but prescriptive as well. Because they outline the areas where possible conflicting priorities may lie and outline how they are able to be handled in the organization in terms of resource allocation such as time, budget, people, etc. Thirdly, the differentiated strategies need to be game changers. They cannot be a cornucopia of more of the same to keep the engine running just a little faster. They have to show that the organization is "playing to win"; not just trying not to lose. Without this, they will never have resounding buy-in at the middle and bottom of the organization where execution really lives, and thus, conflict of priorities and silos will continue to hinder progress.

- Strategic differentiation occurs when all parts of the choir sing their respective parts in harmony to achieve a higher purpose and make unique impact, the music as a symphony of voice.
- Strategic alignment occurs on multiple levels, but it presupposes the ability of each link to articulate their strategic intent. If strategic intent can be understood, both within and without the organization, the alignment process becomes an analytical "e-harmony" process where the actual configuration of the organizations strategy is a consequence of design and implementation strategies.

- **Dynamic capability from execution dimension**: Enterprise capability management in essence consists of a portfolio or matrix of capabilities that are used in various combinations to achieve outcomes. Within that portfolio, a capability will be transient unless managed and maintained over time. Therefore, a typical capability lifecycle spans needs, requirements, acquisition, in-service, obsolescence and disposal. Capability gap is the lack of a capability. A capacity gap is a lack of the "resources" needed by the processes that operationalize a capability to do a given amount of work. Large groups can interact and be able to divide and conquer a complex challenge to accelerate the solution in forming capabilities and capacities if done right. The most important thing when it comes to implementing strategy is to gain the buy-in, or understanding of those who will be affected by it, and cognizant of interconnected digital business ecosystem as well. The dynamic digital organizations need to get away from letting things fall through and start creating "integrated wholes" by utilizing the following correct processes to solve these complexities, ultimately bridging the chasm between strategy and execution.

  - Ability to collaborate with their business counterparts.
  - Understanding of end customer expectations and experience.

- Organizational structure (hierarchy, existing roles and skill sets).
- Technical abilities in social, mobile, analytics or cloud.
- Agility to move quickly, adapt and change course.

- **Organizational democracy from structure dimension**: Organization design is the vehicle through which business strategy is executed and defines the environment in which the talent can unleash the potential. Organizational democracy will begin to become the emergent model; that openness needs to become a leadership competency; that democratic processes will overtake hierarchical control; and that culture of innovation will become a more fundamental organizational asset. In industrial business reality, functional silos are generally constant barriers to business advancement or maturity. More often, organizations are too siloed to be able to relate coherently as a holistic business to the customer's journey. It will take a lot of leadership for the digital pioneers who want to bridge the chasm, to find new ways to hasten their collective best thinking efforts. There is no doubt that the chasm between strategy and execution is very complex in nature. It's never a question of if these problems will happen; it's a question of when and to what degree. The best way to remove these silos and problematic hand-offs is to replace them with a many-to-many infrastructure. Hierarchical structures will transcend into "network structures". It's all about engaging specialized talent so they can converse in ways they wouldn't be able to on their own. This process should be intensive and highly effective, enabling an organization to get all the right people in tackling a challenge from all the right angles all at once, which in turn results in the optimal solution. From customer engagement perspective, creating good content and its distribution to the right personas at the right time is exposing most businesses to huge areas of potential improvement in their customer engagement thinking. There's no easy panacea for organizational democracy. A "whole systems " approach will transcend into an "interconnected systems " approach:

- A coherent integration of across national and international business, social and political systems.
- A greater awareness of the intricacies and the systemic value of organizational systems, processes, people dynamics, technology, resource allocation, supply side variables, market variables, economies of scale, etc.

- **Diversification from management dimension**: "Diversity in thought" is the gold nugget to be found in embracing diversity in the digital era. Especially, in the command-control industrial age, when conformity to expectations is very highly valued, and independent thinkers are seen, by default, as trouble makers. Because at traditional settings, when the human mind perceives the thought differences, an unconscious signal goes off that often sets the mind into a defensive mode of self-protection. If one's unconscious mind is in self-protect mode, then respect for differences will not automatically occur. Digital now opens the new window to see through the complexity from the different angle, based on the latest social collaboration tools and technology maturity, optimistically, the digital nature of hyper-connectivity and cross-boundary collaboration can stimulate the next level of "diversity in thought". As mind-sets are deeply embedded into the ways of thinking with assumptions and bias that pervades an organization. They're rarely reexamined, even when new or contradictory information comes to light.

(1) The real power of social technology comes from the innate appeal of interacting socially and intellectual stimulation that people derive from sharing what they know, expressing opinions and learning what others know and think.
(2) Social technologies enable social behaviors to take place online, endowing these interactions with scale, speed and disruptive economics of the internet; provide platforms for content creation, distribution, consuming, co-creation and transformation of personal and group communication into content.

(3) For scaling collaboration, some companies have created institutional platforms that focus on building longer-term relationships. Sustaining long-term collaboration allows participants to develop subject knowledge over time and focus more directly on business objectives to digital business strategy and digitally enabled innovation and transformation.

- **Design from Customer Experience dimension**: Digital is the age of customers. Explicitly consider user and customer experience and interaction design as a first class citizen. Customer Experience (CX) is the sum of all experiences a customer has with a supplier of goods or services, over the duration of their relationship with that supplier. This can include awareness, discovery, attraction, interaction, purchase, use, cultivation and advocacy. It can also be used to mean an individual experience over one transaction; User Experience (UX) involves a person's behaviors, attitudes, and emotions about using a particular product, system or service. User experience includes the practical, experiential, affective, meaningful and valuable aspects of human-computer interaction and product ownership (wikipedia). The distinction is usually clear in context: In every process, you have to think about how to support executors with the right tools and facilities to enable them to make the process perform. That's not only screens in process management, but also the availability of information, the possibility to ask for help, back up by colleagues etc, together with the business process modeling. Actual real life usage of a system will highlight areas where process design best practices and usability may work against one another. Thus:

  - Budgeting for an iterative development model will ensure that the users are not stuck with the first pretty wire-frame that was put into code.
  - The second has to be with the user interfaces that are easy to use. Appropriate model transformations and quick prototyping facilities grant that business-level designs are

always aligned with user interaction designs that implement them.

- This grants impressive advantages in terms of the speed of delivering the solutions, as well as ease of understanding and usage by customers

The multidimensional digital transformation provides impressive advantages in terms of the speed of delivering the solutions, as well as the ease of understanding and usage by customers. At a high maturity level, organizations have to stretch out in every business dimension for driving the full-fledged digital transformation, in order to adapting to the new world of business: Fast, always "on," highly connected and ultra-competitive.

Digital is not only about any technology. It's not just the products you make or the website you design. It's a core shift in how the business operates. This shift is due to the emerging significance of "digitization" –the use of digital technologies to enhance productivity and agility, uncover customer insights, and create new business models. Digital transformation is not a one-time project or a stand-alone initiative, it is a continuous journey to develop the unique enterprise digital capabilities, integrate them across their organizations and transform into the digital master with high level digital maturity. Digital maturity matters. It matters in every industrial sector. The philosophy and methodology that digital masters use can be selectively adopted by any company that has the digital leadership drive to do so. Digital transformation requires strong leadership to drive change. But it also requires a vision for why, what and how you want to transform. Companies in all industries and regions are experimenting with and benefiting from such digital transformation. Being digital, not just doing digital; from digitally disrupted to digital disrupters, and ultimately businesses strive to become digital master.

INDEX

ACKNOWLEDGEMENT

Wring a book is a journey with 1% of inspiration and 99% of perspiration. Digital Master was born in digital era, with the purpose to throw some light on business's digital transformation, also help today's digital professionals shape game changing digital mindset, because digital is the era for those who have passion in the heart and hunger in the mind. It is the age for life time learning and continuous growth.

The content of Digital Master is based on years of research, numerous professional digital debates and enriched crowd-sourcing brainstorming regarding digital leadership, strategy, culture, innovation, information management, talent management, and digital maturity etc. Innovation is its wing and collective insight is the wind. I am deeply thankful to all for generously giving thoughts and wisdoms.

Also thanks for the courtesy images from FreeDigitalPhotos.net

(1) Digital Master Image 9: the clipart of "Pollination", image courtesy of SweetCrisis at FreeDigitalPhotos.net

(2) Digital Master Image 10: the clipart of "Abstract Tech Background With Globe", image courtesy of cooldesign at FreeDigitalPhotos.net

(3) Digital Master image 21: the clipart of "People And Globe", image courtesy of Vlado at FreeDigitalPhotos.net, and the clipart of "Blue Earth", image courtesy of graur codrin at FreeDigitalPhotos.net

(4) Digital Master Image 23: the clipart of "Earth Globe", image courtesy of phanlop88 at FreeDigitalPhotos.net

ABOUT THE AUTHOR

Pearl Zhu is an innovative "Corporate Global Executive" with more than twenty years of technical and business working experience in strategic planning, Information Technology, software development, ecommerce and international trading, etc. She is a digital visionary who can capture business insight, technology foresight, and perceive digital leadership and management philosophy from multi-dimensional lenses and global perspectives. She is also a forward-thinking digital leader who advocates business innovation and culture evolution.

Pearl is a prolific blogger who creates a professional and popular blog: "Future of CIO", which has reached the 1300+ posting milestones and catching 600, 000 + views from world-wide audience. It covers more than 50+ hot IT and management subjects such as future of leadership, IT trends, digital transformation, organizational culture and management, business strategy and execution, innovation, IT transformation, decision effectiveness, CIO Debate, BPM, Culture Master, talent management and risk intelligence, etc.

Pearl has worked for both Fortune 100 companies to gain variety of experiences and startup to present entrepreneur spirit. Her cross-industrial, cross-functional and cross-cultural backgrounds make her a natural strategic and creative thinker, always see the other side of coin, also inspire her to observe deeper and broader with the fresh eyes and open mind, to become a relentless change agent, the symbol of diversity and the voice for those without voice.

She holds a master's degree in Computer Science from University of Southern California, and she lives in San Francisco Bay Area for 15 years. Digital Master Website: http://www.digitalmastermindset.com
Future of CIO Website: http://futureofcio.blogspot.com

www.ingramcontent.com/pod-product-compliance
Lightning Source LLC
Chambersburg PA
CBHW051220050326
40689CB00007B/740